D1436384

COLLECTED VERSE OF ROBERT SERVICE

COLLECTED VERSE OF
ROBERT SERVICE

LONDON
ERNEST BENN LIMITED
Bouverie House, Fleet Street

First published (Collected Edition) April 1930
Second impression ,, ,, December 1930
Third impression ,, ,, November 1935

Printed in Great Britain

CONTENTS

SONGS OF A SOURDOUGH

CONTENTS

BALLADS OF A CHEECHAKO

CONTENTS

RHYMES OF A ROLLING STONE

vii

CONTENTS

CONTENTS

THE RHYMES OF A
RED-CROSS MAN

CONTENTS

CONTENTS

BALLADS OF A BOHEMIAN

PART ONE

SPRING

I

II

xi

CONTENTS

CONTENTS

PART THREE
LATE SUMMER
I

II

CONTENTS

PART FOUR

WINTER

I

CONTENTS

SONGS OF A SOURDOUGH

To
C. M.

THE lonely sunsets flare forlorn
Down valleys dreadly desolate :
The lordly mountains soar in scorn,
As still as death, as stern as fate.

The lonely sunsets flame and die ;
The giant valleys gulp the night ;
The monster mountains scrape the sky,
Where eager stars are diamond-bright.

So gaunt against the gibbous moon,
Piercing the silence velvet-piled,
A lone wolf howls his ancient rune,
The fell arch-spirit of the Wild.

O outcast land ! O leper land !
Let the lone wolf-cry all express—
The hate insensate of thy hand,
Thy heart's abysmal loneliness.

SONGS OF A SOURDOUGH

THE LAW OF THE YUKON

THIS is the law of the Yukon, and ever she makes
    it plain :

" Send not your foolish and feeble ; send me your
    strong and your sane.

Strong for the red rage of battle ; sane, for I
    harry them sore ;

Send me men girt for the combat, men who are
    grit to the core ;

Swift as the panther in triumph, fierce as the bear
    in defeat,

Sired of a bulldog parent, steeled in the furnace
    heat.

Send me the best of your breeding, lend me your
    chosen ones ;

Them will I take to my bosom, them will I call
    my sons ;

Them will I gild with my treasure, them will I
    glut with my meat ;

But the others—the misfits, the failures—I trample
    under my feet.

Dissolute, damned, and despairful, crippled and
    palsied and slain,

Ye would send me the spawn of your gutters—
    Go ! take back your spawn again.

" Wild and wide are my borders, stern as death is
    my sway ;

From my ruthless throne I have ruled alone for
    a million years and a day ;

Hugging my mighty treasure, waiting for man to
    come :

Till he swept like a turbid torrent, and after him
    swept—the scum.

The pallid pimp of the dead-line, the enervate of
    the pen,

One by one I weeded them out, for all that I
    sought was—Men.

One by one I dismayed them, frighting them sore
    with my glooms ;

One by one I betrayed them unto my manifold
    dooms.

Drowned them like rats in my rivers, starved
    them like curs on my plains,

Rotted the flesh that was left them, poisoned the
    blood in their veins ;

Burst with my winter upon them, searing forevei
    their sight,

Lashed them with fungus-white faces, whimpering
    wild in the night ;

Staggering blind through the storm-whirl, stumbling
    mad through the snow,

Frozen stiff in the ice pack, brittle and bent like
    a bow ;

Featureless, formless, forsaken, scented by wolves
    in their flight,

Left for the wind to make music through ribs that
    are glittering white ;

Gnawing the black crust of failure, searching the
     pit of despair,

Crooking the toe in the trigger, trying to patter
     a prayer ;

Going outside with an escort, raving with lips all
     afoam ;

Writing a cheque for a million, drivelling feebly
     of home ;

Lost like a louse in the burning . . . or else in
     tented town

Seeking a drunkard's solace, sinking and sinking
     down ;

Steeped in the slime at the bottom, dead to a
     decent world,

Lost 'mid the human flotsam, far on the frontier
     hurled ;

In the camp at the bend of the river, with its dozen
     saloons aglare,

Its gambling dens a-riot, its gramophones all
     a-blare ;

Crimped with the crimes of a city, sin-ridden and
     bridled with lies,

In the hush of my mountained vastness, in the
flush of my midnight skies.
Plague-spots, yet tools of my purpose, so natheless
I suffer them thrive,
Crushing my Weak in their clutches, that only my
Strong may survive.

" But the others, the men of my mettle, the men
who would 'stablish my fame,
Unto its ultimate issue, winning me honour, not
shame ;
Searching my uttermost valleys, fighting each step
as they go,
Shooting the wrath of my rapids, scaling my
ramparts of snow ;
Ripping the guts of my mountains, looting the beds
of my creeks,
Them will I take to my bosom, and speak as a
mother speaks.
I am the land that listens, I am the land that
broods ;

Steeped in eternal beauty, crystalline waters and
    woods.

Long have I waited lonely, shunned as a thing
    accurst,

Monstrous, moody, pathetic, the last of the lands
    and the first ;

Visioning camp-fires at twilight, sad with a longing
    forlorn,

Feeling my womb o'er-pregnant with the seed of
    cities unborn.

Wild and wide are my borders, stern as death is
    my sway,

And I wait for the men who will win me—and I
    will not be won in a day ;

And I will not be won by weaklings, subtile, suave,
    and mild,

But by men with the hearts of vikings, and the
    simple faith of a child ;

Desperate, strong, and resistless, unthrottled by
    fear or defeat,

Them will I gild with my treasure, them will I
    glut with my meat.

" Lofty I stand from each sister land, patient and
wearily wise,

With the weight of a world of sadness in my quiet,
passionless eyes ;

Dreaming alone of a people, dreaming alone of
a day,

When men shall not rape my riches, and curse me
and go away ;

Making a bawd of my bounty, fouling the hand
that gave—

Till I rise in my wrath and I sweep on their path
and I stamp them into a grave.

Dreaming of men who will bless me, of women
esteeming me good,

Of children born in my borders, of radiant motherhood ;

Of cities leaping to stature, of fame like a flag
unfurled,

As I pour the tide of my riches in the eager lap
of the world."

This is the Law of the Yukon, that only the Strong
    shall thrive ;
That surely the Weak shall perish, and only the
    Fit survive.
Dissolute, damned, and despairful, crippled and
    palsied and slain,
This is the Will of the Yukon,—Lo ! how she
    makes it plain !

THE PARSON'S SON

*This is the song of the parson's son, as he squats in
    his shack alone,
On the wild, weird nights when the Northern Lights
    shoot up from the frozen zone,
And it's sixty below, and couched in the snow the
    hungry huskies moan.*

" I'm one of the Arctic brotherhood, I'm an old-
    time pioneer.
I came with the first—O God ! how I've cursed
    this Yukon—but still I'm here.
I've sweated athirst in its summer heat, I've
    frozen and starved in its cold ;
I've followed my dreams by its thousand streams,
    I've toiled and moiled for its gold.

15   B

" Look at my eyes—been snow-blind twice ; look
    where my foot's half gone ;
And that gruesome scar on my left cheek where
    the frost-fiend bit to the bone.
Each one a brand of this devil's land, where I've
    played and I've lost the game,
A broken wreck with a craze for ' hooch,' and
    never a cent to my name.

" This mining is only a gamble, the worst is as
    good as the best ;
I was in with the bunch and I might have come
    out right on top with the rest ;
With Cormack. Ladue and Macdonald—O God !
    but it's hell to think
Of the thousands and thousands I've squandered
    on cards and women and drink.

" In the early days we were just a few, and we
    hunted and fished around,
Nor dreamt by our lonely camp-fires of the wealth
    that lay under the ground.

We traded in skins and whiskey, and I've often
slept under the shade.
Of that lone birch tree on Bonanza, where the first
big find was made.

" We were just like a great big family, and every
man had his squaw,
And we lived such a wild, free, fearless life beyond
the pale of the law ;
Till sudden there came a whisper, and it maddened
us every man,
And I got in on Bonanza before the big rush
began.

" Oh, those Dawson days, and the sin and the blaze,
and the town all open wide !
(If God made me in His likeness, sure He let the
devil inside.)
But we all were mad, both the good and the bad,
and as for the women, well—
No spot on the map in so short a space has hustled
more souls to hell.

" Money was just like dirt there, easy to get and
    to spend.

I was all caked in on a dance-hall jade, but she
    shook me in the end.

It put me queer, and for near a year I never drew
    sober breath,

Till I found myself in the bughouse ward with a
    claim staked out on death.

" Twenty years in the Yukon, struggling along its
    creeks ;

Roaming its giant valleys, scaling its god-like
    peaks ;

Bathed in its fiery sunsets, fighting its fiendish
    cold,

Twenty years in the Yukon . . . twenty years—
    and I'm old.

" Old and weak, but no matter, there's ' hooch ' in
    the bottle still.

I'll hitch up the dogs to-morrow, and mush down
    the trail to Bill.

It's so long dark, and I'm lonesome—I'll just lay
    down on the bed,
To-morrow I'll go . . . to-morrow . . . I guess
    I'll play on the red.

" . . . Come, Kit, your pony is saddled. I'm
    waiting, dear, in the court . . .
. . . Minnie, you devil, I'll kill you if you skip
    with that flossy sport . . .
. . . How much does it go to the pan, Bill ? . . .
    play up, School, and play the game . . .
. . . Our Father, which art in heaven, hallowed be
    Thy name . . ."

This was the song of the parson's son, as he lay in
    his bunk alone,
Ere the fire went out and the cold crept in, and his
    blue lips ceased to moan,
And the hunger-maddened malamutes had torn him
    flesh from bone.

THE SPELL OF THE YUKON

I WANTED the gold, and I sought it;
    I scrabbled and mucked like a slave.
Was it famine or scurvy—I fought it,
    I hurled my youth into the grave.
I wanted the gold and I got it—
    Came out with a fortune last fall,—
Yet somehow life's not what I thought it,
    And somehow the gold isn't all.

No! There's the land. (Have you seen it?)
    It's the cussedest land that I know,
From the big, dizzy mountains that screen it,
    To the deep, deathlike valleys below.
Some say God was tired when He made it;
    Some say it's a fine land to shun;
Maybe: but there's some as would trade it
    For no land on earth—and I'm one.

You come to get rich (damned good reason),
    You feel like an exile at first;
You hate it like hell for a season,
    And then you are worse than the worst.
It grips you like some kinds of sinning;
    It twists you from foe to a friend;
It seems it's been since the beginning;
    It seems it will be to the end.

I've stood in some mighty-mouthed hollow
    That's plumb-full of hush to the brim;
I've watched the big, husky sun wallow
    In crimson and gold, and grow dim,
Till the moon set the pearly peaks gleaming,
    And the stars tumbled out, neck and crop;
And I've thought that I surely was dreaming,
    With the peace o' the world piled on top.

The summer—no sweeter was ever;
    The sunshiny woods all athrill;
The greyling aleap in the river,
    The bighorn asleep on the hill.

The strong life that never knows harness;
  The wilds where the caribou call;
The freshness, the freedom, the farness—
  O God! how I'm stuck on it all.

The winter! the brightness that blinds you,
  The white land locked tight as a drum,
The cold fear that follows and finds you,
  The silence that bludgeons you dumb.
The snows that are older than history,
  The woods where the weird shadows slant;
The stillness, the moonlight, the mystery,
  I've bade 'em good-bye—but I can't.

There's a land where the mountains are nameless,
  And the rivers all run God knows where;
There are lives that are erring and aimless,
  And deaths that just hang by a hair;
There are hardships that nobody reckons;
  There are valleys unpeopled and still;
There's a land—oh, it beckons and beckons,
  And I want to go back—and I will.

They're making my money diminish ;
  I'm sick of the taste of champagne.
Thank God ! when I'm skinned to a finish
  I'll pike to the Yukon again.
I'll fight—and you bet it's no sham-fight :
  It's hell !—but I've been there before ;
And it's better than this by a damsite—
  So me for the Yukon once more.

There's gold, and it's haunting and haunting,
  It's luring me on as of old ;
Yet it isn't the gold that I'm wanting
  So much as just finding the gold.
It's the great, big, broad land 'way up yonder,
  It's the forests where silence has lease ;
It's the beauty that thrills me with wonder,
  It's the stillness that fills me with peace.

THE CALL OF THE WILD

HAVE you gazed on naked grandeur where there's
    nothing else to gaze on,
  Set pieces and drop-curtain scenes galore,
Big mountains heaved to heaven, which the blind-
    ing sunsets blazon,
  Black canyons where the rapids rip and roar ?
Have you swept the visioned valley with the green
    stream streaking through it,
  Searched the Vastness for a something you have
    lost ?
Have you strung your soul to silence ?   Then for
    God's sake go and do it ;
  Hear the challenge, learn the lesson, pay the cost.

Have you wandered in the wilderness, the sage-
    brush desolation,
  The bunch-grass levels where the cattle graze !

Have you whistled bits of rag-time at the end of
    all creation,
  And learned to know the desert's little ways ?
Have you camped upon the foothills, have you
    galloped o'er the ranges,
  Have you roamed the arid sun-lands through
    and through ?
Have you chummed up with the mesa ? Do you
    know its moods and changes ?
  Then listen to the wild—it's calling you.

Have you known the Great White Silence, not a
    snow-gemmed twig a-quiver ?
  (Eternal truths that shame our soothing lies.)
Have you broken trail on snowshoes ? mushed
    your huskies up the river,
  Dared the unknown, led the way, and clutched
    the prize ?
Have you marked the map's void spaces, mingled
    with the mongrel races,
  Felt the savage strength of brute in every
    thew ?

And though grim as hell the worst is, can you
    round it off with curses ?
Then hearken to the wild—it's wanting you.

Have you suffered, starved, and triumphed,
    grovelled down, yet grasped at glory,
Grown bigger in the bigness of the whole ?
" Done things " just for the doing, letting babblers
    tell the story.
Seeing through the nice veneer the naked
    soul ?
Have you seen God in His splendours, heard the
    text that nature renders ?
(You'll never hear it in the family pew.)
The simple things, the true things, the silent men
    who do things—
Then listen to the wild—it's calling you.

They have cradled you in custom, they have
    primed you with their preaching,
They have soaked you in convention through
    and through ;

They have put you in a showcase ; you're a credit
    to their teaching—
  But can't you hear the wild ?—it's calling you.
Let us probe the silent places, let us seek what
    luck betide us ;
  Let us journey to a lonely land I know.
There's a whisper on the night-wind, there's a star
    agleam to guide us,
  And the wild is calling, calling . . . let us go.

THE LONE TRAIL

Ye who know the Lone Trail fain would follow it,
Though it lead to glory or the darkness of the pit.
Ye who take the Lone Trail, bid your love good-bye ;
The Lone Trail, the Lone Trail follow till you die.

The trails of the world be countless, and most of
  the trails be tried ;
You tread on the heels of the many, till you come
  where the ways divide ;
And one lies safe in the sunlight, and the other
  is dreary and wan,
Yet you look aslant at the Lone Trail, and the
  Lone Trail lures you on.
And somehow you're sick of the highway, with
  its noise and its easy needs,
And you seek the risk of the by-way, and you reck
  not where it leads.

28

And sometimes it leads to the desert, and the
 tongue swells out of the mouth,
And you stagger blind to the mirage, to die in the
 mocking drouth.
And sometimes it leads to the mountain, to the
 light of the lone camp-fire,
And you gnaw your belt in the anguish of hunger-
 goaded desire.

And sometimes it leads to the Southland, to the
 swamp where the orchid glows,
And you rave to your grave with the fever, and
 they rob the corpse for its clothes.
And sometimes it leads to the Northland, and the
 scurvy softens your bones,
And your flesh dints in like putty, and you spit
 out your teeth like stones.
And sometimes it leads to a coral reef in the wash
 of a weedy sea,
And you sit and stare at the empty glare where
 the gulls wait greedily.
And sometimes it leads to an Arctic trail, and the
 snows where your torn feet freeze,

And you whittle away the useless clay, and crawl
    on your hands and knees.
Often it leads to the dead-pit ; always it leads to
    pain ;
By the bones of your brothers ye know it, but oh,
    to follow you're fain.
By your bones they will follow behind you, till the
    ways of the world are made plain.

Bid good-bye to sweetheart, bid good-bye to friend ;
The Lone Trail, the Lone Trail follow to the end.
Tarry not, and fear not, chosen of the true ;
Lover of the Lone Trail, the Lone Trail waits for you.

THE HEART OF THE SOURDOUGH

THERE where the mighty mountains bare their
    fangs unto the moon ;
There where the sullen sun-dogs glare in the
    snow-bright, bitter noon,
And the glacier-gutted streams sweep down at the
    clarion call of June :

There where the livid tundras keep their tryst
    with the tranquil snows ;
There where the Silences are spawned, and the
    light of hell-fire flows
Into the bowl of the midnight sky, violet, amber,
    and rose :

There where the rapids churn and roar, and the
    ice-floes bellowing run ;

31

Where the tortured, twisted rivers of blood rush
    to the setting sun—
I've packed my kit and I'm going, boys, ere
    another day is gone.

.   .   .   .   .   .

1 knew it would call, or soon or late, as it calls
    the whirring wings ;
It's the olden lure, it's the golden lure, it's the
    lure of the timeless things ;
And to-night, O God of the trails untrod, how
    it whines in my heart-strings !

I'm sick to death of your well-groomed gods, your
    make-believe and your show ;
I long for a whiff of bacon and beans, a snug
    shake-down in the snow,
A trail to break, and a life at stake, and another
    bout with the foe ;

With the raw-ribbed Wild that abhors all life,
    the Wild that would crush and rend ;

I have clinched and closed with the naked North,
 I have learned to defy and defend ;
Shoulder to shoulder we've fought it out—yet the
 Wild must win in the end.

I have flouted the Wild. I have followed its lure,
 fearless, familiar, alone ;
By all that the battle means and makes I claim
 that land for mine own ;
Yet the Wild must win, and a day will come
 when I shall be overthrown.

Then when as wolf-dogs fight we've fought, the
 lean wolf-land and I ;
Fought and bled till the snows are red under the
 reeling sky ;
Even as lean wolf-dog goes down will I go down
 and die.

THE THREE VOICES

THE waves have a story to tell me,
  As I lie on the lonely beach;
Chanting aloft in the pine-tops,
  The wind has a lesson to teach;
But the stars sing an anthem of glory
  I cannot put into speech.

The waves tell of ocean spaces,
  Of hearts that are wild and brave,
Of populous city places,
  Of desolate shores they lave;
Of men who sally in quest of gold
  To sink in an ocean grave.

The wind is a mighty roamer;
  He bids me keep me free,

Clean from the taint of the gold-lust,
   Hardy and pure as he ;
Cling with my love to nature
   As a child to the mother-knee.

But the stars throng out in their glory,
   And they sing of the God in man ;
They sing of the mighty Master,
   Of the loom His fingers span ;
Where a star or a soul is a part of the whole.
   And weft in the wondrous plan.

Here by the camp-fire's flicker,
   Deep in my blanket curled,
I long for the peace of the pine-gloom
   When the scroll of the Lord is unfurled.
And the wind and the wave are silent,
   And world is singing to world.

THE PINES

WE sleep in the sleep of ages, the bleak, barbarian
    pines ;
The grey moss drapes us like sages, and closer
    we lock our lines,
And deeper we clutch through the gelid gloom
    where never a sunbeam shines.

On the flanks of the storm-gored ridges are our
    black battalions massed ;
We surge in a host to the sullen coast, and we
    sing in the ocean blast ;
From empire of sea to empire of snow we grip
    our empire fast.

To the niggard lands were we driven ; 'twixt
   desert and foe are we penned.
To us was the Northland given, ours to stronghold and defend ;
Ours till the world be riven in the crash of the
   utter end.

Ours from the bleak beginning, through the æons
   of death-like sleep ;
Ours from the shock when the naked rock was
   hurled from the hissing deep ;
Ours through the twilight ages of weary glacier-
   creep.

Wind of the East, wind of the West, wandering
   to and fro,
Chant your songs in our topmost boughs, that the
   sons of men may know
The peerless pine was the first to come, and the
   pine will be last to go !

We pillar the halls of perfumed gloom ; we plume
    where the eagles soar ;
The North-wind swoops from the brooding Pole,
    and our ancients crash and roar ;
But where one falls from the crumbling walls
    shoots up a hardy score.

We spring from the gloom of the canyon's womb ;
    in the valley's lap we lie ;
From the white foam-fringe where the breakers
    cringe to the peaks that tusk the sky
We climb, and we peer in the crag-locked mere
    that gleams like a golden eye,—

Gain to the verge of the hog-back ridge where
    the vision ranges free :
Pines and pines and the shadow of pines as far
    as the eye can see ;
A steadfast legion of stalwart knights in dominant
    empery.

Sun, moon and stars, give answer ; shall we not
    staunchly stand
Even as now, forever, wards of the wilder strand,
Sentinels of the stillness. lords of the last lone
    land !

THE HARPY

*There was a woman, and she was wise; woefully
  wise was she;*
*She was old, so old, yet her years all told were but
  a score and three;*
*And she knew by heart, from finish to start, the
  Book of Iniquity.*

There is no hope for such as I, on earth nor yet
  in Heaven;
Unloved I live, unloved I die, unpitied, un-
  forgiven;
A loathèd jade I ply my trade, unhallowed and
  unshriven.

I paint my cheeks, for they are white, and cheeks
of chalk men hate ;
Mine eyes with wine I make to shine, that men
may seek and sate ;
With overhead a lamp of red I sit me down and
wait.

Until they come, the nightly scum, with drunken
eyes aflame ;
Your sweethearts, sons, ye scornful ones—'tis I
who know their shame ;
The gods ye see are brutes to me—and so I play
my game.

For life is not the thing we thought, and not the
thing we plan ;
And woman in a bitter world must do the best
she can ;
Must yield the stroke, and bear the yoke, and
serve the will of man ;

Must serve his need and ever feed the flame of
   his desire ;
Though be she loved for love alone, or be she
   loved for hire ;
For every man since life began is tainted with
   the mire.

And though you know he love you so, and set
   you on love's throne,
Yet let your eyes but mock his sighs, and let
   your heart be stone,
Lest you be left (as I was left) attainted and
   alone.

From love's close kiss to hell's abyss is one sheer
   flight, I trow ;
And wedding-ring and bridal bell are will-o'-wisps
   of woe ;
And 'tis not wise to love too well, and this all
   women know.

Wherefore, the wolf-pack having gorged upon the
 lamb, their prey,
With siren smile and serpent guile I make the wolf-
 pack pay ;
With velvet paws and flensing claws, a tigress
 roused to slay.

One who in youth sought truest truth, and found a
 devil's lies ;
A symbol of the sin of man, a human sacrifice :
Yet shall I blame on man the shame ?   Could it be
 otherwise ?

Was I not born to walk in scorn where others walk
 in pride ?
The Maker marred, and evil-starred I drift upon
 His tide ;
And He alone shall judge His own, so I His judg-
 ment bide.

Fate has written a tragedy; its name is "The
Human Heart."

The theatre is the House of Life, Woman the mummer's
part :

The Devil enters the prompter's box and the play is
ready to start.

THE LURE OF LITTLE VOICES

THERE'S a cry from out the Loneliness—Oh, listen,
    Honey, listen !
  Do you hear it, do you fear it, you're a-holding
    of me so ?
You're a-sobbing in your sleep, dear, and your
    lashes, how they glisten—
  Do you hear the Little Voices all a-begging me
    to go ?

All a-begging me to leave you. Day and night
    they're pleading, praying,
  On the North-wind, on the West-wind, from the
    peak and from the plain ;
Night and day they never leave me—do you know
    what they are saying ?
  " He was ours before you got him, and we want
    him once again."

Yes, they're wanting me, they're haunting me, the
  awful lonely places ;
  They're whining and they're whimpering as if
    each had a soul ;
They're calling from the wilderness, the vast and
    god-like spaces,
  The stark and sullen solitudes that sentinel the
    Pole.

They miss my little camp-fires, ever brightly,
    bravely gleaming
  In the womb of desolation where was never man
    before ;
As comradeless I sought them, lion-hearted, loving,
    dreaming ;
  And they hailed me as a comrade, and they loved
    me evermore.

And now they're all a-crying, and it's no use me
    denying :
  The spell of them is on me and I'm helpless as
    a child ;

My heart is aching, aching, but I hear them sleep-
    ing, waking ;
  It's the Lure of Little Voices, it's the mandate of
    the Wild.

I'm afraid to tell you, Honey, I can take no bitter
    leaving ;
  But softly in the sleep-time from your love I'll
    steal away.
Oh, it's cruel, dearie, cruel, and it's God knows how
    I'm grieving ;
  But His Loneliness is calling and He knows I
    must obey.

THE SONG OF THE WAGE-SLAVE

WHEN the long, long day is over, and the Big Boss
    gives me my pay,
I hope that it won't be hell-fire, as some of the
    parsons say.
And I hope that it won't be heaven, with some of
    the parsons I've met—
All I want is just quiet, just to rest and forget.
Look at my face, toil-furrowed; look at my
    calloused hands;
Master, I've done Thy bidding, wrought in Thy
    many lands—
Wrought for the little masters, big-bellied they be,
    and rich;
I've done their desire for a daily hire, and I die like
    a dog in a ditch.

I have used the strength Thou hast given, Thou
    knowest I did not shirk ;
Threescore years of labour—Thine be the long
    day's work.
And now, Big Master, I'm broken and bent and
    twisted and scarred,
But I've held my job, and Thou knowest, and Thou
    wilt not judge me hard.
Thou knowest my sins are many, and often I've
    played the fool—
Whiskey and cards and women, they made me the
    devil's tool.
I was just like a child with money : I flung it away
    with a curse,
Feasting a fawning parasite, or glutting a harlot's
    purse,
Then back to the woods repentant, back to the
    mill or the mine,
I, the worker of workers, everything in my
    line.
Everything hard but headwork (I'd no more brains
    than a kid),

A brute with brute strength to labour, doing as I
was bid ;

Living in camps with men-folk, a lonely and love-
less life ;

Never knew kiss of sweetheart, never caress of
wife.

A brute with brute strength to labour, and they
were so far above—

Yet I'd gladly have gone to the gallows for one
little look of Love.

I with the strength of two men, savage and shy
and wild—

Yet how I'd ha' treasured a woman, and the
sweet, warm kiss of a child.

Well, 'tis Thy world, and Thou knowest. I
blaspheme and my ways be rude ;

But I've lived my life as I found it, and I've done
my best to be good ;

I, the primitive toiler, half naked, and grimed to
the eyes,

Sweating it deep in their ditches, swining it stark
in their styes.

Hurling down forests before me, spanning tumul-
    tuous streams;

Down in the ditch building o'er me palaces fairer
    than dreams;

Boring the rock to the ore-bed, driving the road
    through the fen,

Resolute, dumb, uncomplaining, a man in a world
    of men.

Master, I've filled my contract, wrought in Thy
    many lands;

Not by my sins wilt Thou judge me, but by the
    work of my hands.

Master, I've done Thy bidding, and the light is
    low in the west,

And the long, long shift is over . . . Master, I've
    earned it—Rest.

GRIN

IF you're up against a bruiser and you're getting
    knocked about—

               Grin.

If you're feeling pretty groggy, and you're licked
    beyond a doubt—

               Grin.

Don't let him see you're funking, let him know
    with every clout,

Though your face is battered to a pulp, your
    blooming heart is stout :

Just stand upon your pins until the beggar knocks
    you out—

               And grin.

This life's a bally battle, and the same advice
    holds true,

               Of grin.

If you're up against it badly, then it's only one
    on you,

                So grin.

If the future's black as thunder, don't let people
    see you're blue ;

Just cultivate a cast-iron smile of joy the whole
    day through ;

If they call you " Little Sunshine," wish that *they'd*
    no troubles, too—

                You may—grin.

Rise up in the morning with the will that, smooth
    or rough,

                You'll grin.

Sink to sleep at midnight, and although you're
    feeling tough,

                Yet grin.

There's nothing gained by whining, and you're not
    that kind of stuff ;

You're a fighter from away back, and you *won't*
    take a rebuff :

Your trouble is that you don't know when you
    have had enough—
                Don't give in.
If Fate should down you, just get up and take
    another cuff ;
You may bank on it that there is no philosophy
    like bluff
                And grin.

THE SHOOTING OF DAN McGREW

A BUNCH of the boys were whooping it up in the
    Malamute saloon ;
The kid that handles the music-box was hitting a
    jag-time tune ;
Back of the bar, in a solo game, sat Dangerous
    Dan McGrew,
And watching his luck was his light-o'-love, the
    lady that's known as Lou.

When out of the night, which was fifty below,
    and into the din and the glare,
There stumbled a miner fresh from the creeks,
    dog-dirty and loaded for bear.

He looked like a man with a foot in the grave,
and scarcely the strength of a louse,
Yet he tilted a poke of dust on the bar, and he
called for drinks for the house.
There was none could place the stranger's face,
though we searched ourselves for a clue ;
But we drank his health, and the last to drink
was Dangerous Dan McGrew.

There's men that somehow just grip your eyes,
and hold them hard like a spell ;
And such was he, and he looked to me like a
man who had lived in hell ;
With a face most hair, and the dreary stare of a
dog whose day is done,
As he watered the green stuff in his glass, and
the drops fell one by one.
Then I got to figgering who he was, and wondering
what he'd do,
And I turned my head—and there watching him
was the lady that's known as Lou.

His eyes went rubbering round the room, and he
    seemed in a kind of daze,
Till at last that old piano fell in the way of his
    wandering gaze.
The rag-time kid was having a drink ; there was
    no one else on the stool,
So the stranger stumbles across the room, and
    flops down there like a fool.
In a buckskin shirt that was glazed with dirt he
    sat, and I saw him sway ;
Then he clutched the keys with his talon hands—
    my God ! but that man could play !

Were you ever out in the Great Alone, when the
    moon was awful clear,
And the icy mountains hemmed you in with a
    silence you most could *hear* ;
With only the howl of a timber wolf, and you
    camped there in the cold,
A half-dead thing in a stark, dead world, clean
    mad for the muck called gold ;

While high overhead, green, yellow, and red, the
    North Lights swept in bars—
Then you've a haunch what the music meant . . .
    hunger and night and the stars.

And hunger not of the belly kind, that's banished
    with bacon and beans ;
But the gnawing hunger of lonely men for a home
    and all that it means ;
For a fireside far from the cares that are, four
    walls and a roof above ;
But oh ! so cramful of cosy joy, and crowned
    with a woman's love ;
A woman dearer than all the world, and true as
    Heaven is true—
(God ! how ghastly she looks through her rouge,—
    the lady that's known as Lou.)

Then on a sudden the music changed, so soft that
    you scarce could hear ;
But you felt that your life had been looted clean
    of all that it once held dear ;

That some one had stolen the woman you loved ;
    that her love was a devil's lie ;
That your guts were gone, and the best for you
    was to crawl away and die.
'Twas the crowning cry of a heart's despair, and
    it thrilled you through and through—
" I guess I'll make it a spread misere," said Danger-
    ous Dan McGrew.

The music almost died away . . . then it burst
    like a pent-up flood ;
And it seemed to say, " Repay, repay," and my
    eyes were blind with blood.
The thought came back of an ancient wrong, and
    it stung like a frozen lash,
And the lust awoke to kill, to kill . . . then the
    music stopped with a crash,

And the stranger turned, and his eyes they burned
    in a most peculiar way ;
In a buckskin shirt that was glazed with dirt he
    sat, and I saw him sway ;

Then his lips went in in a kind of grin, and he
  spoke, and his voice was calm ;
And, " Boys," says he, " you don't know me, and
  none of you care a damn ;
But I want to state, and my words are straight,
  and I'll bet my poke they're true,
That one of you is a hound of hell . . . and that
  one is Dan McGrew."

Then I ducked my head, and the lights went out.
  and two guns blazed in the dark ;
And a woman screamed, and the lights went up,
  and two men lay stiff and stark ;
Pitched on his head, and pumped full of lead, was
  Dangerous Dan McGrew,
While the man from the creeks lay clutched to
  the breast of the lady that's known as Lou.

These are the simple facts of the case, and I guess
  I ought to know ;
They say that the stranger was crazed with
  " hooch," and I'm not denying it's so.

I'm not so wise as the lawyer guys, but strictly
    between us two—
The woman that kissed him and—pinched his
    poke—was the lady that's known as Lou.

THE CREMATION OF SAM McGEE

THERE are strange things done in the midnight
     sun
  By the men who moil for gold ;
The Arctic trails have their secret tales
     That would make your blood run cold ;
The Northern Lights have seen queer sights,
     But the queerest they ever did see
Was that night on the marge of Lake Lebarge
     I cremated Sam McGee.

Now Sam McGee was from Tennessee, where the
     cotton blooms and blows.
Why he left his home in the South to roam round
     the Pole God only knows.

He was always cold, but the land of gold seemed
    to hold him like a spell ;
Though he'd often say in his homely way that
    he'd " sooner live in hell."

On a Christmas Day we were mushing our way
    over the Dawson trail.
Talk of your cold ! through the parka's fold it
    stabbed like a driven nail.
If our eyes we'd close, then the lashes froze, till
    sometimes we couldn't see ;
It wasn't much fun, but the only one to whimper
    was Sam McGee.

And that very night as we lay packed tight in our
    robes beneath the snow,
And the dogs were fed, and the stars o'erhead
    were dancing heel and toe,
He turned to me, and, " Cap," says he, " I'll cash
    in this trip, I guess ;
And if I do, I'm asking that you won't refuse my
    last request."

Well, he seemed so low that I couldn't say no :
    then he says with a sort of moan :
" It's the cursèd cold, and it's got right hold till
    I'm chilled clean through to the bone.
Yet 'taint being dead, it's my awful dread of the
    icy grave that pains :
So I want you to swear that, foul or fair, you'll
    cremate my last remains."

A pal's last need is a thing to heed, so I swore I
    would not fail ;
And we started on at the streak of dawn, but God !
    he looked ghastly pale.
He crouched on the sleigh, and he raved all day
    of his home in Tennessee ;
And before nightfall a corpse was all that was left
    of Sam McGee.

There wasn't a breath in that land of death, and
    I hurried, horror driven,
With a corpse half-hid that I couldn't get rid
    because of a promise given ;

It was lashed to the sleigh, and it seemed to say :
   " You may tax your brawn and brains,
But you promised true, and it's up to you to
   cremate those last remains."

Now a promise made is a debt unpaid, and the
   trail has its own stern code.
In the days to come, though my lips were dumb,
   in my heart how I cursed that load.
In the long, long night, by the lone firelight, while
   the huskies, round in a ring,
Howled out their woes to the homeless snows—O
   God ! how I loathed the thing !

And every day that quiet clay seemed to heavy
   and heavier grow ;
And on I went, though the dogs were spent and
   the grub was getting low ;
The trail was bad, and I felt half mad, but I swore
   I would not give in ;
And I'd often sing to the hateful thing, and it
   hearkened with a grin.

Till I came to the marge of Lake Lebarge. and a
    derelict there lay ;
It was jammed in the ice, but I saw in a trice it
    was called the " Alice May."
And I looked at it, and I thought a bit, and I
    looked at my frozen chum :
Then, " Here," said I, with a sudden cry, " is my
    cre-ma-tor-eum."

Some planks I tore from the cabin floor, and I lit
    the boiler fire ;
Some coal I found that was lying around, and I
    heaped the fuel higher ;
The flames just soared, and the furnace roared—
    such a blaze you seldom see ;
And I burrowed a hole in the glowing coal, and I
    stuffed in Sam McGee.
Then I made a hike, for I didn't like to hear him
    sizzle so ;
And the heavens scowled, and the huskies howled,
    and the wind began to blow.

It was icy cold, but the hot sweat rolled down my
    cheeks, and I don't know why ;
And the greasy smoke in an inky cloak went
    streaking down the sky.

I do not know how long in the snow I wrestled
    with grisly fear ;
But the stars came out and they danced about ere
    again I ventured near ;
I was sick with dread, but I bravely said : " I'll
    just take a peep inside.
I guess he's cooked, and it's time I looked," . . .
    then the door I opened wide.

And there sat Sam, looking cool and calm, in the
    heart of the furnace roar ;
And he wore a smile you could see a mile, and he
    said : " Please close that door.
It's fine in here, but I greatly fear you'll let in the
    cold and storm—
Since I left Plumtree, down in Tennessee, it's the
    first time I've been warm "

There are strange things done in the midnight sun
    By the men who moil for gold ;
The Arctic trails have their secret tales
    That would make your blood run cold.
The Northern Lights have seen queer sights,
    But the queerest they ever did see
Was that night on the marge of Lake Lebarge
    I cremated Sam McGee.

MY MADONNA

I HALED me a woman from the street,
  Shameless, but, oh, so fair !
I bade her sit in the model's seat,
  And I painted her sitting there.

    I hid all trace of her heart unclean ;
      I painted a babe at her breast ;
    I painted her as she might have been
      If the Worst had been the Best.

She laughed at my picture, and went away.
  Then came, with a knowing nod,
A connoisseur, and I heard him say :
  " 'Tis Mary, the Mother of God."

So I painted a halo round her hair,
    And I sold her, and took my fee,
And she hangs in the church of Saint Hilaire,
    Where you and all may see.

UNFORGOTTEN

I KNOW a garden where the lilies gleam,
  And one who lingers in the sunshine there;
  She is than white-stoled lily far more fair,
And oh, her eyes are heaven-lit with dream.

  I know a garret, cold and dark and drear,
    And one who toils and toils with tireless pen,
    Until his brave, sad eyes grow weary—then
  He seeks the stars, pale, silent as a seer.

And ah, it's strange, for desolate and dim
  Between these two there rolls an ocean wide;
  Yet he is in the garden by her side,
And she is in the garret there with him.

THE RECKONING

It's fine to have a blow-out in a fancy restaurant,
With terrapin and canvas-back and all the wine
 you want ;
To enjoy the flowers and music, watch the pretty
 women pass,
Smoke a choice cigar, and sip the wealthy water
 in your glass ;
It's bully in a high-toned joint to eat and drink
 your fill,
But it's quite another matter when you
                              Pay the bill.

It's great to go out every night on fun or pleasure
 bent,
To wear your glad rags always, and to never save
 a cent ;

To drift along regardless, have a good time every
    trip ;
To hit the high spots sometimes, and to let your
    chances slip ;
To know you're acting foolish, yet to go on fooling
    still,
Till Nature calls a show-down, and you
                    Pay the bill.

Time has got a little bill—get wise while yet you
    may,
For the debit side's increasing in a most alarming
    way ;
The things you had no right to do, the things you
    should have done,
They're all put down : it's up to you to pay for
    every one.
So eat, drink, and be merry, have a good time if you
    will,
But God help you when the time comes, and you
                  Foot the bill.

QUATRAINS

One said : Thy life is thine to make or mar,
To flicker feebly, or to soar, a star ;
It lies with thee—the choice is thine, is thine,
To hit the ties or drive thy auto-car.

I answer Her : The choice is mine—ah, no !
We all were made or marred long, long ago.
The parts are written : hear the super wail :
" Who is stage-managing this cosmic show ? "

Blind fools of fate, and slaves of circumstance.
Life is a fiddler, and we all must dance.
From gloom where mocks that will-o'-wisp, Free-
        will,
I heard a voice cry : " Say, give us a chance."

74

Chance! Oh, there is no chance. The scene is
    set.
Up with the curtain! Man, the marionette,
Resumes his part. The gods will work the wires.
They've got it all down fine, you bet, you bet!

It's all decreed : the mighty earthquake crash ;
The countless constellations' wheel and flash ;
The rise and fall of empires, war's red tide,
The composition of your dinner hash.

There's no haphazard in this world of ours :
Cause and effect are grim, relentless powers.
They rule the world. (A king was shot last
    night.
Last night I held the joker and both bowers.)

From out the mesh of fate our heads we thrust.
We can't do what we would, but what we must.
Heredity has got us in a cinch.
(Consoling thought, when you've been on a
    " bust.")

Hark to the song where spheral voices blend :
" There's no beginning, never will be end."
It makes us nutty ; hang the astral chimes !
The table's spread ; come, let us dine, my friend.

THE MEN THAT DON'T FIT IN

THERE'S a race of men that don't fit in,
  A race that can't stay still ;
So they break the hearts of kith and kin,
  And they roam the world at will.
They range the field and they rove the flood,
  And they climb the mountain's crest ;
Theirs is the curse of the gipsy blood,
  And they don't know how to rest.

  If they just went straight they might go far ;
    They are strong and brave and true ;
  But they're always tired of the things that are,
    And they want the strange and new.
  They say : " Could I find my proper groove,
    What a deep mark I would make ! "
  So they chop and change, and each fresh move
  Is only a fresh mistake.

And each forgets, as he strips and runs,
  With a brilliant, fitful pace,
It's the steady, quiet, plodding ones
  Who win in the lifelong race.
And each forgets that his youth has fled,
  Forgets that his prime is past,
Till he stands one day with a hope that's dead
  In the glare of the truth at last.

    He has failed, he has failed ; he has missed
        his chance ;
      He has just done things by half.
    Life's been a jolly good joke on him,
      And now is the time to laugh.
    Ha, ha ! He is one of the Legion Lost ;
      He was never meant to win ;
    He's a rolling stone, and it's bred in the
        bone ;
      He's a man who won't fit in.

MUSIC IN THE BUSH

O'ER the dark pines she sees the silver moon,
    And in the west, all tremulous, a star :
And soothing sweet she hears the mellow tune
    Of cow-bells jangled in the fields afar.

Quite listless, for her daily stent is done,
    She stands, sad exile, at her rose-wreathed door,
And sends her love eternal with the sun
    That goes to gild the land she'll see no more.

The grave, gaunt pines imprison her sad gaze,
    All still the sky and darkling drearily ;
She feels the chilly breath of dear, dead days
    Come sifting through the alders eerily.

Oh, how the roses riot in their bloom !
  The curtains stir as with an ancient pain ;
Her old piano gleams from out the gloom,
  And waits and waits her tender touch in vain.

But now her hands like moonlight brush the
      keys
  With velvet grace. melodious delight ;
And now a sad refrain from overseas
  Goes sobbing on the bosom of the night.

And now she sings.   (O singer in the gloom,
  Voicing a sorrow we can ne'er express,
Here in the Farness where we few have room
  Unshamed to show our love and tenderness,

Our hearts will echo, till they beat no more,
  That song of sadness and of motherland ;
And stretched in deathless love to England's
      shore,
  Some day she'll hearken and she'll understand.)

A prima-donna in the shining past,
  But now a mother growing old and grey,
She thinks of how she held a people fast
  In thrall, and gleaned the triumphs of a day.

She sees a sea of faces like a dream ;
  She sees herself a queen of song once more ;
She sees lips part in rapture, eyes agleam ;
  She sings as never once she sang before.

She sings a wild, sweet song that throbs with
        pain,
  The added pain of life that transcends art,
A song of home, a deep, celestial strain,
  The glorious swan-song of a dying heart.

A lame tramp comes along the railway track,
  A grizzled dog whose day is nearly done :
He passes, pauses, then comes slowly back
  And listens there—an audience of one.

She sings—her golden voice is passion-fraught
    As when she charmed a thousand eager ears ;
He listens trembling, and she knows it not,
    And down his hollow cheeks roll bitter tears.

She ceases and is still, as if to pray ;
    There is no sound, the stars are all alight—
Only a wretch who stumbles on his way,
    Only a vagrant sobbing in the night.

THE RHYME OF THE REMITTANCE MAN

THERE'S a four-pronged buck a-swinging in the
    shadow of my cabin,
  And it roamed the velvet valley till to-day ;
But I tracked it by the river, and I trailed it in
    the cover,
  And I killed it on the mountain miles away.
Now I've had my lazy supper, and the level sun
    is gleaming
  On the water where the silver salmon play ;
And I light my little corn-cob, and I linger softly
    dreaming,
  In the twilight, of a land that's far away.

Far away, so faint and far, is flaming London,
    fevered Paris,
  That I fancy I have gained another star ;

Far away the din and hurry, far away the sin and
    worry,
  Far away—God knows they cannot be too far.
Gilded galley-slaves of Mammon—how my purse-
    proud brothers taunt me !
  I might have been as well-to-do as they
Had I clutched like them my chances, learned
    their wisdom, crushed my fancies,
  Starved my soul and gone to business every
    day.

Well, the cherry bends with blossom, and the
    vivid grass is springing,
  And the star-like lily nestles in the green ;
And the frogs their joys are singing, and my heart
    in tune is ringing,
  And it doesn't matter what I might have
    been.
While above the scented pine-gloom, piling heights
    of golden glory,
  The sun-god paints his canvas in the west ;

I can couch me deep in clover, I can listen to
    the story
  Of the lazy, lapping water—it is best.

While the trout leaps in the river, and the blue
    grouse thrills the cover,
  And the frozen snow betrays the panther's
    track,
And the robin greets the dayspring with the
    rapture of a lover,
  I am happy, and I'll nevermore go back.
For I know I'd just be longing for the little old
    log cabin,
  With the morning-glory clinging to the door,
Till I loathed the city places, cursed the care on
    all the faces,
  Turned my back on lazar London evermore.

So send me far from Lombard Street, and write
    me down a failure ;
  Put a little in my purse and leave me free.

Say: "He turned from Fortune's offering to
      follow up a pale lure,
  He is one of us no longer—let him be."
I am one of you no longer: by the trails my feet
      have broken,
  The dizzy peaks I've scaled, the camp-fire's
      glow,
By the lonely seas I've sailed in—yea, the final
      word is spoken,
  I am signed and sealed to nature. Be it so.

THE LOW-DOWN WHITE

THIS is the pay-day up at the mines, when the
bearded brutes come down ;
There's money to burn in the streets to-night, so
I've sent my klooch to town,
With a haggard face and a ribband of red entwined
in her hair of brown.

And I know at the dawn she'll come reeling home
with the bottles, one, two, three ;
One for herself to drown her shame, and two big
bottles for me,
To make me forget the thing I am and the man
I used to be.

To make me forget the brand of the dog, as I
crouch in this hideous place ;

To make me forget once I kindled the light of
  love in a lady's face,
Where even the squalid Siwash now holds me a
  black disgrace.

Oh, I have guarded my secret well ! And who
  would dream as ı speak
In a tribal tongue like a rogue unhung, 'mid the
  ranch-house tilth and reek,
I could roll to bed with a Latin phrase, and rise
  with a verse of Greek ?

Yet I was a senior prizeman once, and the pride
  of a college eight ;
Called to the bar—my friends were true ! but they
  could not keep me straight ;
Then came the divorce, and I went abroad and
  " died " on the River Plate.

But I'm not dead yet ; though with half a lung
  there isn't time to spare,

And I hope that the year will see me out, and,
    thank God, no one will care—
Save maybe the little slim Siwash girl with the
    rose of shame in her hair.

She will come with the dawn, and the dawn is
    near ; I can see its evil glow,
Like a corpse-light seen through a frosty pane in
    a night of want and woe ;
And yonder she comes, by the bleak bull-pines,
    swift staggering through the snow.

THE LITTLE OLD LOG CABIN

WHEN a man gits on his uppers in a hard-pan sort
 of town,
  An' he ain't got nothin' comin', an' he can't afford
   ter eat.
An' he's in a fix fer lodgin', an' he wanders up an'
 down,
  An' you'd fancy he'd been boozin', he's so
   locoed 'bout the feet ;
When he's feelin' sneakin' sorry, an' his belt is
 hangin' slack,
  An' his face is peaked an' grey-like, an' his heart
   gits down an' whines,
Then he's apt ter git a-thinkin' an' a-wishin' he was
 back
  In the little ol' log cabin in the shadder of the
   pines.

90

When he's on the blazin' desert, an' his canteen's
    sprung a leak,
  An' he's all alone an' crazy, an' he's crawlin'
    like a snail,
An' his tongue's so black an' swollen that it hurts
    him fer to speak,
  An' he gouges down fer water, an' the raven's
    on his trail ;
When he's done with care and cursin', an' he feels
    more like to cry,
  An' he sees ol' Death a-grinnin', an' he thinks
    upon his crimes,
Then he's like ter hev' a vision, as he settles down
    ter die,
  Of the little ol' log cabin an' the roses an' the
    vines.

Oh, the little ol' log cabin, it's a solemn shinin'
    mark
  When a feller gits ter sinnin', an' a-goin' ter
    the wall,

An' folks don't understand him, an' he's gropin in
  the dark,

  An' he's sick of bein' cursed at, an' he's longin'
    fer his call :

When the sun of life's a-sinkin' you can see it
    'way above,

  On the hill from out the shadder in a glory 'gin
    the sky,

An' your mother's voice is callin', an' ner arms
    are stretched in love.

  An' somehow you're glad you're goin', an' you
    ain't a-scared to die ;

When you'll be like a kid again, an' nestle to her
    breast,

  An' never leave its shelter, an' forget, an' love,
    an' rest.

THE YOUNGER SON

IF you leave the gloom of London and you seek
  a glowing land,
  Where all except the flag is strange and
    new,
There's a bronzed and stalwart fellow who will grip
  you by the hand,
  And greet you with a welcome warm and
    true ;
For he's your younger brother, the one you sent
  away,
  Because there wasn't room for him at home ;
And now he's quite contented, and he's glad he
  didn't stay,
  And he's building Britain's greatness o'er the
    foam.

When the giant herd is moving at the rising of
    the sun,
  And the prairie is lit with rose and gold ;
And the camp is all a-bustle, and the busy day's
    begun,
  He leaps into the saddle sure and bold.
Through the round of heat and hurry, through the
    racket and the rout,
  He rattles at a pace that nothing mars ;
And when the night-winds whisper, and camp-fires
    flicker out,
  He is sleeping like a child beneath the stars.

When the wattle-blooms are drooping in the sombre
    she-oak glade,
  And the breathless land is lying in a swoon,
He leaves his work a moment, leaning lightly on
    his spade,
  And he hears the bell-bird chime the Austral noon.
The parakeets are silent in the gum-tree by the
    creek ;
  The ferny grove is sunshine-steeped and still ;

But the dew will gem the myrtle in the twilight
  ere he seek
 His little lonely cabin on the hill.

Around the purple, vine-clad slope the argent river
  dreams ;
 The roses almost hide the house from view ;
A snow-peak of the Winterberg in crimson splen-
  dour gleams ;
 The shadow deepens down on the karroo.
He seeks the lily-scented dusk beneath the orange
  tree :
 His pipe in silence glows and fades and
  glows,
And then two little maids come out and climb
  upon his knee,
 And one is like the lily, one the rose.

He sees his white sheep dapple o'er the green
  New Zealand plain,
 And where Vancouver's shaggy ramparts frown

When the sunlight threads the pine-gloom he is
    fighting might and main
  To clinch the rivets of an Empire down.
You will find him toiling, toiling, in the south or
    in the west,
  A child of nature, fearless, frank and free :
And the warmest heart that beats for you is beating
    in his breast,
  And he sends you loyal greeting o'er the sea.

You've a brother in the Army, you've another in
    the Church ;
  One of you is a diplomatic swell ;
You've had the pick of everything and left him
    in the lurch ;
  And yet I think he's doing very well.
I'm sure his life is happy, and he doesn't envy yours;
  I know he loves the land his pluck has won :
And I fancy in the years unborn, while England's
    fame endures,
  She will come to bless with pride—the Younger
    Son.

THE MARCH OF THE DEAD

THE cruel war was over—oh, the triumph was so
    sweet !
  We watched the troops returning, through our
    tears ;
There was triumph, triumph, triumph down the
    scarlet glittering street,
  And you scarce could hear the music for the
    cheers.

And you scarce could see the house-tops for the
    flags that flew between,
  The bells were pealing madly to the sky ;
And every one was shouting for the Soldiers of
    the Queen,
  And the glory of an age was passing by.

And then there came a shadow. swift and sudden
    dark and drear ;
  The bells were silent, not an echo stirred.
The flags were drooping sullenly, the men forgot
    to cheer ;
  We waited, and we never spoke a word.
The sky grew darker, darker, till from out the
    gloomy rack
  There came a voice that checked the heart with
    dread :
" Tear down, tear down your bunting now, and
    hang up sable black ;
  They are coming—it's the Army of the Dead."

They were coming, they were coming, gaunt and
    ghastly, sad and slow ;
  They were coming, all the crimson wrecks of
    pride ;
With faces seared, and cheeks red smeared, and
    haunting eyes of woe,
  And clotted holes the khaki couldn't hide.

Oh, the clammy brow of anguish ! the livid, foam-
  flecked lips !

The reeling ranks of ruin swept along !

The limb that trailed, the hand that failed, the
  bloody finger-tips !

And oh, the dreary rhythm of their song !

" They left us on the veldt-side, but we felt we
  couldn't stop,

  On this, our England's crowning festal day ;

We're the men of Magersfontein, we're the men of
  Spion Kop,

  Colenso,—we're the men who had to pay.

We're the men who paid the blood-price. Shall
  the grave be all our gain ?

  You owe us.   Long and heavy is the score.

Then cheer us for our glory now, and cheer us for
  our pain,

  And cheer us as ye never cheered before."

The folks were white and stricken, and each tongue
  seemed weighed with lead ;

  Each heart was clutched in hollow hand of ice ;

And every eye was staring at the horror of the dead,
  The pity of the men who paid the price.
They were come, were come to mock us, in the
    first flush of our peace ;
  Through writhing lips their teeth were all
    agleam ;
They were coming in their thousands—oh, would
    they never cease !
  I closed my eyes, and then—it was a dream.

There was triumph, triumph, triumph down the
    scarlet gleaming street ;
  The town was mad, a man was like a boy.
A thousand flags were flaming where the sky and
    city meet ;
  A thousand bells were thundering the joy.
There was music, mirth and sunshine ; but some
    eyes shone with regret :
  And while we stun with cheers our homing
    braves,
O God, in Thy great mercy, let us nevermore forget
  The graves they left behind, the bitter graves.

" FIGHTING MAC "

A LIFE TRAGEDY

A PISTOL-SHOT rings round and round the world :
 In pitiful defeat a warrior lies.
A last defiance to dark Death is hurled,
 A last wild challenge shocks the sunlit skies.
 Alone he falls with wide, wan, woeful eyes :
Eyes that could smile at death—could not face
 shame.

Alone, alone he paced his narrow room,
 In the bright sunshine of that Paris day ;
Saw in his thought the awful hand of doom ;
 Saw in his dream his glory pass away ;
 Tried in his heart, his weary heart, to pray :
" O God ! who made me, give me strength to face
The spectre of this bitter, black disgrace."

 *   *   *   *   *   *

The burn brawls darkly down the shaggy glen,
  The bee-kissed heather blooms around the door
He sees himself a barefoot boy again,
  Bending o'er page of legendary lore.
  He hears the pibroch, grips the red claymore,
Runs with the Fiery Cross a clansman true,
Sworn kinsman of Rob Roy and Roderick Dhu.

Eating his heart out with a wild desire,
  One day, behind his counter trim and neat,
He hears a sound that sets his brain afire—
  The Highlanders are marching down the street.
  Oh, how the pipes shrill out, the mad drums
      beat !
" On to the gates of Hell, my Gordons gay ! "
He flings his hated yardstick far away.

He sees the sullen pass, high-crowned with snow,
  Where Afghans cower with eyes of gleaming hate.
He hurls himself against the hidden foe.
  They try to rally—ah, too late, too late !
  Again, defenceless, with fierce eyes that wait

For death, he stands, like baited bull at bay,
And flouts the Boers, that mad Majuba day.

He sees again the murderous Soudan,
   Blood-slaked and rapine swept. He seems to
      stand
Upon the gory plain of Omdurman.
   Then Magersfontein, and supreme command
   Over his Highlanders. To shake his hand
A King is proud, and princes call him friend,
And glory crowns his life—and now the end.

The awful end. His eyes are dark with doom ;
   He hears the shrapnel shrieking overhead :
He sees the ravaged ranks, the flame - stabbed
      gloom.
   Oh, to have fallen ! the battle-field his bed,
   With Wauchope and his glorious brother-dead.
Why was he saved for this, for this ? And now
He raises the revolver to his brow.

   .   .   .   .   .   .

In many a Highland home, framed with rude art,
   You'll find his portrait, rough-hewn, stern and
      square :
It's graven in the Fuyam fellah's heart ;
   The Ghurka reads it at his evening prayer ;
   The raw lands know it, where the fierce suns
      glare ;
The Dervish fears it.   Honour to his name,
Who holds aloft the shield of England's fame.

Mourn for our hero, men of Northern race !
   We do not know his sin ; we only know
His sword was keen. He laughed death in the
      face,
   And struck, for Empire's sake, a giant blow.
   His arm was strong.   Ah ! well they learnt, the
      foe.
The echo of his deeds is ringing yet,
Will ring for aye.   All else . . . let us forget.

THE WOMAN AND THE ANGEL

An angel was tired of heaven, as he lounged in
    the golden street ;
His halo was tilted sideways, and his harp lay mute
    at his feet ;
So the Master stooped in His pity, and gave him
    a pass to go,
For the space of a moon, to the earth-world, to
    mix with the men below.

He doffed his celestial garments, scarce waiting
    to lay them straight ;
He bade goodbye to Peter, who stood by the
    golden gate ;
The sexless singers of heaven chanted a fond
    farewell,
And the imps looked up as they pattered on the
    red-hot flags of hell.

Never was seen such an angel : eyes of a heavenly
    blue,

Features that shamed Apollo, hair of a golden
    hue ;

The women simply adored him, his lips were like
    Cupid's bow ;

But he never ventured to use them—and so they
    voted him slow.

Till at last there came One Woman, a marvel of
    loveliness,

And she whispered to him : " Do you love me ? "
    And he answered that woman, " Yes."

And she said : " Put your arms around me, and
    kiss me, and hold me—so—"

But fiercely he drew back, saying : " This thing is
    wrong, and I know."

Then sweetly she mocked his scruples, and softly
    she him beguiled :

" You, who are verily man among men, speak with
    the tongue of a child.

We have outlived the old standards ; we have
    burst, like an over-tight thong,
The ancient, outworn, puritanic traditions of Right
    and Wrong."

Then the Master feared for His angel, and called
    him again to His side,
For oh, the woman was wondrous, and oh, the
    angel was tried.
And deep in his hell sang the Devil, and this was
    the strain of his song :
* The ancient, outworn, puritanic traditions of
    Right and Wrong."

THE RHYME OF THE RESTLESS ONES

WE couldn't sit and study for the law ;
    The stagnation of a bank we couldn't stand :
For our riot blood was surging, and we didn't need
        much urging
To excitements and excesses that are banned.
So we took to wine and drink and other things,
    And the devil in us struggled to be free ;
Till our friends rose up in wrath, and they pointed
        out the path,
And they paid our debts and packed us o'er the
        sea.

Oh, they shook us off and shipped us o'er the
        foam,
To the larger lands that lure a man to roam ;
        And we took the chance they gave
        Of a far and foreign grave,
And we bade goodbye for evermore to home.

And some of us are climbing on the peak,
   And some of us are camping on the plain ;
By pine and palm you'll find us, with never claim
     to bind us,
By track and trail you'll meet us once again.

We are fated serfs to freedom—sky and sea ;
   We have failed where slummy cities overflow ;
But the stranger ways of earth know our pride and
     know our worth,
And we go into the dark as fighters go.

Yes, we go into the night as brave men go,
Though our faces they be often streaked with woe ;
     Yet we're hard as cats to kill,
     And our hearts are reckless still,
And we've danced with death a dozen times or so.

And you'll find us in Alaska after gold,
   And you'll find us herding cattle in the South.

We like strong drink and fun ; and when the race
    is run,
  We often die with curses in our mouth.

We are wild as colts unbroke, but never mean ;
  Of our sins we've shoulders broad to bear the
    blame ;
But we'll never stay in town, and we'll never
    settle down,
  And we'll never have an object or an aim.

No, there's that in us that time can never tame ;
And life will always seem a careless game ;
      And they'd better far forget—
      Those who say they love us yet—
Forget, blot out with bitterness our name.

NEW YEAR'S EVE

It's cruel cold on the water-front, silent and dark
   and drear ;
  Only the black tide weltering, only the hissing
    snow ;
And I, alone, like a storm-tossed wreck, on this
   night of the glad New Year,
  Shuffling along in the icy wind, ghastly and
    gaunt and slow.

They're playing a tune in McGuffy's saloon, and
   it's cheery and bright in there
  (God ! but I'm weak—since the bitter dawn, and
    never a bite of food) ;
I'll just go over and slip inside—I mustn't give
   way to despair—

                E

Perhaps I can bum a little booze if the boys are
feeling good.

They'll jeer at me, and they'll sneer at me, and
they'll call me a whiskey soak ;
("Have a drink ? Well, thankee kindly, sir, I
don't mind if I do.")
A drivelling, dirty gin-joint fiend, the butt of the
bar-room joke ;
Sunk and sodden and hopeless—"Another ?
Well, here's to you ! "

McGuffy is showing a bunch of the boys how Bob
Fitzsimmons hit ;
The barman is talking of Tammany Hall, and
why the ward boss got fired ;
I'll just sneak into a corner, and they'll let me
alone a bit ;
The room is reeling round and round . . . O
God, but I'm tired, I'm tired. . . .

.   .   .   .   .

Roses she wore on her breast that night. Oh, but
their scent was sweet ;
Alone we sat on the balcony, and the fan-palms
arched above ;
The witching strain of a waltz by Strauss came
up to our cool retreat,
And I prisoned her little hand in mine, and I
whispered my plea of love.

Then sudden the laughter died on her lips, and
lowly she bent her head ;
And oh, there came in the deep, dark eyes a
look that was heaven to see,
And the moments went, and I waited there, and
never a word was said,
And she plucked from her bosom a rose of red,
and shyly gave it to me.

Then the music swelled to a crash of joy, and the
lights blazed up like day ;
And I held her fast to my throbbing heart, and
I kissed her bonny brow ;

" She is mine, she is mine for evermore ! " the
    violins seemed to say.
And the bells were ringing the New Year in—
    O God ! I can hear them now.

Don't you remember that long, last waltz, with its
    sobbing, sad refrain ?
    Don't you remember that last goodbye, and the
        dear eyes dim with tears ?
Don't you remember that golden dream, with
    never a hint of pain,
    Of lives that would blend like an angel-song in
        the bliss of the coming year ?

Oh, what have I lost ! What have I lost ! Ethel,
    forgive, forgive !
    The red, red rose is faded now, and it's fifty
        years ago.
'Twere better to die a thousand deaths than live
    each day as I live !
    I have sinned, I have sunk to the lowest depths
        —but oh, I have suffered so !

Hark ! Oh hark ! I can hear the bells ! . . .
    Look ! I can see her there,
  Fair as a dream . . . but it fades . . . And now
    —I can hear the dreadful hum
Of the crowded court . . . See ! the Judge looks
    down . . . NOT GUILTY, my Lord, I swear . . .
  The bells, I can hear the bells again . . . Ethel,
    I come, I come ! . . .
      .   .   .   .   .

"Rouse up, old man, it's twelve o'clock. You
    can't sleep here, you know.
  Say ! ain't you got no sentiment ? Lift up your
    muddled head ;
Have a drink to the glad New Year, a drop before
    you go—
  You darned old dirty hobo . . . My God !
    Here, boys ! He's DEAD ! "

COMFORT

Say ! You've struck a heap of trouble—
  Bust in business, lost your wife ;
No one cares a cent about you,
  You don't care a cent for life ;
Hard luck has of hope bereft you,
  Health is failing, wish you'd die—
Why, you've still the sunshine left you,
  And the big, blue sky.

  Sky so blue it makes you wonder
    If it's heaven shining through ;
  Earth so smiling 'way out yonder,
    Sun so bright it dazzles you ;
  Birds a-singing, flowers a-flinging
    All their fragrance on the breeze ;
  Dancing shadows, green, still meadows—
    Don't you mope, you've still got these.

116

These, and none can take them from you ;
 These, and none can weigh their worth.
What ! you're tired and broke and beaten ?—
 Why, you're rich—you've got the earth !
Yes, if you're a tramp in tatters,
 While the blue sky bends above,
You've got nearly all that matters.
 You've got God, and God is love.

PREMONITION

'Twas a year ago and the moon was bright
(Oh, I remember so well, so well),
I walked with my love in a sea of light,
And the voice of my sweet was a silver bell.

And sudden the moon grew strangely dull,
And sudden my love had taken wing ;
I looked on the face of a grinning skull,
I strained to my heart a ghastly thing.

'Twas but fantasy, for my love lay still
In my arms with her tender eyes aglow,
And she wondered why my lips were chill,
Why I was silent and kissed her so.

118

A year has gone and the moon is bright,
    A gibbous moon like a ghost of woe :
I sit by a new-made grave to-night,
    And my heart is broken—it's strange, you
    know.

THE TRAMPS

CAN you recall, dear comrade, when we tramped
    God's land together,
  And we sang the old, old Earth-song, for our
    youth was very sweet ;
When we drank and fought and lusted, as we
    mocked at tie and tether,
  Along the road to Anywhere, the wide world
    at our feet.

Along the road to Anywhere, when each day had
    its story ;
  When time was yet our vassal, and life's jest
    was still unstale ;
When peace unfathomed filled our hearts as,
    bathed in amber glory,
  Along the road to Anywhere we watched the
    sunsets pale.

120

Alas ! the road to Anywhere is pitfalled with
    disaster ;

  There's hunger, want, and weariness, yet O we
      loved it so !

As on we tramped exultantly, and no man was
    our master,

  And no man guessed what dreams were ours,
      as swinging heel and toe,

We tramped the road to Anywhere, the magic
    road to Anywhere,

  The tragic road to Anywhere, such dear, dim
      years ago.

L'ENVOI

You who have lived in the Land,
  You who have trusted the trail ;
You who are strong to withstand,
  You who are swift to assail ;
Songs have I sung to beguile,
  Vintage of desperate years
Hard as a harlot's smile,
  Bitter as unshed tears.

    Little of joy or mirth,
      Little of ease I sing ;
    Sagas of men of earth,
      Humanly suffering,
    Such as you all have done ;
      Savagely faring forth,
      Sons of the midnight sun,
        Argonauts of the North.

Far in the land God forgot
   Glimmers the lure of your trail :
Still in your lust are you taught
   Even to win is to fail.
Still must you follow and fight
   Under the vampire wing ;
There in the long, long night
   Hoping and vanquishing.

   Husbandmen of the Wild,
      Reaping a barren gain ;
   Scourged by desire, reconciled
      Unto disaster and pain ;
   These my songs are for you,
      You who are seared with the brand ;
   God knows I have tried to be true ;
      Please God you will understand.

BALLADS OF A CHEECHAKO

BALLADS DE A CHEECHAKO

BALLADS OF A CHEECHAKO

TO THE MAN OF THE HIGH NORTH

My rhymes are rough, and often in my rhyming
I've drifted, silver-sailed, on seas of dream,
Hearing afar the bells of Elfland chiming,
Seeing the groves of Arcadie agleam.

I was the thrall of Beauty that rejoices
From peak snow-diademed to regal star ;
Yet to mine aerie ever pierced the voices,
The pregnant voices of the Things That Are.

The Here, the Now, the vast Forlorn around us ;
The gold-delirium, the ferine strife ;
The lusts that lure us on, the hates that hound us ;
Our red rags in the patch-work quilt of Life.

The nameless men who nameless rivers travel,
And in strange valleys greet strange deaths alone ;
The grim, intrepid ones who would unravel
The mysteries that shroud the Polar Zone.

These will I sing, and if one of you linger
  Over my pages in the Long, Long Night,
And on some lone line lay a calloused finger,
  Saying : " It's human-true—it hits me right " ;
Then will I count this loving toil well spent ;
Then will I dream awhile—content. content.

MEN OF THE HIGH NORTH

Men of the High North, the wild sky is blazing;
   Islands of opal float on silver seas;
Swift splendours kindle, barbaric, amazing;
   Pale ports of amber, golden argosies.
Ringed all around us the proud peaks are glowing;
   Fierce chiefs in council, their wigwam the sky;
Far, far below us the big Yukon flowing,
   Like threaded quicksilver, gleams to the eye.

Men of the High North, you who have known it;
   You in whose hearts its splendours have abode;
Can you renounce it, can you disown it?
   Can you forget it, its glory and its goad?
Where is the hardship, where is the pain of it?
   Lost in the limbo of things you've forgot;
Only remain the guerdon and gain of it;
   Zest of the foray, and God, how you fought!

You who have made good, you foreign faring;
   You money magic to far lands has whirled;
Can you forget those days of vast daring,
   There with your soul on the Top o' the World?

Nights when no peril could keep you awake on
  Spruce boughs you spread for your couch in
    the snow ;
Taste all your feasts like the beans and the bacon
  Fried at the camp-fire at forty below ?

Can you remember your huskies all going,
  Barking with joy and their brushes in air ;
You in your parka, glad-eyed and glowing,
  Monarch, your subjects the wolf and the bear ?
Monarch, your kingdom unravisht and gleaming ;
  Mountains your throne, and a river your car ;
Crash of a bull moose to rouse you from dreaming ;
  Forest your couch, and your candle a star.

You who this faint day the High North is luring
  Unto her vastness, taintlessly sweet ;
You who are steel-braced, straight-lipped, en-
    during,
  Dreadless in danger and dire in defeat :
Honour the High North ever and ever,
  Whether she crown you, or whether she slay ;
Suffer her fury, cherish and love her—
  He who would rule he must learn to obey.

Men of the High North, fierce mountains love you ;
  Proud rivers leap when you ride on their breast.
See, the austere sky, pensive above you,
  Dons all her jewels to smile on your rest.

Children of Freedom, scornful of frontiers,
  We who are weaklings honour your worth.
Lords of the wilderness, Princes of Pioneers,
  Let's have a rouse that will ring round the
  earth.

THE BALLAD OF THE NORTHERN
LIGHTS

ONE of the Down and Out—that's me. Stare at
   me well, ay, stare !
Stare and shrink—say ! you wouldn't think that
   I was a millionaire.
Look at my face, it's crimped and gouged—one
   of them death-mask things ;
Don't seem the sort of man, do I, as might be
   the pal of kings ?
Slouching along in smelly rags, a bleary-eyed,
   no-good bum ;
A knight of the hollow needle, pard, spewed from
   the sodden slum.
Look me all over from head to foot ; how much
   would you think I was worth ?
A dollar ? a dime ? a nickel ? Why, *I'm the
   wealthiest man on earth.*

No, don't you think that I'm off my base. You'll
   sing a different tune
If only you'll let me spin my yarn. Come over
   to this saloon ;

Wet my throat—it's as dry as chalk, and seeing
as how it's you,
I'll tell the tale of a Northern trail, and so help
me God, it's true.
I'll tell of the howling wilderness and the haggard
Arctic heights,
Of a reckless vow that I made, and how *I staked
the Northern Lights*.

Remember the year of the Big Stampede and the
trail of Ninety-eight,
When the eyes of the world were turned to the
North, and the hearts of men elate;
Hearts of the old dare-devil breed thrilled at the
wondrous strike,
And to every man who could hold a pan came
the message, " Up and hike."
Well, I was there with the best of them, and I
knew I would not fail.
You wouldn't believe it to see me now; but wait
till you've heard my tale.

You've read of the trail of Ninety-eight, but its
woe no man may tell;
It was all of a piece and a whole yard wide, and
the name of the brand was " Hell."
We heard the call and we staked our all; we
were plungers playing blind,
And no man cared how his neighbour fared, and
no man looked behind;

For a ruthless greed was born of need, and the
    weakling went to the wall,
And a curse might avail where a prayer would
    fail, and the gold lust crazed us all.

Bold were we, and they called us three the
    " Unholy Trinity " ;
There was Ole Olson, the Sailor Swede, and the
    Dago Kid and me.
We were the discards of the pack, the foreloopers
    of Unrest,
Reckless spirits of fierce revolt in the ferment of
    the West.
We were bound to win and we revelled in the
    hardships of the way.
We staked our ground and our hopes were crowned,
    and we hoisted out the pay.
We were rich in a day beyond our dreams, it
    was gold from the grass-roots down ;
But we weren't used to such sudden wealth, and
    there was the siren town.
We were crude and careless frontiersmen, with
    much in us of the beast ;
We could bear the famine worthily, but we lost
    our heads at the feast.
The town looked mighty bright to us, with a
    bunch of dust to spend,
And nothing was half too good them days, and
    every one was our friend.

Wining meant more than mining then, and life
    was a dizzy whirl,
Gambling and dropping chunks of gold down the
    neck of a dance-hall girl ;
Till we went clean mad, it seems to me, and we
    squandered our last poke,
And we sold our claim, and we found ourselves
    one bitter morning—broke.

The Dago Kid he dreamed a dream of his mother's
    aunt who died—
In the dawn-light dim she came to him, and she
    stood by his bedside,
And she said : " Go forth to the highest North
    till a lonely trail ye find ;
Follow it far and trust your star, and fortune will
    be kind."
But I jeered at him, and then there came the
    Sailor Swede to me,
And he said : " I dreamed of my sister's son,
    who croaked at the age of three.
From the herded dead he sneaked and said :
    ' Seek you an Arctic trail ;
'Tis pale and grim by the Polar rim, but seek and
    ye shall not fail.' "
And lo ! that night I too did dream of my mother's
    sister's son,
And he said to me : " By the Arctic Sea there's
    a treasure to be won.

Follow and follow a lone moose trail, till you
    come to a valley grim,
On the slope of the lonely watershed that borders
    the Polar brim."
Then I woke my pals, and soft we swore by the
    mystic Silver Flail,
'Twas the hand of Fate, and to-morrow straight
    we would seek the lone moose trail.

We watched the groaning ice wrench free, crash
    on with a hollow din ;
Men of the wilderness were we, freed from the
    taint of sin.
The mighty river snatched us up and it bore us
    swift along ;
The days were bright, and the morning light was
    sweet with jewelled song.
We poled and lined up nameless streams, portaged
    o'er hill and plain ;
We burnt our boat to save the nails, and built
    our boat again ;
We guessed and groped, North, ever North, with
    many a twist and turn ;
We saw ablaze in the deathless days the splendid
    sunsets burn.
O'er soundless lakes where the grayling makes a
    rush at the clumsy fly ;
By bluffs so steep that the hard-hit sheep falls
    sheer from out the sky ;

By lilied pools where the bull moose cools and
    wallows in huge content ;
By rocky lairs where the pig-eyed bears peered
    at our tiny tent.
Through the black canyon's angry foam we hurled
    to dreamy bars,
And round in a ring the dog-nosed peaks bayed
    to the mocking stars.
Spring and summer and autumn went ; the sky
    had a tallow gleam,
Yet North and ever North we pressed to the land
    of our Golden Dream.

So we came at last to a tundra vast and dark and
    grim and lone ;
And there was the little lone moose trail, and we
    knew it for our own.
By muskeg hollow and nigger-head it wandered
    endlessly ;
Sorry of heart and sore of foot, weary men were
    we.
The short-lived sun had a leaden glare and the
    darkness came too soon,
And stationed there with a solemn stare was the
    pinched, anaemic moon.
Silence and silvern solitude till it made you dumbly
    shrink,
And you thought to hear with an outward ear the
    things you thought to think.

Oh, it was wild and weird and wan, and ever in
    camp o' nights
We would watch and watch the silver dance of the
    mystic Northern Lights.
And soft they danced from the Polar sky and
    swept in primrose haze ;
And swift they pranced with their silver feet, and
    pierced with a blinding blaze.
They danced a cotillion in the sky ; they were
    rose and silver shod ;
It was not good for the eyes of man—'twas a sight
    for the eyes of God.
It made us mad and strange and sad, and the
    gold whereof we dreamed
Was all forgot, and our only thought was of the
    lights that gleamed.
Oh, the tundra sponge it was golden brown, and
    some was a bright blood-red ;
And the reindeer moss gleamed here and there
    like the tombstones of the dead.
And in and out and around about the little trail
    ran clear,
And we hated it with a deadly hate and we feared
    with a deadly fear.
And the skies of night were alive with light, with
    a throbbing, thrilling flame ;
Amber and rose and violet, opal and gold it
    came.
It swept the sky like a giant scythe, it quivered
    back to a wedge ;

Argently bright, it cleft the night with a wavy
    golden edge.
Pennants of silver waved and streamed, lazy
    banners unfurled ;
Sudden splendours of sabres gleamed, lightning
    javelins were hurled.
There in our awe we crouched and saw with our
    wild, uplifted eyes
Charge and retire the hosts of fire in the battle-
    field of the skies.

But all things come to an end at last, and the
    muskeg melted away,
And frowning down to bar our path a muddle of
    mountains lay.
And a gorge sheered up in granite walls, and the
    moose trail crept betwixt ;
'Twas as if the earth had gaped too far and her
    stony jaws were fixt.
Then the winter fell with a sudden swoop, and
    the heavy clouds sagged low,
And earth and sky were blotted out in a whirl of
    driving snow.

We were climbing up a glacier in the neck of a
    mountain pass,
When the Dago Kid slipped down and fell into
    a deep crevasse.
When we got him out one leg hung limp, and
    his brow was wreathed with pain,

And he says : " 'Tis badly broken, boys, and I'll
    never walk again.
It's death for all if ye linger here, and that's no
    curséd lie ;
Go on, go on while the trail is good, and leave
    me down to die."
He raved and swore, but we tended him with
    our uncouth, clumsy care.
The camp-fire gleamed and he gazed and dreamed
    with a fixed and curious stare.
Then all at once he grabbed my gun and he put
    it to his head,
And he says : " I'll fix it for you, boys ! "—them
    are the words he said.

So we sewed him up in a canvas sack and we
    slung him to a tree ;
And the stars like needles stabbed our eyes, and
    woeful men were we.
And on we went on our woeful way, wrapped in
    a daze of dream,
And the Northern Lights in the crystal nights
    came forth with a mystic gleam.
They danced and they danced the devil-dance
    over the naked snow ;
And soft they rolled like a tide upshoaled with
    a ceaseless ebb and flow.
They rippled green with a wondrous sheen, they
    fluttered out like a fan :

They spread with a blaze of rose-pink rays never
    yet seen of man.
They writhed like a brood of angry snakes,
    hissing and sulphur pale;
Then swift they changed to a dragon vast, lash-
    ing a cloven tail.
It seemed to us, as we gazed aloft with an ever-
    lasting stare,
The sky was a pit of bale and dread, and a
    monster revelled there.
We climbed the rise of a hog-back range that
    was desolate and drear,
When the Sailor Swede had a crazy fit, and he
    got to talking queer.
He talked of his home in Oregon and the peach-
    trees all in bloom,
And the fern head-high, and the topaz sky, and
    the forest's scented gloom.
He talked of the sins of his misspent life, and
    then he seemed to brood,
And I watched him there like a fox a hare, for
    I knew it was not good.
And sure enough in the dim dawn-light I missed
    him from the tent,
And a fresh trail broke through the crusted snow,
    and I knew not where it went.
But I followed it o'er the seamless waste, and I
    found him at shut of day,
Naked there as a new-born babe—so I left him
    where he lay.

Day after day was sinister, and I fought fierce-
    eyed despair,
And I clung to life, and I struggled on, I knew
    not why nor where.
I packed my grub in short relays, and I cowered
    down in my tent,
And the world around was purged of sound like
    a frozen continent.
Day after day was dark as death, but ever and
    ever at nights,
With a brilliancy that grew and grew, blazed up
    the Northern Lights.
They rolled around with a soundless sound like
    softly bruiséd silk ;
They poured into the bowl of the sky with the
    gentle flow of milk.
In eager, pulsing violet their wheeling chariots
    came,
Or they poised above the Polar rim like a coronal
    of flame.
From depths of darkness fathomless their lancing
    rays were hurled,
Like the all-combining searchlights of the navies
    of the world.
There on the roof-pole of the world as one be-
    witched I gazed,
And howled and grovelled like a beast as the
    awful splendours blazed.
My eyes were seared, yet thralled I peered through
    the parka hood nigh blind ;

But I staggered on to the lights that shone, and
  never I looked behind.
There is a mountain round and low that lies by
  the Polar rim,
And I climbed its height in a whirl of light, and
  I peered o'er its jaggéd brim ;
And there in a crater deep and vast, ungained,
  unguessed of men,
The mystery of the Arctic world was flashed into
  my ken.
For there these poor dim eyes of mine beheld
  the sight of sights—
That hollow ring was the source and spring of the
  mystic Northern Lights.

Then I staked that place from crown to base,
  and I hit the homeward trail.
Ah, God ! it was good, though my eyes were
  blurred, and I crawled like a sickly snail.
In that vast white world where the silent sky
  communes with the silent snow,
In hunger and cold and misery I wandered to and fro.
But the Lord took pity on my pain, and He led
  me to the sea,
And some ice-bound whalers heard my moan, and
  they fed and sheltered me.
They fed the feeble scarecrow thing that stumbled
  out of the wild
With the ravaged face of a mask of death and
  the wandering wits of a child—

                                                F

A craven, cowering bag of bones that once had
    been a man.
They tended me and they brought me back to
    the world, and here I am.

Some say that the Northern Lights are the glare
    of the Arctic ice and snow ;
And some that it's electricity, and nobody seems
    to know.
But I'll tell you now—and if I lie, may my lips
    be stricken dumb—
It's a *mine*, a mine of the precious stuff that men
    call radium.
It's a million dollars a pound, they say, and there's
    tons and tons in sight.
You can see it gleam in a golden stream in the
    solitudes of night.
And it's mine, all mine—and say ! if you have
    a hundred plunks to spare,
I'll let you have the chance of your life, I'll sell
    you a quarter share.
You turn it down ? Well, I'll make it ten, seeing
    as you are my friend.
Nothing doing ? Say ! don't be hard—have you
    got a dollar to lend ?
Just a dollar to help me out, I know you'll treat
    me white ;
I'll do as much for you some day . . . God bless
    you, sir ; good-night.

THE BALLAD OF THE BLACK FOX SKIN

I

THERE was Claw-fingered Kitty and Windy Ike
    living the life of shame,
When unto them in the Long, Long Night came
    the man-who-had-no-name ;
Bearing his prize of a black fox pelt, out of the
    Wild he came.

His cheeks were blanched as the flume-head foam
    when the brown spring freshets flow ;
Deep in their dark, sin-calcined pits were his
    sombre eyes aglow ;
They knew him far for the fitful man who spat
    forth blood on the snow.

" Did ever you see such a skin ? " quoth he ;
    " there's nought in the world so fine—
Such fulness of fur as black as the night, such
    lustre, such size, such shine ;
It's life to a one-lunged man like me ; it's London,
    it's women, it's wine.

"The Moose-hides called it the devil-fox, and
    swore that no man could kill;
That he who hunted it, soon or late, must surely
    suffer some ill;
But I laughed at them and their old-squaw tales.
    Ha! Ha! I'm laughing still.

"For look ye, the skin—it's as smooth as sin, and
    black as the core of the Pit.
By gun or by trap, whatever the hap, I swore I
    would capture it;
By star and by star afield and afar, I hunted and
    would not quit.

"For the devil-fox, it was swift and sly, and it
    seemed to fleer at me;
I would wake in fright by the camp-fire light,
    hearing its evil glee;
Into my dream its eyes would gleam, and its
    shadow would I see.

"It sniffed and ran from the ptarmigan I had
    poisoned to excess;
Unharmed it sped from my wrathful lead ('twas
    as if I shot by guess);
Yet it came by night in the stark moonlight to
    mock at my weariness.

"I tracked it up where the mountains hunch like
    the vertebrae of the world;

I tracked it down to the death-still pits where the
  avalanche is hurled ;
From the glooms to the sacerdotal snows, where
  the carded clouds are curled.

" From the vastitudes where the world protrudes
  through clouds like seas up-shoaled,
I held its track till it led me back to the land I
  had left of old—
The land I had looted many moons. I was weary
  and sick and cold.

" I was sick, soul-sick, of the futile chase, and
  there and then I swore
The foul fiend fox might scathless go, for I would
  hunt no more ;
Then I rubbed mine eyes in a vast surprise—it
  stood by my cabin door.

" A rifle raised in the wraith-like gloom, and a
  vengeful shot that sped ;
A howl that would thrill a cream-faced corpse—
  and the demon fox lay dead. . . .
Yet there was never a sign of wound, and never
  a drop he bled.

" So that was the end of the great black fox, and
  here is the prize I've won ;
And now for a drink to cheer me up—I've mushed
  since the early sun ;

We'll drink a toast to the sorry ghost of the fox
    whose race is run."

II

Now Claw-fingered Kitty and Windy Ike, bad as
    the worst were they ;
In their road-house down by the river-trail they
    waited and watched for prey ;
With wine and song they joyed night long, and
    they slept like swine by day.

For things were done in the Midnight Sun that
    no tongue will ever tell ;
And men there be who walk earth free, but whose
    names are writ in hell—
Are writ in flames with the guilty names of
    Fournier and Labelle.

Put not your trust in a poke of dust would ye
    sleep the sleep of sin ;
For there be those who would rob your clothes
    ere yet the dawn comes in ;
And a prize likewise in a woman's eyes is a peer-
    less black fox skin.

Put your faith in the mountain cat if you lie
    within his lair ;
Trust the fangs of the mother-wolf, and the claws
    of the lead-ripped bear ;

But oh, of the wiles and the gold-tooth smiles of
    a dance-hall wench beware !

Wherefore it was beyond all laws that lusts of
    man restrain,
A man drank deep and sank to sleep never to
    wake again ;
And the Yukon swallowed through a hole the cold
    corpse of the slain.

III

The black fox skin a shadow cast from the roof
    nigh to the floor ;
And sleek it seemed and soft it gleamed, and the
    woman stroked it o'er ;
And the man stood by with a brooding eye, and
    gnashed his teeth and swore.

When thieves and thugs fall out and fight there's
    fell arrears to pay ;
And soon or late sin meets its fate, and so it fell
    one day
That Claw-fingered Kitty and Windy Ike fanged
    up like dogs at bay.

" The skin is mine, all mine," she cried ; " I did
    the deed alone."
" It's share and share with a guilt-yoked pair,"
    he hissed in a pregnant tone ;

And so they snarled like malamutes over a mildewed bone.

And so they fought, by fear untaught, till haply
    it befell
One dawn of day she slipped away to Dawson
    town to sell
The fruit of sin, this black fox skin that had made
    their lives a hell.

She slipped away as still he lay, she clutched the
    wondrous fur ;
Her pulses beat, her foot was fleet, her fear was
    as a spur ;
She laughed with glee, she did not see him rise
    and follow her.

The bluffs uprear and grimly peer far over Dawson
    town ;
They see its lights a blaze o' nights and harshly
    they look down ;
They mock the plan and plot of man with grim,
    ironic frown.

The trail was steep ; 'twas at the time when
    swiftly sinks the snow ;
All honeycombed, the river ice was rotting down
    below ;
The river chafed beneath its rind with many a
    mighty throe.

And up the swift and oozy drift a woman climbed
   in fear,
Clutching to her a black fox fur as if she held it
   dear ;
And hard she pressed it to her breast—then Windy
   Ike drew near.

She made no moan—her heart was stone—she
   read his smiling face,
And like a dream flashed all her life's dark horror
   and disgrace ;
A moment only—with a snarl he hurled her into
   space.

She rolled for nigh an hundred feet ; she bounded
   like a ball ;
From crag to crag she carromed down through
   snow and timber fall ; . . .
A hole gaped in the river ice ; the spray flashed—
   that was all.

A bird sang for the joy of spring, so piercing
   sweet and frail ;
And blinding bright the land was dight in gay
   and glittering mail ;
And with a wondrous black fox skin a man slid
   down the trail.

IV

A wedge-faced man there was who ran along the
    river bank,
Who stumbled through each drift and slough, and
    ever slipped and sank,
And ever cursed his Maker's name, and ever
    " hooch " he drank.

He travelled like a hunted thing, hard harried,
    sore distrest ;
The old grandmother moon crept out from her
    cloud-quilted nest ;
The aged mountains mocked at him in their
    primeval rest.

Grim shadows diapered the snow ; the air was
    strangely mild ;
The valley's girth was dumb with mirth, the
    laughter of the wild ;
The still, sardonic laughter of an ogre o'er a child.

The river writhed beneath the ice ; it groaned
    like one in pain,
The yawning chasms opened wide, and closed
    and yawned again ;
And sheets of silver heaved on high until they
    split in twain.

From out the road-house by the trail they saw a
    man afar
Make for the narrow river-reach where the swift
    cross-currents are ;
Where, frail and worn, the ice is torn and the
    angry waters jar.

But they did not see him crash and sink into the
    icy flow ;
They did not see him clinging there, gripped by
    the undertow,
Clawing with bleeding finger-nails at the jagged
    ice and snow.

They found a note beside the hole where he had
    stumbled in :
" Here met his fate by evil luck a man who lived
    in sin,
And to the one who loves me least I leave this
    black fox skin."

And strange it is ; for, though they searched the
    river all around,
No trace or sign of black fox skin was ever after
    found ;
Though one man said he saw the tread of *hoofs*
    deep in the ground.

THE BALLAD OF PIOUS PETE

" The North has got him."—Yukonism.

I TRIED to refine that neighbour of mine, honest
    to God, I did.
I grieved for his fate, and early and late I watched
    over him like a kid.
I gave him excuse, I bore his abuse in every way
    that I could ;
I swore to prevail ; I camped on his trail ; I
    plotted and planned for his good.
By day and by night I strove in men's sight to
    gather him into the fold,
With precept and prayer, with hope and despair,
    in hunger and hardship and cold.
I followed him into Gehennas of sin, I sat where
    the sirens sit ;
In the shade of the Pole, for the sake of his soul,
    I strove with the powers of the Pit.

I shadowed him down to the scrofulous town ; I
    dragged him from dissolute brawls ;
But I killed the galoot when he started to shoot
    electricity into my walls.

God knows what I did he should seek to be rid
    of one who would save him from shame.
God knows what I bore that night when he swore
    and bade me make tracks from his claim.
I started to tell of the horrors of hell, when sudden
    his eyes lit like coals ;
And " Chuck it," says he, " don't persecute me
    with your cant and your saving of souls."
I'll swear I was mild as I'd be with a child, but
    he called me the son of a slut ;
And, grabbing his gun with a leap and a run, he
    threatened my face with the butt.
So what could I do (I leave it to you) ? With
    curses he harried me forth ;
Then he was alone, and I was alone, and over
    us menaced the North.

Our cabins were near ; I could see, I could hear ;
    but between us there rippled the creek ;
And all summer through, with a rancour that grew,
    he would pass me and never would speak.
Then a shuddery breath like the coming of Death
    crept down from the peaks far away ;
The water was still ; the twilight was chill ; the
    sky was a tatter of gray.
Swift came the Big Cold, and opal and gold the
    lights of the witches arose ;
The frost-tyrant clinched, and the valley was
    cinched by the stark and cadaverous snows.

The trees were like lace where the star-beams
could chase, each leaf with a jewel agleam.
The soft white hush lapped the Northland and
wrapped us round in a crystalline dream ;
So still I could hear quite loud in my ear the
swish of the pinions of time ;
So bright I could see, as plain as could be, the
wings of God's angels ashine.

As I read in the Book I would oftentimes look
to that cabin just over the creek.
Ah me, it was sad and evil and bad, two neigh-
bours who never would speak !
I knew that full well like the devil in hell he was
hatching out, early and late,
A system to bear through the frost-spangled air
the warm, crimson waves of his hate.
I only could peer and shudder and fear—'twas
ever so ghastly and still ;
But I knew over there in his lonely despair he
was plotting me terrible ill.
I knew that he nursed a malice accurst, like the
blast of a winnowing flame ;
I pleaded aloud for a shield, for a shroud—Oh,
God ! then calamity came.

Mad ! If I'm mad then you too are mad ; but
it's all in the point of view.
If you'd looked at them things gallivantin' on
wings, all purple and green and blue ;

If you'd noticed them twist, as they mounted and
    hissed like scorpions dim in the dark ;
If you'd seen them rebound with a horrible sound,
    and spitefully spitting a spark ;
If you'd watched *It* with dread, as it hissed by your
    bed, that thing with the feelers that crawls—
You'd have settled the brute that attempted to
    shoot electricity into your walls.

Oh, some they were blue, and they slithered right
    through ; they were silent and squashy and
    round ;
And some they were green ; they were wriggly
    and lean ; they writhed with so hateful a
    sound.
My blood seemed to freeze ; I fell on my knees ;
    my face was a white splash of dread.
Oh, the Green and the Blue, they were gruesome
    to view ; but the worst of them all were the
    Red.
They came through the door, they came through
    the floor, they came through the moss-creviced
    logs.
They were savage and dire ; they were whiskered
    with fire ; they bickered like malamute dogs.
They ravined in rings like iniquitous things ; they
    gulped down the Green and the Blue.
I crinkled with fear whene'er they drew near, and
    nearer and nearer they drew.

And then came the crown of Horror's grim crown,
    the monster so loathsomely red.
Each eye was a pin that shot out and in, as, squid-
    like, it oozed to my bed ;
So softly it crept with feelers that swept and
    quivered like fine copper wire ;
Its belly was white with a sulphurous light, its
    jaws were a-drooling with fire.
It came and it came ; I could breathe of its flame,
    but never a wink could I look.
I thrust in its maw the Fount of the Law ; I
    fended it off with the Book.
I was weak—oh, so weak—but I thrilled at its
    shriek, as wildly it fled in the night ;
And deathlike I lay till the dawn of the day.   (Was
    ever so welcome the light ?)

I loaded my gun at the rise of the sun ; to his
    cabin so softly I slunk.
My neighbour was there in the frost-freighted air,
    all wrapped in a robe in his bunk.
It muffled his moans ; it outlined his bones, as
    feebly he twisted about ;
His gums were so black, and his lips seemed to
    crack, and his teeth all were loosening out.
'Twas a death's head that peered through the
    tangle of beard ; 'twas a face I will never
    forget ;
Sunk eyes full of woe, and they troubled me so
    with their pleadings and anguish, and yet

As I rested my gaze in a misty amaze on the
    scurvy degenerate wreck,
I thought of the Things with the dragon-fly wings,
    then laid I my gun on his neck.
He gave out a cry that was faint as a sigh, like a
    perishing malamute,
And he says unto me, " I'm converted," says he ;
    " for Christ's sake, Peter, don't shoot ! "
They're taking me out with an escort about, and
    under a sergeant's care ;
I am humbled indeed, for I'm 'cuffed to a Swede
    that thinks he's a millionaire.
But it's all Gospel true what I'm telling to you—
    up there where the Shadow falls—
That I settled Sam Noot when he started to shoot
    electricity into my walls.

THE BALLAD OF BLASPHEMOUS BILL

I TOOK a contract to bury the body of blasphemous
  Bill MacKie,
Whenever, wherever or whatsoever the manner of
  death he die—
Whether he die in the light o' day or under the
  peak-faced moon ;
In cabin or dance-hall, camp or dive, mucklucks
  or patent shoon ;
On velvet tundra or virgin peak, by glacier, drift
  or draw ;
In muskeg hollow or canyon gloom, by avalanche,
  fang or claw ;
By battle, murder or sudden wealth, by pestilence,
  hooch or lead—
I swore on the Book I would follow and look till
  I found my tombless dead.

For Bill was a dainty kind of cuss, and his mind
  was mighty sot
On a dinky patch with flowers and grass in a
  civilised bone-yard lot.

And where he died or how he died, it didn't
    matter a damn
So long as he had a grave with frills and a tomb-
    stone " epigram."
So I promised him, and he paid the price in good
    cheechako coin
(Which the same I blowed in that very night down
    in the Tenderloin).
Then I painted a three-foot slab of pine : " Here
    lies poor Bill MacKie,"
And I hung it up on my cabin wall and I waited
    for Bill to die.

Years passed away, and at last one day came a
    squaw with a story strange,
Of a long-deserted line of traps 'way back of the
    Bighorn range ;
Of a little hut by the great divide, and a white
    man stiff and still,
Lying there by his lonesome self, and I figured it
    must be Bill.
So I thought of the contract I'd made with him,
    and I took down from the shelf
The swell black box with the silver plate he'd
    picked out for hisself ;
And I packed it full of grub and " hooch," and I
    slung it on the sleigh ;
Then I harnessed up my team of dogs and was off
    at dawn of day.

You know what it's like in the Yukon wild when
    it's sixty-nine below ;
When the ice-worms wriggle their purple heads
    through the crust of the pale blue snow ;
When the pine-trees crack like little guns in the
    silence of the wood,
And the icicles hang down like tusks under the
    parka hood ;
When the stove-pipe smoke breaks sudden off, and
    the sky is weirdly lit,
And the careless feel of a bit of steel burns like a
    red-hot spit ;
When the mercury is a frozen ball, and the frost-
    fiend stalks to kill—
Well, it was just like that that day when I set out
    to look for Bill.

Oh, the awful hush that seemed to crush me down
    on every hand,
As I blundered blind with a trail to find through
    that blank and bitter land ;
Half dazed, half crazed in the winter wild, with its
    grim heart-breaking woes,
And the ruthless strife for a grip on life that only
    the sourdough knows !
North by the compass, North I pressed ; river and
    peak and plain
Passed like a dream I slept to lose and I waked
    to dream again.

River and plain and mighty peak—and who could
    stand unawed ?
As their summits blazed, he could stand undazed
    at the foot of the throne of God.
North, aye, North, through a land accurst, shunned
    by the scouring brutes,
And all I heard was my own harsh word and the
    whine of the malamutes,
Till at last I came to a cabin squat, built in the
    side of a hill,
And I burst in the door, and there on the floor,
    frozen to death, lay Bill.

Ice, white ice, like a winding-sheet, sheathing each
    smoke-grimed wall ;
Ice on the stove-pipe, ice on the bed, ice gleaming
    over all ;
Sparkling ice on the dead man's chest, glittering
    ice in his hair,
Ice on his fingers, ice in his heart, ice in his glassy
    stare ;
Hard as a log and trussed like a frog, with his
    arms and legs outspread.
I gazed at the coffin I'd brought for him, and I
    gazed at the gruesome dead,
And at last I spoke : " Bill liked his joke ; but
    still, goldarn his eyes,
A man had ought to consider his mates in the way
    he goes and dies."

Have you ever stood in an Arctic hut in the shadow
  of the Pole,
With a little coffin six by three and a grief you
  can't control ?
Have you ever sat by a frozen corpse that looks
  at you with a grin,
And that seems to say : " You may try all day,
  but you'll never jam me in ? "
I'm not a man of the quitting kind, but I never
  felt so blue
As I sat there gazing at that stiff and studying
  what I'd do.
Then I rose and I kicked off the husky dogs that
  were nosing round about,
And I lit a roaring fire in the stove, and I started
  to thaw Bill out.

Well, I thawed and thawed for thirteen days but
  it didn't seem no good ;
His arms and legs stuck out like pegs, as if they
  was made of wood.
Till at last I said : " It ain't no use—he's froze too
  hard to thaw ;
He's obstinate, and he won't lie straight, so I guess
  I got to—*saw*."
So I sawed off poor Bill's arms and legs, and I
  laid him snug and straight
In the little coffin he picked hisself, with the
  dinky silver plate ;

And I came nigh near to shedding a tear as I
nailed him safely down ;
Then I stowed him away in my Yukon sleigh, and
I started back to town.

So I buried him as the contract was in a narrow
grave and deep,
And there he's waiting the Great Clean-up, when
the Judgment sluice-heads sweep ;
And I smoke my pipe and I meditate in the light
of the Midnight Sun,
And sometimes I wonder if they *was*, the awful
things I done.
And as I sit and the parson talks, expounding ot
the Law,
I often think of poor old Bill—*and how hard he
was to saw.*

THE BALLAD OF ONE-EYED MIKE

*This is the tale that was told to me by the man with
 the crystal eye,
As I smoked my pipe in the camp-fire light, and the
 Glories swept the sky;
As the Northlights gleamed and curved and streamed,
 and the bottle of " hooch " was dry.*

A man once aimed that my life be shamed, and
 wrought me a deathly wrong;
I vowed one day I would well repay, but the heft
 of his hate was strong.
He thonged me East and he thonged me West;
 he harried me back and forth,
Till I fled in fright from his peerless spite to the
 bleak, bald-headed North.

And there I lay, and for many a day I hatched
 plan after plan,
For a golden haul of the wherewithal to crush
 and to kill my man;

And there I strove, and there I clove through the
    drift of icy streams ;
And there I fought, and there I sought for the
    pay-streak of my dreams.

So twenty years, with their hopes and fears and
    smiles and tears and such,
Went by and left me long bereft of hope of the
    Midas touch ;
About as fat as a chancel rat, and lo ! despite my
    will,
In the weary fight I had clean lost sight of the
    man I sought to kill.

'Twas so far away, that evil day when I prayed
    the Prince of Gloom
For the savage strength and the sullen length of
    life to work his doom.
Nor sign nor word had I seen or heard, and it
    happed so long ago ;
My youth was gone and my memory wan, and I
    willed it even so.

It fell one night in the waning light by the Yukon's
    oily flow,
I smoked and sat as I marvelled at the sky's port-
    winey glow ;
Till it paled away to an absinthe gray, and the
    river seemed to shrink,

All wobbly flakes and wriggling snakes and goblin
  eyes a-wink.

'Twas weird to see and it 'wildered me in a queer,
  hypnotic dream,
Till I saw a spot like an inky blot come floating
  down the stream ;
It bobbed and swung ; it sheered and hung ; it
  romped round in a ring ;
It seemed to play in a tricksome way ; it sure was
  a merry thing.

In freakish flights strange oily lights came fluttering
  round its head,
Like butterflies of a monster size—then I knew it
  for the Dead.
Its face was rubbed and slicked and scrubbed as
  smooth as a shaven pate ;
In the silver snakes that the water makes it gleamed
  like a dinner-plate.

It gurgled near, and clear and clear and large and
  large it grew ;
It stood upright in a ring of light and it looked
  me through and through.
It weltered round with a woozy sound, and ere I
  could retreat,
With the witless roll of a sodden soul it wantoned
  to my feet.

And here I swear by this Cross I wear, I heard
    that " floater " say :
" I am the man from whom you ran, the man you
    sought to slay.
That you may note and gaze and gloat, and say
    ' Revenge is sweet,'
In the grit and grime of the river's slime I am
    rotting at your feet.

" The ill we rue we must e'en undo, though it rive
    us bone from bone ;
So it came about that I sought you out, for I
    prayed I might atone.
I did you wrong, and for long and long I sought
    where you might live ;
And now you're found, though I'm dead and
    drowned, I beg you to forgive."

So sad it seemed, and its cheek-bones gleamed, and
    its fingers flicked the shore ;
And it lapped and lay in a weary way, and its
    hands met to implore ;
That I gently said : " Poor, restless dead, I would
    never work you woe ;
Though the wrong you rue you can ne'er undo, I
    forgave you long ago."

Then, wonder-wise, I rubbed my eyes and I woke
    from a horrid dream

The moon rode high in the naked sky, and some-
    thing bobbed in the stream,
It held my sight in a patch of light, and then it
    sheered from the shore ;
It dipped and sank by a hollow bank, and I never
    saw it more.

This was the tale he told to me, that man so warped
    and gray,
Ere he slept and dreamed, and the camp-fire gleamed
    in his eye in a wolfish way—
That crystal eye that raked the sky in the weird
    Auroral ray.

THE BALLAD OF THE BRAND

'TWAS up in a land long famed for gold, where
women were far and rare,
Tellus, the smith, had taken to wife a maiden
amazingly fair ;
Tellus, the brawny worker in iron, hairy and
heavy of hand,
Saw her and loved her and bore her away from
the tribe of a Southern land ;
Deeming her worthy to queen his home and
mother him little ones,
That the name of Tellus, the master smith, might
live in his stalwart sons.

Now there was little of law in the land, and evil
doings were rife,
And every man who joyed in his home guarded
the fame of his wife ;
For there were those of the silver tongue and the
honeyed art to beguile,
Who would cozen the heart from a woman's
breast and damn her soul with a smile.

And there were women too quick to heed a look
    or a whispered word,
And once in a while a man was slain, and the ire
    of the King was stirred ;
So far and wide he proclaimed his wrath, and
    this was the law he willed :
" That whosoever killeth a man, even shall he be
    killed."

Now Tellus, the smith, he trusted his wife ; his
    heart was empty of fear.
High on the hill was the gleam of their hearth, a
    beacon of love and cheer.
High on the hill they builded their bower, where
    the broom and the bracken meet ;
Under a grove of oaks it was, hushed and
    drowsily sweet.
Here he enshrined her, his dearest saint, his idol,
    the light of his eye ;
Her kisses rested upon his lips as brushes a
    butterfly.
The weight of her arms around his neck was light
    as the thistle down ;
And sweetly she studied to win his smile, and
    gently she mocked his frown.

And when at the close of the dusty day his
    clangorous toil was done,
She hastened to meet him down the way all lit
    by the amber sun.

Their dove-cot gleamed in the golden light, a
    temple of stainless love ;
Like the hanging cup of a big blue flower was
    the topaz sky above.
The roses and lilies yearned to her, as swift
    through their throng she pressed ;
A little white, fragile, fluttering thing that lay like
    a child on his breast.
Then the heart of Tellus, the smith, was proud,
    and sang for the joy of life.
And there in the bronzing summertide he thanked
    the gods for his wife.

Now there was one called Philo, a scribe, a man
    of exquisite grace,
Carved like the god Apollo in limb, fair as Adonis
    in face ;
Eager and winning of manner, full of such
    radiant charm,
Womenkind fought for his favour and loved to
    their uttermost harm.
Such was his craft and his knowledge, such was
    his skill at the game.
Never was woman could flout him, so be he
    plotted her shame.
And so he drank deep of pleasure, and then it
    fell on a day
He gazed on the wife of Tellus and marked her
    out for his prey.

Tellus, the smith, was merry, and the time of the
    year it was June,
So he said to his stalwart helpers : " Shut down
    the forge at noon.
Go ye and joy in the sunshine, rest in the coolth
    of the grove,
Drift on the dreamy river, every man with his
    love."
Then to himself : " Oh, Beloved, sweet will be
    your surprise ;
To-day will we sport like children, laugh in each
    other's eyes ;
Weave gay garlands of poppies, crown each other
    with flowers,
Pull plump carp from the lilies, rifle the ferny
    bowers.
To-day with feasting and gladness the wine of
    Cyprus will flow ;
To-day is the day we were wedded only a twelve-
    month ago."

The larks trilled high in the heavens ; his heart
    was lyric with joy ;
He plucked a posy of lilies ; he sped like a love-
    sick boy.
He stole up the velvety pathway—his cottage was
    sunsteeped and still ;
Vines honeysuckled the window ; softly he peeped
    o'er the sill.

The lilies dropped from his fingers ; devils were
    choking his breath ;
Rigid with horror, he stiffened ; ghastly his face
    was as death.
Like a nun whose faith in the Virgin is met with
    a prurient jibe,
He shrank—'twas the wife of his bosom in the
    arms of Philo, the scribe.

Tellus went back to his smithy ; he reeled like a
    drunken man ;
His heart was riven with anguish ; his brain was
    brooding a plan.
Straight to his anvil he hurried ; started his
    furnace aglow ;
Heated his iron and shaped it with savage and
    masterful blow.
Sparks showered over and round him ; swiftly
    under his hand
There at last it was finished—a hideous and in-
    famous Brand.

That night the wife of his bosom, the light of joy
    in her eyes,
Kissed him with words of rapture ; but he knew
    that her words were lies.
Never was she so beguiling, never so merry of
    speech
(For passion ripens a woman as the sunshine
    ripens a peach).

He clenched his teeth into silence ; he yielded up
    to her lure,
Though he knew that her breasts were heaving
    from the fire of her paramour.
" To-morrow," he said, " to-morrow "—he wove
    her hair in a strand,
Twisted it round his fingers and smiled as he
    thought of the Brand.

The morrow was come, and Tellus swiftly stole
    up the hill.
Butterflies drowsed in the noon-heat ; coverts
    were sunsteeped and still.
Softly he padded the pathway unto the porch,
    and within
Heard he the low laugh of dalliance, heard he
    the rapture of sin.
Knew he her eyes were mystic with light that no
    man should see,
No man kindle and joy in, no man on earth save
    he.
And never for him would it kindle. The blood-
    lust surged in his brain ;
Through the senseless stone could he see them,
    wanton and warily fain.
Horrible ! Heaven he sought for, gained it and
    gloried and fell—
Oh, it was sudden—headlong into the nethermost
    hell. . . .

Was this he, Tellus, this marble ?   Tellus . . . not
    dreaming a dream ?
Ah ! sharp-edged as a javelin, was that a woman's
    scream ?
Was it a door that shattered, shell-like, under his
    blow ?
Was it his saint, that strumpet, dishevelled and
    cowering low ?
Was it her lover, that wild thing, that twisted and
    gouged and tore ?
Was it a man he was crushing, whose head he
    beat on the floor ?
Laughing the while at its weakness, till sudden he
    stayed his hand—
Through the red ring of his madness flamed the
    thought of the Brand.

Then bound he the naked Philo with thongs that
    cut in the flesh,
And the wife of his bosom, fear-frantic, he gagged
    with a silken mesh,
Choking her screams into silence ; bound her
    down by the hair ;
Dragged her lover unto her under her frenzied
    stare
In the heat of the hearth-fire embers he heated
    the hideous Brand ;
Twisting her fingers open, he forced its haft in
    her hand.

He pressed it downward and downward ; she felt
the living flesh sear ;
She saw the throe of her lover ; she heard the
scream of his fear.
Once, twice and thrice he forced her, heedless of
prayer and shriek—
Once on the forehead of Philo, twice in the soft
of his cheek.

Then (for the thing was finished) he said to the
woman : " See
How you have branded your lover ! Now will I
let him go free."
He severed the thongs that bound him, laughing :
" Revenge is sweet,"
And Philo, sobbing in anguish, feebly rose to his
feet.
The man who was fair as Apollo, god-like in
woman's sight,
Hideous now as a satyr, fled to the pity of night.

*Then came they before the Judgment Seat, and thus
spoke the Lord of the Land :*
*" He who seeketh his neighbour's wife shall suffer the
doom of the Brand.*
*Brutish and bold on his brow be it stamped, deep in
his cheek let it sear,*
*That every man may look on his shame, and shudder
and sicken and fear.*

He shall hear their mock in the market-place, their
    fleering jibe at the feast,
He shall seek the caves and the shroud of night, and
    the fellowship of the beast.
Outcast forever from homes of men, far and far shall
    he roam.
Such be the doom, sadder than death, of him who
    shameth a home."

THE BALLAD OF HARD-LUCK HENRY

Now wouldn't you expect to find a man an awful
    crank
That's staked out nigh three hundred claims, and
    every one a blank ;
That's followed every fool stampede, and seen the
    rise and fall
Of camps where men got gold in chunks and he
    got none at all ;
That's prospected a bit of ground and sold it for
    a song
To see it yield a fortune to some fool that came
    along ;
That's sunk a dozen bed-rock holes, and not a
    speck in sight,
Yet sees them take a million from the claims to
    left and right ?
Now aren't things like that enough to drive a
    man to booze ?
But Hard-Luck Smith was hoodoo-proof—he knew
    the way to lose.

'Twas in the fall of nineteen four—leap-year I've
    heard them say—

When Hard-Luck came to Hunker Creek and
    took a hillside lay.
And lo ! as if to make amends for all the futile
    past,
Late in the year he struck it rich, the real pay-
    streak at last.
The riffles of his sluicing-box were choked with
    speckled earth,
And night and day he worked that lay for all
    that he was worth.
And when in chill December's gloom his lucky
    lease expired,
He found that he had made a stake as big as he
    desired.

One day while meditating on the waywardness of
    fate,
He felt the ache of lonely man to find a fitting
    mate ;
A petticoated pard to cheer his solitary life,
A woman with soft, soothing ways, a confidant, a
    wife.
And while he cooked his supper on his little Yukon
    stove,
He wished that he had staked a claim in Love's
    rich treasure-trove ;
When suddenly he paused and held aloft a Yukon
    egg,
For there in pencilled letters was the magic name
    of Peg.

You know these Yukon eggs of ours—some pink,
    some green, some blue—
A dollar per, assorted tints, assorted flavours too.
The supercilious cheechako might designate them
    high,
But one acquires a taste for them and likes them
    by-and-by.
Well, Hard-Luck Henry took this egg and held it
    to the light,
And there was more faint pencilling that sorely
    taxed his sight.
At last he made it out, and then the legend ran
    like this—
" Will Klondike miner write to Peg, Plumhollow,
    Squashville, Wis. ? "

That night he got to thinking of this far-off, un-
    known fair ;
It seemed so sort of opportune, an answer to his
    prayer.
She flitted sweetly through his dreams, she haunted
    him by day,
She smiled through clouds of nicotine, she cheered
    his weary way.
At last he yielded to the spell ; his course of love
    he set—
Wisconsin his objective point ; his object, Margaret.

With every mile of sea and land his longing grew
    and grew.

He practised all his pretty words, and these, I
   fear, were few.
At last, one frosty evening, with a cold chill down
   his spine,
He found himself before her house, the threshold
   of the shrine.
His courage flickered to a spark, then glowed
   with sudden flame—
He knocked; he heard a welcome word; she
   came—his goddess came.
Oh, she was fair as any flower, and huskily he
   spoke:
"I'm all the way from Klondike, with a mighty
   heavy poke.
I'm looking for a lassie, one whose Christian name
   is Peg,
Who sought a Klondike miner, and who wrote it
   on an egg."

The lassie gazed at him a space, her cheeks grew
   rosy red;
She gazed at him with tear-bright eyes, then
   tenderly she said:
"Yes, lonely Klondike miner, it is true my name
   is Peg.
It's also true I longed for you and wrote it on an
   egg.
My heart went out to some one in that land of
   night and cold;

But oh, I fear that Yukon egg must have been
      mighty old.
I waited long, I hoped and feared ; you should
      have come before ;
I've been a wedded woman now for eighteen
      months or more.
I'm sorry, since you've come so far, you ain't the
      one that wins ;
But won't you take a step inside—*I'll let you see
      the twins.*"

THE MAN FROM ELDORADO

I

He's the man from Eldorado, and he's just arrived
  in town,
  In moccasins and oily buckskin shirt.
He's gaunt as any Indian, and pretty nigh as
  brown ;
  He's greasy, and he smells of sweat and dirt.
He sports a crop of whiskers that would shame a
  healthy hog ;
  Hard work has racked his joints and stooped
  his back ;
He slops along the sidewalk followed by his yellow
  dog,
  But he's got a bunch of gold-dust in his sack.

He seems a little wistful as he blinks at all the
  lights,
  And maybe he is thinking of his claim
And the dark and dwarfish cabin where he lay
  and dreamed at nights,
  (Thank God, he'll never see the place again !)

185

Where he lived on tinned tomatoes, beef embalmed and sourdough bread,
  On rusty beans and bacon furred with mould ;
His stomach's out of kilter and his system full of lead,
  But it's over, and his poke is full of gold.

He has panted at the windlass, he has loaded in the drift,
  He has pounded at the face of oozy clay ;
He has taxed himself to sickness, dark and damp and double shift,
  He has laboured like a demon night and day.
And now, praise God, it's over, and he seems to breathe again
  Of new-mown hay, the warm, wet, friendly loam ;
He sees a snowy orchard in a green and dimpling plain,
  And a little vine-clad cottage, and it's—Home.

II

He's the man from Eldorado, and he's had a bite and sup,
  And he's met in with a drouthy friend or two ;
He's cached away his gold-dust, but he's sort of bucking up,
  So he's kept enough to-night to see him through.
His eye is bright and genial, his tongue no longer lags ;

His heart is brimming o'er with joy and mirth ;
He may be far from savoury, he may be clad in
   rags,
   But to-night he feels as if he owns the earth.

Says he : " Boys, here is where the shaggy North
      and I will shake ;
   I thought I'd never manage to get free.
I kept on making misses ; but at last I've got my
      stake ;
   There's no more thawing frozen muck for me.
I am going to God's Country, where I'll live the
      simple life ;
   I'll buy a bit of land and make a start ;
I'll carve a little homestead, and I'll win a little
      wife,
   And raise ten little kids to cheer my heart."

They signified their sympathy by crowding to the
      bar ;
   They bellied up three deep and drank his health.
He shed a radiant smile around and smoked a
      rank cigar ;
   They wished him honour, happiness and wealth.
They drank unto his wife to be—that unsuspect-
      ing maid ;
   They drank unto his children half a score ;
And when they got through drinking, very tenderly
      they laid
   The man from Eldorado on the floor.

III

He's the man from Eldorado, and he's only start-
      ing in
   To cultivate a thousand-dollar jag.
His poke is full of gold-dust and his heart is full of
      sin,
   And he's dancing with a girl called Muckluck
      Mag.
She's as light as any fairy; she's as pretty as a
      peach;
   She's mistress of the witchcraft to beguile;
There's sunshine in her manner, there is music in
      her speech,
   And there's concentrated honey in her smile.

Oh, the fever of the dance-hall and the glitter
      and the shine,
   The beauty, and the jewels, and the whirl,
The madness of the music, the rapture of the
      wine,
   The languorous allurement of a girl!
She is like a lost madonna; he is gaunt, unkempt
      and grim;
   But she fondles him and gazes in his eyes;
Her kisses seek his heavy lips, and soon it seems
      to him
   He has staked a little claim in Paradise.

"Who's for a juicy two-step?" cries the master
  of the floor ;
  The music throbs with soft, seductive beat.
There's glitter, gilt and gladness ; there are pretty
  girls galore ;
  There's a woolly man with moccasins on feet.
They know they've got him going ; he is buying
  wine for all ;
  They crowd around as buzzards at a feast,
Then when his poke is empty they boost him
  from the hall,
  And spurn him in the gutter like a beast.

He's the man from Eldorado, and he's painting
  red the town ;
  Behind he leaves a trail of yellow dust ;
In a whirl of senseless riot he is ramping up and
  down ;
  There's nothing checks his madness and his lust.
And soon the word is passed around—it travels
  like a flame ;
  They fight to clutch his hand and call him friend,
The chevaliers of lost repute, the dames of sorry
  fame ;
  Then comes the grim awakening—the end.

IV

He's the man from Eldorado, and he gives a
  grand affair :

There's feasting, dancing, wine without restraint.
The smooth Beau Brummels of the bar, the faro
    men, are there ;
  The tinhorns and purveyors of red paint ;
The sleek and painted women, their predacious
    eyes aglow—
  Sure Klondike City never saw the like ;
Then Muckluck Mag proposed the toast, " The
    giver of the show,
  The livest sport that ever hit the pike."

The " live one " rises to his feet ; he stammers to
    reply—
  And then there comes before his muddled brain
A vision of green vastitudes beneath an April sky,
  And clover pastures drenched with silver rain.
He knows that it can never be, that he is down
    and out ;
  Life leers at him with foul and fetid breath ;
And then amid the revelry, the song and cheer
    and shout,
  He suddenly grows grim and cold as death.

He grips the table tensely, and he says : " Dear
    friends of mine,
  I've let you dip your fingers in my purse ;
I've crammed you at my table, and I've drowned
    you in my wine,
  And I've little left to give you but—my curse.

I've failed supremely in my plans ; it's rather late
    to whine ;
  My poke is mighty weasened up and small.
I thank you each for coming here ; the happiness
    is mine—
  And now, you thieves and harlots, take it all."

He twists the thong from off his poke ; he swings
    it o'er his head ;
  The nuggets fall around their feet like grain.
They rattle over roof and wall ; they scatter, roll
    and spread ;
  The dust is like a shower of golden rain.
The guests a moment stand aghast, then grovel on
    the floor ;
  They fight, and snarl, and claw, like beasts of
    prey ;
And then, as everybody grabbed and everybody
    swore,
  The man from Eldorado slipped away.

v

He's the man from Eldorado, and they found him
    stiff and dead,
  Half covered by the freezing ooze and dirt.
A clotted Colt was in his hand, a hole was in his
    head,
  And he wore an old and oily buckskin shirt.

His eyes were fixed and horrible, as one who
    hails the end ;
  The frost had set him rigid as a log ;
And there, half lying on his breast. his last and
    only friend,
  There crouched and whined a mangy yellow
    dog

MY FRIENDS

THE man above was a murderer, the man below
    was a thief ;
And I lay there in the bunk between, ailing
    beyond belief ;
A weary armful of skin and bone, wasted with
    pain and grief.

My feet were froze, and the lifeless toes were
    purple and green and gray ;
The little flesh that clung to my bones, you could
    punch it in holes like clay ;
The skin on my gums was a sullen black, and
    slowly peeling away.

I was sure enough in a direful fix, and often I
    wondered why
They did not take the chance that was left and
    leave me alone to die,
Or finish me off with a dose of dope—so utterly
    lost was I.

But no ; they brewed me the green-spruce tea.
    and nursed me there like a child ;

And the homicide he was good to me, and bathed
  my sores and smiled ;
And the thief he starved that I might be fed, and
  his eyes were kind and mild.

Yet they were woefully wicked men, and often at
  night in pain
I heard the murderer speak of his deed and dream
  it over again ;
1 heard the poor thief sorrowing for the dead self
  he had slain.

I'll never forget that bitter dawn, so evil, askew
  and gray,
When they wrapped me round in the skins of
  beasts and they bore me to a sleigh,
And we started out with the nearest post an
  hundred miles away.

I'll never forget the trail they broke, with its
  tense, unuttered woe ;
And the crunch, crunch, crunch, as their snowshoes sank through the crust of the hollow
  snow ;
And my breath would fail, and every beat of my
  heart was like a blow.

And oftentimes I would die the death, yet wake
  up to life anew ;
The sun would be all ablaze on the waste, and the
  sky a blighting blue,

And the tears would rise in my snow-blind eyes
    and furrow my cheeks like dew.

And the camps we made when their strength out-
    played and the day was pinched and wan ;
And oh, the joy of that blessed halt, and how I
    did dread the dawn ;
And how I hated the weary men who rose and
    dragged me on.

And oh, how I begged to rest, to rest—the snow
    was so sweet a shroud ;
And oh, how I cried when they urged me on, cried
    and cursed them aloud ;
Yet on they strained, all racked and pained, and
    sorely their backs were bowed.

And then it was all like a lurid dream, and I
    prayed for a swift release.
From the ruthless ones who would not leave me
    to die alone in peace ;
Till I wakened up and I found myself at the post
    of the Mounted Police.

And there was my friend the murderer, and there
    was my friend the thief,
With bracelets of steel around their wrists, and
    wicked beyond belief :
But when they come to God's judgment seat—
    may I be allowed the brief.

THE PROSPECTOR

I STROLLED up old Bonanza, where I staked in
    Ninety-eight,
  A-purpose to revisit the old claim.
I kept thinking mighty sadly of the funny ways of
    Fate,
  And the lads who once were with me in the
    game.
Poor boys, they're down-and-outers, and there's
    scarcely one to-day
  Can show a dozen colours in his poke ;
And me, I'm still prospecting, old and battered,
    gaunt and gray,
  And I'm looking for a grub-stake, and I'm
    broke.

I strolled up old Bonanza. The same old moon
    looked down ;
  The same old landmarks seemed to yearn to
    me ;
But the cabins all were silent, and the flat, once
    like a town,
  Was mighty still and lonesome-like to see.

There were piles and piles of tailings where we
    toiled with pick and pan,
  And turning round a bend I heard a roar,
And there a giant gold-ship of the very newest
    plan
  Was tearing chunks of pay-dirt from the shore.

It wallowed in its water-bed ; it burrowed, heaved
    and swung ;
  It gnawed its way ahead with grunts and sighs ;
Its bill of fare was rock and sand ; the tailings
    were its dung ;
  It glared around with fierce electric eyes.
Full fifty buckets crammed its maw ; it bellowed
    out for more ;
  It looked like some great monster in the gloom.
With two to feed its sateless greed, it worked for
    seven score,
  And I sighed : " Ah, old-time miner, here's your
    doom ! "

The idle windlass turns to rust ; the sagging sluice-
    box falls ;
  The holes you digged are water to the brim ;
Your little sod-roofed cabins with the snugly moss-
    chinked walls
  Are deathly now and mouldering and dim.
The battle-field is silent where of old you fought
    it out ;
  The claims you fiercely won are lost and sold ;

But there's a little army that they'll never put to
      rout—
  The men who simply live to seek the gold.

The men who can't remember when they learned
      to swing a pack,
  Or in what lawless land the quest began ;
The solitary seeker with his grub-stake on his back
  The restless buccaneer of pick and pan.
On the mesas of the Southland, on the tundras of
      the North,
  You will find us, changed in face but still the
      same ;
And it isn't need, it isn't greed that sends us
      faring forth—
  It's the fever, it's the glory of the game.

For once you've panned the speckled sand and
      seen the bonny dust,
  Its peerless brightness blinds you like a spell ;
It's little else you care about ; you go because you
      must,
  And you feel that you could follow it to hell.
You'd follow it in hunger, and you'd follow it in
      cold ;
  You'd follow it in solitude and pain ;
And when you're stiff and battened down let
      some one whisper " Gold,"
  You're lief to rise and follow it again.

Yet look you, if I find the stuff it's just like so
    much dirt ;
  I fling it to the four winds like a child.
It's wine and painted women and the things that
    do me hurt,
  Till I crawl back, beggared, broken, to the Wild.
Till I crawl back, sapped and sodden, to my
    grub-stake and my tent—
  There's a city, there's an army (hear them
    shout).
There's the gold in millions, millions, but I haven't
    got a cent ;
  And oh, it's me, it's me that found it out.

It was my dream that made it good, my dream
    that made me go
  To lands of dread and death disprized of man ;
But oh, I've known a glory that their hearts will
    never know,
  When I picked the first big nugget from my pan.
It's still my dream, my dauntless dream, that
    drives me forth once more
  To seek and starve and suffer in the Vast ;
That heaps my heart with eager hope, that
    glimmers on before—
  My dream that will uplift me to the last.

Perhaps I am stark crazy, but there's none of you
    too sane ;
  It's just a little matter of degree.

My hobby is to hunt out gold ; it's fortressed in
    my brain ;
  It's life and love and wife and home to me.
And I'll strike it, yes, I'll strike it ; I've a hunch
    I cannot fail ;
  I've a vision, I've a prompting, I've a call ;
I hear the hoarse stampeding of an army on my
    trail,
  To the last, the greatest gold camp of them all.

Beyond the shark-tooth ranges sawing savage at
    the sky
  There's a lowering land no white man ever
    struck ;
There's gold, there's gold in millions, and I'll find
    it if I die,
  And I'm going there once more to try my luck.
Maybe I'll fail—what matter ? It's a mandate, it's
    a vow ;
  And when in lands of dreariness and dread
You seek the last lone frontier, far beyond your
    frontiers now,
  You will find the old prospector, silent, dead.

You will find a tattered tent-pole with a ragged robe
    below it ;
  You will find a rusted gold-pan on the sod ;
You will find the claim I'm seeking, with my bones
    as stakes to show it ;
  But I've sought the last Recorder, and He's—God.

THE BLACK SHEEP

"The aristocratic ne'er-do-well in Canada frequently finds
his way into the ranks of the Royal North-West Mounted
Police."—*Extract.*

> *Hark to the ewe that bore him :*
> *"What has muddied the strain ?*
> *Never his brothers before him*
> *Showed the hint of a stain."*
> *Hark to the tups and wethers ;*
> *Hark to the old gray ram :*
> *"We're all of us white, but he's black as night,*
> *And he'll never be worth a damn."*

I'm up on the bally wood-pile at the back of the
    barracks yard ;
"A damned disgrace to the force, sir," with a
    comrade standing guard ;
Making the bluff I'm busy, doing my six months'
    hard.

"Six months' hard and dismissed, sir." Isn't that
    rather hell ?
And all because of the liquor laws and the wiles
    of a native belle—
Some " hooch " I gave to a siwash brave who
    swore that he wouldn't tell.

At least they *say* that I did it.   It's so in the town
    report.
All that I can recall is a night of revel and
    sport,
When I woke with a " head " in the guard-room,
    and they dragged me sick into court.

And the O.C. said : " You are guilty," and I said
    never a word ;
For, hang it, you see I couldn't—I didn't know
    what had occurred,
And, under the circumstances, denial would be
    absurd.

But the one that cooked my bacon was Grubbe,
    of the City Patrol.
He fagged for my room at Eton, and didn't I
    devil his soul !
And now he is getting even, landing me down in
    the hole.

Plugging away on the wood-pile ; doing chores
    round the square.
There goes an officer's lady—gives me a haughty
    stare—
Me that's an earl's own nephew—that is the
    hardest to bear.

To think of the poor old mater awaiting her pro-
    digal son.

Tho' I broke her heart with my folly, I was
 always the white-haired one.
(That fatted calf that they're cooking will surely
 be overdone.)

I'll go back and yarn to the Bishop; I'll dance
 with the village belle;
I'll hand round tea to the ladies, and everything
 will be well.
Where I have been won't matter; what I have
 seen I won't tell.

I'll soar to their ken like a comet. They'll see me
 with never a stain;
But will they reform me ?—far from it. We pay
 for our pleasure with pain;
But the dog will return to his vomit, the hog to
 his wallow again.

I've chewed on the rind of creation, and bitter
 I've tasted the same.
Stacked up against hell and damnation, I've man-
 aged to stay in the game;
I've had my moments of sorrow; I've had my
 seasons of shame.

That's past; when one's nature's a cracked one,
 it's too jolly hard to mend.

So long as the road is level, so long as I've cash
    to spend,
I'm bound to go to the devil, and it's all the same
    in the end.

The bugle is sounding for stables ; the men troop
    off through the gloom :
An orderly laying the tables sings in the bright
    mess-room.
(I'll wash in the prison bucket, and brush with the
    prison broom.)

I'll lie in my cell and listen ; I'll wish that I
    couldn't hear
The laugh and the chaff of the fellows swigging
    the canteen beer ;
The nasal tone of the gramophone playing " The
    Bandolier."

And it seems to me, though it's misty, that night
    of the flowing bowl,
That the man who potlatched the whiskey and
    landed me into the hole
*Was Grubbe, that unmerciful bounder, Grubbe, of the
    City Patrol.*

THE TELEGRAPH OPERATOR

I will not wash my face ;
   I will not brush my hair ;
I " pig " around the place—
   There's nobody to care.
Nothing but rock and tree ;
   Nothing but wood and stone.
Oh, God, it's hell to be
   Alone, alone, alone !

Snow-peaks and deep-gashed draws
   Corral me in a ring.
I feel as if I was
   The only living thing
On all this blighted earth ;
   And so I frowst and shrink,
And crouching by my hearth
   I hear the thoughts I think.

I think of all I miss—
   The boys I used to know ;
The girls I used to kiss ;
   The coin I used to blow ;

The bars I used to haunt ;
    The racket and the row ;
The beers I didn't want
    (I wish I had 'em now).

Day after day the same,
    Only a little worse ;
No one to grouch or blame—
    Oh, for a loving curse !
Oh, in the night I fear,
    Haunted by nameless things,
Just for a voice to cheer,
    Just for a hand that clings !

Faintly as from a star
    Voices come o'er the line ;
Voices of ghosts afar,
    Not in this world of mine ;
Lives in whose loom I grope ;
    Words in whose weft I hear
Eager the thrill of hope,
    Awful the chill of fear.

I'm thinking out aloud ;
    I reckon that is bad ;
(The snow is like a shroud)—
    Maybe I'm going mad.
Say ! wouldn't that be tough ?
    This awful hush that hugs
And chokes one is enough
    To make a man go " bugs."

There's not a thing to do ;
  I cannot sleep at night ;
No wonder I'm so blue ;
  Oh, for a friendly fight !
The din and rush of strife ;
  A music-hall aglow ;
A crowd, a city, life—
  Dear God, I miss it so !

Here, you have moped enough !
  Brace up and play the game !
But say, it's awful tough—
  Day after day the same
(I've said that twice, I bet).
  Well, there's not much to say.
I wish I had a pet,
  Or something I could play.

Cheer up ! don't get so glum
  And sick of everything ;
The worst is yet to come ;
  God help you till the Spring.
God shield you from the Fear ;
  Teach you to laugh, not moan
Ha ! ha ! it sounds so queer—
  Alone, alone, alone !

H

THE WOOD-CUTTER

The sky is like an envelope,
  One of those blue official things :
And, sealing it, to mock our hope,
  The moon, a silver wafer, clings.
What shall we find when death gives leave
To read—our sentence or reprieve ?

I'm holding it down on God's scrap-pile, up on
      the fag-end of earth ;
  O'er me a menace of mountains, a river that
      grits at my feet ;
Face to face with my soul-self, weighing my life
      at its worth ;
  Wondering what I was made for, here in my
      last retreat.

Last ! Ah, yes, it's the finish. Have ever you
      heard a man cry ?
  (Sobs that rake him and rend him, right from
      the base of the chest.)
That's how I've cried, oh, so often ; and now
      that my tears are dry,

I sit in the desolate quiet and wait for the
   infinite Rest.

Rest ! Well, it's restful around me ; it's quiet clean
   to the core.
   The mountains pose in their ermine, in golden
      the hills are clad ;
The big, blue, silt-freighted Yukon seethes by my
   cabin door,
   And I think it's only the river that keeps me
      from going mad.

By day it's a ruthless monster, a callous, insatiate
   thing,
   With oily bubble and eddy, with sudden
      swirling of breast ;
By night it's a writhing Titan, sullenly murmuring,
   Ever and ever goaded, and ever crying for rest.

It cries for its human tribute, but me it will never
   drown.
   I've learned the lore of my river ; my river
      obeys me well.
I hew and I launch my cordwood, and raft it to
   Dawson town,
   Where wood means wine and women, and,
      incidentally, hell.

Hell and the anguish thereafter. Here as I sit
    alone
    I'd give the life I have left me to lighten some
        load of care :
(The bitterest part of the bitter is being denied
        to atone ;
    Lips that have mocked at Heaven lend them-
        selves ill to prayer).

Impotent as a beetle pierced on the needle of Fate ;
    A wretch in a cosmic death-cell, peaks for my prison
        bars ;
'Whelmed by a world stupendous, lonely and listless
        I wait,
    Drowned in a sea of silence, strewn with confetti
        of stars.

See ! from far up the valley a rapier pierces the
    night,
    The white search-ray of a steamer. Swiftly,
        serenely it nears ;
A proud, white, alien presence, a glittering galley
    of light,
    Confident-poised, triumphant, freighted with
        hopes and fears.

I look as one looks on a vision ; I see it pulsating by ;
    I glimpse joy-radiant faces ; I hear the thresh
        of the wheel.

Hoof-like my heart beats a moment ; then silence
swoops from the sky.
Darkness is piled upon darkness. God only
knows how I feel.

Maybe you've seen me sometimes ; maybe you've
pitied me then—
The lonely waif of the wood-camp, here by
my cabin door.
Some day you'll look and see not ; futile and outcast of men,
I shall be far from your pity, resting forevermore.

*My life was a problem in ciphers, a weary and profit-
less sum.*
*Slipshod and stupid I worked it, dazed by negation
and doubt.*
*Ciphers the total confronts me.   Oh, Death, with thy
moistened thumb,*
Stoop like a petulant schoolboy, wipe me forever out!

THE SONG OF THE MOUTH-ORGAN

(With apologies to the singer of the " Song of the Banjo.")

I'M a homely little bit of tin and bone ;
  I'm beloved by the Legion of the Lost ;
I haven't got a " vox humana " tone,
  And a dime or two will satisfy my cost.
I don't attempt your high-falutin' flights ;
  I am more or less uncertain on the key ;
But I tell you, boys, there's lots and lots of nights
  When you've taken mighty comfort out of me.

I weigh an ounce or two, and I'm so small
  You can pack me in the pocket of your vest ;
And when at night so wearily you crawl
  Into your bunk and stretch your limbs to rest,
You take me out and play me soft and low,
  The simple songs that trouble your heartstrings ;
The tunes you used to fancy long ago,
  Before you made a rotten mess of things.

Then a dreamy look will come into your eyes,
  And you break off in the middle of a note ;
And then, with just the dreariest of sighs,
  You drop me in the pocket of your coat.

212

But somehow I have bucked you up a bit ;
   And, as you turn around and face the wall,
You don't feel quite so spineless and unfit—
   You're not so bad a fellow after all.

Do you recollect the bitter Arctic night ;
   Your camp beside the canyon on the trail ;
Your tent a tiny square of orange light ;
   The moon above consumptive-like and pale ;
Your supper cooked, your little stove aglow ;
   You tired, but snug and happy as a child ?
Then 'twas " Turkey in the Straw " till your lips
      were nearly raw,
   And you hurled your bold defiance at the Wild.

Do you recollect the flashing, lashing pain ;
   The gulf of humid blackness overhead ;
The lightning making rapiers of the rain ;
   The cattle-horns like candles of the dead ;
You sitting on your bronco there alone,
   In your slicker, saddle-sore and sick with cold ?
Do you think the silent herd did not hear " The
      Mocking Bird,"
   Or relish " Silver Threads among the Gold " ?

Do you recollect the wild Magellan coast ;
   The head-winds and the icy, roaring seas ;
The nights you thought that everything was lost ;
   The days you toiled in water to your knees ;
The frozen ratlines shrieking in the gale ;

The hissing steeps and gulfs of livid foam :
When you cheered your messmates nine with " Ben
                Bolt " and " Clementine,"
    And " Dixie Land " and " Seeing Nellie Home " ?

Let the jammy banjo voice the Younger Son,
    Who waits for his remittance to arrive ;
I represent the grimy, gritty one,
    Who sweats his bones to keep himself alive ;
Who's up against the real thing from his birth ;
    Whose heritage is hard and bitter toil ;
I voice the weary, smeary ones of earth,
    The helots of the sea and of the soil.

I'm the Steinway of strange mischief and mis-
                chance ;
    I'm the Stradivarius of blank defeat ;
In the down-world, when the devil leads the dance,
    I am simply and symbolically meet ;
I'm the irrepressive spirit of mankind ;
    I'm the small boy playing knuckle down with
                Death ;
At the end of all things known, where God's
                rubbish-heap is thrown,
    I shrill impudent triumph at a breath.

I'm a humble little bit of tin and horn ;
    I'm a byword, I'm a plaything, I'm a jest ;
The virtuoso looks on me with scorn ;

But there's times when I am better than the
    best.
Ask the stoker and the sailor of the sea ;
  Ask the mucker and the hewer of the pine ;
Ask the herder of the plain, ask the gleaner of the
    grain—
  There's a lowly, loving kingdom—and it's mine.

THE TRAIL OF NINETY-EIGHT

1

Gold! We leapt from our benches. Gold! We
    sprang from our stools.
Gold! We wheeled in the furrow, fired with the
    faith of fools.
Fearless, unfound, unfitted, far from the night
    and the cold,
Heard we the clarion summons, followed the
    master-lure—Gold!

Men from the sands of the Sunland; men from
    the woods of the West;
Men from the farms and the cities, into the
    Northland we pressed.
Graybeards and striplings and women, good men
    and bad men and bold,
Leaving our homes and our loved ones, crying
    exultantly—" Gold ! "

Never was seen such an army, pitiful, futile,
    unfit;

Never was seen such a spirit, manifold courage
and grit ;
Never has been such a cohort under one banner
unrolled
As surged to the ragged-edged Arctic, urged by
the arch-tempter—Gold.

" Farewell ! " we cried to our dearests ; little we
cared for their tears.
" Farewell ! " we cried to the humdrum and the
yoke of the hireling years ;
Just like a pack of school-boys, and the big crowd
cheered us goodbye.
Never were hearts so uplifted, never were hopes
so high.

The spectral shores flitted past us, and every
whirl of the screw.
Hurled us nearer to fortune, and ever we planned
what we'd do—
Do with the gold when we got it—big, shiny
nuggets like plums,
There in the sand of the river, gouging it out
with our thumbs.

And one man wanted a castle, another a racing
stud ;
A third would cruise in a palace yacht like a
red-necked prince of blood.

And so we dreamed and we vaunted, millionaires
    to a man,
Leaping to wealth in our visions long ere the
    trail began.

II

We landed in wind-swept Skagway. We joined
    the weltering mass,
Clamouring over their outfits, waiting to climb the
    Pass.
We tightened our girths and our pack-straps ; we
    linked on the Human Chain,
Struggling up to the summit, where every step
    was a pain.

Gone was the joy of our faces, grim and haggard
    and pale ;
The heedless mirth of the shipboard was changed
    to the care of the trail.
We flung ourselves in the struggle, packing our
    grub in relays,
Step by step to the summit in the bale of the
    winter days.

Floundering deep in the sump-holes, stumbling
    out again ;
Crying with cold and weakness, crazy with fear
    and pain.

Then from the depths of our travail, ere our
    spirits were broke,
Grim, tenacious and savage, the lust of the trail
    awoke.

" Klondike or bust ! " rang the slogan ; every man
    for his own.
Oh, how we flogged the horses, staggering skin
    and bone !
Oh, how we cursed their weakness, anguish they
    could not tell,
Breaking their hearts in our passion, lashing them
    on till they fell !

For grub meant gold to our thinking, and all that
    could walk must pack ;
The sheep for the shambles stumbled, each with
    a load on its back ;
And even the swine were burdened, and grunted
    and squealed and rolled,
And men went mad in the moment, huskily
    clamouring " Gold ! "

Oh, we were brutes and devils, goaded by lust
    and fear !
Our eyes were strained to the summit ; the weak-
    lings dropped to the rear,
Falling in heaps by the trail-side, heart-broken,
    limp and wan ;

But the gaps closed up in an instant, and heedless the chain went on.

Never will I forget it, there on the mountain face,
Antlike, men with their burdens. clinging in icy
    space ;
Dogged, determined and dauntless, cruel and callous and cold,
Cursing, blaspheming, reviling, and ever that
    battlecry—" Gold ! "

Thus toiled we, the army of fortune, in hunger
    and hope and despair,
Till glacier, mountain and forest vanished, and,
    radiantly fair,
There at our feet lay Lake Bennett, and down to
    its welcome we ran :
The trail of the land was over, the trail of the
    water began.

III

We built our boats and we launched them.
    Never has been such a fleet ;
A packing-case for a bottom, a mackinaw for a
    sheet.
Shapeless, grotesque, lopsided, flimsy, makeshift
    and crude,
Each man after his fashion builded as best he
    could.

Each man worked like a demon, as prow to rudder
we raced ;
The winds of the Wild cried " Hurry ! " the voice
of the waters, " Haste ! "
We hated those driving before us ; we dreaded
those pressing behind ;
We cursed the slow current that bore us ; we
prayed to the God of the wind.

Spring ! and the hillsides flourished, vivid in
jewelled green ;
Spring ! and our hearts' blood nourished envy and
hatred and spleen.
Little cared we for the Spring-birth ; much cared
we to get on—
Stake in the Great White Channel, stake ere the
best be gone.

The greed of the gold possessed us ; pity and
love were forgot ;
Covetous visions obsessed us ; brother with
brother fought.
Partner with partner wrangled, each one claiming
his due ;
Wrangled and halved their outfits, sawing their
boats in two.

Thuswise we voyaged Lake Bennett, Tagish, then
Windy Arm,

Sinister, savage and baleful, boding us hate and
    harm.
Many a scow was shattered there on that iron
    shore ;
Many a heart was broken straining at sweep and
    oar.

We roused Lake Marsh with a chorus, we drifted
    many a mile ;
There was the canyon before us—cave-like its
    dark defile ;
The shores swept faster and faster ; the river
    narrowed to wrath ;
Waters that hissed disaster reared upright in our
    path.

Beneath us the green tumult churning, above us
    the cavernous gloom ;
Around us, swift twisting and turning, the black,
    sullen walls of a tomb.
We spun like a chip in a mill-race ; our hearts
    hammered under the test ;
Then—oh, the relief on each chill face !—we
    soared into sunlight and rest.

Hand sought for hand on the instant. Cried
    we, " Our troubles are o'er ! "
Then, like a rumble of thunder, heard we a
    canorous roar.

Leaping and boiling and seething, saw we a
    cauldron afume ;
There was the rage of the rapids, there was the
    menace of doom.

The river springs like a racer, sweeps through
    a gash in the rock ;
Butts at the boulder-ribbed bottom, staggers and
    rears at the shock ;
Leaps like a terrified monster, writhes in its fury
    and pain ;
Then with the crash of a demon springs to the
    onset again.

Dared we that ravening terror ; heard we its din
    in our ears ;
Called on the Gods of our fathers, juggled forlorn
    with our fears ;
Sank to our waists in its fury, tossed to the sky
    like a fleece ;
Then, when our dread was the greatest, crashed
    into safety and peace.

But what of the others that followed, losing their
    boats by the score ?
Well could we see them and hear them, strung
    down that desolate shore.
What of the poor souls that perished ? Little of
    them shall be said—
On to the Golden Valley, pause not to bury
    the dead.

Then there were days of drifting, breezes soft
   as a sigh ;
Night trailed her robe of jewels over the floor
   of the sky.
The moonlit stream was a python, silver, sinuous,
   vast,
That writhed on a shroud of velvet—well, it
   was done at last.

There were the tents of Dawson, there the scar
   of the slide ;
Swiftly we poled o'er the shallows, swiftly leapt
   o'er the side.
Fires fringed the mouth of Bonanza ; sunset
   gilded the dome ;
The test of the trail was over—thank God, thank
   God, we were Home !

THE BALLAD OF GUM-BOOT BEN

*He was an old prospector with a vision bleared
    and dim.*
*He asked me for a grubstake, and the same I
    gave to him.*
*He hinted of a hidden trove, and when I made
    so bold*
To question his veracity, this is the tale he told.

"I do not seek the copper streak, nor yet the
    yellow dust ;
I am not fain for sake of gain to irk the
    frozen crust ;
Let fellows gross find gilded dross, far other is
    my mark ;
Oh, gentle youth, this is the truth—I go to seek
    the Ark.

"I prospected the Pelly bed, I prospected the
    White ;
The Nordenscold for love of gold I piked from
    morn till night ;

225

Afar and near for many a year I led the wild
stampede,
Until I guessed that all my quest was vanity and
greed.

" Then came I to a land I knew no man had ever
seen,
A haggard land, forlornly spanned by mountains
lank and lean ;
The nitchies said 'twas full of dread, of smoke
and fiery breath,
And no man dare put foot in there for fear of
pain and death.

" But I was made all unafraid, so, careless and alone,
Day after day I made my way into that land
unknown ;
Night after night by camp-fire light I crouched in
lonely thought ;
Oh, gentle youth, this is the truth—I knew not
what I sought.

" I rose at dawn ; I wandered on.   'Tis somewhat
fine and grand
To be alone and hold your own in God's vast
awesome land ;
Come woe or weal, 'tis fine to feel a hundred
miles between
The trails you dare and pathways where the feet
of men have been.

" And so it fell on me a spell of wander-lust was
cast.

The land was still and strange and chill, and
cavernous and vast ;

And sad and dead, and dull as lead, the valleys
sought the snows ;

And far and wide on every side the ashen peaks
arose.

" The moon was like a silent spike that pierced
the sky right through ;

The small stars popped and winked and hopped
in vastitudes of blue ;

And unto me for company came creatures of the
shade,

And formed in rings and whispered things that
made me half afraid.

" And strange though be, 'twas borne on me that
land had lived of old,

And men had crept and slain and slept where
now they toiled for gold ;

Through jungles dim the mammoth grim had
sought the oozy fen,

And on his track, all bent of back, had crawled
the hairy men.

" And furthermore, strange deeds of yore in this
dead place were done.

They haunted me, as wild and free I roamed
from sun to sun ;

Until I came where sudden flame uplit a terraced
    height,
A regnant peak that seemed to seek the coronal
    of night.

" I scaled the peak ; my heart was weak, yet on
    and on I pressed.
Skyward I strained until I gained its dazzling
    silver crest ;
And there I found, with all around a world
    supine and stark,
Swept clean of snow, a flat plateau, and on it
    lay—the Ark.

" Yes, there, I knew, by two and two the beasts
    did disembark,
And so in haste I ran and traced in letters on
    the Ark
My human name—Ben Smith's the same. And
    now I want to float
A syndicate to haul and freight to town that
    noble boat."

I met him later in a bar and made a gay remark
Anent an ancient miner and an option on the Ark.
He gazed at me reproachfully, as only topers can ;
But what he said I can't repeat—he was a bad old
*   man.*

CLANCY OF THE MOUNTED POLICE

In the little Crimson Manual it's written plain
    and clear
That who would wear the scarlet coat shall say
    goodbye to fear ;
Shall be a guardian of the right, a sleuth-hound
    of the trail—
In the little Crimson Manual there's no such
    word as " fail "—
Shall follow on though heavens fall, or hell's
    top-turrets freeze,
Half round the world, if need there be, on
    bleeding hands and knees.
It's duty, duty, first and last, the Crimson
    Manual saith ;
The Scarlet Rider makes reply : " It's duty—to
    the death."
And so they sweep the solitudes, free men from
    all the earth ;
And so they sentinel the woods, the wilds that
    know their worth ;
And so they scour the startled plains and mock
    at hurt and pain,

And read their Crimson Manual, and find their
　　duty plain.
Knights of the lists of unrenown, born of the
　　frontier's need,
Disdainful of the spoken word, exultant in the
　　deed ;
Unconscious heroes of the waste, proud players
　　of the game,
Props of the power behind the throne, upholders
　　of the name ;
For thus the Great White Chief hath said, " In
　　all my lands be peace,"
And to maintain his word he gave his West the
　　Scarlet Police.

Livid-lipped was the valley, still as the grave of
　　God ;
　　Misty shadows of mountain thinned into mists
　　　of cloud ;
Corpselike and stark was the land, with a quiet
　　that crushed and awed,
　　And the stars of the weird sub-arctic glimmered
　　　over its shroud.

Deep in the trench of the valley two men
　　stationed the Post,
　　Seymour and Clancy the reckless, fresh from
　　　the long patrol ;
Seymour, the sergeant, and Clancy—Clancy who
　　made his boast

He could cinch like a bronco the Northland,
    and cling to the prongs of the Pole.

Two lone men on detachment, standing for law
    on the trail;
    Undismayed in the vastness, wise with the
        wisdom of old—
Out of the night hailed a half-breed telling a
    pitiful tale,
    " White man starving and crazy on the banks
        of the Nordenscold."

Up sprang the red-haired Clancy, lean and
    eager of eye;
    Loaded the long toboggan, strapped each dog
        at its post;
Whirled his lash at the leader; then, with a
    whoop and a cry,
    Into the Great White Silence faded away like
        a ghost.

The clouds were a misty shadow, the hills were
    a shadowy mist;
    Sunless, voiceless and pulseless, the day was a
        dream of woe;
Through the ice-rifts the river smoked and
    bubbled and hissed;
    Behind was a trail fresh broken, in front
    the untrodden snow.

Ahead of the dogs ploughed Clancy, haloed by
    steaming breath ;
  Through peril of open water, through ache of
    insensate cold ;
Up rivers wantonly winding in a land affianced
    to death,
  Till he came to a cowering cabin on the
    banks of the Nordenscold.

Then Clancy loosed his revolver, and he strode
    through the open door ;
  And there was the man he sought for, crouch-
    ing beside the fire ;
The hair of his beard was singeing, the frost
    on his back was hoar,
  And ever he crooned and chanted as if he
    never would tire :—

*" I panned and I panned in the shiny sand, and
    I sniped on the river bar ;*
*But I know, I know, that it's down below that
    the golden treasures are ;*
*So I'll wait and wait till the floods abate, and I'll
    sink a shaft once more,*
*And I'd like to bet that I'll go home yet with a brass
    band playing before."*

He was nigh as thin as a sliver, and he whined
    like a Moose-hide cur ;

So Clancy clothed him and nursed him as a
    mother nurses a child ;
Lifted him on the toboggan, wrapped him in
    robes of fur,
    Then with the dogs sore straining started to
        face the Wild.

Said the Wild, " I will crush this Clancy, so
        fearless and insolent ;
    For him will I loose my fury, and blind and
        buffet and beat ;
Pile up my snows to stay him ; then when his
    strength is spent,
    Leap on him from my ambush and crush him
        under my feet.

" Him will I ring with my silence, compass him
        with my cold ;
Closer and closer clutch him unto mine icy
    breast ;
Buffet him with my blizzards, deep in my snows
    enfold,
    Claiming his life as my tribute, giving my
        wolves the rest."

Clancy crawled through the vastness ; o'er him
        the hate of the Wild ;
    Full on his face fell the blizzard ; cheering his
        huskies he ran ;

Fighting, fierce-hearted and tireless, snows that
　　drifted and piled,
　With ever and ever behind him singing the
　　crazy man.

    " Sing hey, sing ho, for the ice and snow,
      And a heart that's ever merry ;
    Let us trim and square with a lover's care
      (For why should a man be sorry ?)
    A grave deep, deep, with the moon a-peep,
      A grave in the frozen mould.
    Sing hey, sing ho, for the winds that blow,
    And a grave deep down in the ice and snow,
      A grave in the land of gold."

Day after day of darkness, the whirl of the
　　seething snows ;
　Day after day of blindness, the swoop of the
　　stinging blast ;
On through a blur of fury the swing of staggering
　　blows ;
　On through a world of turmoil, empty, inane and
　　vast.

Night with its writhing storm-whirl, night despair-
　　ingly black ;
　Night with its hours of terror, numb and end-
　　lessly long ;
Night with its weary waiting, fighting the shadows
　　back,

And ever the crouching madman singing his crazy song.

Cold with its creeping terror, cold with its sudden clinch ;
  Cold so utter you wonder if 'twill ever again be warm ;
Clancy grinned as he shuddered, " Surely it isn't a cinch
  Being wet-nurse to a looney in the teeth of an arctic storm."

The blizzard passed and the dawn broke, knife-edged and crystal clear ;
  The sky was a blue-domed iceberg, sunshine outlawed away ;
Ever by snowslide and ice-rip haunted and hovered the Fear ;
  Ever the Wild malignant poised and panted to slay.

The lead-dog freezes in harness—cut him out of the team !
  The lung of the wheel-dog's bleeding—shoot him and let him lie !
On and on with the others—lash them until they scream !
  " Pull for your lives, you devils ! On ! To halt is to die."

There in the frozen vastness Clancy fought with
    his foes ;
  The ache of the stiffened fingers, the cut of the
    snowshoe thong ;
Cheeks black-raw through the hood-flap, eyes that
    tingled and closed,
  And ever to urge and cheer him quavered the
    madman's song.

Colder it grew and colder, till the last heat left
    the earth,
  And there in the great stark stillness the bale
    fires glinted and gleamed,
And the Wild all around exulted and shook with
    a devilish mirth,
  And life was far and forgotten the ghost of a
    joy once dreamed.

Death ! And one who defied it, a man of the
    Mounted Police ;
  Fought it there to a standstill long after hope
    was gone ;
Grinned through his bitter anguish, fought with-
    out let or cease,
  Suffering, straining, striving, stumbling, strug-
    gling on.

Till the dogs lay down in their traces, and rose
    and staggered and fell ;
  Till the eyes of him dimmed with shadows, and
    the trail was so hard to see ;

Till the Wild howled out triumphant, and the
world was a frozen hell—
    Then said Constable Clancy : " I guess that it's
up to me."

Far down the trail they saw him, and his hands
they were blanched like bone ;
    His face was a blackened horror, from his eye-
lids the salt rheum ran ;
His feet he was lifting strangely, as if they were
made of stone,
    But safe in his arms and sleeping he carried
the crazy man.

So Clancy got into Barracks, and the boys made
rather a scene ;
    And the O.C. called him a hero, and was nice
as a man could be ;
But Clancy gazed down his trousers at the place
where his toes had been,
    And then he howled like a husky, and sang in
a shaky key :—

*" When I go back to the old love that's true to the
finger-tips,*
*I'll say : ' Here's bushels of gold, love,' and I'll kiss
my girl on the lips ;*
*' It's yours to have and to hold, love.'   It's the proud,
proud boy I'll be,*
*When I go back to the old love that's waited so long
for me."*

LOST

" Black is the sky, but the land is white—
(O the wind, the snow and the storm !)—
Father, where is our boy to-night ?
Pray to God he is safe and warm."

" Mother, mother, why should you fear
Safe is he, and the Arctic moon
Over his cabin shines so clear—
Rest and sleep, 'twill be morning soon."

"It's getting dark awful sudden. Say, this is
mighty queer !
Where in the world have I got to ? It's still
and black as a tomb.
I reckoned the camp was yonder, I figured the
trail was here—
Nothing ! Just draw and valley packed with
quiet and gloom ;
Snow that comes down like feathers, thick and
gobby and gray ;
Night that looks spiteful ugly—seems that I've
lost my way.

238

"The cold's got an edge like a jackknife—it
    must be forty below ;
  Leastways that's what it seems like—it cuts so
    fierce to the bone.
The wind's getting real ferocious ; it's heaving and
    whirling the snow ;
  It shrieks with a howl of fury, it dies away to
    a moan ;
Its arms sweep round like a banshee's, swift and
    icily white,
And buffet and blind and beat me. Lord ! it's
    a hell of a night.

"I'm all tangled up in a blizzard. There's only
    one thing to do—
  Keep on moving and moving ; it's death, it's
    death if I rest.
Oh, God ! if I see the morning, if only I struggle
    through,
  I'll say the prayers I've forgotten since I lay
    on my mother's breast.
I seem going round in a circle ; maybe the camp
    is near.
  Say ! did somebody holler ? Was it a light I
    saw ?
Or was it only a notion ? I'll shout, and maybe
    they'll hear—
  No ! the wind only drowns me—shout till my
    throat is raw.
                          I

" The boys are all round the camp-fire wondering
    when I'll be back.
  They'll soon be starting to seek me; they'll
    scarcely wait for the light.
What will they find, I wonder, when they come
    to the end of my track—
  A hand stuck out of a snowdrift, frozen and
    stiff and white.
That's what they'll strike, I reckon; that's how
    they'll find their pard.
  A pie-faced corpse in a snowbank—curse you,
    don't be a fool!
Play the game to the finish; bet on your very
    last card;
  Nerve yourself for the struggle. Oh, you coward,
    keep cool!

" I'm going to lick this blizzard; I'm going to live
    the night.
  It can't down me with its bluster—I'm not the
    kind to be beat.
On hands and knees will I buck it; with every
    breath will I fight;
  It's life, it's life that I fight for—never it seemed
    so sweet.
I know that my face is frozen; my hands are
    numblike and dead;
  But oh, my feet keep a-moving, heavy and hard
    and slow;

They're trying to kill me, kill me, the night that's
　　black overhead,
　The wind that cuts like a razor, the whipcord
　　lash of the snow.
Keep a-moving, a-moving; don't, don't stumble,
　　you fool !
　Curse this snow that's a-piling a-purpose to
　　block my way.
It's heavy as gold in the rocker, it's white and
　　fleecy as wool ;
　It's soft as a bed of feathers, it's warm as a
　　stack of hay.
Curse on my feet that slip so, my poor tired,
　　stumbling feet—
　I guess they're a job for the surgeon, they feel
　　so queerlike to lift—
I'll rest them just for a moment—oh, but to rest
　　is sweet !
　The awful wind cannot get me, deep, deep down
　　in the drift."

　　" *Father, a bitter cry I heard,*
　　　Out of the night so dark and wild.
　　Why is my heart so strangely stirred ?
　　　'Twas like the voice of our erring child."

　　" *Mother, mother, you only heard*
　　　A waterfowl in the locked lagoon—
　　Out of the night a wounded bird—
　　　Rest and sleep, 'twill be morning soon."

Who is it talks of sleeping ?   I'll swear that some-
        body shook
    Me hard by the arm for a moment, but how
        on earth could it be ?
See how my feet are moving—awfully funny they
        look—
    Moving as if they belonged to a some one that
        wasn't me.
The wind down the night's long alley bowls me
        down like a pin ;
    I stagger and fall and stagger, crawl arm-deep
        in the snow.
Beaten back to my corner, how can I hope to
        win ?
    And there is the blizzard waiting to give me
        the knockout blow.

Oh, I'm so warm and sleepy !   No more hunger
        and pain.
    Just to rest for a moment ; was ever rest such
        a joy ?
Ha ! what was that ? I'll swear it, somebody
        shook me again ;
    Somebody seemed to whisper : " Fight to the
        last, my boy."
Fight ! That's right, I must struggle. I know
        that to rest means death ;
    Death, but then what does death mean ?—ease
        from a world of strife.

Life has been none too pleasant; yet with my
  failing breath
  Still and still must I struggle, fight for the gift
  of life.

     *   *   *   *   *   *

Seems that I must be dreaming!   Here is the
  old home trail;
  Yonder a light is gleaming; oh, I know it so
  well!
The air is scented with clover; the cattle wait
  by the rail;
  Father is through with the milking; there goes
  the supper-bell.

     *   *   *   *   *   *

Mother, your boy is crying, out in the night and
  cold;
  Let me in and forgive me, I'll never be bad
  any more:
I'm, oh, so sick and so sorry: please, dear mother,
  don't scold—
  It's just your boy, and he wants you. . . .
  Mother, open the door. . . .

    *" Father, father, I saw a face
      Pressed just now to the window-pane!
    Oh, it gazed for a moment's space,
      Wild and wan, and was gone again!"*

" *Mother, mother, you saw the snow*
   Drifted down from the maple-tree
(Oh, the wind that is sobbing so !
   Weary and worn and old are we)—
Only the snow and a wounded loon—
   Rest and sleep, 'twill be morning soon."

L'ENVOI

WE talked of yesteryears, of trails and treasure.
   Of men who played the game and lost or won ;
Of mad stampedes, of toil beyond all measure,
   Of camp-fire comfort when the day was done.
We talked of sullen nights by moon-dogs haunted,
   Of bird and beast and tree, of rod and gun ;
Of boat and tent, of hunting-trip enchanted
   Beneath the wonder of the midnight sun ;
Of bloody-footed dogs that gnawed the traces,
   Of prisoned seas, wind-lashed and winter-locked.
The ice-grey dawn was pale upon our faces,
   Yet still we filled the cup and still we talked.

The city street was dimmed.   We saw the glitter
   Of moon-picked brilliants on the virgin snow,
And down the drifted canyon heard the bitter,
   Relentless slogan of the winds of woe.
The city was forgot, and, parka-skirted,
   We trod that leagueless land that once we knew ;
We saw stream past, down valleys glacier-girted,
   The wolf-worn legions of the caribou ;

We smoked our pipes, o'er scenes of triumph dwelling ;
*   Of deeds of daring, dire defeats, we talked ;*
And other tales that lost not in the telling,
*   Ere to our beds uncertainly we walked.*

And so, dear friends, in gentler valleys roaming,
*   Perhaps, when on my printed page you look,*
Your fancies by the firelight may go homing
*   To that lone land that haply you forsook.*
And if perchance you hear the silence calling,
*   The frozen music of star yearning heights,*
Or, dreaming, see the seines of silver trawling
*   Across the sky's abyss on vasty nights,*
You may recall that sweep of savage splendour,
*   That land that measures each man at his worth,*
And feel in memory, half fierce, half tender,
*   The brotherhood of men that know the North.*

THE END

RHYMES OF A ROLLING STONE

I have no doubt at all the Devil grins
    As seas of ink I spatter;
Ye Gods, forgive my " literary" sins—
    The other kind don't matter.

PRELUDE

I sing no idle songs of dalliance days,
  No dreams Elysian inspire my rhyming;
I have no Celia to enchant my lays,
  No pipes of Pan have set my heart to chiming
I am no wordsmith dripping gems divine
  Into the golden chalice of a sonnet;
If love songs witch you, close this book of mine,
          Waste no time on it.

Yet bring I to my work an eager joy,
  A lusty love of life and all things human
Still in me leaps the wonder of the boy,
  A pride in man, a deathless faith in woman.
Still red blood calls, still rings the valiant fray;
  Adventure beacons through the summer gloaming.
Oh, long and long and long will be the day
          Ere I come homing!

This earth is ours to love: lute, brush and pen,
  They are but tongues to tell of life sincerely;
The thaumaturgic Day, the might of men,
  O God of Scribes, grant us to grave them clearly!
Grant heart that homes in heart, then all is well.
  Honey is honey-sweet, howe'er the hiving.
Each to his work, his wage at evening bell
  The strength of striving.

251

RHYMES OF
A ROLLING STONE

A ROLLING STONE

THERE'S sunshine in the heart of me,
  My blood sings in the breeze;
The mountains are a part of me,
  I'm fellow to the trees.
My golden youth I'm squandering,
  Sun-libertine am I;
A-wandering, a-wandering,
  Until the day I die.

I was once, I declare, a Stone Age man,
  And I roomed in the cool of a cave;
I have known, I will swear, in a new life-span,
  The fret and the sweat of a slave:
For far over all that folks hold worth,
  There lives and there leaps in me
A love of the lowly things of earth,
  And a passion to be free.

To pitch my tent with no prosy plan.
  To range and to change at will ;
To mock at the mastership of man,
  To seek Adventure's thrill.
Carefree to be, as a bird that sings,
  To go my own sweet way ;
To reck not at all what may befall,
  But to live and to love each day.

To make my body a temple pure
  Wherein I dwell serene ;
To care for the things that shall endure,
  The simple, sweet and clean.
To oust out envy and hate and rage,
  To breathe with no alarm ;
For Nature shall be my anchorage,
  And none shall do me harm.

To shun all lures that debauch the soul,
  The orgied rites of the rich ;
To eat my crust as a rover must
  With the rough-neck down in the ditch.
To trudge by his side whate'er betide ;
  To share his fire at night ;
To call him friend to the long trail-end,
  And to read his heart aright.

To scorn all strife, and to view all life
 With the curious eyes of a child ;
From the plangent sea to the prairie,
 From the slum to the heart of the Wild.
From the red-rimmed star to the speck of sand,
 From the vast to the greatly small ;
For I know that the whole for good is planned,
 And I want to see it all.

To see it all, the wide world-way,
 From the fig-leaf belt to the Pole ;
With never a one to say me nay,
 And none to cramp my soul.
In belly-pinch I will pay the price,
 But God ! let me be free ;
For once I know in the long ago,
 They made a slave of me.

In a flannel shirt from earth's clean dirt,
 Here, pal, is my calloused hand !
Oh, I love each day as a rover may,
 Nor seek to understand.
To *enjoy* is good enough for me ;
 The gipsy of God am I ;
Then here's a hail to each flaring dawn !
And here's a cheer to the night that's gone !
And may I go a-roaming on
 Until the day I die !

Then every star shall sing to me
    Its song of liberty ;
And every morn shall bring to me
    Its mandate to be free.
In every throbbing vein of me
    I'll feel the vast Earth-call :
O body, heart and brain of me,
    Praise Him who made it all !

THE SOLDIER OF FORTUNE

'DENY your God!" they ringed me with their
    spears ;
  Blood-crazed were they, and reeking from the
    strife ;
Hell-hot their hate, and venom-fanged their sneers,
  And one man spat on me and nursed a knife.
And there was I, sore wounded and alone,
  I, the last living of my slaughtered band.
Oh, sinister the sky, and cold as stone !
  In one red laugh of horror reeled the land.
And dazed and desperate I faced their spears,
  And like a flame out-leaped that naked knife,
And like a serpent stung their bitter jeers :
  " Deny your God, and we will give you life."

Deny my God ! Oh, life was very sweet !
  And it is hard in youth and hope to die ;
And there my comrades dear lay at my feet,
  And in that blear of blood soon must I lie.

And yet . . . I almost laughed—it seemed so odd,
  For long and long had I not vainly tried
To reason out and body forth my God,
  And prayed for light, and doubted—and *denied.*
Denied the Being I could not conceive,
  Denied a life-to-be beyond the grave. . . .
And now they ask me, who do not believe,
  Just to deny, to voice my doubt, to save
This life of mine that sings so in the sun,
  The bloom of youth yet red upon my cheek,
My only life !—O fools ! 'tis easy done,
  I will deny . . . and yet I do not speak.

" Deny your God ! " their spears are all agleam,
  And I can see their eyes with blood-lust shine ;
Their snarling voices shrill into a scream,
  And, mad to slay, they quiver for the sign.
Deny my God ! yes, I could do it well ;
  Yet if I did, what of my race, my name ?
How they would spit on me, these dogs of hell !
  Spurn me, and put on me the brand of shame.
A white man's honour ! what of that, I say ?
  Shall these black curs cry " Coward " in my
    face ?

They who would perish for their gods of clay—
  Shall I defile my country and my race ?

My country ! what's my country to me now ?
  Soldier of Fortune, free and far I roam ;
All men are brothers in my heart, I vow ;
  The wide and wondrous world is all my home.
My country ! reverent of her splendid Dead,
  Her heroes proud, her martyrs pierced with
    pain :
For me her puissant blood was vainly shed ;
  For me her drums of battle beat in vain,
And free I fare, half-heedless of her fate :
  No faith, no flag, I owe—then why not seek
This last loop-hole of life ?   Why hesitate ?
  I will deny . . . and yet I do not speak.

"Deny your God ! " their spears are poised on
    high,
  And tense and terrible they wait the word ;
And dark and darker glooms the dreary sky,
  And in that hush of horror no thing stirred.
Then, through the ringing terror and sheer hate
  Leaped there a vision to me—Oh, how far !
A face, Her face . . . through all my stormy fate
  A joy, a strength, a glory and a star.

Beneath the pines, where lonely camp-fires gleam,
  In seas forlorn, amid the deserts drear,
How I had gladdened to that face of dream !
  And never, never had it seemed so dear.

O silken hair that veils the sunny brow !
  O eyes of grey, so tender and so true !
O lips of smiling sweetness ! must I now
  Forever and forever go from you ?
Ah, yes, I must . . . for if I do this thing,
  How can I look into your face again ?
Knowing you think me more than half a king.
  I with my craven heart, my honour slain.
No ! no ! my mind's made up. I gaze above,
  Into that sky insensate as a stone ;
Not for my creed, my country, but my Love
  Will I stand up and meet my death alone.
Then, though it be to utter dark I sink,
  The God that dwells in me is not denied ;
" Best " triumphs over " Beast "—and so I think
  Humanity itself is glorified. . . .

"And now, my butchers, I embrace my fate.
  Come ! let my heart's blood slake the thirsty
    sod.
Curst be the life you offer ! Glut your hate !
  Strike ! Strike, you dogs ! I'll *not* deny my
    God."
I saw the spears that seemed a-leap to slay,
  All quiver earthward at the headman's nod ;
And in a daze of dream I heard him say :
  " Go, set him free who serves so well his God ! "

THE GRAMOPHONE AT FOND-DU-LAC

Now Eddie Malone got a swell grammyfone, to
    draw all the trade to his store ;
An' sez he : " Come along for a season of song,
    which the like ye had niver before."
Then Dogrib an' Slave, an' Yellow-knife brave, an'
    Cree in his dinky canoe,
Confluated near, to see an' to hear Ed's grammy-
    fone make its dayboo.

Then Ed turned the crank, an' there on the bank
    they squatted like bumps on a log.
For acres around there wasn't a sound, not even the
    howl of a dog.
When out of the horn there sudden was born
    such a marvellous elegant tone ;
An' then like a spell on that auddyence fell the voice
    of its first grammyfone.

" *Bad medicine !* " cried Old Tom, the One-eyed,
    an' made for to jump in the lake ;
But no one gave heed to his little stampede, so he
    guessed he had made a mistake.
Then Roll-in-the-Mud, a chief of the blood, observed
    in choice Chippewayan :
" You've brought us canned beef, an' it's now my
    belief, that this here's a case of ' *canned man.*' "

Well, though I'm not strong on the Dago in song,
    that sure got me goin' for fair.
There was Crusoe an' Scotty an' Ma'am Shoeman,
    Hank, an' Melber an' Bonchy was there.
'Twas silver an' gold, an' sweetness untold, to hear
    all them big guinneys sing ;
An' thick all around an' inhalin' the sound, them
    Indians formed in a ring.

So solemn they sat, an' they smoked an' they spat,
    but their eyes sort o' glistened an' shone :
Yet niver a word of approvin' occurred till that
    guy Harry Lauder came on.
Then hunter of moose an' squaw an' papoose jest
    laughed till their stummicks was sore ;
Six times Eddie set back that record an' yet they
    hollered an' hollered for more.

I'll never forget that frame-up, you bet ; them
    caverns of sunset agleam ;
Them still peaks aglow, them shadders below, an'
    the lake like a petrified dream ;
The teepees that stood by the edge of the wood ;
    the evenin' star blinkin' alone ;
The peace an' the rest, an' final an' best, the music
    of Ed's grammyfone.

Then sudden an' clear there rang on my ear a song
    mighty simple an' old ;
Heart-hungry an' high it thrilled to the sky, all
    about " silver threads in the gold."
'Twas tender to tears, an' it brung back the years
    the mem'ries that hallow an' yearn ;
'Twas home-love an' joy, 'twas the thought of my
    boy . . . an' right there I vowed I'd return.

Big Four-finger Jack was right at my back, an' I
    saw with a kind o' surprise,
He gazed at the lake with a heartful of ache, an'
    the tears irrigated his eyes.
An' sez he : " Cuss me, pard ! but that there hits
    me hard ; I've a mother does nuthin' but wait.
She's turned eighty-three, an' she's only got me,
    an' I'm scared it'll soon be too late."

   *   *   *   *   *   *

On Fond-du-lac's shore I'm hearin' once more that
    blessed old grammyfone play.
The summer's all gone, an' I'm still livin' on in the
    same old haphazardous way.
Oh, I cut out the booze, an' with muscles an' thews
    I corralled all the coin to go back ;
But it wasn't to be—he'd a mother, you see—so
    I—*slipped it to Four-finger Jack.*

THE LAND OF BEYOND

Have ever you heard of the Land of Beyond,
   That dreams at the gates of the day ?
Alluring it lies at the skirts of the skies,
   And ever so far away ;
Alluring it calls : O ye the yoke galls,
   And ye of the trail overfond,
With saddle and pack, by paddle and track,
   Let's go to the Land of Beyond !

Have ever you stood where the silences brood,
   And vast the horizons begin,
At the dawn of the day to behold far away
   The goal you would strive for and win ?
Yet, ah ! in the night when you gain to the height,
   With the vast pool of heaven star-spawned,
Afar and agleam, like a valley of dream,
   Still mocks you a Land of Beyond.

Thank God ! there is always a Land of Beyond
  For us who are true to the trail ;
A vision to seek, a beckoning peak,
  A farness that never will fail ;
A pride in our soul that mocks at a goal,
  A manhood that irks at a bond,
And try how we will, unattainable still,
  Behold it, our Land of Beyond

SUNSHINE

I

FLAT as a drum-head stretch the haggard snows ;
  The mighty skies are palisades of light ;
The stars are blurred ; the silence grows and grows ;
  Vaster and vaster vaults the icy night.
Here in my sleeping-bag I cower and pray :
" Silence and night, have pity ; stoop and slay."

I have not slept for many, many days.
  I close my eyes with weariness—that's all.
I still have strength to feed the drift-wood blaze
  That flickers weirdly on the icy wall.
I still have strength to pray : " God rest her soul,
Here in the awful shadow of the Pole."

There in the cabin's alcove low she lies,
  Still candles gleaming at her head and feet ;
All snow-drop white, ash-cold, with closèd eyes,
  Lips smiling, hands at rest—O God, how sweet !

How all unutterably sweet she seems . . .
Not dead, not dead, indeed — she dreams, she
    dreams.

II

" Sunshine," I called her, and she brought, I vow,
    God's blessed sunshine to this life of mine.
I was a rover, of the breed who plough
    Life's furrow in a far-flung, lonely line ;
The wilderness my home, my fortune cast
In a wild land of dearth, barbaric, vast.

When did I see her first ?   Long had I lain
    Groping my way to life through fevered gloom.
Sudden the cloud of darkness left my brain ;
    A velvet bar of sunshine pierced the room,
And in that mellow glory aureoled
She stood, she stood, all golden in its gold.

Sunshine ! O miracle ! the earth grew glad ;
    Radiant each blade of grass, each living thing.
What a huge strength, high hope, proud will I
    had !
    All the wide world with rapture seemed to ring.
Would she but wed me ?   Yes : then fared we
    forth
Into the vast, unvintageable North.

III

In Muskrat Land the conies leap,
   The wavies linger in their flight ;
The jewelled, snake-like rivers creep ;
   The sun, sad rogue, is out all night ;
The great wood-bison paws the sand,
In Muskrat Land, in Muskrat Land.

In Muskrat Land dim streams divide
   The tundras belted by the sky.
How sweet in slim canoe to glide,
   And dream, and let the world go by !
Build gay camp-fires on greening strand !
In Muskrat Land, in Muskrat Land.

IV

And so we dreamed and drifted, she and I ;
   And how she loved that free. unfathomed life !
There, in the peach-bloom of the midnight sky,
   The silence welded us, true man and wife.
Then North and North invincibly we pressed
Beyond the Circle, to the world's white crest.

And on the wind-flailed Arctic waste we stayed,
   Dwelt with the Huskies by the Polar sea.
Fur had they, white fox, marten, mink, to trade
   And we had food-stuff, bacon, flour and tea.

So we made snug, chummed up with all the band :
Sudden the Winter swooped on Husky Land.

V

What was that ill so sinister and dread,
  Smiting the tribe with sickness to the bone ?
So that we waked one morn to find them fled ;
  So that we stood and stared, alone, alone.
Bravely she smiled and looked into my eyes ;
  Laughed at their troubled, stern, foreboding
    pain ;
Gaily she mocked the menace of the skies,
  Turned to our cheery cabin once again,
Saying : " 'Twill soon be over, dearest one,
The long, long night : then O the sun, the sun ! "

VI

God made a heart of gold, of gold,
  Shining and sweet and true ;
Gave it a home of fairest mould,
  Blest it, and called it—You.

God gave the rose its grace of glow,
  And the lark its radiant glee ;
But, better than all, I know, I know
  God gave you, Heart, to me.

VII

She was all sunshine in those dubious days ;
  Our cabin beaconed with defiant light ;
We chattered by the friendly drift-wood blaze ;
  Closer and closer cowered the hag-like night.
A wolf-hound would have been a welcome sound,
  And there was none in all that stricken land ;
Yet with such silence, darkness, death around,
  Learned we to love as few can understand.
Spirit with spirit fused, and soul to soul,
There in the sullen shadow of the Pole.

VIII

What was that haunting horror of the night ?
  Brave was she ; buoyant, full of sunny cheer.
Why was her face so small, so strangely white ?
  Then did I turn from her, heart-sick with fear ;
Sought in my agony the outcast snows ;
  Prayed in my pain to that insensate sky ;
Grovelled and sobbed and cursed, and then arose :
  " Sunshine !   O heart of gold ! to die ! to die ! "

IX

She died on Christmas Day—it seems so sad
  That one you love should die on Christmas Day

Head-bowed I knelt by her ; O God ! I had
  No tears to shed, no moan, no prayer to pray.
I heard her whisper : " Call me, will you, dear ?
  They say Death parts, but I won't go away.
I will be with you in the cabin here ;
  Oh, I will plead with God to let me stay !
Stay till the Night is gone, till Spring is nigh,
Till sunshine comes . . . be brave . . . I'm tired
    . . . good-bye. . . ."

X

For weeks, for months I had not seen the sun ;
  The minatory dawns are leprous pale ;
The felon days malinger one by one ;
  How like a dream Life is ! how vain ! how
    stale !
I, too, am faint ; that vampire-like disease
  Has fallen on me ; weak and cold am I,
Hugging a tiny fire in fear I freeze :
  The cabin must be cold, and so I try
To bear the frost, the frost that fights decay,
The frost that keeps her beautiful alway.

XI

She lies within an icy vault ;
It glitters like a cave of salt.

All marble-pure and angel-sweet
With candles at her head and feet,
Under an ermine robe she lies.
I kiss her hands, I kiss her eyes :
" Come back, come back, O Love, I pray,
Into this house, this house of clay !
Answer my kisses soft and warm ;
Nestle again within my arm.
Come ! for I know that you are near ;
Open your eyes and look, my dear.
Just for a moment break the mesh ;
Back from the spirit leap to flesh.
Weary I wait ; the night is black ;
Love of my life, come back, come back ! "

XII

Last night maybe I was a little mad,
    For as I prayed despairful by her side,
Such a strange, antic visioning I had :
    Lo ! it did seem *her eyes were open wide.*
Surely I must have dreamed ! I stared once
        more . . .
    No, 'twas a candle's trick, a shadow cast.
There were her lashes locking as before.
    (Oh, but it filled me with a joy so vast !)
No, 'twas a freak, a fancy of the brain.
(Oh, but to-night I'll try again, again !)

XIII

It was no dream ; now do I know that Love
  Leapt from the starry battlements of Death ;
For in my vigil as I bent above,
  Calling her name with eager, burning breath,
Sudden there came a change ; again I saw
  The radiance of the rose-leaf stain her cheek ;
Rivers of rapture thrilled in sunny thaw ;
  Cleft were her coral lips as if to speak ;
Curved were her tender arms as if to cling
  Open the flower-like eyes of lucent blue,
Looking at me with love so pitying
  That I could fancy Heaven shining through.
" Sunshine," I faltered, " stay with me, oh, stay ! "
  Yet ere I finished, in a moment's flight,
There in her angel purity she lay—
  Ah ! but I know she'll come again to-night.
Even as radiant sword leaps from the sheath,
Soul from the body leaps—we call it Death.

XIV

Even as this line I write,
  Do I know that she is near ;
Happy am I, every night
  Comes she back to bid me cheer ;
Kissing her, I hold her fast ;
Win her into life at last.

Did I dream that yesterday
  On yon mountain ridge a glow
Soft as moonstone paled away,
  Leaving less forlorn the snow ?
Could it be the sun ? Oh, fain
Would I see the sun again !

Oh, to see a coral dawn
  Gladden to a crocus glow !
Day's a spectre dim and wan,
  Dancing on the furtive snow ;
Night's a cloud upon my brain :
Oh, to see the sun again !

You who find us in this place,
  Have you pity in your breast ;
Let us in our last embrace
  Under earth sun-hallowed rest.
Night's a claw upon my brain :
Oh, to see the sun again !

xv

The Sun ! at last the Sun ! I write these lines,
  Here on my knees, with feeble, fumbling hand
Look ! in yon mountain cleft a radiance shines,
  Gleam of a primrose—see it thrill, expand,

Grow glorious.   Dear God be praised ! it streams
  Into the cabin in a gush of gold.
Look ! there she stands, the angel of my dreams,
  All in the radiant shimmer aureoled ;
First as I saw her from my bed of pain ;
  First as I loved her when the darkness passed.
Now do I know that Life is not in vain ;
  Now do I know God cares, at last, at last !
Light outlives dark, joy grief, and Love's the sum :
Heart of my heart ! Sunshine ! I come . . . I
    come . . .

THE IDEALIST

Oh, you who have daring deeds to tell !
And you who have felt Ambition's spell !
Have you heard of the louse who longed to dwell
    In the golden hair of a queen ?
He sighed all day and he sighed all night,
And no one could understand it quite,
For the head of a slut is a louse's delight,
    But he pined for the head of a queen.

So he left his kinsfolk in merry play,
And off by his lonesome he stole away,
From the home of his youth so bright and gay,
    And gloriously unclean.
And at last he came to the palace gate,
And he made his way in a manner straight
(For a louse may go where a man must wait)
    To the tiring-room of the queen.

The queen she spake to her tiring-maid :
" There's something the matter, I'm afraid.
To-night ere for sleep my hair ye braid,
   Just see what may be seen."
And lo, when they combed that shining hair,
They found him alone in his glory there,
And he cried : " I die, but I do not care,
   For I've lived in the head of a queen ! "

ATHABASKA DICK

WHEN the boys come out from Lac Labiche in
    the lure of the early Spring,
  To take the pay of the " Hudson's Bay," as
    their fathers did before,
They are all aglee for the jamboree, and they make
    the Landing ring
  With a whoop and a whirl, and a " Grab your
    girl," and a rip and a skip and a roar.
For the spree of Spring is a sacred thing, and the
    boys must have their fun ;
  Packer and tracker and half-breed Cree, from
    the boat to the bar they leap ;
And then when the long flotilla goes, and the last
    of their pay is done,
  The boys from the bank of Lac Labiche swing
    to the heavy sweep.
And oh, how they sigh ! and their throats are
    dry, and sorry are they and sick :
Yet there's none so cursed with a lime-kiln thirst
    as that Athabaska Dick.

279

He was long and slim and lean of limb, but strong
    as a stripling bear ;
    And by the right of his skill and might he guided
        the Long Brigade.
All water-wise were his laughing eyes, and he
    steered with a careless care,
    And he shunned the shock of foam and rock,
        till they came to the Big Cascade.
And here they must make the long *portage*, and
    the boys sweat in the sun ;
    And they heft and pack, and they haul and
        track, and each must do his trick ;
But their thoughts are far in the Landing bar,
    where the founts of nectar run :
    And no man thinks of such gorgeous drinks as
        that Athabaska Dick.

'Twas the close of day, and his long boat lay just
    over the Big Cascade,
    When there came to him one Jack-pot Jim,
        with a wild light in his eye ;
And he softly laughed, and he led Dick aft, all
    eager, yet half afraid,
    And snugly stowed in his coat he showed a
        pilfered flask of " rye."

And in haste he slipped, or in fear he tripped,
    but—Dick in warning roared—
And there rang a yell, and it befell that Jim
    was overboard.

Oh, I heard a splash, and quick as a flash I knew
    he could not swim.
  I saw him whirl in the river swirl, and thresh
    his arms about.
In a queer, strained way I heard Dick say: "I'm
    going after him,"
  Throw off his coat, leap down the boat—and
    then I gave a shout:
"Boys, grab him, quick! You're crazy, Dick:
    Far better one than two!
  Hell, man! You know you've got no show!
    It's sure and certain death . . ."
And there we hung, and there we clung, with
    beef and brawn and thew,
  And sinews cracked and joints were racked, and
    panting came our breath;
And there we swayed and there we prayed, till
    strength and hope were spent—
Then Dick, he threw us off like rats and after
    Jim he went.

With a mighty urge amid the surge of river-rage
    he leapt,
  And gripped his mate and desperate he fought
    to gain the shore ;
With teeth agleam he bucked the stream, yet swift
    and sure he swept
  To meet the mighty cataract that waited all
    aroar.
And there we stood like carven wood, our faces
    sickly white,
  And watched him as he beat the foam, and
    inch by inch he lost ;
And nearer, nearer drew the fall, and fiercer grew
    the fight,
  Till on the very cascade crest a last farewell
    he tossed.
Then down and down and down they plunged into
    that pit of dread ;
And mad we tore along the shore to claim our
    bitter dead.

And from that hell of frenzied foam, that crashed
    and fumed and boiled,
  Two little bodies bubbled up, and they were
    heedless then ;

And oh, they lay like senseless clay ! and bitter
    hard we toiled,
  Yet never, never gleam of hope, and we were
    weary men.
And moments mounted into hours, and black was
    our despair ;
  And faint were we, and we were fain to give them
    up as dead,
When suddenly I thrilled with hope : " Back,
    boys ! and give him air ;
I feel the flutter of his heart . . ." And, as the
    word I said,
Dick gave a sigh, and gazed around, and saw our
    breathless band ;
  And saw the sky's blue floor above, all strewn
    with golden fleece ;
And saw his comrade Jack-pot Jim, and touched
    him with his hand ;
  And then there came into his eyes a look of
    perfect peace.
And as there, at his very feet, the thwarted river
    raved,
I heard him murmur low and deep : " Thank
    God ! the *whiskey's* saved."

CHEER

It's a mighty good world, so it is, dear lass,
　When even the worst is said.
There's a smile and a tear, a sigh and a cheer,
　But better be living than dead ;
A joy and a pain, a loss and a gain ;
　There's honey and maybe some gall :
Yet still I declare, foul weather or fair,
　It's a mighty good world after all.

For look, lass ! at night when I break from the
　　　fight,
　My Kingdom's awaiting for me ;
There's comfort and rest, and the warmth of your
　　　breast,
　And little ones climbing my knee.
There's fire-light and song—Oh, the world may be
　　　wrong,
　Its empires may topple and fall :
My home is my care—if gladness be there,
　It's a mighty good world after all.

284

O heart of pure gold ! I have made you a fold,
  It's sheltered, sun-fondled and warm.
O little ones, rest ! I have fashioned a nest ;
  Sleep on ! you are safe from the storm.
For there's no foe like fear, and there's no friend
      like cheer,
  And sunshine will flash at our call ;
So crown Love as King, and let us all sing—
  "It's a mighty good world after all."

THE RETURN

THEY turned him loose ; he bowed his head,
   A felon, bent and grey.
His face was even as the Dead,
   He had no word to say.

He sought the home of his old love,
   To look on her once more ;
And where her roses breathed above,
   He cowered beside the door.

She sat there in the shining room ;
   Her hair was silver grey.
He stared and stared from out the gloom ;
   He turned to go away.

Her roses rustled overhead.
   She saw, with sudden start.
" I knew that you would come," she said,
   And held him to her heart.

Her face was rapt and angel-sweet;
She touched his hair of grey;
❋　　*　　*　　*　　*　　❋
　　　But he, sob-shaken, at her feet,
　　　Could only pray and pray.

THE JUNIOR GOD

THE Junior God looked from his place
  In the conning-towers of heaven,
And he saw the world through the span of space
  Like a giant golf-ball driven.
And because he was bored, as some gods are,
  With high celestial mirth,
He clutched the reins of a shooting star,
  And he steered it down to earth.

The Junior God, 'mid leaf and bud,
  Passed on with a weary air,
Till lo ! he came to a pool of mud,
  And some hogs were rolling there.
Then in he plunged with gleeful cries,
  And down he lay supine ;
For they had no mud in paradise,
  And they likewise had no swine.

The Junior God forgot himself;
  He squelched mud through his toes;
With the careless joy of a wanton boy
  His reckless laughter rose.
Till, tired at last, in a brook close by,
  He washed off every stain;
Then softly up to the radiant sky
  He rose, a god again.

The Junior God now heads the roll
  In the list of heaven's peers;
He sits in the House of High Control,
  And he regulates the spheres.
Yet does he wonder, do you suppose,
  If, even in gods divine,
The best and wisest may not be those
  Who have wallowed awhile with the swine?

THE NOSTOMANIAC

On the ragged edge of the world I'll roam,
And the home of the wolf shall be my home,
And a bunch of bones on the boundless snows
The end of my trail . . . who knows, who knows!

I'm dreaming to-night in the fire-glow, alone in
  my study tower,
  My books battalioned around me, my Kipling
    flat on my knee ;
But I'm not in the mood for reading, I haven't
    moved for an hour ;
  Body and brain I'm weary, weary the heart of
    me ;
Weary of crushing a longing it's little I under-
    stand,
  For I thought that my trail was ended, I thought
    I had earned my rest ;
But oh, it's stronger than life is, the call of the
    hearthless land !
  And I turn to the North in my trouble, as a
    child to the mother-breast.

Here in my den it's quiet; the sea-wind taps on
　　the pane;
　There's comfort and ease and plenty, the smile
　　of the South is sweet.
All that a man might long for, fight for and seek
　　in vain,
　Pictures and books and music, pleasure my last
　　retreat.
Peace! I thought I had gained it, I swore that my
　　tale was told;
　By my hair that is grey I swore it, by my eyes
　　that are slow to see;
Yet what does it all avail me? to-night, to-night
　　as of old,
　Out of the dark I hear it—the Northland calling
　　to me.

And I'm daring a rampageous river that runs the
　　devil knows where;
　My hand is athrill on the paddle, the birch-
　　bark bounds like a bird.
Hark to the rumble of rapids! Here in my morris
　　chair,
　Eager and tense I'm straining—isn't it most
　　absurd?

Now in the churn and the lather, foam that hisses
   and stings,
 Leap I, keyed for the struggle, fury and fume
   and roar ;
Rocks are spitting like hell-cats—Oh, it's a sport
   for kings,
 Life on a twist of the paddle . . . there's my
   " Kim " on the floor.

How I thrill and I vision ! Then my camp of a
   night ;
 Red and gold of the fire-glow, net afloat in the
   stream ;
Scent of the pines and silence, little " pal " pipe
   alight,
 Body a-purr with pleasure, sleep untroubled of
   dream :
Banquet of paystreak bacon ! moment of joy
   divine,
 When the bannock is hot and gluey, and the
   teapot's nearing the boil !
Never was wolf so hungry, stomach cleaving to
   spine . . .
 Ha ! there's my servant calling, says that dinner
   will spoil.

What do I want with dinner ? Can I eat any
　　more ?
　Can I sleep as I used to ? . . . Oh, I abhor this
　　life !
Give me the Great Uncertain, the Barren Land
　　for a floor,
　The Milky Way for a roof-beam, splendour and
　　space and strife :
Something to fight and die for—the limpid Lake
　　of the Bear,
　The Empire of Empty Bellies, the dunes where
　　the Dogribs dwell ;
Big things, real things, live things . . . here in
　　my morris chair,
　How I ache for the Northland ! " Dinner and
　　servants "—Hell !

Am I too old, I wonder ? Can I take one trip
　　more ?
　Go to the granite-ribbed valleys, flooded with
　　sunset wine,
Peaks that pierce the aurora, rivers I must
　　explore,
　Lakes of a thousand islands, millioning hordes
　　of the Pine ?

Do they miss me, I wonder, valley and peak and
        plain ?
    Whispering each to the other : " Many a moon
        has passed . . .
Where has he gone, our lover ? Will he come
        back again ?
    Star with his fires our tundra, leave us his bones
        at last ? "

Yes, I'll go back to the Northland, back to the
        way of the bear,
    Back to the muskeg and mountain, back to the
        ice-leaguered sea.
Old am I ! What does it matter ? Nothing I
        would not dare ;
    Give me a trail to conquer—Oh, it is " meat "
        to me !
I will go back to the Northland, feeble and blind
        and lame ;
Sup with the sunny-eyed Husky, eat moose-nose
        with the Cree ;
Play with the Yellow-knife bastards, boasting my
        blood and my name :
    I will go back to the Northland, for the North-
        land is calling to me.

Then give to me paddle and whiplash, and give
    to me tumpline and gun ;
  Give to me salt and tobacco, flour and a gunny
    of tea ;
Take me up over the Circle, under the flamboyant
    sun ;
  Turn me foot-loose like a savage—that is the
    finish of me.
I know the trail I am seeking, it's up by the Lake
    of the Bear ;
  It's down by the Arctic Barrens, it's over to
    Hudson's Bay ;
Maybe I'll get there—maybe : death is set by a
    hair . . .
  Hark ! it's the Northland calling ! now must
    I go away . . .

    Go to the Wild that waits for me ;
    Go where the moose and the musk-ox be ;
    Go to the wolf and the secret snows ;
    Go to my fate . . . who knows, who knows !

AMBITION

THEY brought the mighty chief to town;
  They showed him strange, unwonted sights;
Yet as he wandered up and down,
  He seemed to scorn their vain delights.
His face was grim, his eye lacked fire,
  As one who mourns a glory dead;
And when they sought his heart's desire:
  " Me like-um tooth same gold," he said

A dental place they quickly found.
  He neither moaned nor moved his head.
They pulled his teeth so white and sound;
  They put in teeth of gold instead.
Oh, never saw I man so gay,
  His very being seemed to swell:
" Ha, ha ! " he cried, " Now Injun say
  Me heap big chief, *me look like hell !* "

TO SUNNYDALE

THERE lies the trail to Sunnydale,
  Amid the lure of laughter.
Oh, how can we unhappy be
  Beneath its leafy rafter !
Each perfect hour is like a flower,
  Each day is like a posy.
How can you say the skies are grey ?
  You're wrong, my friend, they're rosy.

With right good will let's climb the hill,
  And leave behind all sorrow.
Oh, we'll be gay ! a bright to-day
  Will make a bright to-morrow.
Oh, we'll be strong ! the way is long
  That never has a turning ;
The hill is high, but there's the sky,
  And how the West is burning !

And if through chance of circumstance
  We have to go bare-foot, sir,
We'll not repine—a friend of mine
  Has got no feet to boot, sir.
This Happiness a habit is,
  And Life is what we make it:
See ! there's the trail to Sunnydale !
  Up, friend ! and let us take it.

THE BLIND AND THE DEAD

She lay like a saint on her copper couch;
  Like an angel asleep she lay,
In the stare of the ghoulish folks that slouch
  Past the Dead and sneak away.

Then came old Jules of the sightless gaze,
  Who begged in the streets for bread.
Each day he had come for a year of days,
  And groped his way to the Dead.

" What's the Devil's Harvest to-day ? " he cried;
  " A wanton with eyes of blue !
I've known too many a such," he sighed;
  " Maybe I know this . . . mon Dieu ! "

He raised the head of the heedless Dead;
  He fingered the frozen face . . .
Then a deathly spell on the watchers fell—
  God ! it was still, that place !

He raised the head of the careless Dead ;
   He fumbled a vagrant curl ;
And then with his sightless smile he said :
   " It's only my little girl."

" Dear, my dear, did they hurt you so !
   Come to your daddy's heart . . ."
Aye, and he held so tight, you know,
   They were hard to force apart.

No ! Paris isn't always gay ;
   And the morgue has its stories, too :
You are a writer of tales, you say—
   Then there is a tale for you.

THE ATAVIST

WHAT are you doing here, Tom Thorne, on the
 white top-knot of the world,
  Where the wind has the cut of a naked knife
   and the stars are rapier keen ?
Hugging a smudgy willow fire, deep in a lynx
 robe curled,
  You that's a lord's own son, Tom Thorne—
   what does your madness mean ?

Go home, go home to your clubs, Tom Thorne !
 home to your evening dress !
  Home to your place of power and pride, and
   the feast that waits for you !
Why do you linger all alone in the splendid
 emptiness,
  Scouring the Land of the Little Sticks on the
   trail of the caribou ?

Why did you fall off the Earth, Tom Thorne,
    out of our social ken ?
  What did your deep damnation prove ? What
    was your dark despair ?
Oh, with the width of a world between, and years
    to the count of ten,
  If they cut out your heart to-night, Tom Thorne,
    her name would be graven there.

And you fled afar for the thing called Peace,
    and you thought you would find it here,
  In the purple tundras vastly spread, and the
    mountains whitely piled ;
It's a weary quest and a dreary quest, but I think
    that the end is near ;
  For they say that the Lord has hidden it in the
    secret heart of the Wild.

And you know that heart as few men know, and
    your eyes are fey and deep,
  With a " something lost " come welling back
    from the raw, red dawn of life :
With woe and pain have you greatly lain, till out
    of abysmal sleep
  The soul of the Stone Age leaps in you, alert
    for the ancient strife.

And if you came to our feast again, with its pomp
and glee and glow,
 I think you would sit stone-still, Tom Thorne,
and see in a daze of dream
A mad sun goading to frenzied flame the glittering
gems of the snow,
 And a monster musk-ox bulking black against
the blood-red gleam.

I think you would see berg-battling shores, and
stammer and halt and stare
 With a sudden sense of the frozen void, serene
and vast and still ;
And the aching gleam and the hush of dream,
and the track of a great white bear,
 And the primal lust that surged in you as you
sprang to make your kill.

I think you would hear the bull-moose call, and
the glutted river roar,
 And spy the hosts of the caribou shadow the
shining plain ;
And feel the pulse of the silences, and stand elate
once more
 On the verge of the yawning vastitudes that
call to you in vain.

L

For I think you are one with the stars and the sun,
        and the wind and the wave and the dew ;
  And the peaks untrod that yearn to God and
        the valleys undefiled ;
Men soar with wings, and they bridle kings, but
        what is it all to you,
  Wise in the ways of the wilderness, and strong
        with the strength of the Wild ?

You have spent your life, you have waged your
        strife where never we play a part ;
  You have held the throne of the Great Unknown,
        you have ruled a kingdom vast :

   *   *   *   *   *   *

*But to-night there's a strange, new trail for you,
        and you go, O weary heart !*
  *To the peace and rest of the Great Unguessed
        . . . at last, Tom Thorne, at last.*

THE SCEPTIC

My Father Christmas passed away
   When I was barely seven.
At twenty-one, alack-a-day,
   I lost my hope of heaven.

Yet not in either lies the curse:
   The hell of it's because
I don't know which loss hurt the worse—
   My God or Santa Claus.

THE ROVER

'

OH. how good it is to be
Foot-loose and heart-free !
Just my dog and pipe and I, underneath the vast
sky ;
Trail to try and goal to win, white road and cool
inn ;
Fields to lure a lad afar, clear spring and still
star ;
Lilting feet that never tire, green dingle, faggot
fire ;
None to hurry, none to hold, heather hill and
hushed fold ;
Nature like a picture-book, laughing leaf and
bright brook ;
Every day a jewel bright, set serenely in the
night ;
Every night a holy shrine, radiant for a day divine.

306

Weathered cheek and kindly eye, let the wanderer
   go by.
Woman-love and wistful heart, let the gipsy one
   depart.
For the farness and the road are his glory and
   his goad.
Oh, the lilt of youth and Spring ! Eyes laugh and
   lips sing.
>   Yea, but it is good to be
>   Foot-loose and heart-free !

II

>   Yet how good it is to come
>   Home at last, home, home !

On the clover swings the bee, overhead's the hale
   tree.
Sky of turquoise gleams through, yonder glints
   the lake's blue.
In a hammock let's swing, weary of wandering ;
Tired of wild, uncertain lands, strange faces, faint
   hands.
Has the wondrous world gone cold ? Am I
   growing old, old ?
Grey and weary . . . let me dream, glide on the
   tranquil stream.

Oh, what joyous days I've had, full, fervid, gay,
   glad !
Yet there comes a subtle change, let the stripling
   rove, range.
From sweet roving comes sweet rest, after all,
   home's best.
And if there's a little bit of woman-love with it,
I will count my life content, God-blest and well
   spent . . .

      Oh, but it is good to be
      Foot-loose and heart-free !
      Yet how good it is to come
      Home at last, home, home ,

BARB-WIRE BILL

At dawn of day the white land lay all gruesome-
  like and grim,

When Bill McGee he says to me : " We've *got* to
  do it, Jim.

We've got to make Fort Liard quick. I know the
  river's bad,

But, oh ! the little woman's sick . . . why ! don't
  you savvy, lad ? ''

And me ! Well, yes, I must confess it wasn't
  hard to see

Their little family group of two would soon be
  one of three.

And so I answered, careless-like : " Why, Bill !
  you don't suppose

I'm scared of that there ' babbling brook ' ?
  Whatever you say—goes."

309

A real live man was Barb-wire Bill, with insides
copper-lined ;
For " barb-wire " was the brand of " hooch " to
which he most inclined.
They knew him far ; his igloos are on Kittiegazuit
strand.
They knew him well, the tribes who dwell within
the Barren Land.
From Koyokuk to Kuskoquim his fame was every-
where ;
And he did love, all life above, that little Julie
Claire,
The lithe, white slave-girl he had bought for seven
hundred skins,
And taken to his wickiup to make his moccasins.

We crawled down to the river bank, and feeble
folk were we,
That Julie Claire from God-knows-where, and
Barb-wire Bill and me.
From shore to shore we heard the roar the heaving
ice-floes make,
And loud we laughed, and launched our raft, and
followed in their wake.
The river swept and seethed and leapt, and caught
us in its stride ;

And on we hurled amid a world that crashed on
every side.

With sullen din the banks caved in ; the shore-
ice lanced the stream ;

The naked floes like spooks arose, all jigging and
agleam.

Black anchor-ice of strange device shot upward
from its bed,

As night and day we cleft our way, and arrow-like
we sped.

But " Faster still ! " cried Barb-wire Bill, and
looked the live-long day

In dull despair at Julie Claire, where white like
death she lay,

And sometimes he would seem to pray and some
times seem to curse,

And bent above with eyes of love, yet ever she
grew worse.

And as we plunged and leapt and lunged, her face
was plucked with pain,

And I could feel his nerves of steel a-quiver at
the strain.

And in the night he gripped me tight as I lay
fast asleep :

The river's kicking like a steer . . . run out the
forward sweep !

That's Hell-gate Canyon right ahead ; I know ot
    old its roar,
And . . . I'll be damned ! *the ice is jammed !*
    We've got to make the shore."

With one wild leap I gripped the sweep. The
    night was black as sin.
The float-ice crashed and ripped and smashed,
    and stunned us with its din.
And near and near, and clear and clear I heard
    the canyon boom ;
And swift and strong we swept along to meet our
    awful doom.
And as with dread I glimpsed ahead the death
    that waited there,
My only thought was of the girl, the little Julie
    Claire ;
And so, like demon mad with fear, I panted at
    the oar,
And foot by foot, and inch by inch, we worked
    the raft ashore.

The bank was staked with grinding ice, and as we
    scraped and crashed,
I only knew one thing to do, and through my
    mind it flashed :

Yet while I groped to find the rope, I heard Bill's
    savage cry :
" That's my job, lad ! It's me that jumps. I'll
    snub this raft or die ! "
I saw him leap, I saw him creep, I saw him gain
    the land ;
I saw him crawl, I saw him fall, then run with
    rope in hand.
And then the darkness gulped him up, and down
    we dashed once more,
And nearer, nearer drew the jam, and thunder-
    like its roar.
Oh, God ! all's lost . . . from Julie Claire there
    came a wail of pain,
And then—the rope grew sudden taut, and quivered
    at the strain ;
It slacked and slipped, it whined and gripped, and
    oh, I held my breath !
And there we hung and there we swung right in
    the jaws of death.

A little strand of hempen rope, and how I watched
    it there,
With all around a hell of sound, and darkness
    and despair ;

A little strand of hempen rope, I watched it all
    alone,
And somewhere in the dark behind I heard a woman
    moan ;
And somewhere in the dark ahead I heard a man
    cry out,
Then silence, silence, silence fell, and mocked my
    hollow shout.
And yet once more from out the shore I heard
    that cry of pain,
A moan of mortal agony, then all was still again.

That night was hell with all the frills, and when
    the dawn broke dim,
I saw a lean and level land, but never sign of him.
I saw a flat and frozen shore of hideous device,
I saw a long-drawn strand of rope that vanished
    through the ice.
And on that treeless, rockless shore I found my
    partner—dead.
No place was there to snub the raft, so—*he had
    served instead !*
And with the rope lashed round his waist, in last
    defiant fight,
He'd thrown himself beneath the ice, that closed
    and gripped him tight ;

And there he'd held us back from death, as fast
  in death he lay . . .
Say, boy! I'm not the pious brand, but—I just
  tried to pray.

And then I looked to Julie Claire, and sore abashed
  was I,
For from the robes that covered her *I heard—a
  baby cry.* . . .

    *   *   *   *   *   *

Thus was Love conqueror of death, and life for
  life was given ;
And though no saint on earth, d'ye think Bill's
  squared hisself with Heaven !

" ? "

IF you had the choice of two women to wed,
  (Though of course the idea is quite absurd).
And the first from her heels to her dainty head
  Was charming in every sense of the word :
And yet in the past (I grieve to state)
She never had been exactly " straight."

And the second—she was beyond all cavil,
  A model of virtue, I must confess ;
And yet, alas ! she was dull as the devil,
  And rather a dowd in the way of dress ;
Though what she was lacking in wit and beauty
She more than made up for in " sense of duty."

Now, suppose you must wed, and make no blunder,
  And either would love you, and let you win her—
Which of the two would you choose, I wonder,
  The stolid saint or the sparkling sinner ?

316

JUST THINK!

JUST think! some night the stars will gleam
  Upon a cold, grey stone,
And trace a name with silver beam,
  And lo! 'twill be your own.

That night is speeding on to greet
  Your epitaphic rhyme.
Your life is but a little beat
  Within the heart of Time.

A little gain, a little pain,
  A laugh, lest you may moan;
A little blame, a little fame,
  A star-gleam on a stone.

317

THE LUNGER

Jack would laugh an' joke all day :
Never saw a lad so gay ;
Singin' like a medder lark,
Loaded to the Plimsoll mark
With God's sunshine was that boy ;
Had a strangle-hoit on Joy.
Held his head 'way up in air,
Left no callin'-cards on Care ;
Breezy, buoyant, brave and true ;
Sent his sunshine out to you ;
Cheerfulest when clouds were black—
    Happy Jack !   Oh, Happy Jack !

Sittin' in my shack alone
I could hear him in his own,
Singin' far into the night,
Till it didn't seem just right
One man should corral the fun,
Live his life so in the sun ;

Didn't seem quite natural
Not to have a grouch at all ;
Not a trouble, not a lack—
    Happy Jack !   Oh, Happy Jack !

He was plumbful of good cheer
Till he struck that low-down year ;
Got so thin, so little to him,
You could most see daylight through him.
Never was his eye so bright,
Never was his cheek so white.
Seemed as if somethin' was wrong,
Sort o' quaver in his song.
Same old smile, same hearty voice :
" Bless you, boys ! let's all rejoice ! "
But old Doctor shook his head :
" Half a lung," was all he said.
Yet that half was surely right,
For I heard him every night,
Singin', singin' in his shack—
    Happy Jack !   Oh, Happy Jack !

Then one day a letter came
Endin' with a female name ;
Seemed to get him in the neck,
Sort o' pile-driver effect ;

Paled his lip and plucked his breath,
Left him starin' still as death.
Somethin' had gone awful wrong,
Yet that night he sang his song.
Oh, but it was good to hear !
For there clutched my heart a fear,
So that I quaked listenin'
Every night to hear him sing.
But each day he laughed with me,
An' his smile was full of glee.
Nothin' seemed to set him back—
   Happy Jack !   Oh, Happy Jack !

Then one night the singin' stopped .
Seemed as if my heart just flopped ;
For I'd learned to love the boy
With his gilt-edged line of joy,
With his glorious gift of bluff,
With his splendid fightin' stuff.
Sing on, lad, and play the game !
O dear God ! . . . no singin' came,
But there surged to me instead—
Silence, silence, deep and dread ;
Till I shuddered, tried to pray,
Said : " He's maybe gone away."
Oh, yes, he had gone away,
Gone forever and a day.

But he'd left behind him there,
In his cabin, pinched and bare,
His poor body, skin and bone,
His sharp face, cold as a stone,
An' his stiffened fingers pressed
Somethin' bright upon his breast:
Locket with a silken curl,
Poor, sweet portrait of a girl.
Yet I reckon at the last
How defiant-like he passed;
For there sat upon his lips
Smile that death could not eclipse;
An' within his eyes lived still
Joy that dyin' could not kill.

An' now when the nights are long,
How I miss his cheery song!
How I sigh an' wish him back!
　Happy Jack!　Oh, Happy Jack!

THE MOUNTAIN AND THE LAKE

I KNOW a mountain thrilling to the stars,
   Peerless and pure, and pinnacled with snow ;
Glimpsing the golden dawn o'er coral bars,
   Flaunting the vanisht sunset's garnet glow ;
Proudly patrician, passionless, serene ;
   Soaring in silvered steeps where cloud - surfs
      break ;
Virgin and vestal—Oh, a very Queen !
   And at her feet there dreams a quiet lake.

My lake adores my mountain—well I know,
   For I have watched it from its dawn-dream
      start,
Stilling its mirror to her splendid snow,
   Framing her image in its trembling heart ;
Glassing her graciousness of greening wood.
   Kissing her throne, melodiously mad,
Thrilling responsive to her every mood,
   Gloomed with her sadness, gay when she is
      glad.

My lake has dreamed and loved since time was
    born ;
  Will love and dream till time shall cease to be ;
Gazing to Her in worship half forlorn,
  Who looks towards the stars and will not see—
My peerless mountain, splendid in her scorn. . . .
    Alas ! poor little lake ! Alas ! poor me !

THE HEADLINER AND THE BREADLINER

MOKO, the Educated Ape, is here,
  The pet of vaudeville, so the posters say,
  And every night the gaping people pay
To see him in his panoply appear ;
To see him pad his paunch with dainty cheer,
  Puff his perfecto, swill champagne, and sway
  Just like a gentleman, yet all in play,
Then bow himself off stage with brutish leer.

And as to-night, with noble knowledge crammed,
  I 'mid this human compost take my place,
I, once a poet, now so dead and damned,
  The woeful tears half freezing on my face :
" O God ! " I cry, " let me but take his shape,
  Moko's, the Blest, the Educated Ape."

DEATH IN THE ARCTIC

I

I TOOK the clock down from the shelf;
"At eight," said I, "I shoot myself,"
It lacked a *minute* of the hour,
And as I waited all a-cower,
A skinful of black, boding pain,
Bits of my life came back again. . . .

"Mother, there's nothing more to eat—
Why don't you go out on the street?
Always you sit and cry and cry;
Here at my play I wonder why.
Mother, when you dress up at night,
Red are your cheeks, your eyes are bright;
Twining a riband in your hair,
Kissing good-bye you go down-stair
Then I'm as lonely as can be.
Oh, how I wish you were with me!
Yet when you go out on the street,
Mother, there's always lots to eat." . . .

II

For days the igloo has been dark ;
But now the rag wick sends a spark
That glitters in the icy air,
And wakes frost sapphires everywhere ;
Bright, bitter flames, that adder-like
Dart here and there, yet fear to strike
The gruesome gloom wherein *they* lie,
My comrades, oh, so keen to die !
And I, the last—well, here I wait
The clock to strike the hour of eight. . . .

" Boy, it is bitter to be hurled
Nameless and naked on the world ;
Frozen by night and starved by day,
Curses and kicks and clouts your pay.
But you must fight !   Boy, look on me !
Anarch of all earth-misery ;
Beggar and tramp and shameless sot ;
Emblem of ill, in rags that rot.
Would you be foul and base as I ?
Oh, it is better far to die !
Swear to me now you'll fight and fight,
Boy, or I'll kill you here to-night." . . .

III

Curse this silence soft and black !
Sting, little light, the shadows back !
Dance, little flame with freakish glee !
Twinkle with brilliant mockery !
Glitter on ice-robed roof and floor !
Jewel the bear-skin of the door !
Gleam in my beard, illume my breath,
Blanch the clock face that times my death !
But do not pierce that murk so deep,
Where in their sleeping-bags they sleep !
But do not linger where they lie,
They who had all the luck to die ! . . .

" There is nothing more to say ;
Let us part and go our way.
Since it seems we can't agree,
I will go across the sea.
Proud of heart and strong am I ;
Not for woman will I sigh ;
Hold my head up gay and glad :
You can find another lad." . . .

IV

Above the igloo piteous flies
Our frayed flag to the frozen skies.
Oh, would you know how earth can be
A hell—go north of Eighty-three !
Go, scan the snows day after day,
And hope for help, and pray and pray ;
Have seal-hide and sea-lice to eat ;
Melt water with your body's heat ;
Sleep all the fell, black winter through
Beside the dear, dead men you knew.
(The walrus blubber flares and gleams—
O God ! how long a minute seems !) . . .

" *Mary, many a day has passed,*
  Since that morn of hot-head youth.
Come I back at last, at last,
  Crushed with knowing of the truth ;
How through bitter, barren years
  You loved me, and me alone ;
Waited, wearied, wept your tears—
Oh, could I atone, atone,
I would pay a million-fold !
  Pay you for the love you gave.
Mary, look down as of old—
  I am kneeling by your grave." . . .

V

Olaf, the Blonde, was the first to go ;
Bitten his eyes were by the snow ;
Sightless and sealed his eyes of blue,
So that he died before I knew.
Here in these poor weak arms he died :
" Wolves will not get you, lad," I lied ;
" For I will watch till Spring come round ;
Slumber you shall beneath the ground."
Oh, how I lied !   I scarce can wait :
Strike, little clock, the hour of eight ! . . .

" Comrade, can you blame me quite ?
The horror of the long, long night
Is on me, and I've borne with pain
So long, and hoped for help in vain.
So frail am I, and blind and dazed ;
With scurvy sick, with silence crazed.
Beneath the Arctic's heel of hate,
Avid for Death I wait, I wait.
Oh, if I falter, fail to fight,
Can you, dear comrade, blame me quite ? "

VI

Big Eric gave up months ago.
But seldom do men suffer so.
His feet sloughed off, his fingers died,
His hands shrunk up and mummified.
I had to feed him like a child ;
Yet he was valiant, joked and smiled,
Talked of his wife and little one
(Thanks be to God that I have none),
Passed in the night without a moan,
Passed, and I'm here, alone, alone. . .

" I've got to kill you, Dick.
  Your life for mine, you know
Better to do it quick,
  A swift and sudden blow.
See ! here's my hand to lick ;
  A hug before you go—
God ! but it makes me sick ;
  Old dog, I love you so.
Forgive, forgive me, Dick—
  A swift and sudden blow."

VII

Often I start up in the dark,
  Thinking the sound of bells to hear.
Often I wake from sleep : " Oh, hark !
  Help . . . it is coming . . . near and near."
Blindly I reel toward the door ;
  There the snow billows bleak and bare ;
Blindly I seek my den once more,
  Silence and darkness and despair.
Oh, it is all a dreadful dream !
  Scurvy and cold and death and dearth ;
I will awake to warmth and gleam,
  Silvery seas and greening earth.
Life is a dream, its wakening,
Death, gentle shadow of God's wing. . . .

" Tick, little clock, my life away !
Even a second seems a day.
Even a minute seems a year,
Peopled with ghosts that press and peer
Into my face so charnel white,
Lit by the devilish, dancing light.
Tick, little clock ! mete out my fate :
Tortured and tense I wait, I wait." . . .

VIII

Oh, I have sworn ! the hour is nigh :
When it strikes eight I die, I die.
Raise up the gun—it stings my brow—
When it strikes eight . . . all ready . . . *now*—

    *   *   *   *   *   *

Down from my hand the weapon dropped ;
Wildly I stared . . .

THE CLOCK HAD STOPPED.

IX

Phantoms and fears and ghosts have gone.
    Peace seems to nestle in my brain.
Lo ! the clock stopped, I'm living on ;
    Heart-sick I was, and less than sane.
Yet do I scorn the thing I planned,
    Hearing a voice : " O coward, fight ! "
Then the clock stopped . . . whose was the hand ?
    Maybe 'twas God's—ah, well, all's right.
Heap on me darkness, fold on fold !
    Pain ! wrench and rack me !   What care I ?
Leap on me, hunger, thirst and cold !
    I will await my time to die ;
Looking to Heaven that shines above ;
Looking to God, and love . . . and love.

x

Hark ! what is that ?   Bells, dogs again !
Is it a dream ?   I sob and cry.
See ! the door opens, fur-clad men
    Rush to my rescue ; frail am I ;
Feeble and dying, dazed and glad.
    There is the pistol where it dropped.
" Boys, it was hard—but I'm not mad . . .
    Look at the clock—it stopped, it stopped.
Carry me out.   The heavens smile.
    See there's an arch of gold above.
Now, let me rest a little while—
    Looking to God and love . . . and love."

DREAMS ARE BEST

I just think that dreams are best,
  Just to sit and fancy things;
Give your gold no acid test,
  Try not how your silver rings;
Fancy women pure and good,
  Fancy men upright and true:
Fortressed in your solitude,
  Let Life be a dream to you.

For I think that Thought is all;
  Truth's a minion of the mind;
Love's ideal comes at call;
  As ye seek so shall ye find.
But ye must not seek too far;
  Things are never what they seem :
Let a star be just a star,
  And a woman—just a dream.

O you Dreamers, proud and pure,
   You have gleaned the sweet of life !
Golden truths that shall endure
   Over pain and doubt and strife.
I would rather be a fool
   Living in my Paradise,
Than the leader of a school,
   Sadly sane and weary-wise

O you Cynics with your sneers,
   Fallen brains and hearts of brass.
Tweak me by my foolish ears,
   Write me down a simple ass !
I'll believe the real " you "
   Is the " you " without a taint ;
I'll believe each woman, too,
   But a slightly damaged saint.

Yes, I'll smoke my cigarette,
   Vestured in my garb of dreams,
And I'll borrow no regret ;
   All is gold that golden gleams.
So I'll charm my solitude
   With the faith that Life is blest.
Brave and noble, bright and good . . .
   Oh, I think that dreams are best !

M

THE QUITTER

WHEN you're lost in the Wild, and you're scared
    as a child,
  And Death looks you bang in the eye,
And you're sore as a boil, it's according to Hoyle
  To cock your revolver and . . . die.
But the Code of a Man says: "Fight all you
    can,"
  And self-dissolution is barred
In hunger and woe, oh, it's easy to blow . . .
  It's the hell-served-for-breakfast that's hard.

"You're sick of the game!" Well, now, that's a
    shame.
  You're young and you're brave and you're bright.
"You've had a raw deal!" I know—but don't
    squeal,
  Buck up, do your damnedest, and fight.
It's the plugging away that will win you the day,
  So don't be a piker, old pard!
Just draw on your grit; it's so easy to quit:
  It's the keeping-your-chin-up that's hard.

It's easy to cry that you're beaten—and die ;
  It's easy to crawfish and crawl ;
But to fight and to fight when hope's out of sight—
  Why, that's the best game of them all !
And though you come out of each gruelling bout
  All broken and beaten and scarred,
Just have one more try—it's dead easy to die.
  It's the keeping-on-living that's hard.

THE clover was in blossom, an' the year was at
the June,
When Flap-jack Billy hit the town, likewise
O'Flynn's saloon.
The frost was on the fodder an' the wind was
growin' keen,
When Billy got to seein' snakes in Sullivan's
shebeen.

Then in meandered Deep-hole Dan, once comrade
of the cup :
" Oh, Billy, for the love of Mike, why don't ye
sober up ?
I've got the gorgus recipay, 'tis smooth an' slick
as silk—
Jest quit yer strangle-holt on hooch, an' irrigate
with milk.
Lackteeal flooid is the lubrication you require :

Yer nervus frame-up's like a bunch of snarled
piano wire.

You want to get it coated up with addypose
tishoo,

So's it will work elastic-like, an' milk's the dope
for you."

Well, Billy was complyable, an' in a month, it's
strange,

That cow-juice seemed to oppyrate a most amazin'
change.

"Call up the water-wagon, Dan, an' book my seat,"
sez he.

"'Tis mighty queer," sez Deep-hole Dan, "'twas
just the same with me."

They shanghaied little Tom O'Shane, they cached
him safe away.

An' though he objurgated some, they "cured"
him night an' day;

An' pretty soon there came the change amazin'
to explain :

"I'll never take another drink," sez Timothy
O'Shane.

They tried it out on Spike Muldoon, that toper
of renown ;

They put it over Grouch McGraw, the terror of
the town.

They roped in " tanks " from far and near, an'
    every test was sure,
An' like a flame there ran the fame of Deep-hole's
    Cow-juice Cure.

" It's mighty queer," sez Deep-hole Dan, " I'm
    puzzled through and through ;
It's only milk from Riley's ranch, no other milk
    will do."
An' it jest happened on that night, with no pre-
    dictive plan,
He left some milk from Riley's ranch a-settin' in
    a pan ;
An' picture his amazement when he poured that
    milk next day—
There in the bottom of the pan a dozen " colours "
    lay.

" Well, what d'ye know 'bout that ? " sez Dan ;
    " Gosh-ding my dasted eyes,
We've been an' had the Gold Cure, Bill, an' none
    of us was wise !
The milk's free-millin', that's a cinch : there's
    colours everywhere.
Now, let us figger this thing out—how does the
    dust git there ?

'Gold from the grass-roots down,' they say—why,
    Bill ! we've got it cold—
Them cows what nibbles up the grass, jest nibbles
    up the gold.
We're blasted, bloomin' millionaires ; dissemble
    an' lie low :
We'll follow them gold-bearin' cows, an' prospect
    where they go.''

An' so it came to pass, fer weeks them miners
    might be found
A-sneakin' round on Riley's ranch, an' snipin' at
    the ground ;
Till even Riley stops an' stares, an' presently
    allows :
"Them boys appear to take a mighty interest in
    cows.''
An' night an' day they shadowed each auriferous
    bovine,
An' panned the grass-roots on their trail, yet nivver
    gold they seen.
An' all that season, secret-like, they worked an'
    nothin' found ;
An' there was colours in the milk, but none was
    in the ground.
An' mighty desperate was they, an' down upon
    their luck,

When sudden, inspiration-like, the source of it
    they struck.
An' where d'ye think they traced it to ? It grieves
    my heart to tell—
In the black sand at the bottom of that wicked
    milkman's *well.*

WHILE THE BANNOCK BAKES

LIGHT up your pipe again, old chum, and sit
    awhile with me ;
  I've got to watch the bannock bake—how rest-
    ful is the air !
You'd little think that we were somewhere north
    of Sixty-three.
  Though where I don't exactly know, and don't
    precisely care.
The man-size mountains palisade us round on
    every side ;
  The river is a-flop with fish, and ripples silver-
    clear ;
The midnight sunshine brims yon cleft—we think
    it's the Divide ;
  We'll get there in a month, maybe, or maybe
    in a year.

It doesn't matter, does it, pal ? We're of that
    breed of men
    With whom the world of wine and cards and
        women disagree ;
Your trouble was a roofless game of poker now
    and then,
    And " raising up my elbow," that's what got
        away with me.
We're merely " Undesirables," artistic more or
    less ;
    My norny hands are Chopin-wise ; you quote
        your Browning well ;
And yet we're fooling round for gold in this damned
    wilderness :
    The joke is, if we found it, we would both go
        straight to hell.

Well, maybe we won't find it—and at least we've
    got the " life."
    We're both as brown as berries, and could wrestle
        with a bear :
(That bannock's raising nicely, pal ; just jab it
    with your knife.)
    Fine specimens of manhood they would reckon
        us out there.
It's the tracking and the packing and the poling
    in the sun ;

It's the sleeping in the open, it's the rugged,
  unfaked food ;
It's the snow-shoe and the paddle, and the camp-
  fire and the gun,
  And when I think of what I was, I know that
  it is good.

Just think of how we've poled all day up this
  strange little stream ;
  Since life began no eye of man has seen this
  place before ;
How fearless all the wild things are ! the banks
  with goose-grass gleam,
  And there's a bronzy muskrat sitting sniffing at
  his door.
A mother duck with brood of ten comes squatter-
  ing along ;
  The tawny, white-winged ptarmigan are flying
  all about ;
And in that swirly, golden pool, a restless, gleaming
  throng,
  The trout are waiting till we condescend to
  take them out.

Ah, yes, it's good ! I'll bet that there's no doctor
  like the Wild :
  (Just turn that bannock over there ; it's getting
  nicely brown) :

I might be in my grave by now, forgotten and
    reviled,
  Or rotting like a sickly cur in some far, foreign
    town.
I might be that vile thing I was—it all seems
    like a dream ;
  I owed a man a grudge one time that only life
    could pay ;
And yet it's half-forgotten now—how petty these
    things seem !
  (But that's " another story," pal ; I'll tell it
    you some day.)

How strange two " irresponsibles " should chum
    away up here ;
  But round the Arctic Circle friends are few and
    far between.
We've shared the same camp-fire and tent for
    nigh on seven year,
  And never had a word that wasn't cheering and
    serene.
We've halved the toil and split the spoil, and
    borne each other's pack ;
  By all the Wild's freemasonry we're brothers,
    tried and true ;

We've swept on danger side by side, and fought
    it back to back,
  And you would die for me, old pal, and I would
    die for you.

Now there was that time I got lost in Rory Bory
    Land,
  (How quick the blizzards sweep on one across
    that Polar sea !)
You formed a rescue crew of One, and saw a
    frozen hand
  That stuck out of a drift of snow—and, partner,
    it was Me.
But I got even, did I not, that day the paddle
    broke ?
  White water on the Coppermine—a rock—a
    split canoe—
Two fellows struggling in the foam (one couldn't
    swim a stroke) :
  A half-drowned man I dragged ashore . . . and,
    partner, it was You.

     *   *   *   *   *   *

In Rory Borealis Land the winter's long and
    black ;
  The silence seems a solid thing, shot through
    with wolfish woe ;

And rowelled by the eager stars the skies vault
  vastly back,
  And man seems but a little mite in that weird-
  lit plateau.
Nothing to do but smoke and yarn of wild and
  mis-spent lives,
  Beside the camp-fire there we sat—what tales
  you told to me
Of love and hate, and chance and fate, and
  temporary wives !
  In Rory Borealis Land, beside the Arctic Sea.

One yarn you told me in those days I can remember
  still ;
  It seemed as if I visioned it, so sharp you
  sketched it in ;
Bellona was the name, I think ; a coast town in
  Brazil,
  Where nobody did anything but serenade and sin.
I saw it all—the jewelled sea, the golden scythe
  of sand,
  The stately pillars of the palms, the feathery
  bamboo,
The red-roofed houses and the swart, sun-dominated
  land,
  The people ever children, and the heavens ever
  blue.

You told me of that girl of yours, that blossom of
  old Spain,
  All glamour, grace and witchery, all passion,
    verve and glow.
How maddening she must have been ! You made
  me see her plain,
  There by our little camp-fire, in the silence and
    the snow.
You loved her and she loved you. She'd a husband
  too, I think ;
  A doctor chap, you told me, whom she treated
    like a dog,
A white man living on the beach, a hopeless slave
  to drink—
  (Just turn that bannock over there, that's
    propped against the log).

That story seemed to strike me, pal—it happens
  every day :
  You had to go away awhile, then somehow it
    befell
The doctor chap discovered, gave her up, and
  went away ;
  You came back, tired of her in time . . . there's
    nothing more to tell.
Hist ! see those willows silvering where swamp
  and river meet !

Just reach me up my rifle, quick ; that's Mister
Moose, I know—
There now, *I've got him dead to rights* . . . but,
hell ! we've lots to eat !
I don't believe in taking life—we'll let the
beggar go.

Heigh-ho ! I'm tired ; the bannock's cooked ; it's
time we both turned in.
The morning mist is coral-kissed, the morning
sky is gold.
The camp-fire's a confessional—what funny yarns
we spin !
It sort of made me think a bit, that story that
you told.
The fig-leaf belt and Rory Bory are such odd
extremes,
Yet after all how very small this old world
seems to be . . .
Yes, that was quite a yarn, old pal. and yet to me
it seems
You missed the point : the point is that the
" doctor chap " . . . was *me*.

THE LOST MASTER

"AND when I come to die," he said,
"Ye shall not lay me out in state,
Nor leave your laurels at my head,
    Nor cause your men of speech orate;
No monument your gift shall be,
    No column in the Hall of Fame;
But just this line ye grave for me:
        'He played the game.'"

So when his glorious task was done,
    It was not of his fame we thought;
It was not of his battles won,
    But of the pride with which he fought;
But of his zest, his ringing laugh,
    His trenchant scorn of praise or blame:
And so we graved his epitaph,
        "He played the game."

And so we, too, in humbler ways
   Went forth to fight the fight anew,
And heeding neither blame nor praise,
   We held the course he set us true.
And we, too, find the fighting sweet ;
   And we, too, fight for fighting's sake ;
And though we go down in defeat,
   And though our stormy hearts may break,
We will not do our Master shame :
We'll play the game, please God.
      We'll play the game.

LITTLE MOCCASINS

Come out, O Little Moccasins, and frolic on the
    snow !
  Come out, O tiny beaded feet, and twinkle in
      the light !
I'll play the old Red River reel, you used to love
    it so :
  Awake, O Little Moccasins, and dance for me
      to-night !

Your hair was all a gleamy gold, your eyes a corn-
    flower blue ;
  Your cheeks were pink as tinted shells, you
      stepped light as a fawn,
Your mouth was like a coral bud, with seed pearls
    peeping through ;
  As gladdening as Spring you were, as radiant as
      dawn.

353

Come out, O Little Moccasins ! I'll play so soft
    and low,
    The songs you loved, the old heart-songs that
        in my mem'ry ring ;
O child, I want to hear you now beside the camp-
    fire glow !
    With all your heart a-throbbing in the simple
        words you sing.

For there was only you and I, and you were all
    to me ;
    And round us were the barren lands, but little
        did we fear ;
Of all God's happy, happy folks the happiest
    were we . . .
    (Oh, call her, poor old fiddle mine, and maybe
        she will hear !)

Your mother was a half-breed Cree, but you
    were white all through ;
    And I your father was—but, well, that's neither
        here not there ;
I only know, my little Queen, that all my world
    was you,
    And now that world can end to-night, and I
        will never care.

For there's a tiny wooden cross that pricks up
    through the snow :
  (Poor little Moccasins ! you're tired, and so you
    lie at rest.)
And there's a grey-haired, weary man beside the
    camp-fire glow :
  (O fiddle mine ! the tears to-night are drumming
    on your breast.)

THE WANDERLUST

THE Wanderlust has lured me to the seven lonely
    seas,
  Has dumped me on the tailing-piles of dearth ;
The Wanderlust has haled me from the morris
    chairs of ease,
  Has hurled me to the ends of all the earth.
How bitterly I've cursed it, oh, the Painted Desert
    knows,
  The wraithlike heights that hug the pallid
    plain,
The all-but-fluid silence—yet the longing grows
    and grows,
  And I've got to glut the Wanderlust again.

  Soldier, sailor, in what a plight I've been !
  Tinker, tailor, oh, what a sight I've seen !
  And I'm hitting the trail in the morning, boys,

And you won't see my heels for dust ;
For it's " all day " with you
When you answer the cue
Of the Wan-der-lust.

The Wanderlust has got me . . . by the belly-
aching fire,
By the fever and the freezing and the pain ;
By the darkness that just drowns you, by the wail
of home desire,
I've tried to break the spell of it—in vain.
Life might have been a feast for me, now there
are only crumbs ;
In rags and tatters, beggar-wise I sit ;
Yet there's no rest or peace for me, imperious it
drums,
The Wanderlust, and I must follow it.

Highway, by-way, many a mile I've done ;
Rare way, fair way, many a height I've won ;
But I'm pulling my freight in the morning,
boys,
And it's over the hills or bust !
For there's never a cure
When you list to the lure
Of the Wan-der-lust.

The Wanderlust has taught me . . . it has
      whispered to my heart
Things all you stay-at-homes will never know.
The white man and the savage are but three short
      days apart,
    Three days of cursing, crawling, doubt and woe.
Then it's down to chewing muclucs, to the water
      you can *eat*,
    To fish you bolt with nose held in your hand.
When you get right down to cases, it's King Grub
      that rules the races,
    And the Wanderlust will help you understand.

    Haunting, taunting, that is the spell of it ;
    Mocking, baulking, that is the hell of it ;
    But I'll shoulder my pack in the morning,
      boys,
      And I'm going because I must ;
      For it's so-long to all
      When you answer the call
        Of the Wan-der-lust.

The Wanderlust has blest me . . . in a ragged
      blanket curled,
  I've watched the gulf of Heaven foam with
      stars ;

I've walked with eyes wide open to the wonder of
    the world,
  I've seen God's flood of glory burst its bars.
I've seen the gold a-blinding in the riffles of the
    sky,
  Till I fancied me a bloated plutocrat ;
But I'm freedom's happy bond-slave, and I will
    be till I die,
  And I've got to thank the Wanderlust for that.

    Wild heart, child heart, all of the world your
        home.
    Glad heart, mad heart, what can you do but
        roam ?
    Oh, I'll beat it once more in the morning,
        boys,
      With a pinch of tea and a crust ;
      For you cannot deny
      When you hark to the cry
        Of the Wan-der-lust.

The Wanderlust will claim me at the finish for its
    own.
  I'll turn my back on men and face the Pole.
Beyond the Arctic outposts I will venture all alone ;
  Some Never-never Land will be my goal.

Thank God! there's none will miss me, for I've
     been a bird of flight;
And in my moccasins I'll take my call;
    For the Wanderlust has ruled me,
    And the Wanderlust has schooled me,
And I'm ready for the darkest trail of all.

     Grim land, dim land, oh, how the vastness
       calls!
     Far land, star land, oh, how the stillness
       falls!
     For you never can tell if it's heaven or hell,
       And I'm taking the trail on trust;
       But I haven't a doubt
       That my soul will leap out
        On its Wan-der-lust.

THE TRAPPER'S CHRISTMAS EVE

IT's mighty lonesome-like and drear.
  Above the Wild the moon rides high,
And shows up sharp and needle-clear
  The emptiness of earth and sky :
No happy homes with love aglow ;
  No Santa Claus to make believe :
Just snow and snow, and then more snow :
  It's Christmas Eve, it's Christmas Eve.

And here am I where all things end,
  And Undesirables are hurled ;
A poor old man without a friend,
  Forgot and dead to all the world ;
Clean out of sight and out of mind. . . .
  Well, maybe it is better so ;
We all in life our level find,
  And mine, I guess. is pretty low.

361

Yet as I sit with pipe alight
  Beside the cabin-fire, it's queer
This mind of mine must take to-night
  The backward trail of fifty year.
The school-house and the Christmas tree ;
  The children with their cheeks aglow ;
Two bright blue eyes that smile on me . . .
  Just half a century ago.

Again (it's maybe forty years),
  With faith and trust almost divine,
These same blue eyes, abrim with tears,
  Through depths of love look into mine.
A parting, tender, soft and low,
  With arms that cling and lips that cleave—
Ah me ! it's all so long ago,
  Yet seems so sweet this Christmas Eve.

Just thirty years ago again . . .
  We say a bitter, *last* good-bye ;
Our lips are white with wrath and pain ;
  Our little children cling and cry.
Whose was the fault ?   It matters not,
  For man and woman both deceive ;
It's buried now and all forgot.
  Forgiven, too, this Christmas Eve.

And she (God pity me) is dead ;
  Our children men and women grown.
I like to think that they are wed,
  With little children of their own,
That crowd around their Christmas tree . . .
  I would not ever have them grieve,
Nor shed a single tear for me,
  To mar their joy this Christmas Eve.

Stripped to the buff and gaunt and still
  Lies all the land in grim distress.
Like lost soul wailing, long and shrill,
  A wolf-howl cleaves the emptiness.
Then hushed as Death is everything.
  The moon rides haggard and forlorn . . .
" O hark the herald angels sing ! "
  God bless all men—it's Christmas morn.

THE WORLD'S ALL RIGHT

Be honest, kindly, simple, true ;
Seek good in all, scorn but pretence ;
Whatever sorrow come to you,
Believe in Life's Beneficence !

The World's all right ; serene I sit,
And cease to puzzle over it.
There's much that's mighty strange, no doubt ;
But Nature knows what she's about ;
And in a million years or so
We'll know more than to-day we know.
Old Evolution's under way—
What ho ! the World's all right, I say.

Could things be other than they are ?
All's in its place, from mote to star.
The thistledown that flits and flies
Could drift no hairsbreadth otherwise.

What is, must be ; with rhythmic laws
All Nature chimes, Effect and Cause.
The sand-grain and the sun obey—
    What ho ! the World's all right, I say.

Just try to get the Cosmic touch,
The sense that " you " don't matter much.
A million stars are in the sky ;
A million planets plunge and die.
A million million men are sped ;
A million million wait ahead.
Each plays his part and has his day—
    What ho ! the World's all right, I say.

Just try to get the Chemic view :
A million million lives made " you."
In lives a million you will be
Immortal down Eternity ;
Immortal on this earth to range,
With never death, but ever change.
You always were, and will be aye—
    What ho ! the World's all right, I say.

Be glad ! And do not blindly grope
For Truth that lies beyond our scope :
A sober plot informeth all
Of Life's uproarious carnival.

Your day is such a little one,
A gnat that lives from sun to sun;
Yet gnat and you have parts to play—
     What ho! the World's all right, I say.

And though it's written from the start,
Just act your best your little part.
Just be as happy as you can,
And serve your kind, and die—a man.
Just live the good that in you lies,
And seek no guerdon of the skies;
Just make your Heaven here, to-day—
     What ho! the World's all right, I say.

Remember! in Creation's swing
The Race and not the man's the thing.
There's battle, murder, sudden death,
And pestilence, with poisoned breath.
Yet quick forgotten are such woes;
On, on the stream of Being flows.
Truth, Beauty, Love maintain their sway—
     What ho! the World's all right, I say.

The World's all right; serene I sit,
And joy that I am part of it;
And put my trust in Nature's plan,
And try to aid her all I can;

Content to pass, if in my place
I've served the uplift of the Race.
Truth! Beauty! Love! O Radiant Day—
    What ho! the World's all right, I say.

THE BALDNESS OF CHEWED-EAR

WHEN Chewed-ear Jenkins got hitched up to
    Guinneyveer McGee,
His flowin' locks, ye recollect, wuz frivolous an'
    free ;
But in old Hymen's jack-pot, it's a most amazin'
    thing,
Them flowin' locks jest disappeared like snowballs
    in the Spring ;
Jest seemed to wilt an' fade away like dead leaves
    in the Fall,
An' left old Chewed-ear balder than a whitewashed
    cannon ball.

Now Missis Chewed-ear Jenkins, that wuz Guin-
    neyveer McGee,
    Wuz jest about as fine a draw as ever made a
        pair ;

But when the boys got joshin' an' suggested it
    was she
  That must be inflooenshul for the old man's
    slump in hair—
  Why! Missis Chewed-ear Jenkins jest went
    clean up in the air.

"To demonstrate," sez she that night, " the lovin'
    wife I am,
I've bought a dozen bottles of Bink's Anty-
    Dandruff Balm.
'Twill make yer hair jest sprout an' curl like
    squash-vines in the sun,
An' I propose to sling it on till every drop is done."
That hit old Chewed-ear's funny side, so he lays
    back an' hollers :
"The day you raise a hair, old girl, you'll git a
    thousand dollars."

Now, whether 'twas the prize or not 'tis mighty
    hard to say,
But Chewed-ear didn't seem to have much comfort
    from that day.
With bottles of that dandruff dope she followed
    at his heels,
An' sprinkled an' massaged him even when he ate
    his meals.

She waked him from his beauty sleep with tender,
    lovin' care,
An' rubbed and scrubbed assiduous, yet never
    sign of hair.

Well, naturally all the boys soon tumbled to the joke,
An' at the Wow-wow's Social 'twas Cold-deck
    Davis spoke :
" The little woman's workin' mighty hard on
    Chewed-ear's crown ;
Let's give her for a three-fifth's share a hundred
    dollars down.
We stand to make five hundred clear—boys,
    drink in whiskey straight :
' The Chewed-ear Jenkins Hirsute Propagation
    Syndicate.' "

The boys wuz on, an' soon chipped in the necessary
    dust ;
   They primed up a committy to negotiate the deal ;
Then Missis Jenkins yielded, bein' rather in disgust,
   An' all wuz signed an' witnessed, an' invested
    with a seal.
They rounded up old Chewed-ear, an' they broke
    it what they'd done ;
   Allowed they'd bought an interest in his chance
    of raisin' hair ;

They yanked his hat off anxious-like, opinin' one
    by one,
  Their magnifyin'-glasses showed fine prospects
    everywhere.
They bought Hairlene, an' Thatchem, an' Jay's
    Cappillery Juice,
  An' Seven Something Sisters, an' Macassar an'
    Bay Rum,
An' every one insisted on his speshul right to
    sluice
  His speshul line of lotion onto Chewed-ear's
    cranium.
They only got the merrier the more the old man
    roared,
An' shares in " Jenkins Hirsute " went sky-highin'
    on the board.

The Syndicate wuz hopeful that they'd demon-
    strate the pay,
An' Missis Jenkins laboured in her perseverin'
    way.
The boys discussed on " surface rights," an' " out-
    crops," an' so on,
An' planned to have it " crown " surveyed, an'
    blueprints of it drawn.
They ran a base line, sluiced an' yelled, an' every
    one wuz glad

Except the balance of the property, an' he wuz
      " mad."
" It gives me pain," he interjects, " to squash yer
      glowin' dream,
But you wuz fools when you got in on this here
      ' Hirsute ' scheme.
You'll never raise a hair on me "—when lo ! that
      very night,
Preparin' to retire, he got a most unpleasant
      fright :
For on that shinin' dome of his, so prominently
      bare,
He felt the baby outcrop of a second growth of
      hair.

A thousand dollars ! Sufferin' Cæsar ! Well, it
      must be saved !
He grabbed his razor recklesslike, an' shaved an'
      shaved an' shaved.
An' when his head wuz smooth again he gives a
      mighty sigh,
An' sneaks away, an' buys some Hair Destroyer
      on the sly.
So there wuz Missis Jenkins with " Restorer "
      wagin' fight,
An' Chewed-ear with " Destroyer " circumventin'
      her at night.

The battle wuz a mighty one ; his nerves wuz on
the strain,
An' yet in spite of all he did that hair began to
gain.

The situation grew intense, so quietly one day,
He gave his shareholders the slip, an' made his
get-away.
Jest like a criminal he skipped, an' aimed to
defalcate
The Chewed-ear Jenkins Hirsute Propagation
Syndicate.
His guilty secret burned him, an' he sought the
city's din :
" I've got to get a wig," sez he, " to cover up my
sin.
It's growin', growin', night an' day ; it's most
amazin' hair " ;
An' when he looked at it that night, he
shuddered with despair.
He shuddered an' suppressed a cry at what his
optics seen—
For on my word of honour, boys, that hair wuz
growin' *green*.
At first he guessed he'd get some dye, an' try to
dye it black ;

An' then he saw 'twas Nemmysis wuz layin' on
    his track.
He must jest face the music, an' confess the thing
    he'd done,
An' pay the boys an' Guinneyveer the money they
    had won.
An' then there came a big idee—it thrilled him
    like a shock :
Why not control the Syndicate by buyin' up the
    stock ?

An' so next day he hurried back with smoothly
    shaven pate,
An' for a hundred dollars he bought up the
    Syndicate.
'Twas mighty frenzied finance an' the boys set up
    a roar,
But " Hirsutes " from the market wuz withdrawn
    for evermore.
An' to this day in Nuggetsville they tell the tale
    how slick
The Syndicate sold out too soon, and Chewed-
    ear turned the trick.

THE MOTHER

THERE will be a singing in your heart,
  There will be a rapture in your eyes;
You will be a woman set apart,
  You will be so wonderful and wise.
You will sleep, and when from dreams you start,
  As of one that wakes in Paradise,
There will be a singing in your heart,
  There will be a rapture in your eyes.

There will be a moaning in your heart,
  There will be an anguish in your eyes;
You will see your dearest ones depart,
  You will hear their quivering good-byes.
Yours will be the heartache and the smart,
  Tears that scald and lonely sacrifice;
There will be a moaning in your heart,
  There will be an anguish in your eyes.

There will come a glory in your eyes,
  There will come a peace within your heart ;
Sitting 'neath the quiet evening skies,
  Time will dry the tear and dull the smart.
You will know that you have played your part ;
  Yours shall be the love that never dies :
You, with Heaven's peace within your heart,
  You, with God's own glory in your eyes.

THE DREAMER

The lone man gazed and gazed upon his gold,
  His sweat, his blood, the wage of weary days;
But now how sweet, how doubly sweet to hold
  All gay and gleamy to the camp-fire blaze.
The evening sky was sinister and cold;
  The willows shivered, wanly lay the snow;
The uncommiserating land, so old,
  So worn, so grey, so niggard in its woe,
Peered through its ragged shroud. The lone man
      sighed,
  Poured back the gaudy dust into its poke,
Gazed at the seething river listless-eyed,
  Loaded his corn-cob pipe as if to smoke;
Then crushed with weariness and hardship crept
Into his ragged robe, and swiftly slept.

        •   •   •   •   •   •

Hour after hour went by ; a shadow slipped
  From vasts of shadow to the camp-fire flame ;
  Gripping a rifle with a deadly aim,
A gaunt and hairy man with wolfish eyes. . . .

      *   *   *   *   *   *

The sleeper dreamed. and lo ! this was his dream :
  He rode a streaming horse across a moor.
Sudden 'mid pit-black night a lightning gleam
  Showed him a wayside inn, forlorn and poor.
A sullen host unbarred the creaking door,
  And led him to a dim and dreary room,
Wherein he sat and poked the fire a-roar,
    So that weird shadows jigged athwart the
      gloom.
He ordered wine.   'Od's blood ! but he was
    tired.
  What matter ! Charles was crushed and George
    was King ;
His party high in power ; how he aspired !
  Red guineas packed his purse, too tight to
    ring.
The firelight gleamed upon his silken hose,
  His silver buckles and his powdered wig.
What ho ! more wine ! He drank, he slowly rose
  What made the shadows dance that madcap jig !

He clutched the candle, steered his way to bed,
And in a trice was sleeping like the dead.

* * * * * *

Across the room there crept, so shadow soft,
 His sullen host, with naked knife agleam,
(A gaunt and hairy man with wolfish eyes.) . . .
 And as he lay, the sleeper dreamed a dream :

* * * * * *

'Twas in a ruder land, a wilder day.
 A rival princeling sat upon his throne,
Within a dungeon dark and foul he lay,
 With chains that bit and festered to the bone.
They haled him harshly to a vaulted room,
 Where One gazed on him with malignant eye ;
And in that devil-face he read his doom,
 Knowing that ere the dawn-light he must die.
Well, he was sorrow-glutted ; let them bring
 Their prize assassins to the bloody work.
His kingdom lost, yet would he die a King,
 Peerless and proud, as when he faced the Turk.
Ah, God ! the glory of that great Crusade !
 The bannered pomp, the gleam, the splendid
  urge !

The crash of reeking combat, blade to blade !
   The reeling ranks, blood-avid and a-surge !
For long he thought ; then feeling o'er him creep
Vast weariness, he fell into a sleep.

      *   *   *   *   *   *

The cell door opened ; soft the headsman came,
   Within his hand a mighty axe agleam,
(A gaunt and hairy man with wolfish eyes.) . . .
   And as he lay, the sleeper dreamed a dream :

      *   *   *   *   *   *

'Twas in a land unkempt, of life's red dawn,
   Where in his sanded cave he dwelt alone ;
Sleeping by day, or sometimes worked upon
   His flint-head arrows and his knives of stone ;
By night stole forth and slew the savage boar,
   So that he loomed a hunter of loud fame,
And many a skin of wolf and wild-cat wore,
   And counted many a flint-head to his name ;
Wherefore he walked the envy of the band,
   Hated and feared, but matchless in his skill
Till lo ! one night deep in that shaggy land,
   He tracked a yearling bear and made his kill ;
Then over-worn he rested by a stream,
And sank into a sleep too deep for dream.

      *   *   *   *   *   *

Hunting his food a rival caveman crept
  Through those dark woods, and marked him
    where he lay ;
Cowered and crawled upon him as he slept,
  Poising a mighty stone aloft to slay—
(A gaunt and hairy man with wolfish eyes.) . . .

    *   *   *   *   *   *

The great stone crashed. The Dreamer shrieked
    and woke,
  And saw, fear-blinded, in his dripping cell,
A gaunt and hairy man, who with one stroke
  Swung a great axe of steel that flashed and
    fell. . . .

So that he woke amid his bedroom gloom,
  And saw, hair-poised, a naked, thirsting knife,
A gaunt and hairy man with eyes of doom—
  And then the blade plunged down to drink his
    life. . . .

So that he woke, wrenched back his robe, and
    looked,
  And saw beside his dying fire upstart
A gaunt and hairy man with finger crooked—
  A rifle rang, a bullet searched his heart. . . .

    *   *   *   *   *   *

The morning sky was sinister and cold.
  Grotesque the Dreamer sprawled. and did not
    rise.
For long and long there gazed upon some gold
  A gaunt and hairy man with wolfish eyes.

AT THIRTY-FIVE

THREE score and ten, the Psalmist saith,
  And half my course is well-nigh run ;
I've had my flout at dusty death,
  I've had my whack of feast and fun.
I've mocked at those who prate and preach
  I've laughed with any man alive ;
But now with sobered heart I reach
  The Great Divide of Thirty-five.

And looking back I must confess
  I've little cause to feel elate.
I've played the mummer more or less ;
  I fumbled fortune, flouted fate.
I've vastly dreamed and little done ;
  I've idly watched my brothers strive :
Oh, I have loitered in the sun
  By primrose paths to Thirty-five !

And those who matched me in the race,
    Well, some are out and trampled down;
The others jog with sober pace;
    Yet one wins delicate renown.
O midnight feast and famished dawn!
    O gay, hard life, with hope alive!
O golden youth, forever gone,
    How sweet you seem at Thirty-five!

Each of our lives is just a book
    As absolute as Holy Writ;
We humbly read, and may not look
    Ahead, nor change one word of it.
And here are joys and here are pains;
    And here we fail and here we thrive;
O wondrous volume! What remains
    When we reach chapter Thirty-five?

The very best, I dare to hope.
    Ere Fate writes Finis to the tome;
A wiser head, a wider scope,
    And for the gipsy heart, a home;
A songful home, with loved ones near.
    With joy, with sunshine all alive:
Watch me grow younger every year—
    Old Age! thy name is Thirty-five!

THE SQUAW-MAN

THE cow-moose comes to water, and the beaver's
    overbold,
  The net is in the eddy of the stream ;
The tepee stars the vivid sward with russet, red
    and gold,
  And in the velvet gloom the fire's agleam.
The night is ripe with quiet, rich with incense
    of the pine ;
  From sanctuary lake I hear the loon :
The peaks are bright against the blue, and drenched
    with sunset wine,
  And like a silver bubble is the moon.

Cloud-high I climbed but yesterday ; a hundred
    miles around
  I looked to see a rival fire agleam.
As in a crystal lens it lay, a land without a bound.
  All lure, and virgin vastitude, and dream.

The great sky roared exultantly, the great earth
    bared its breast,
  All river-veined and patterned with the pine ;
The heedless hordes of caribou were streaming
    to the West,
  A land of lustrous mystery—and mine.

Yea, mine to frame my Odyssey : Oh, little do
    they know
  My conquest and the kingdom that I keep !
The meadows of the musk-ox where the laughing
    grasses grow,
  The rivers where the careless conies leap.
Beyond the silent Circle, where white men are
    fierce and few,
  I lord it, and I mock at man-made law ;
Like a flame upon the water is my little light
    canoe,
  And yonder in the fireglow is my squaw.

A squaw-man ! yes, that's what I am ; sneer at
    me if you will.
  I've gone the grilling pace that cannot last ;
With bawdry, bridge and brandy—Oh, I've drunk
    enough to kill
  A dozen such as you, but that is past.

I've swung round to my senses, found the place
    where I belong ;
The City made a madman out of me ;
But here beyond the Circle, where there's neither
    right nor wrong,
    I leap from life's strait-jacket, and I'm free.

Yet ever in the far forlorn, by trails of lone
    desire ;
    Yet ever in the dawn's white leer of hate ;
Yet ever by the dripping kill, beside the drowsy
    fire,
    There comes the fierce heart-hunger for a mate.
There comes the mad blood-clamour for a woman's
    clinging hand,
    Love-humid eyes, the velvet of a breast :
And so I sought the Bonnet-plumes, and chose
    from out the band
    The girl I thought the sweetest and the best.

O wistful women I have loved before my dark
    disgrace !
O women fair and rare in my home land !
Dear ladies, if I saw you now I'd turn away my
    face,
    Then crawl to kiss your footprints in the sand !

And yet—that day the rifle jammed—a wounded
    moose at bay—
  A roar, a charge . . . I faced it with my knife:
A shot from out the willow-scrub, and there the
    monster lay . . .
  Yes, little Laughing Eyes, you saved my life.

The man must have the woman, and we're all
    brutes more or less,
  Since first the male ape shinned the family tree;
And yet I think I love her with a husband's
    tenderness,
  And yet I know that she would die for me.
Oh, if I left you, Laughing Eyes, and nevermore
    came back,
  God help you, girl! I know what you would
    do . . .
I see the lake wan in the moon, and from the
    shadow black,
  There drifts a little *empty* birch canoe.

We're here beyond the Circle, where there's never
    wrong nor right;
  We aren't spliced according to the law;
But by the gods I hail you on this hushed and holy
    night
  As the mother of my children, and my squaw.

I see your little slender face set in the firelight
    glow ;
  I pray that I may never make it sad ;
I hear you croon a baby song, all slumber-soft
    and low—
  God bless you, little Laughing Eyes! I'm glad.

HOME AND LOVE

Just Home and Love ! the words are small,
    Four little letters unto each ;
And yet you will not find in all
    The wide and gracious range of speech
Two more so tenderly complete :
    When angels talk in Heaven above,
I'm sure they have no words more sweet
        Than Home and Love.

Just Home and Love ! it's hard to guess
    Which of the two were best to gain.
Home without Love is bitterness ;
    Love without home is often pain.
No ! each alone will seldom do ;
    Somehow they travel hand and glove :
If you win one you must have two,
        Both Home and Love.

And if you've both, well, then I'm sure
　　You ought to sing the whole day long ;
It doesn't matter if you're poor
　　With these to make divine your song.
And so I praisefully repeat,
　　When angels talk in Heaven above,
There are no words more simply sweet
　　　　Than Home and Love.

I'M SCARED OF IT ALL

I'M scared of it all, God's truth! so I am:
    It's too big and brutal for me.
My nerve's on the raw and I don't give a damn
    For all the " hoorah " that I see.
I'm pinned between subway and overhead train,
    Where automobillies swoop down:
Oh, I want to go back to the timber again—
    I'm scared of the terrible town.

I want to go back to my lean, ashen plains;
    My rivers that flash into foam;
My ultimate valleys where solitude reigns;
    My trail from Fort Churchill to Nome.
My forests packed full of mysterious gloom,
    My ice-fields agrind and aglare:
The city is deadfalled with danger and doom—
    I know that I'm safer up there.

I watch the wan faces that flash in the street:
  All kinds and all classes I see.
Yet never a one in the million I meet
  Has the smile of a comrade for me.
Just jaded and panting like dogs in a pack;
  Just tensed and intent on the goal:
O God! but I'm lonesome—I wish I was back,
  Up there in the land of the Pole.

I wish I was back on the Hunger Plateaus,
  And seeking the lost caribou;
I wish I was up where the Coppermine flows
  To the kick of my little canoe.
I'd like to be far on some weariful shore,
  In the land of the Blizzard and Bear:
Oh, I wish I was snug in the Arctic once more
  For I know I am safer up there!

I prowl in the canyons of dismal unrest;
  I cringe—I'm so weak and so small.
I can't get my bearings, I'm crushed and oppressed
  With the haste and the waste of it all.
The slaves and the madmen, the lust and the sweat,
  The fear in the faces I see;
The getting, the spending, the fever, the fret—
  It's too bleeding cruel for me.

I feel it's all wrong, but I can't tell you why—
   The palace, the hovel next door ;
The insolent towers that sprawl to the sky,
   The crush and the rush and the roar.
I'm trapped like a fox and I fear for my pelt ;
   I cower in the crash and the glare ;
Oh, I want to be back in the avalanche belt,
   For I know that it's safer up there !

I'm scared of it all.   Oh, afar I can hear
   The voice of my solitudes call !
We're nothing but brute with a little veneer,
   And nature is best after all.
There's tumult and terror abroad in the street ;
   There's menace and doom in the air ;
I've got to get back to my thousand-mile beat ;
The trail where the cougar and silver-tip meet ;
The snows and the camp-fire, with wolves at my
     feet ;
   Good-bye, for it's safer up there.

       To be forming good habits up there ;
       To be starving on rabbits up there ;
         In your hunger and woe,
         Though it's sixty below,
      Oh, I know that it's safer up there !

A SONG OF SUCCESS

Ho ! we were strong, we were swift, we were brave.
   Youth was a challenge, and Life was a fight.
All that was best in us gladly we gave,
   Sprang from the rally, and leapt for the height.
Smiling is Love in a foam of Spring flowers :
   Harden our hearts to him—on let us press !
Oh, what a triumph and pride shall be ours !
   See where it beacons, the star of success !

Cares seem to crowd on us—so much to do :
   New fields to conquer, and time's on the wing.
Grey hairs are showing, a wrinkle or two ;
   Somehow our footstep is losing its spring.
Pleasure's forsaken us, Love ceased to smile :
   Youth has been funeralled ; Age travels fast.
Sometimes we wonder : Is it worth while ?
   There ! we have gained to the summit at last.

Aye, we have triumphed !   Now must we haste,
  Revel in victory . . . why ! what is wrong ?
Life's choicest vintage is flat to the taste—
  Are we too late ?   Have we laboured too long ?
Wealth, power, fame we hold . . . ah ! but the
      truth :
  Would we not give this vain glory of ours
For one mad, glad year of glorious youth,
  Life in the Springtide, and Love in the flowers !

THE SONG OF THE CAMP-FIRE

I

Heed me, feed me, I am hungry, I am red-tongued
with desire ;
  Boughs of balsam, slabs of cedar, gummy faggots
  of the pine,
Heap them on me, let me hug them to my eager
heart of fire,
  Roaring, soaring up to heaven as a symbol and
  a sign.
Bring me knots of sunny maple, silver birch and
tamarack ;
  Leaping, sweeping, I will lap them with my
  ardent wings of flame ;
I will kindle them to glory, I will beat the darkness
back ;
  Streaming, gleaming, I will goad them to my
  glory and my fame.
Bring me gnarly limbs of live-oak, aid me in my
frenzied fight ;
  Strips of iron-wood, scaly blue-gum, writhing
  redly in my hold ;

With my lunge of lurid lances, with my whips
　　　that flail the night,
　They will burgeon into beauty, they will foliate
　　　in gold.
Let me star the dim sierras, stab with light the
　　　inland seas ;
　Roaming wind and roaring darkness ! seek no
　　　mercy at my hands ;
I will mock the marly heavens, lamp the purple
　　　prairies,
　I will flaunt my deathless banners down the far,
　　　unhouseled lands.
In the vast and vaulted pine-gloom where the
　　　pillared forests frown,
　By the sullen, brutish rivers running where God
　　　only knows,
On the starlit coral beaches when the combers
　　　thunder down,
　In the death-spell of the barrens, in the shudder
　　　of the snows ;
In a blazing belt of triumph from the palm-leaf to
　　　the pine,
　As a symbol of defiance, lo! the wilderness I span ;
And my beacons burnt exultant as an everlasting
　　　sign
　Of unending domination, of the mastery of
　　　Man ;

I, the Life, the fierce Uplifter, I that weaned him
    from the mire ;
  I, the angel and the devil; I, the tyrant and the
    slave ;
I, the Spirit of the Struggle ; I, the mighty God of
    Fire ;
  I, the Maker and Destroyer ; I, the Giver and
    the Grave.

II

Gather round me, boy and grey-beard, frontiers-
    men of every kind.
Few are you, and far and lonely, yet an army
    forms behind :
By your camp-fires shall they know you, ashes
    scattered to the wind.

Peer into my heart of solace, break your bannock
    at my blaze ;
Smoking, stretched in lazy shelter, build your
    castles as you gaze ;
Or, it may be, deep in dreaming, think of dim,
    unhappy days.

Let my warmth and glow caress you, for your
    trails are grim and hard ;
o

Let my arms of comfort press you, hunger-hewn
and battle-scarred :
O my lovers ! how I bless you with your lives so
madly marred !

For you seek the silent spaces, and their secret
lore you glean ;
For you win the savage races, and the brutish Wild
you wean ;
And I gladden desert places, where camp-fire has
never been.

From the Pole unto the Tropics is there trail ye
have not dared ?
And because you hold death lightly, so by death
shall you be spared,
(As the sages of the ages in their pages have
declared.)

On the roaring Arkilinik in a leaky bark canoe ;
Up the cloud of Mount McKinley, where the
avalanche leaps through ;
In the furnace of Death Valley, when the mirage
glimmers blue.

Now a smudge of wiry willows on the weary
Kuskoquim ;

Now   a   flare   of   gummy   pine-knots   where
    Vancouver's scaur is grim ;
Now a gleam of sunny ceiba, when the Cuban
    beaches dim.

Always, always God's Great Open : lo ! I burn
    with keener light
In the corridors of silence, in the vestibules of
    night ;
'Mid the ferns and grasses gleaming, was there
    ever gem so bright ?

Not for weaklings, not for women, like my brother
    of the hearth ;
Ring your songs of wrath around me, I was made
    for manful mirth,
In the lusty, gusty greatness, on the bald spots
    of the earth.

Men, my masters ! Men, my lovers ! ye have
    fought and ye have bled ;
Gather round my ruddy embers, softly glowing is
    my bed ;
By my heart of solace dreaming, rest ye and be
    comforted !

III

I am dying, O my masters ! by my fitful flame ye
        sleep ;
    My purple plumes of glory droop forlorn.
Grey ashes choke and cloak me, and above the
        pines there creep
    The stealthy silver moccasins of morn.
There comes a countless army, it's the Legion of
        the Light ;
    It tramps in gleaming triumph round the world ;
And before its jewelled lances all the shadows of
        the night
    Back in to abysmal darknesses are hurled.

Leap to life again, my lovers ! ye must toil and
        never tire ;
    The day of daring, doing, brightens clear,
When the bed of spicy cedar and the jovial camp-
        fire
    Must only be a memory of cheer.
There is hope and golden promise in the vast
        portentous dawn ;
    There is glamour in the glad, effluent sky :
Go and leave me ; I will dream of you and love
        you when you're gone ;
    I have served you, O my masters ! let me die.

A little heap of ashes, grey and sodden by the
    rain,
  Wind-scattered, blurred and blotted by the
    snow :
Let that be all to tell of me, and glorious again,
  Ye things of greening gladness, leap and glow !
A black scar in the sunshine by the palm-leaf or
    the pine,
  Blind to the night and dead to all desire ;
Yet oh, of life and uplift what a symbol and a
    sign !
Yet oh, of power and conquest what a destiny is
    mine !
A little heap of ashes—Yea ! a miracle divine,
  The footprint of a god, all-radiant Fire.

HER LETTER

" I'M taking pen in hand this night, and hard it
    is for me ;
  My poor old fingers tremble so, my hand is stiff
    and slow,
And even with my glasses on I'm troubled sore to
    see . . .
  You'd little know your mother, boy ; you'd
    little, little know.
You mind how brisk and bright I was, how straight
    and trim and smart ;
  'Tis weariful I am the now, and bent and frail
    and grey.
I'm waiting at the road's end, lad ; and all that's
    in my heart,
  Is just to see my boy again before I'm called
    away.

"Oh, well I mind the sorry day you crossed the
    gurly sea ;
  'Twas like the heart was torn from me, a waeful
    wife was I.
You said that you'd be home again in two years,
    maybe three ;
  But nigh a score of years have gone, and still
    the years go by.
I know it's cruel hard for you, you've bairnies of
    your own ;
  I know the siller's hard to win, and folks have
    used you ill :
But oh, think of your mother, lad, that's waiting
    by her lone !
  And even if you canna come—*just write and say
    you will.*

"Aye, even though there's little hope, just promise
    that you'll try.
  It's weary, weary waiting, lad ; just say you'll
    come next year.
I'm thinking there will be no ' next ' ; I'm thinking
    soon I'll lie
  With all the ones I've laid away . . . but oh,
    the hope will cheer !
You know you're all that's left to me, and we are
    seas apart ;

But if you'll only *say* you'll come, then will I
  hope and pray.
I'm waiting by the grave-side, lad ; and all that's
  in my heart
Is just to see my boy again before I'm called
  away."

THE MAN WHO KNEW

THE Dreamer visioned Life as it might be,
   And from his dream forthright a picture grew,
A painting all the people thronged to see,
   And joyed therein—till came the Man Who
      Knew,
Saying : " 'Tis bad.   Why do ye gape, ye fools ?
He painteth not according to the schools.'·

The Dreamer probed Life's mystery of woe,
   And in a book he sought to give the clue ;
The people read, and saw that it was so,
   And read again—then came the Man Who
      Knew,
Saying : " Ye witless ones ! this book is vile :
It hath not got the rudiments of style."

Love smote the Dreamer's lips, and silver-clear
   He sang a song so sweet, so tender true,

That all the market-place was thrilled to hear,
  And listened rapt — till came the Man Who
    Knew,
Saying : " His technique's wrong ; he singeth ill.
Waste not your time." The singer's voice was
    still.

And then the people roused as if from sleep,
  Crying : " What care we if it be not Art !
Hath he not charmed us, made us laugh and
    weep ?
  Come, let us crown him where he sits apart."
Then, with his picture spurned, his book unread,
His song unsung, they found their Dreamer—
    dead.

THE LOGGER

In the moonless, misty night, with my little pipe
    alight,
  I am sitting by the camp-fire's fading cheer ;
Oh, the dew is falling chill on the dim, deer-
    haunted hill,
  And the breakers in the bay are moaning drear.
The toilful hours are sped, the boys are long
    abed,
  And I alone a weary vigil keep ;
In the sightless, sullen sky I can hear the night-
    hawk cry,
  And the frogs in frenzied chorus from the
    creek.

And somehow the ember's glow brings me back
    the long ago,
  The days of merry laughter and light song ;
When I sped the hours away with the gayest of
    the gay
  In the giddy whirl of fashion's festal throng.

Oh, I ran a grilling race and I little recked the
pace,
    For the lust of youth ran riot in my blood ;
But at last I made a stand in this God-forsaken
land
        Of the pine-tree and the mountain and the
flood.

And now I've got to stay, with an overdraft to
pay
    For pleasure in the past with future pain ;
And I'm not the chap to whine, for if the chance
were mine
    I know I'd choose the old life once again.
With its woman's eyes ashine, and its flood of
golden wine ;
    Its fever and its frolic and its fun ;
The old life with its din, its laughter and its sin—
    And chuck me in the gutter when it's done.

Ah, well ! it's past and gone, and the memory is
wan,
    That conjures up each old familiar face ;
And here by fortune hurled, I am dead to all the
world,
        And I've learned to lose my pride and keep my
place.

My ways are hard and rough, and my arms are
    strong and tough,
  And I hew the dizzy pine till darkness falls ;
And sometimes I take a dive, just to keep my
    heart alive,
  Among the gay saloons and dancing-halls.

In the distant, dinful town just a little drink, to
    drown
  The cares that crowd and canker in my brain ;
Just a little joy to still set my pulses all athrill,
  Then back to brutish labour once again.
And things will go on so until one day I shall
    know
  That Death has got me cinched beyond a doubt :
Then I'll crawl away from sight, and morosely
    in the night
  My weary, wasted life will peter out.

Then the boys will gather round, and they'll launch
    me in the ground,
  And pile on stones the timber wolf to foil ;
And the moaning pine will wave overhead a
    nameless grave,
  Where the blacksnake in the sunshine loves to
    coil.

And they'll leave me there alone, and perhaps
    with softened tone
  Speak of me sometimes in the camp-fire's glow
As a played-out, broken chum, who has gone to
    Kingdom Come,
  And who went the pace in England long ago.

THE PASSING OF THE YEAR

My glass is filled, my pipe is lit,
    My den is all a cosy glow ;
And snug before the fire I sit,
    And wait to *feel* the old year go.
I dedicate to solemn thought
    Amid my too-unthinking days,
This sober moment, sadly fraught
    With much of blame, with little praise.

Old Year ! upon the Stage of Time
    You stand to bow your last adieu ;
A moment, and the prompter's chime
    Will ring the curtain down on you.
Your mien is sad, your step is slow ;
    You falter as a Sage in pain ;
Yet turn, Old Year, before you go,
    And face your audience again.

413

That sphynx-like face, remote, austere,
  Let us all read, whate'er the cost :
O Maiden ! why that bitter tear ?
  Is it for dear one you have lost ?
Is it for fond illusion gone ?
  For trusted lover proved untrue ?
O sweet girl-face, so sad, so wan,
  What hath the Old Year meant to you ?

And you, O neighbour on my right,
  So sleek, so prosperously clad !
What see you in that aged wight
  That makes your smile so gay and glad ?
What opportunity unmissed ?
  What golden gain, what pride of place ?
What splendid hope ?   O Optimist !
  What read you in that withered face ?

And you, deep shrinking in the gloom,
  What find you in that filmy gaze ?
What menace of a tragic doom ?
  What dark, condemning yesterdays ?
What urge to crime, what evil done ?
  What cold, confronting shape of fear ?
O haggard, haunted, hidden One,
  What see you in the dying year ?

And so from face to face I flit,
  The countless eyes that stare and stare ;
Some are with approbation lit,
  And some are shadowed with despair.
Some show a smile and some a frown ;
  Some joy and hope, some pain and woe :
Enough !   Oh, ring that curtain down !
  Old weary year ! it's time to go.

My pipe is out, my glass is dry ;
  My fire is almost ashes too :
But once again, before you go,
  And I prepare to meet the New :
Old Year ! a parting word that's true,
  For we've been comrades, you and I—
I thank God for each day of you ;
  There ! bless you now ! Old Year, good-bye !

THE GHOSTS

Smith, great writer of stories, drank; found it
  immortalized his pen;
Fused in his brain-pan, else a blank, heavens of
  glory now and then;
Gave him the magical genius touch; God-given
  power to gouge out, fling
Flat in your face a soul-thought—Bing! Twiddle
  your heart-strings in his clutch.
" Bah ! " said Smith, " let my body lie stripped
  to the buff in swinish shame,
If I can blaze in the radiant sky out of adoring
  stars my name.
Sober am I nonentitized; drunk am I more than
  half a god.
Well, let the flesh be sacrificed; spirit shall speak
  and shame the clod.
Who would not gladly, gladly give Life to do
  one thing that will live ? "

Smith had a friend, we'll call him Brown ; dearer
  than brothers were those two.
When in the wassail Smith would drown, Brown
  would rescue and pull him through.
When Brown was needful Smith would lend ; so
  it fell as the years went by,
Each on the other would depend : then at the last
  Smith came to die.

There Brown sat in the sick man's room, still as
  a stone in his despair ;
Smith bent on him his eyes of doom, shook back
  his lion mane of hair ;
Said : " Is there one in my chosen line, writer of
  forthright tales, my peer ?
Look in that little desk of mine ; there is a package,
  bring it here.
Story of stories, gem of all ; essence and triumph,
  key and clue ;
Tale of a loving woman's fall ; soul swept hellward,
  and God ! it's true,
I was the man—Oh, yes, I've paid, paid with
  mighty and mordant pain.
Look ! here's the masterpiece I've made out of
  my sin, my manhood slain.

Art supreme! yet the world would stare, know
    my mistress and blaze my shame.
I have a wife and daughter—there! take it and
    thrust it in the flame."

Brown answered : " Master, you have dipped pen
    in your heart, your phrases sear.
Ruthless, unflinching, you have stripped naked
    your soul and set it here.
Have I not loved you well and true ?   See!
    between us the shadows drift ;
This bit of blood and tears means You—oh, let
    me have it, a parting gift.
Sacred I'll hold it, a trust divine ; sacred your
    honour, her dark despair ;
Never shall it see printed line : here, by the living
    God I swear."
Brown on a Bible laid his hand ; Smith, great
    writer of stories, sighed :
" Comrade, I trust you, and understand.   Keep
    my secret ! "   And so he died.

Smith was buried—upsoared his sales ; lured you
    his books in every store ;
Exquisite, whimsy, heart - wrung tales ;   men
    devoured them and craved for more.

So when it slyly got about Brown had a post-
  humous manuscript,
Jones, the publisher, sought him out, into his
  pocket deep he dipped.
" A thousand dollars ? " Brown shook his head.
    " The story is not for sale," he said.

Jones went away, then others came. Tempted
  and taunted, Brown was true.
Guarded at friendship's shrine, the fame of the
  unpublished story grew and grew.
It's a long, long lane that has no end, but some
  lanes end in the Potter's field ;
Smith to Brown had been more than friend :
  patron, protector, spur and shield.
Poor, loving-wistful, dreamy Brown, long and lean,
  with a smile askew,
Friendless he wandered up and down, gaunt as a
  wolf, as hungry, too.
Brown with his lilt of saucy rhyme, Brown with
  his tilt of tender mirth,
Garretless in the gloom and grime, singing his
  glad, mad songs of earth :
So at last with a faith divine, down and down
  to the Hunger-line.

There as he stood in a woeful plight, tears a-freeze
    on his sharp cheek-bones,
Who should chance to behold his plight but the
    publisher, the plethoric Jones;
Peered at him for a little while, held out a bill:
    " *Now*, will you sell ? "
Brown scanned it with his twisted smile: " A
    thousand dollars ! you go to hell ! "
Brown enrolled in the homeless host, sleeping
    anywhere, anywhen;
Suffered, strove, became a ghost, slave of the
    lamp for other men;
For What's-his-name and So-and-so in the abyss
    his soul he stripped,
Yet in his want, his worst of woe, held he fast
    to the manuscript.
Then one day as he chewed his pen, half in hunger
    and half despair.
Creaked the door of his garret den; Dick, his
    brother, was standing there.
Down on the pallet bed he sank, ashen his face,
    his voice a wail:
" Save me, brother ! I've robbed the bank;
    to-morrow it's ruin, capture, gaol.
Yet there's a chance : I could to-day pay back
    the money, save our name;
You have a manuscript, they say, worth a thousand
    —think man ! the shame. . . ."

Brown with his heart pain-pierced the while, with
    his stern, starved face, and his lips stone-pale,
Shuddered and smiled his twisted smile : " Brother,
    I guess you go to gaol."

While poor Brown in the leer of dawn wrestled
    with God for the sacred fire,
Came there a woman weak and wan, out of the
    mob, the murk, the mire ;
Frail as a reed, a fellow ghost, weary with woe,
    with sorrowing ;
Two pale souls in the legion lost ; lo ! Love bent
    with a tender wing,
Taught them a joy so deep, so true, it seemed
    that the whole world-fabric shook,
Thrilled and dissolved in radiant dew : then
    Brown made him a golden book,
Full of the faith that Life is good, that the earth
    is a dream divinely fair,
Lauding his gem of womanhood, in many a lyric
    rich and rare ;
Took it to Jones, who shook his head : " I will
    consider it," he said.
While he considered, Brown's wife lay clutched
    in the tentacles of pain ;
Then came the doctor, grave and grey ; spoke of
    decline, of nervous strain ;

Hinted Egypt, the South of France—Brown with
  terror was tiger-gripped.
Where was the money ? What the chance !
  Pitiful God ! . . . the manuscript !
A thousand dollars—his only hope ! He gazed
  and gazed at the garret wall . . .
Reached at last for the envelope, turned to his
  wife and told her all.
Told of his friend, his promise true ; told like his
  very heart would break ;
" Oh, my dearest ! what shall I do ? Shall I not
  sell it for your sake ? "
Ghostlike she lay, as still as doom ; turned to the
  wall her weary head ;
Icy-cold in the pallid gloom, silent as death . . .
  at last she said :
" Do, my husband ! Keep your vow ! Guard his
  secret and let me die . . .
Oh, my dear, I must tell you now—*the woman
  he loved and wronged was I ;*
Darling ! I haven't long to live : I never told
  you—forgive, forgive ! "

For a long, long time Brown did not speak ; sat
  bleak-browed in the wretched room ;
Slowly a tear stole down his cheek, and he kissed
  her hand in the dismal gloom.

To break his oath, to brand her shame ; his well-
    loved friend, his worshipped wife ;
To keep his vow, to save her name, yet at the
    cost of what ? Her life !
A moment's space did he hesitate, a moment of
    pain and dread and doubt,
Then he broke the seals and, stern as fate, un-
    folded the sheets and spread them out . . .
On his knees by her side he limply sank, peering
    amazed—*each page was blank.*

(For oh, the supremest of our art are the stories
    we do not dare to tell,
Locked in the silence of the heart, for the awful
    records of Heav'n and Hell.)

Yet those two in the silence there seemed less
    weariful than before.
Hark ! a step on the garret stair. a postman
    knocks at the flimsy door.
" Registered letter ! " Brown thrills with fear ;
    opens and reads, then bends above :
" Glorious tidings ! Egypt, dear ! The book is
    accepted—life and love ! "

GOOD-BYE, LITTLE CABIN

O DEAR little cabin, I've loved you so long,
    And now I must bid you good-bye !
I've filled you with laughter, I've thrilled you
        with song,
    And sometimes I've wished I could cry.
Your walls they have witnessed a weariful fight,
    And rung to a won Waterloo :
But oh, in my triumph I'm dreary to-night—
    Good-bye, little cabin, to you !

Your roof is bewhiskered, your floor is aslant,
    Your walls seem to sag and to swing ;
I'm trying to find just your faults, but I can't—
    You poor, tired, heart-broken old thing !
I've seen when you've been the best friend that
        I had,
    Your light like a gem on the snow ;
You're sort of a part of me—Gee ! but I'm sad :
    I hate, little cabin, to go.

Below your cracked window red raspberries
  climb ;
  A hornet's nest hangs from a beam ;
Your rafters are scribbled with adage and rhyme,
  And dimmed with tobacco and dream.
" Each day has its laugh," and " Don't worry, just
  work."
  Such mottoes reproachfully shine.
Old calendars dangle—what memories lurk
  About you, dear cabin of mine !

I hear the world-call and the clang of the fight ;
  I hear the hoarse cry of my kind ;
Yet well do I know, as I quit you to-night,
  It's Youth that I'm leaving behind.
And often I'll think of you, empty and black,
  Moose antlers nailed over your door :
Oh, if I should perish my ghost will come back
  To dwell in you, cabin, once more !

How cold, still and lonely, how weary you seem !
  A last wistful look and I'll go.
Oh, will you remember the lad with his dream !
  The lad that you comforted so.

The shadows enfold you, it's drawing to night ;
　The evening star needles the sky :
And huh ! but it's stinging and stabbing my
　　sight—
　God bless you, old cabin, good-bye !

HEART O' THE NORTH

AND when I come to the dim trail-end,
  I who have been Life's rover,
This is all I would ask, my friend,
  Over and over and over :

A little space on a stony hill,
  With never another near me,
Sky o' the North that's vast and still,
  With a single star to cheer me ;

Star that gleams on a moss-grey stone
  Graven by those who love me—
There would I lie alone, alone,
  With a single pine above me ;

Pine that the north wind whinnies through—
  Oh, I have been Life's lover,
But there I'd lie and listen to
  Eternity passing over.

THE SCRIBE'S PRAYER

WHEN from my fumbling hand the tired pen falls,
  And in the twilight weary droops my head ;
While to my quiet heart a still voice calls,
  Calls me to join my kindred of the Dead :
Grant that I may, O Lord, ere rest be mine,
Write to Thy praise one radiant, ringing line.

For all of worth that in this clay abides,
  The leaping rapture and the ardent flame,
The hope, the high resolve, the faith that guides ;
  All, all is Thine, and liveth in Thy name :
Lord, have I dallied with the sacred fire !
Lord, have I trailed Thy glory in the mire !

E'en as a toper from the dram-shop reeling,
  Sees in his garret's blackness, dazzling fair,
All that he might have been, and, heart-sick, kneeling,
  Sobs in the passion of a vast despair :

So my ideal self haunts me alway—
When the accounting comes, how shall I pay?

For in the dark I grope, nor understand ;
* And in my heart fight selfishness and sin :*
Yet, Lord, I do not seek Thy helping hand ;
* Rather let me my own salvation win :*
Let me through strife and penitential pain
Onward and upward to the heights attain.

Yea, let me live my life, its meaning seek ;
* Bear myself fitly in the ringing fight ;*
Strive to be strong that I may aid the weak ;
* Dare to be true—O God ! the Light, the Light !*
Cometh the Dark so soon ?   I've mocked Thy word,
* Yet do I know Thy Love : have mercy, Lord.*

THE RHYMES OF A RED-CROSS MAN

To the Memory of

MY BROTHER

LIEUTENANT ALBERT SERVICE

CANADIAN INFANTRY

KILLED IN ACTION, FRANCE

August 1916.

THE RHYMES
OF A RED-CROSS MAN

FOREWORD

I've tinkered at my bits of rhymes
In weary, woeful, waiting times ;
In doleful hours of battle-din,
Ere yet they brought the wounded in ;
Through vigils of the fateful night,
In lousy barns by candle-light ;
In dug-outs, sagging and aflood,
On stretchers stiff and bleared with blood ;
By ragged grove, by ruined road,
By hearths accurst where Love abode ;
By broken altars, blackened shrines
I've tinkered at my bits of rhymes.

I've solaced me with scraps of song
The desolated ways along :
Through sickly fields all shrapnel-sown,
And meadows reaped by death alone ;
By blazing cross and splintered spire,
By headless Virgin in the mire ;

By gardens gashed amid their bloom,
By gutted grave, by shattered tomb ;
Beside the dying and the dead
Where rocket green and rocket red
In trembling pools of poising light
With flowers of flame festoon the night.
Ah me ! by what dark ways of wrong
I've cheered my heart with scraps of song.

So here's my sheaf of war-won verse,
And some is bad, and some is worse.
And if at times I curse a bit,
You needn't read that part of it ;
For through it all like horror runs
The red resentment of the guns.
And you yourself would mutter when
You took the things that once were men,
And sped them through that zone of hate
To where the dripping surgeons wait ;
And wonder too if in God's sight
War ever, ever can be right.

Yet may it not be, crime and war
But effort misdirected are ?
And if there's good in war and crime,
There may be in my bits of rhyme,
My songs from out the slaughter mill :
So take or leave them as you will.

THE CALL

(*France, August First*, 1914.)

FAR and near, high and clear,
    Hark to the call of War !
Over the gorse and the golden dells,
Ringing and swinging of clamorous bells,
Praying and saying of wild farewells :
    War ! War ! War !

High and low, all must go :
    Hark to the shout of War !
Leave to the women the harvest yield ;
Gird ye, men, for the sinister field ;
A sabre instead of a scythe to wield :
    War ! Red War !

Rich and poor, lord and boor,
    Hark to the blast of War !
Tinker and tailor and millionaire,
Actor in triumph and priest in prayer,
Comrades now in the hell out there,
    Sweep to the fire of War !

Prince and page, sot and sage,
        Hark to the roar of War !
Poet, professor and circus clown,
Chimney-sweeper and fop o' the town,
Into the pot and be melted down :
        Into the pot of War !

Women all, hear the call,
        The pitiless call of War !
Look your last on your dearest ones,
Brothers and husbands, fathers, sons :
Swift they go to the ravenous guns,
        The gluttonous guns of War.

Everywhere thrill the air
        The maniac bells of War.
There will be little of sleeping to-night ;
There will be wailing and weeping to-night ;
Death's red sickle is reaping to-night :
        War ! War ! War !

THE FOOL

" But it isn't playing the game," he said,
And he slammed his books away ;
" The Latin and Greek I've got in my head
Will do for a duller day."
" Rubbish ! " I cried ; " the bugle's call
Isn't for lads from school."
D'ye think he'd listen ?   Oh, not at all :
So I called him a fool, a fool.

Now there's his dog by his empty bed,
And the flute he used to play,
And his favourite bat . . . but Dick he's dead,
Somewhere in France, they say :
Dick with his rapture of song and sun,
Dick of the yellow hair,
Dicky whose life had but begun,
Carrion-cold out there.

Look at his prizes all in a row
Surely a hint of fame.
Now he's finished with, nothing to show:
Doesn't it seem a shame ?
Look from the window !   All you see
Was to be his one day :
Forest and furrow, lawn and lea,
And he goes and chucks it away.

Chucks it away to die in the dark.
Somebody saw him fall,
Part of him mud, part of him blood,
The rest of him—not at all.
And yet I'll bet he was never afraid,
And he went as the best of 'em go,
For his hand was clenched on his broken blade,
And his face was turned to the foe.

And I called him a fool . . . Oh, blind was I !
And the cup of my grief's abrim.
Will Glory o' England ever die
So long as we've lads like him ?
So long as we've fond and fearless fools,
Who, spurning fortune and fame,
Turn out with the rallying cry of their schools,
Just bent on playing the game.

A fool ! Ah no ! He was more than wise.
His was the proudest part.
He died with the glory of faith in his eyes,
And the glory of love in his heart.
And though there's never a grave to tell,
Nor a cross to mark his fall,
Thank God ! we know that he " batted well "
In the last great Game of all.

THE VOLUNTEER

Sez I : My Country calls ?   Well, let it call.
I grins perlitely and declines with thanks.
Go, let 'em plaster every blighted wall,
'Ere's *one* they don't stampede into the ranks.
Them politicians with their greasy ways ;
Them empire-grabbers — fight for 'em ?   No
    fear !
I've seen this mess a-comin' from the days
Of Algyserious and Aggydear :
      I've felt me passion rise and swell,
      But . . . wot the 'ell, Bill ?   Wot the 'ell?

Sez I : My Country ? Mine ? I likes their cheek.
Me mud-bespattered by the cars they drive,
Wot makes my measly thirty bob a week,
And sweats red blood to keep meself alive !
Fight for the right to slave that they may spend,
Them in their mansions, me 'ere in my slum ?
No, let 'em fight wot's something to defend :
But me, I've nothin',—let the Kaiser come.
      And so I cusses 'ard and well,
      But . . . wot the 'ell, Bill ?   Wot the 'ell?

Sez I : If they would do the decent thing,
And shield the missis and the little 'uns,
Why, even *I* might shout God save the King,
And face the chances of them 'ungry guns.
But we've got three, another on the way ;
It's that wot makes me snarl and set me jor :
The wife and nippers wot of 'em, I say,
If I gets knocked out in this blasted war ?
      Gets proper busted by a shell,
      But . . . wot the 'ell, Bill ? Wot the 'ell ?

Ay, wot the 'ell's the use of all this talk ?
To-day some boys in blue was passin' me,
And some of 'em they 'ad no legs to walk,
And some of 'em they 'ad no eyes to see.
And—well, I couldn't look 'em in the face,
And so I'm goin', goin' to declare
I'm under forty-one and take me place
To face the music with the bunch out there.
      A fool, you say ! Maybe you're right.
      I'll 'ave no peace unless I fight.
      I've ceased to think ; I only know
      I've gotta go, Bill, gotta go.

THE CONVALESCENT

. . . So I walked among the willows very quietly
    all night ;
There was no moon at all, at all ; no timid star
    alight ;
There was no light at all, at all ; I wint from tree to
    tree,
And I called him as his mother called, but he nivver
    answered me.

Oh I called him all the night-time, as I walked the
    wood alone ;
And I listened and I listened, but I nivver heard a
    moan ;
Then I found him at the dawnin', when the sorry
    sky was red :
I was lookin' for the livin', but I only round the
    dead.

Sure I know that it was Shamus by the silver cross
    he wore ;
But the bugles they were callin', and I heard the
    cannon roar.

Oh I had no time to tarry, so I said a little prayer,
And I clasped his hands together, and I left him
lyin' there.

Now the birds are singin', singin', and I'm home
in Donegal,
And it's Springtime, and I'm thinkin' that I only
dreamed it all ;
I dreamed about that evil wood, all crowded with
its dead,
Where I knelt beside me brother when the battle-
dawn was red.

Where I prayed beside me brother ere I wint to
fight anew :
Such dreams as these are evil dreams ; I can't
believe it's true.
Where all is love and laughter, sure it's hard to
think of loss. . . .
But mother's sayin' nothin', and she clasps—*a
silver cross.*

THE MAN FROM ATHABASKA

OH the wife she tried to tell me that 'twas nothing
    but the thrumming
Of a wood-pecker a-rapping on the hollow of a tree ;
And she thought that I was fooling when I said it
    was the drumming
Of the mustering of legions, and 'twas calling
    unto me ;
'Twas calling me to pull my freight and hop across
    the sea.

And a-mending of my fish-nets sure I started up in
    wonder,
For I heard a savage roaring and 'twas coming
    from afar ;
Oh the wife she tried to tell me that 'twas only
    summer thunder,
And she laughed a bit sarcastic when I told her it
    was War ;
'Twas the chariots of battle where the mighty
    armies are.

Then down the lake came Half-breed Tom with
   russet sail a-flying,
And the word he said was " War " again, so what
   was I to do ?
Oh the dogs they took to howling, and the missis
   took to crying,
As I flung my silver foxes in the little birch canoe :
Yes, the old girl stood a-blubbing till an island hid
   the view.

Says the factor : " Mike, you're crazy ! They have
   soldier men a-plenty.
You're as grizzled as a badger, and you've sixty
   year or so."
" But I haven't missed a scrap," says I, " since I
   was one and twenty.
And shall I miss the biggest ? You can bet your
   whiskers—no ! "
So I sold my furs and started . . . and that's
   eighteen months ago.

For I joined the Foreign Legion, and they put me
   for a starter
In the trenches of the Argonne with the Boche a
   step away ;
And the partner on my right hand was an *apache*
   from Montmartre ;

On my left there was a millionaire from Pitts-
burg, U.S.A.
(Poor fellow ! They collected him in bits the other
day.)

But I'm sprier than a chipmunk, save a touch of
the lumbago,
And they calls me Old Methoosalah, and *blagues*
me all the day.
I'm their exhibition sniper, and they work me like a
Dago,
And laugh to see me plug a Boche a half a mile
away.
Oh I hold the highest record in the regiment. they
say.

And at night they gather round me, and I tell them
of my roaming
In the Country of the Crepuscule beside the
Frozen Sea ;
Where the musk-ox runs unchallenged, and the
cariboo goes homing,
And they sit like little children, just as quiet as
can be :
Men of every crime and colour, how they harken
unto me !

And I tell them of the Furland, of the tumpline and
 the paddle,
Of secret rivers loitering, that no one will explore;
And I tell them of the ranges, of the pack-strap
 and the saddle,
And they fill their pipes in silence, and their eyes
 beseech for more ;
While above the star-shells fizzle and the high
 explosives roar.

And I tell of lakes fish-haunted, where the big bull
 moose are calling,
And forests still as sepulchres with never trail or
 track ;
And valleys packed with purple gloom, and mountain peaks appalling,
And I tell them of my cabin on the shore at Fond
 du Lac ;
And I find myself a-thinking : Sure I wish that I
 was back.

So I brag of bear and beaver while the batteries are
 roaring,
And the fellows on the firing steps are blazing at
 the foe ;
And I yarn of fur and feather when the *marmites*
 are a-soaring,

And they listen to my stories, seven *poilus* in a row,
Seven lean and lousy *poilus* with their cigarettes
aglow.

And I tell them when it's over how I'll hike for
Athabaska,
And those seven greasy *poilus* they are crazy to
go too.
And I'll give the wife the " pickle-tub " I promised,
and I'll ask her
The price of mink and marten, and the run of
cariboo,
And I'll get my traps in order, and I'll start to
work anew.

For I've had my fill of fighting, and I've seen a
nation scattered,
And an army swung to slaughter, and a river red
with gore,
And a city all a-smoulder, and . . . as if it really
mattered,
For the lake is yonder dreaming, and my cabin's
on the shore ;
And the dogs are leaping madly, and the wife is
singing gladly,
And I'll rest in Athabaska, and I'll leave it nevermore.

THE RED RETREAT

*Tramp, tramp, the grim road, the road from Mons
to Wipers*
*(I've 'ammered out this ditty with me bruised and
bleedin' feet);*
*Tramp, tramp, the dim road—we didn't 'ave no
pipers,*
*And bellies that was 'oller was the drums we 'ad to
beat.*
*Tramp, tramp, the bad road, the bits o' kiddies
crying there.*
The fell birds a-flyin' there, the 'ouses all aflame;
*Tramp, tramp, the sad road, the pals I left a-lyin'
there,*
*Red there, and dead there. . . . Oh blimy, it's a
shame!*

A-singin' " 'Oo's Yer Lady Friend ? " we started
out from 'Arver,
A-singin' till our froats was dry—we didn't care
a 'ang;
The Frenchies 'ow they lined the way, and slung
us their palaver,

And all we knowed to arnser was the one word
    " vang " ;
They gave us booze and caporal, and cheered for
    us like crazy,
And all the pretty gels was out to kiss us as we
    passed ;
And 'ow they all went dotty when we 'owled the
    Marcelaisey !
Oh, Gawd ! Them was the 'appy days, the days
    too good to last.

We started out for God Knows Where, we started
    out a-roarin' ;
We 'ollered : " 'Ere We Are Again," and 'struth !
    but we was dry.
The dust was gummin' up our ears, and 'ow the
    sweat was pourin' ;
The road was long, the sun was like a brazier in
    the sky,
We wondered where the 'Uns was—we wasn't long
    a-wonderin',
For down a scruff of 'ill-side they rushes like a
    flood ;
Then oh ! 'twas music 'eavenly, our batteries
    a-thunderin',
And arms and legs went soarin' in the fountain of
    their blood.

For on they came like bee swarms, a-hochin' and
  a-singin' ;
We pumped the bullets into 'em ; we couldn't miss
  a shot.
But though we mowed 'em down like grass, like
  grass was they a-springin',
And all our 'ands was blistered, for our rifles was
  so 'ot.
We roared with battle-fury, and we lammed the
  stuffin' out of 'em,
And then we fixed our bay'nets and we spitted 'em
  like meat.
You should 'ave 'eard the beggars squeal ; you
  should 'ave seen the rout of 'em,
And 'ow we cussed and wondered when the word
  came : " Retreat ! "

Retreat ! That was the 'ell of it. It fair upset our
  'abits,
A-runnin' from them blighters over 'alf the roads
  of France ;
A-scurryin' before 'em like a lot of blurry
  rabbits,
And knowin' we could smash 'em if we just 'ad 'alf
  a chance.

Retreat ! That was the bitter bit, a-limpin' and
    a-blunderin' ;
All day and night a-hoofin' it and sleepin' on our
    feet ;
A-fightin' rearguard actions for a bit of rest, and
    wonderin'
If sugar beets or mangels was the 'olesomest to eat.

Ho yus, there isn't many left that started out so
    cheerily ;
There was no bands a-playin' and we 'ad no autmo-
    beels.
Our tummies they was 'oller, and our 'eads was
    'angin' wearily,
And if we stopped to light a fag the 'Uns was
    on our 'eels.
That rotten road ! I can't forget the kids and
    mothers flyin' there,
The bits of barns a-blazin' and the 'orrid sights I
    sor ;
The stiffs that lined the wayside, me own pals
    a-lyin' there,
Their faces covered over wiv a little 'eap of stror.

Tramp, tramp, the red road, the wicked bullets
    'ummin'
(*I've panted out this ditty with me 'ot 'ard breath*).

*Tramp, tramp, the dread road, the Boches all
    a-comin',*
The lootin' and the shootin' and the shrieks o' death.
*Tramp, tramp, the fell road, the mad 'orde pursuin'
    there,*
*And 'ow we 'urled it back again, them grim, grey
    waves ;*
*Tramp, tramp, the 'ell road, the 'orror and the ruin
    there,*
*The graves of me mateys there, the grim, sour
    graves.*

THE HAGGIS OF PRIVATE McPHEE

"HAE ye heard whit ma auld mither's postit tae
me ?
It fair maks me hamesick," says Private McPhee.
"And whit did she send ye ? " says Private McPhun,
As he cockit his rifle and bleezed at a Hun.
"A haggis !   A *haggis* ! " says Private McPhee ;
"The brawest big haggis I ever did see.
And think !   It's the morn when fond memory
turns
Tae haggis and whuskey—the Birthday o' Burns.
We maun find a dram ; then we'll ca' in the rest
O' the lads, and we'll hae a Burns' Nicht wi' the
best."

"Be ready at sundoon," snapped Sergeant McCole ;
"I want you two men for the List'nin' Patrol."
Then Private McPhee looked at Private McPhun :
"I'm thinkin', ma lad, we're confoundedly done."
Then Private McPhun looked at Private McPhee :
"I'm thinkin', auld chap, it's a' aff wi' oor spree."

But up spoke their crony, wee Wullie McNair :
" Jist lea' yer braw haggis for me tae prepare ;
And as for the dram, if I search the camp roun',
We maun hae a drappie tae jist haud it doon.
Sae rin, lads, and think, though the nicht it be
    black,
O' the haggis that's waitin' ye when ye get back."

My ! but it wis waesome on Naebuddy's Land,
And the deid they were rottin' on every hand.
And the rockets like corpse candles hauntit the
    sky,
And the winds o' destruction went shudderin'
    by.
There wis skelpin' o' bullets and skirlin' o' shells,
And breengin' o' bombs and a thoosand death-
    knells ;
But cooryin' doon in a Jack Johnson hole
Little fashed the twa men o' the List'nin' Patrol.
For sweeter than honey and bricht as a gem
Wis the thocht o' the haggis that waitit for them.

Yet alas ! in oor moments o' sunniest cheer
Calamity's aften maist cruelly near.
And while the twa talked o' their puddin' divine
The Boches below them were howkin' a mine.

And while the twa cracked o' the feast they would
hae,
The fuse it wis burnin' and burnin' away.
Then sudden a roar like the thunner o' doom,
A hell-leap o' flame . . . then the wheesht o' the
tomb.

" Haw, Jock ! Are ye hurtit ? " says Private
McPhun.
" Ay, Geordie, they've got me ; I'm fearin' I'm
done.
It's ma leg ; I'm jist thinkin' it's aff at the knee ·
Ye'd best gang and leave me," says Private
McPhee.
" Oh leave ye I wunna," says Private McPhun ;
" And leave ye I canna, for though I micht run,
It's no faur I wud gang, it's no muckle I'd see :
I'm blindit, and that's whit's the maitter wi' me."
Then Private McPhee sadly shakit his heid :
" If we bide here for lang, we'll be bidin' for deid.
And yet, Geordie lad, I could gang weel content
If I'd tasted that haggis ma auld mither sent."
" That's droll," says McPhun ; " ye've jist speakit
ma mind.
Oh I ken it's a terrible thing tae be blind ;
And yet it's no' that that embitters ma lot—
It's missin' that braw muckle haggis ye've got."

For a while they were silent; then up once again
Spoke Private McPhee, though he whussilt wi'
    pain :
" And why should we miss it ?   Between you and
    me
We've legs for tae run, and we've eyes for tae see.
You lend me your shanks and I'll lend you ma
    sicht,
And we'll baith hae a kyte-fu' o' haggis the nicht."

Oh the sky it wis dourlike and dreepin' a wee,
When Private McPhun gruppit Private McPhee.
Oh the glaur it wis fylin' and crieshin' the grun',
When Private McPhee guidit Private McPhun.
" Keep clear o' them corpses—they're maybe no
    deid !
Haud on !   There's a big muckle crater aheid.
Look oot !   There's a sap ; we'll be haein' a
    coup.
A staur-shell !   For Godsake !   Doun', lad, on yer
    daup.
Bear aff tae yer richt. . . . Aw yer jist daein' fine :
Before the nicht's feenished on haggis we'll dine."

There wis death and destruction on every hand ;
There wis havoc and horror on Naebuddy's Land.

And the shells bickered doun wi' a crump and a
    glare,
And the hameless wee bullets were dingin' the air.
Yet on they went staggerin', cooryin' doun
When the stutter and cluck o' a Maxim crept roun'.
And the legs o' McPhun they were sturdy and
    stoot,
And McPhee on his back kept a bonnie look-oot.
" On, on, ma brave lad !   We're no faur frae the
    goal ;
I can hear the braw sweerin' o' Sergeant McCole."

But strength has its leemit, and Private McPhun,
Wi' a sab and a curse fell his length on the grun'.
Then Private McPhee shoutit doon in his ear :
" Jist think o' the haggis !   I smell it from here.
It's gushin' wi' juice, it's embaumin' the air ;
It's steamin' for us, and we're—jist—aboot—
    there."
Then Private McPhee answers :   " Dommit, auld
    chap !
For the sake o' that haggis I'll gang till I drap."
And he gets on his feet wi' a heave and a strain,
And onward he staggers in passion and pain.
And the flare and the glare and the fury increase,
Till you'd think they'd jist taken a' hell on a
    lease.

And on they go reelin' in peetifu' plight,
And someone is shoutin' away on their right ;
And someone is runnin', and noo they can hear
A sound like a prayer and a sound like a cheer ;
And swift through the crash and the flash and the
    din,
The lads o' the Hielands are bringin' them in.

" They're baith sairly woundit, but is it no' droll
Hoo they rave aboot haggis ? " says Sergeant
    McCole.
When hirplin alang comes wee Wullie McNair,
And they a' wonnert why he wis greetin' sae sair.
And he says : " I'd jist liftit it oot o' the pot,
And there it lay steamin' and savoury hot,
When sudden I dooked at the fleech o' a shell,
And it *drapped on the haggis and dinged it tae hell.*"

And oh, but the lads were fair taken aback ;
Then sudden the order wis passed tae attack,
And up from the trenches like lions they leapt,
And on through the nicht like a torrent they swept.
On, on, wi' their bayonets thirstin' before !
On, on tae the foe wi' a rush and a roar !
And wild to the welkin their battle-cry rang,
And doon on the Boches like tigers they sprang :
And there wisna a man but had death in his 'ee,
For he thocht o' the haggis o' Private McPhee.

THE LARK

FROM wrath-red dawn to wrath-red dawn,
The guns have brayed without abate ;
And now the sick sun looks upon
The bleared, blood-boltered fields of hate
As if it loathed to rise again.
How strange the hush !   Yet sudden, hark !
From yon down-trodden gold of grain,
The leaping rapture of a lark.

A fusillade of melody,
That sprays us from yon trench of sky ;
A new amazing enemy
We cannot silence though we try ;
A battery on radiant wings,
That from yon gap of golden fleece
Hurls at us hopes of such strange things
As joy and home and love and peace.

462

Pure heart of song ! do you not know
That we are making earth a hell ?
Or is it that you try to show
Life still is joy and all is well ?
Brave little wings ! Ah, not in vain
You beat into that bit of blue :
Lo ! we who pant in war's red rain
Lift shining eyes, see Heaven too.

THE ODYSSEY OF 'ERBERT 'IGGINS

Me and Ed and a stretcher
Out on the nootral ground.
(If there's one dead corpse, I'll betcher
There's a 'undred smellin' around.)
Me and Eddie O'Brian,
Both of the R.A.M.C.
" It's a 'ell of a night
For a soul to take flight,"
As Eddie remarks to me.
Me and Ed crawlin' 'omeward,
Thinkin' our job is done.
When sudden and clear.
Wot do we 'ear :
'Owl of a wounded 'Un.

" Got to take 'im," snaps Eddy :
" Got to take all we can.
'E may be a Germ
Wiv the 'eart of a worm

But, blarst 'im ! ain't 'e a man ? "
So 'e sloshes out fixin' a dressin'
('E'd always a medical knack),
When that wounded 'Un
'E rolls to 'is gun,
And 'e plugs me pal in the back.

Now what would you do ?   I arst you.
There was me slaughtered mate,
There was that 'Un
(I'd collered 'is gun),
A-snarlin' 'is 'ymn of 'ate.
Wot did I do ?   'Ere, whisper. . . .
'E'd a shiny bald top to 'is 'ead,
But when I got through,
Between me and you,
It was 'orrid and jaggy and red.

" 'Ang on like a limpet, Eddy.
Thank Gord ! you ain't dead after all."
It's slow and it's sure and it's steady
(Which is 'ard, for 'e's big and I'm small).
The rockets are shootin' and shinin',
It's rainin' a perishin' flood,
The bullets are buzzin' and whinin',
And I'm up to me stern in the mud.
There's all kinds of 'owlin' and 'ootin' ;

It's black as a bucket of tar ;
Oh, I'm doin' my bit,
But I'm 'avin' a fit,
And I wish I was 'ome wiv Mar.
" Stick on like a plaster, Eddy.
Old sport, you're a-slakin' your grip."
Gord ! But I'm crocky already ;
My feet, 'ow they slither and slip !
There goes the biff of a bullet.
The Boches have got us for fair
Another one—*Whut !*
The son of a slut !
'E managed to miss by a 'air.
'Ow ! Wot was it jabbed at me shoulder ?
Gave it a dooce of a wrench.
Is it Eddy or me
Wot's a-bleedin' so free ?
Crust ! but it's long to the trench.
I ain't just as strong as a Sandow,
And Ed ain't a flapper by far ;
I'm blamed if I understand 'ow
We've managed to get where we are,
But 'ere's for a bit of a breather.
" Steady there, Ed, 'arf a mo'.
Old pal, it's all right ;
It's a 'ell of a fight,
But are we down-'earted ? No-o-o."

Now war is a funny thing, ain't it ?
It's the rummiest sort of a go.
For when it's most real,
It's then that you feel
You're a-watchin' a cinema show.
'Ere's me wot's a barber's assistant.
Hey presto ! It's somewheres in France.
And I'm 'ere in a pit
Where a coal-box 'as 'it,
And it's all like a giddy romance.

The ruddy quick-firers are spittin',
The 'eavies are bellowin' 'ate,
And 'ere I am cashooly sittin',
And 'oldin' the 'ead of me mate.
Them gharstly green star-shells is beamin',
'Ot shrapnel is poppin' like rain,
And I'm sayin': "Bert 'Iggins, you're dreamin',
And you'll wake up in 'Ampstead again.

You'll wake up and 'ear yourself sayin' :
' Would you like, sir, to 'ave a shampoo ? '
'Stead of sheddin' yer blood
In the rain and the mud,
Which is some'ow the right thing to do ;
Which is some'ow yer 'oary-eyed dooty,
Wot you're doin' the best wot you can,
For 'Ampstead and 'ome and beauty,
And you've been and you've slaughtered a man,

A feller wot punctured your partner ;
Oh, you 'ammered 'im 'ard on the 'ead,
And you still see 'is eyes
Starin' bang at the skies,
And you ain't even sorry 'e's dead.
But you wish you was back in your diggin's
Asleep on your mouldy old stror.
Oh, you're doin' yer bit, 'Erbert 'Iggins,
But you ain't just enjoyin' the war."

" 'Ang on like a hoctopus, Eddy.
It's us for the bomb-belt again.
Except for the shrap
Which 'as 'it me a tap,
I'm feelin' as right as the rain.
It's my silly old feet wot are slippin',
It's as dark as a 'ogs'ead o' sin,
But don't be oneasy, my pippin,
I'm goin' to pilot you in.
It's my silly old 'ead wot is reelin'.
The bullets is buzzin' like bees.
Me shoulder's red-'ot,
And I'm bleedin' a lot,
And me legs is on'inged at the knees.
But we're staggerin' nearer and nearer.
Just stick it, old sport, play the game.

I make 'em out clearer and clearer,
Our trenches a-snappin' with flame.
Oh, we're stumblin' closer and closer.
'Ang on there, lad ! Just one more try.
Did you say : Put you down ? Damn it, no, sir !
I'll carry you in if I die.
By cracky ! old feller, they've seen us.
They're sendin' out stretchers for two.
Let's give 'em the hoorah between us
('Anged lucky we aren't booked through).
My flipper is mashed to a jelly.
A bullet 'as tickled your spleen.
We've shed lots of gore
And we're leakin' some more,
But—wot a hoccasion it's been !
Ho ! 'Ere comes the rescuin' party.
They're crawlin' out cautious and slow.
Come ! Buck up and greet 'em, my 'earty,
Shoulder to shoulder—so.
They mustn't think we was down-'earted.
Old pal, we was never down-'earted.
If they arsts us if we was down-'earted
We'll 'owl in their fyces : ' No-o-o.' "

A SONG OF WINTER WEATHER

It isn't the foe that we fear ;
It isn't the bullets that whine :
It isn't the business career
Of a shell, or the bust of a mine ;
It isn't the snipers who seek
To nip our young hopes in the bud :
No, it isn't the guns,
And it isn't the Huns—
It's the MUD,

      MUD,

         MUD.

It isn't the *mêlée* we mind.
That often is rather good fun.
It isn't the shrapnel we find
Obtrusive when rained by the ton ;
It isn't the bounce of the bombs
That gives us a positive pain :
It's the strafing we get
When the weather is wet—
It's the RAIN,

      RAIN,

         RAIN.

It isn't because we lack grit
We shrink from the horrors of war.
We don't mind the battle a bit;
In fact that is what we are for;
It isn't the rum-jars and things
Make us wish we were back in the fold:
It's the fingers that freeze
In the boreal breeze—
It's the COLD,
        COLD,
          COLD.

        Oh, the rain, the mud, and the cold,
        The cold, the mud, and the rain;
        With weather at zero it's hard for a
           hero
        From language that's rude to
           refrain.
        With porridgy muck to the knees,
        With sky that's a-pouring a flood,
        Sure the worst of our foes
        Are the pains and the woes
        Of the RAIN.
              the COLD.
                  and the MUD.

TIPPERARY DAYS

OH, weren't they the fine boys! You never saw
    the beat of them,
Singing all together with their throats bronze-bare;
Fighting-fit and mirth-mad, music in the feet of
    them,
Swinging on to glory and the wrath out there.
Laughing by and chaffing by, frolic in the smiles
    of them,
On the road, the white road, all the afternoon;
Strangers in a strange land, miles and miles and
    miles of them,
Battle-bound and heart-high, and singing this tune:

> *It's a long way to Tipperary,*
> *It's a long way to go;*
> *It's a long way to Tipperary,*
> *And the sweetest girl I know.*
> *Good-bye, Piccadilly,*
> *Farewell, Leicester Square:*
> *It's a long, long way to Tipperary,*
> *But my heart's right there.*

Come Yvonne and Juliette! Come Mimi and
    cheer for them !
Throw them flowers and kisses as they pass you by
Aren't they the lovely lads ! Haven't you a tear
    for them
Going out so gallantly to dare and die ?
What is it they're singing so ? Some high hymn
    of Motherland ?
Some immortal chanson of their Faith and King ?
Marseillaise or Brabançon, anthem of that other
    land,
Dears, let us remember it, that song they sing :

    " *C'est un chemin long ' to Tepararee,'*
      C'est un chemin long, c'est vrai ;
      C'est un chemin long ' to Tepararee,'
      Et la belle fille qu'je connais ;
      Bonjour, Peekadeely !
      Au revoir, Lestaire Squaire !
      C'est un chemin long ' to Tepararee,'
      Mais mon cœur ' ees zaire.' "

The gallant old " Contemptibles " ! There isn't
    much remains of them,
So full of fun and fitness, and a-singing in their
    pride ;
For some are cold as clabber and the corby picks
    the brains of them,

I'm gay !   You bet I *am* gay ;
But I wasn't a while ago.
If you'd seen me even to-day,
The darndest picture of woe,
With this Caliban mug of mine.
So ravaged and raw and red,
Turned to the wall—in fine,
Wishing that I was dead. . . .
What has happened since then,
Since I lay with my face to the wall,
The most despairing of men ?
Listen !   I'll tell you all.

That *poilu* across the way,
With the shrapnel wound in his head,
Has a sister : she came to-day
To sit awhile by his bed.
All morning I heard him fret :
" Oh, when will she come, Fleurette ? "

Then sudden, a joyous cry ;
The tripping of little feet ;
The softest, tenderest sigh ;
A voice so fresh and sweet ;
Clear as a silver bell,
Fresh as the morning dews :
" *C'est toi, c'est toi, Marcel !*
Mon frère, comme je suis heureuse ! "

So over the blanket's rim
I raised my terrible face,
And I saw—how I envied him!
A girl of such delicate grace;
Sixteen, all laughter and love;
As gay as a linnet, and yet
As tenderly sweet as a dove;
Half woman, half child—Fleurette.

Then I turned to the wall again.
(I was awfully blue, you see.)
And I thought with a bitter pain :
" Such visions are not for me."
So there like a log I lay,
All hidden, I thought, from view,
When sudden I heard her say :
" Ah ! Who is that *malheureux* ? "
Then briefly I heard him tell
(However he came to know)
How I'd smothered a bomb that fell
Into the trench, and so
None of my men were hit,
Though it busted me up a bit.

Well, I didn't quiver an eye,
And he chattered and there she sat ;
And I fancied I heard her sigh—
Though I wouldn't just swear to that.

And maybe she wasn't so bright,
Though she talked in a merry strain,
And I closed my eyes ever so tight,
Yet I saw her ever so plain :
Her dear little tilted nose,
Her delicate dimpled chin,
Her mouth like a budding rose,
And the glistening pearls within ;
Her eyes like the violet :
Such a rare little queen—Fleurette.

And at last when she rose to go,
The light was a little dim,
And I ventured to peep, and so
I saw her, graceful and slim,
And she kissed him and kissed him, and oh
How I envied and envied him !

So when she was gone I said
In rather a dreary voice
To him of the opposite bed :
" Ah, friend, how you must rejoice !
But me, I'm a thing of dread.
For me nevermore the bliss,
The thrill of a woman's kiss."

Then I stopped, for lo ! she was there,
And a great light shone in her eyes

And me! I could only stare,
I was taken so by surprise,
When gently she bent her head:
"*May I kiss you, Sergeant?*" she said.
Then she kissed my burning lips
With her mouth like a scented flower,
And I thrilled to the finger-tips,
And I hadn't even the power
To say: "God bless you, dear!"
And I felt such a precious tear
Fall on my withered cheek,
And darn it! I couldn't speak.

And so she went sadly away,
And I knew that my eyes were wet.
Ah, not to my dying day
Will I forget, forget!
Can you wonder now I am gay?
God bless her, that little Fleurette!

FUNK

WHEN your marrer bone seems 'oller,
And you're glad you ain't no taller,
And you're all a-shakin' like you 'ad the chills;
When your skin creeps like a pullet's,
And you're duckin' all the bullets,
And you're green as gorgonzola round the gills;
When your legs seem made of jelly,
And you're squeamish in the belly,
And you want to turn about and do a bunk:
For Gawd's sake, kid, don't show it!
Don't let your mateys know it—
You're just sufferin' from funk, funk, funk.

Of course there's no denyin'
That it ain't so easy tryin'
To grin and grip your rifle by the butt,
When the 'ole world rips asunder,
And you sees yer pal go under,
As a bunch of shrapnel sprays 'im on the
    nut;

I admit it's 'ard contrivin',
When you 'ears the shells arrivin',
To discover you're a bloomin' bit o' spunk ;
But, my lad, you've got to do it,
And your God will see you through it,
For wot 'E 'ates is funk, funk, funk.
So stand up, son ; look gritty,
And just 'um a lively ditty,
And only be afraid to be afraid ;
Just 'old yer rifle steady,
And 'ave yer bay'nit ready,
For that's the way good soldier-men is made.
And if you 'as to die,
As it sometimes 'appens, why,
Far better die a 'ero than a skunk ;
A-doin' of yer bit,
And so—to 'ell with it,
There ain't no bloomin' funk, funk, funk.

OUR HERO

"Flowers, only flowers—bring me dainty posies,
Blossoms for forgetfulness," that was all he said;
So we sacked our gardens, violets and roses,
Lilies white and bluebells laid we on his bed.
Soft his pale hands touched them, tenderly
    caressing;
Soft into his tired eyes came a little light;
Such a wistful love-look, gentle as a blessing;
There amid the flowers waited he the night.

"I would have you raise me; I can see the West
    then:
I would see the sun set once before I go."
So he lay a-gazing, seemed to be at rest then,
Quiet as a spirit in the golden glow.
So he lay a-watching rosy castles crumbling,
Moats of blinding amber, bastions of flame,
Rugged rifts of opal, crimson turrets tumbling;
So he lay a-dreaming till the shadows came.

"Open wide the window; there's a lark a-singing;
There's a glad lark singing in the evening sky.
How it's wild with rapture, radiantly winging:
Oh it's good to hear that when one has to die.
I am horror-haunted from the hell they found me;
I am battle-broken, all I want is rest.
Ah! It's good to die so, blossoms all around me,
And a kind lark singing in the golden West."

"Flowers, song and sunshine, just one thing is
        wanting,
Just the happy laughter of a little child."
So we brought out dearest, Doris all-enchanting;
Tenderly he kissed her; radiant he smiled.
"In the golden peace-time you will tell the story
How for you and yours, sweet, bitter deaths were
        ours. . . .
God bless little children!" So he passed to glory,
So we left him sleeping, still amid the flow'rs.

MY MATE

I'VE been sittin' starin', starin' at 'is muddy pair of
  boots,
And tryin' to convince meself it's 'im.
(Look out there, lad!   That sniper—'e's a dysey
  when 'e shoots ;
'E'll be layin' of you out the same as Jim.)
Jim as lies there in the dug-out wiv 'is blanket
  round 'is 'ead,
To keep 'is brains from mixin' wiv the mud ;
And 'is face as white as putty, and his overcoat all
  red,
Like 'e's spilt a bloomin' paint-pot—but it's blood.

And I'm tryin' to remember of a time we wasn't
  pals.
'Ow often we've played 'ookey, 'im and me ;
And sometimes it was music-'alls, and sometimes it
  was gals,
And even there we 'ad no disagree.
For when 'e copped Maria Jones, the one I liked
  the best,

I shook 'is 'and and loaned 'im 'arf a quid ;
I saw 'im through the parson's job, I 'elped 'im
  make 'is nest,
I even stood god-farther to the kid.

So when the war broke out, sez 'e : " Well, wot
  abaht it, Joe ? "
" Well, wot abaht it, lad ? " sez I to 'im.
'Is missis made a awful fuss, but 'e was mad to go
('E always was 'igh-sperrited was Jim).
Well, none of it's been 'eaven, and the most of it's
  been 'ell,
But we've shared our baccy, and we've 'alved our
  bread.
We'd all the luck at Wipers, and we shaved through
  Noove Chapelle,
And . . . that snipin' barstard gits 'im on the 'ead.

Now wot I wants to know is, why it wasn't me
  was took ?
I've only got meself, 'e stands for three.
I'm plainer than a louse, while 'e was 'andsome as a
  dook ;
'E always *was* a better man than me.
'E was goin' 'ome next Toosday ; 'e was 'appy as a
  lark,
And 'e'd just received a letter from 'is kid ;

And 'e struck a match to show me, as we stood
    there in the dark,
When . . . that bleedin' bullet got 'im on the lid.

'E was killed so awful sudden that 'e 'adn't time to
    die,
'E sorto jumped, and came down wiv a thud.
Them corpsy-lookin' star-shells kept a-streamin' in
    the sky,
And there 'e lay like nothin' in the mud.
And there 'e lay so quiet wiv no mansard to 'is 'ead,
And I'm sick, and blamed if I can understand :
The pots of 'alf and 'alf we've 'ad, and *zip !* like
    that—'e's dead,
Wiv the letter of 'is nipper in 'is 'and.

There's some as fights for freedom and there's
    some as fights for fun,
But me, my lad, I fights for bleedin' 'ate.
You can blame the war and blast it, but I 'opes it
    won't be done
Till I gets the bloomin' blood-price for me mate.
It'll take a bit o' bayonet to level up for Jim ;
Then if I'm spared I think I'll 'ave a bid
Wiv 'er that was Mariar Jones to take the place
    of 'im,
To sorter be a farther to 'is kid.

MILKING TIME

THERE's a drip of honeysuckle in the deep green
  lane ;
There's old Martin jogging homeward on his worn
  old wain ;
There are cherry petals falling, and a cuckoo calling,
  calling,
And a score of larks (God bless 'em) . . . but it's
  all pain, pain.
For you see I am not really there at all, not at all ;
For you see I'm in the trenches where the crump-
  crumps fall ;
And the bits o' shells are screaming and it's only
  blessed dreaming
That in fancy I am seeming back in old Saint Pol.

Oh I've thought of it so often since I've come down
  here ;
And I never dreamt that any place could be so
  dear ;

The silvered whinstone houses, and the rosy men
  in blouses.
And the kindly, white-capped women with their
  eyes spring-clear.
And mother's sitting knitting where her roses
  climb,
And the angelus is calling with a soft, soft chime,
And the sea-wind comes caressing, and the light's
  a golden blessing,
And Yvonne, Yvonne is guessing that it's milking
  time.

Oh it's Sunday, for she's wearing of her 'broidered
  gown ;
And she draws the pasture pickets and the cows
  come down ;
And their feet are powdered yellow, and their
  voices honey-mellow,
And they bring a scent of clover, and their eyes are
  brown.
And Yvonne is dreaming after, but her eyes are
  blue ;
And her lips are made for laughter, and her white
  teeth too ;
And her mouth is like a cherry, and a dimple mock·
  ing merry
Is lurking in the very cheek she turns to you.

So I walk beside her kindly, and she laughs at
    me ;
And I heap her arms with lilac from the lilac
    tree ;
And a golden light is welling, and a golden peace
    is dwelling,
And a thousand birds are telling how it's good
    to be.
And what are pouting lips for if they can't be
    kissed ?
And I've filled her arms with blossom so she can't
    resist ;
And the cows are sadly straying, and her mother
    must be saying
That Yvonne is long delaying . . . *God! How*
    close that missed !

A nice polite reminder that the Boche are nigh ;
That we're here to fight like devils, and if need be
    die ;
That from kissing pretty wenches to the frantic
    firing-benches
Of the battered, tattered trenches is a far, far cry.
Yet still I'm sitting dreaming in the glare and
    grime ;
And once again I'm hearing of them church-bells
    chime ;

And how I wonder whether in the golden summer
  weather
We will fetch the cows together when it's milking
  time ! . . .

English voice, months later :
" *Ow, Bill ! A rottin' Frenchy. Whew ! 'E ain't
  'arf prime. . . .*"

YOUNG FELLOW MY LAD

" WHERE are you going, Young Fellow My Lad,
On this glittering morn of May ? "
" I'm going to join the Colours, Dad ;
They're looking for men, they say."
" But you're only a boy, Young Fellow My Lad ;
You aren't obliged to go."
" I'm seventeen and a quarter, Dad,
And ever so strong, you know."

*　　*　　*　　*　　*　　*

" So you're off to France, Young Fellow My Lad,
And you're looking so fit and bright."
" I'm terribly sorry to leave you, Dad,
But I feel that I'm doing right."
" God bless you and keep you, Young Fellow My
Lad,
You're all of my life, you know."
" Don't worry.　I'll soon be back, dear Dad,
And I'm awfully proud to go."

*　　*　　*　　*　　*　　*

" Why don't you write, Young Fellow My Lad ?
I watch for the post each day ;
And I miss you so, and I'm awfully sad,
And it's months since you went away.
And I've had the fire in the parlour lit,
And I'm keeping it burning bright
Till my boy comes home ; and here I sit
Into the quiet night."

*   *   *   *   *   *

" What is the matter, Young Fellow My Lad ?
No letter again to-day,
Why did the postman look so sad,
And sigh as he turned away ?
I hear them tell that we've gained new ground,
But a terrible price we've paid :
God grant, my boy, that you're safe and sound ;
But oh I'm afraid, afraid."

*   *   *   *   *   *

" They've told me the truth, Young Fellow My
    Lad :
You'll never come back again.
(*Oh God ! the dreams and the dreams I've had,*
And the hopes I've nursed in vain !)
For you passed in the night, Young Fellow My Lad,
And you proved in the cruel test
Of the screaming shell and the battle hell
That my boy was one of the best."

" So you'll live, you'll live, Young Fellow My
     Lad,
In the gleam of the evening star,
In the woodnote wild and the laugh of the child,
In all sweet things that are.
And you'll never die, my wonderful boy,
While life is noble and true ;
For all our beauty and hope and joy
We will owe to our lads like you."

A SONG OF THE SANDBAGS

No, Bill, I'm not a-spooning out no patriotic tosh
(The cove be'ind the sandbags ain't a death-or-
    glory cuss).
And though I strafes 'em good and 'ard I doesn't
    'ate the Boche,
I guess they're mostly decent, just the same as most
    of us.
I guess they loves their 'omes and kids as much as
    you or me ;
And just the same as you or me they'd rather shake
    than fight ;
And if we'd 'appened to be born at Berlin-on-the-
    Spree,
We'd be out there, with 'Ans and Fritz, dead sure
    that we was right.

    A-standin' up to the sandbags,
    It's funny the thoughts wot come ;
    Starin' into the darkness,
    'Earin' the bullets 'um ;

(Zing! Zip! Ping! Rip!
'Ark 'ow the bullets 'um!)
A-leanin' against the sandbags
Wiv me rifle under me ear,
Oh, I've 'ad more thoughts on a sentry-go
Than I used to 'ave in a year.

I wonder, Bill, if 'Ans and Fritz is wonderin' like
　me
Wot's at the bottom of it all? Wot all the
　slaughter's for?
'E thinks 'e's right (of course 'e ain't), but this we
　both agree,
If them as made it 'ad to fight, there wouldn't be
　no war.
If them as lies in feather beds while we kips in the
　mud ;
If them as makes their fortoons while we fights for
　'em like 'ell ;
If them as slings their pots of ink just 'ad to sling
　their blood :
By Crust ! I'm thinkin' there'ud be another tale to
　tell.

Shiverin' up to the sandbags,
With a hicicle 'stead of a spine,
Don't it seem funny the things you think
'Ere in the firin' line :

B

(*Wee! Whut! Ziz! Zut!*
Lord! 'Ow the bullets whine!)
Hunkerin' down when a star-shell
Cracks in a sputter of light,
You can jaw to yer soul by the sandbags
Most any old time o' night.

They talks o' England's glory and a-'oldin' of our
trade,
Of Empire and 'igh destiny until we're fair film-
flammed ;
But if it's for the likes o' that that bloody war is
made,
Then wot I say is : Empire and 'igh destiny be
damned !
There's only one good cause, Bill, for poor blokes
like us to fight :
That's self-defence, for 'earth and 'ome, and them
that bears our name :
And that's wot I'm a-doin' by the sandbags 'ere to-
night. . . .
But Fritz out there will tell you 'e's a-doin' of the
same.

Starin' over the sandbags,
Sick of the 'ole damn thing ;
Firin' to keep meself awake,
'Earin' the bullets sing.

(Hiss! Twang! Tsing! Pang!
Saucy the bullets sing.)
Dreamin' 'ere by the sandbags
Of a day when war will cease,
When 'Ans and Fritz and Bill and me
Will clink our mugs in fraternity,
And the Brotherhood of Labour will be
The Brotherhood of Peace.

ON THE WIRE

Oh God, take the sun from the sky !
It's burning me, scorching me up.
God, can't You hear my cry ?
Water !   A poor, little cup !
It's laughing, the cursed sun !
See how it swells and swells
Fierce as a hundred hells !
God, will it never have done ?
It's searing the flesh on my bones ;
It's beating with hammers red
My eyeballs into my head ;
It's parching my very moans.
See !   It's the size of the sky,
And the sky is a torrent of fire,
Foaming on me as I lie
Here on the wire . . . the wire. . . .

Of the thousands that wheeze and hum
Heedlessly over my head,
Why can't a bullet come,
Pierce to my brain instead,

498

Blacken for ever my brain,
Finish for ever my pain ?
Here in the hellish glare
Why must I suffer so ?
Is it God doesn't care ?
Is it God doesn't know ?
Oh, to be killed outright,
Clean in the clash of the fight !
That is a golden death,
That is a boon ; but this . . .
Drawing an anguished breath
Under a hot abyss,
Under a stooping sky
Of seething, sulphurous fire,
Scorching me up as I lie
Here on the wire . . . the wire. . . !

Hasten, Oh God, Thy night !
Hide from my eyes the sight
Of the body I stare and see
Shattered so hideously.
I can't believe that it's mine.
My body was white and sweet,
Flawless and fair and fine,
Shapely from head to feet ;
Oh no, I can never be
The thing of horror I see

Under the rifle fire,
Trussed on the wire . . . the wire. . . .
Of night and of death I dream ;
Night that will bring me peace,
Coolness and starry gleam,
Stillness and death's release :
Ages and ages have passed—
Lo ! it is night at last.
Night ! but the guns roar out,
Night ! but the hosts attack.
Red and yellow and black
Geysers of doom upspout.
Silver and green and red
Star-shells hover and spread.
Yonder off to the right
Fiercely kindles the fight ;
Roaring near and more near,
Thundering now in my ear ;
Close to me, close . . . Oh, hark !
Someone moans in the dark.
I hear, but I cannot see,
I hear as the rest retire,
Someone is caught like me,
Caught on the wire . . . the wire. . .

Again the shuddering dawn,
Weird and wicked and wan ;

Again, and I've not yet gone.
The man whom I heard is dead.
Now I can understand :
A bullet hole in his head,
A pistol gripped in his hand.
Well, he knew what to do,—
Yes, and now I know too . . .

Hark the resentful guns !
Oh, how thankful am I
To think my beloved ones
Will never know how I die !
I've suffered more than my share ;
I'm shattered beyond repair ;
I've fought like a man the fight,
And now I demand the right
(God ! how his fingers cling !)
To do without shame this thing.
Good ! there's a bullet still ;
Now I am ready to fire ;
Blame me, God, if You will,
Here on the wire . . . the wire. . . .

BILL'S GRAVE

I'M gatherin' flowers by the wayside to lay on the
grave of Bill ;
I've sneaked away from the billet, 'cause Jim
wouldn't understand ;
'E'd call me a silly fat'ead, and larf till it made 'im
ill,
To see me 'ere in the cornfield, wiv a big bookay in
me 'and.

For Jim and me we are rough 'uns, but Bill was
one o' the best ;
We 'listed and learned together to larf at the wust
wot comes ;
Then Bill copped a packet proper, and took 'is
departure West,
So sudden 'e 'adn't a minit to say good-bye to 'is
chums.

And they took me to where 'e was planted, a sort
    of a measly mound,
And, thinks I, 'ow Bill would be tickled, bein' so
    soft and queer,
If I gathered a bunch o' them wild-flowers, and
    sort of arranged them round
Like a kind of a bloody head-piece . . . and that's
    the reason I'm 'ere.

But not for the love of glory I wouldn't 'ave Jim
    to know.
'E'd call me a slobberin' Cissy, and larf till 'is sides
    was sore ;
I'd 'ave larfed at meself meself too, it isn't so long
    ago ;
But some'ow it changes a feller, 'avin' a taste of
    war.

It 'elps a man to be 'elpful, to know wot 'is pals is
    worth
(Them golden poppies is blazin' like lamps some
    fairy 'as lit) ;
I'm fond o' them big white dysies. . . . Now Jim's
    o' the salt o' the earth ;
But 'e 'as got a tongue wot's a terror, and 'e ain't
    sentimental a bit.

I likes them blue chaps wot's 'idin' so shylike
 among the corn.
Won't Bill be glad ! We was allus thicker 'n
 thieves, us three.
Why ! 'Oo's that singin' so 'earty ! *Jim !* And as
 sure as I'm born,
'E's there in the giddy cornfields, a-gatherin'
 flowers like me.

Quick ! Drop me posy be'ind me. I watches 'im
 for a while,
Then I says : " Wot 'o, there, Chummy ! Wot
 price the little bookay ? "
And 'e starts like a bloke wot's guilty, and 'e says
 with a sheepish smile :
" She's a bit of orl right, the widder wot keeps the
 estaminay."

So 'e goes away in a 'urray, and I wishes 'im best
 'o luck,
And I picks up me bunch o' wild-flowers, and the
 light's gettin' sorto dim,
When I makes me way to the boneyard, and . .
 I stares like a man wot's stuck,
For wot do I see ? *Bill's grave-mound strewn with
 the flowers of Jim.*

Of course I won't never tell 'im, bein' a tactical lad ;
And Jim parley-voos to the widder : " Trez beans,
    lamoor ; compree ? "
Oh, 'e'd die of shame if 'e knew I knew; but say !
    won't Bill be glad
When 'e stares through the bleedin' clods and
    sees the blossoms of Jim and me !

JEAN DESPREZ

Oh ye whose hearts are resonant, and ring to
　　War's romance,
Hear ye the story of a boy, a peasant boy of
　　France ;
A lad uncouth and warped with toil, yet who, when
　　trial came,
Could feel within his soul upleap and soar the
　　sacred flame ;
Could stand upright, and scorn and smite, as only
　　heroes may :
Oh, harken ! Let me try to tell the tale of Jean
　　Desprez.

With fire and sword the Teuton horde was ravag-
　　ing the land,
And there was darkness and despair, grim death
　　on every hand ;
Red fields of slaughter sloping down to ruin's
　　black abyss ;
The wolves of war ran evil-fanged, and little did
　　they miss.

And on they came with fear and flame, to burn and
    loot and slay.

Until they reached the red-roofed croft, the home
    of Jean Desprez.

" Rout out the village, one and all ! " the Uhlan
    Captain said.

" Behold ! Some hand has fired a shot. My trum-
    peter is dead.

Now shall they Prussian vengeance know ; now
    shall they rue the day,

For by this sacred German slain, ten of these dogs
    shall pay."

They drove the cowering peasants forth, women
    and babes and men,

And from the last, with many a jeer, the Captain
    chose he ten ;

Ten simple peasants, bowed with toil ; they stood,
    they knew not why,

Against the grey wall of the church, hearing their
    children cry ;

Hearing their wives and mothers wail, with faces
    dazed they stood.

A moment only. . . . *Ready! Fire!* They
    weltered in their blood.

But there was one who gazed unseen, who heard
    the frenzied cries,

Who saw these men in sabots fall before their
    children's eyes ;
A Zouave wounded in a ditch, and knowing death
    was nigh,
He laughed with joy : " Ah ! here is where I settle
    ere I die."
He clutched his rifle once again, and long he aimed
    and well. . . .
A shot !   Beside his victims ten the Uhlan Captain
    fell.

They dragged the wounded Zouave out ; their rage
    was like a flame.
With bayonets they pinned him down, until their
    Major came.
A blonde, full-blooded man he was, and arrogant
    of eye ;
He stared to see with shattered skull his favourite
    Captain lie.
" Nay, do not finish him so quick, this foreign
    swine," he cried ;
" Go nail him to the big church door : he shall be
    crucified."

With bayonets through hands and feet they nailed
    the Zouave there,
And there was anguish in his eyes, and horror in
    his stare ;

" Water !   A single drop ! " he moaned ; but how
    tney jeered at him,
And mocked him with an empty cup, and saw his
    sight grow dim ;
And as in agony of death with blood his lips were
    wet,
The Prussian Major gaily laughed, and lit a
    cigarette.

But 'mid the white-faced villagers who cowered in
    horror by,
Was one who saw the woeful sight, who heard the
    woeful cry :
" Water !   One little drop, I beg !   For love of
    Christ who died. . . ."
It was the little Jean Desprez who turned and stole
    aside ;
It was the little bare-foot boy who came with cup
    abrim,
And walked up to the dying man, and gave the
    drink to him.

A roar of rage !   They seize the boy ; they tear
    him fast away.
The Prussian Major swings around ; no longer is
    he gay.

His teeth are wolfishly a-gleam; his face all dark
    with spite :
" Go, shoot the brat," he snarls, " that dare defy
    our Prussian might.
Yet stay ! I have another thought. I'll kindly
    be, and spare ;
Quick ! give the lad a rifle charged, and set him
    squarely there,
And bid him shoot, and shoot to kill. Haste !
    Make him understand.
The dying dog he fain would save shall perish by
    his hand.
And all his kindred they shall see, and all shall
    curse his name,
Who bought his life at such a cost, the price of
    death and shame."

They brought the boy, wild-eyed with fear; they
    made him understand ;
They stood him by the dying man, a rifle in his
    hand.
" Make haste ! " said they ; " the time is short, and
    you must kill or die."
The Major puffed his cigarette, amusement in his
    eye.
And then the dying Zouave heard, and raised his
    weary head :

" Shoot, son, 'twill be the best for both ; shoot swift
    and straight," he said.
" Fire first and last, and do not flinch ; for lost to
    hope am I ;
And I will murmur : *Vive La France !* and bless
    you ere I die."

Half-blind with blows the boy stood there ; he
    seemed to swoon and sway ;
Then in that moment woke the soul of little Jean
    Desprez.
He saw the woods go sheening down ; the larks
    were singing clear ;
And oh ! the scents and sounds of spring, how
    sweet they were ! how dear !
He felt the scent of new-mown hay, a soft breeze
    fanned his brow ;
Oh, God ! the paths of peace and toil ! How
    precious were they now !
The summer days and summer ways, how bright
    with hope and bliss !
The autumn such a dream of gold , . . and all
    must end in this :
This shining rifle in his hand, that shambles all
    around ;
The Zouave there with dying glare ; the blood upon
    the ground ;

The brutal faces round him ringed, the evil eyes
  aflame ;
That Prussian bully standing by, as if he watched
  a game.
" Make haste and shoot," the Major sneered ; " a
  minute more I give ;
A minute more to kill your friend, if you yourself
  would live."

They only saw a bare-foot boy, with blanched and
  twitching face ;
They did not see within his eyes the glory of his
  race ;
The glory of a million men who for fair France
  have died,
The splendour of self-sacrifice that will not be
  denied.
Yet . . . he was but a peasant boy, and oh ! but
  life was sweet. . . .
" Your minute's nearly gone, my lad," he heard a
  voîce repeat.
" Shoot !   Shoot ! " the dying Zouave moaned ;
  " Shoot !   Shoot ! " the soldiers said.
Then Jean Desprez reached out and shot . . . *the
  Prussian Major dead !*

GOING HOME

I'M goin' 'ome to Blighty—ain't I glad to 'ave the
    chance !
I'm loaded up wiv fightin', and I've 'ad my fill o'
    France ;
I'm feelin' so excited-like, I want to sing and dance,
       For I'm goin' 'ome to Blighty in the
        mawnin'.

I'm goin' 'ome to Blighty : can you wonder as I'm
      gay ?
I've got a wound I wouldn't sell for 'alf a year o'
      pay ;
A harm that's mashed to jelly in the nicest sort o'
      way,
       For it takes me 'ome to Blighty in the
        mawnin'.

'Ow everlastin' keen I was on gettin' to the front !
I'd ginger for a dozen, and I 'elped to bear the
    brunt ;
But Cheese and Crust ! I'm crazy, now I've done
    me little stunt,
       To sniff the air of Blighty in the mawnin'.

I've looked upon the wine that's white, and on the
    wine that's red ;
I've looked on cider flowin', till it fairly turned me
    'ead ;
But oh, the finest scoff will be, when all is done and
    said,
        A pint o' Bass in Blighty in the mawnin' !

I'm goin' back to Blighty, which I left to strafe the
    'Un ;
I've fought in bloody battles, and I've 'ad a 'eap of
    fun ;
But now me flipper's busted, and I fink me dooty's
    done,
        And I'll kiss me gel in Blighty in the
          mawnin'.

Oh, there be furrin' lands to see, and some of 'em
    be fine ;
And there be furrin' gels to kiss, and scented
    furrin' wine ;
But there's no land like England, and no other gel
    like mine :
        Thank Gawd for dear old Blighty in the
          mawnin'.

COCOTTE

When a girl's sixteen, and as poor as she's
    pretty,
And she hasn't a friend and she hasn't a home,
Heigh-ho! She's as safe in Paris city
As a lamb night-strayed where the wild wolves
    roam;
And that was I; oh, it's seven years now
(Some water's run down the Seine since then),
And I've almost forgotten the pangs and the tears
    now,
And I've almost taken the measure of men.

Oh, I found me a lover who loved me only,
Artist and poet, and almost a boy.
And my heart was bruised, and my life was
    lonely,
And him I adored with a wonderful joy.
If he'd come to me with his pockets empty,
How we'd have laughed in a garret gay!

515

But he was rich, and in radiant plenty
We lived in a villa at Viroflay.

Then came the War, and of bliss bereft me;
Then came the call, and he went away;
All that he had in the world he left me,
With the rose-wreathed villa at Viroflay.
Then came the news and the tragic story:
My hero, my splendid lover was dead,
Sword in hand on the field of glory,
And he died with my name on his lips, they said.

So here am I in my widow's mourning,
The weeds I've really no right to wear;
And women fix me with eyes of scorning,
Call me " cocotte," but I do not care.
And men look at me with eyes that borrow
The brightness of love, but I turn away;
Alone, say I, I will live with Sorrow,
In my little villa at Viroflay.

And lo! I'm living alone with *Pity*,
And they say that pity from love's not far;
Let me tell you all: last week in the city
I took the metro at Saint Lazare;
And the carriage was crowded to overflowing,
And when there entered at Chateaudun

Two wounded *poilus* with medals showing,
I eagerly gave my seat to one.

You should have seen them : they'd slipped death's
        clutches,
But sadder a sight you will rarely find ;
One had a leg off and walked on crutches,
The other, a bit of a boy, was blind.
And they both sat down, and the lad was trying
To grope his way as a blind man tries ;
And half of the women around were crying,
And some of the men had tears in their eyes.

How he stirred me, this blind boy, clinging
Just like a child to his crippled chum.
But I did not cry. Oh no ; a singing
Came to my heart for a year so dumb.
Then I knew that at three-and-twenty
There is wonderful work to be done,
Comfort and kindness and joy in plenty,
Peace and light and love to be won.

Oh, thought I, could mine eyes be given
To one who will live in the dark alway !
To love and to serve—'twould make life Heaven
Here in my villa at Viroflay.

So I left my *poilus* : and now you wonder
Why to-day I am so elate. . . .
Look ! In the glory of sunshine yonder
They're bringing my blind boy in at the gate.

MY BAY'NIT

WHEN first I left Blighty they gave me a bay'nit,
And told me it 'ad to be smothered wiv gore;
But blimey! I 'aven't been able to stain it,
So far as I've gone, wiv the vintage of war.
For ain't it a fraud! When a Boche and yours
    truly
Gits into a mix in the grit and the grime,
'E jerks up 'is 'ands wiv a yell, and 'e's duly
            Part of me outfit every time.

        Left, right, Hans and Fritz!
        Goose step, keep up yer mits!
        Oh my, ain't it a shyme!
        Part of me outfit every time.

At toastin' a biscuit me bay'nit's a dandy;
I've used it to open a bully beef can;
For pokin' the fire it comes in werry 'andy;
For any old thing but for stickin' a man.

'Ow often I've said : " 'Ere, I'm goin' to press you
Into a 'Un till you're seasoned for prime,"
And fiercely I rushes to do it, but bless you !
        Part of me outfit every time.

        Lor, yus ; *don't* they look glad ?
        Right O ! 'Owl Kamerad !
        Oh my, always the syme !
        Part of me outfit every time.

I'm 'untin' for someone to christen me bay'nit,
Some nice juicy Chewton wot's fightin' in France ;
I'm fairly down'earted—'ow *can* yer explain it ?
I keeps gettin' prisoners every chance.
As soon as they sees me they ups and surrenders,
Extended like monkeys wot's tryin' to climb ;
And I uses me bay'nit—to slit their suspenders—
        Part of me outfit every time.

        Four 'Uns ; lor, wot a bag !
        'Ere, Fritz, sample a fag !
        Oh my, ain't it a gyme !
        Part of me outfit every time.

CARRY ON !

It's easy to fight when everything's right,
And you're mad with the thrill and the glory ;
It's easy to cheer when victory's near,
And wallow in fields that are gory.
It's a different song when everything's wrong,
When you're feeling infernally mortal ;
When it's ten against one, and hope there is none,
Buck up, little soldier, and chortle :

> Carry on ! Carry on !
> There isn't much punch in your blow.
> You're glaring and staring and hitting out
>   blind ;
> You're muddy and bloody, but never you mind.
> Carry on ! Carry on !
> You haven't the ghost of a show.
> It's looking like death, but while you've a
>   breath,
> Carry on, my son ! Carry on !

And so in the strife of the battle of life
It's easy to fight when you're winning ;
It's easy to slave, and starve and be brave,
When the dawn of success is beginning.
But the man who can meet despair and defeat
With a cheer, there's the man of God's choosing ;
The man who can fight to Heaven's own height
Is the man who can fight when he's losing.

Carry on ! Carry on !
Things never were looming so black ;
But show that you haven't a cowardly streak,
And though you're unlucky you never are
weak.
Carry on ! Carry on !
Brace up for another attack.
It's looking like hell, but—you never can tell :
Carry on, old man ! Carry on !

There are some who drift out in the deserts of
doubt,
And some who in brutishness wallow ;
There are others, I know, who in piety go,
Because of a Heaven to follow.
But to labour with zest, and to give of your best,
For the sweetness and joy of the giving ;
To help folks along with a hand and a song :
Why, there's the real sunshine of living.

Carry on !   Carry on !
Fight the good fight and true ;
Believe in your mission, greet life with a cheer ;
There's big work to do and that's why you are
here.
Carry on !   Carry on !
Let the world be the better for you ;
And at last when you die, let this be your cry :
Carry on, my soul !   Carry on !

OVER THE PARAPET

ALL day long when the shells sail over
I stand at the sandbags and take my chance;
But at night, at night I'm a reckless rover,
And over the parapet gleams Romance.
Romance! Romance! How I've dreamed it, writing
Dreary old records of money and mart,
Me with my head chuckful of fighting
And the blood of vikings to thrill my heart.

But little I thought that my time was coming,
Sudden and splendid, supreme and soon;
And here I am with the bullets humming
As I crawl and I curse the light of the moon.
Out alone, for adventure thirsting,
Out in mysterious No Man's Land;
Prone with the dead when a star-shell, bursting,
Flares on the horrors on every hand.

There are ruby stars and they drip and wiggle ;
And the grasses gleam in a light blood-red ;
There are emerald stars, and their tails they
     wriggle,
And ghastly they glare on the face of the dead.
But the worst of all are the stars of whiteness,
That spill in a pool of pearly flame,
Pretty as gems in their silver brightness,
And etching a man for a bullet's aim.

Yet oh, it's great to be here with danger,
Here in the weird, death-pregnant dark,
In the devil's pasture a stealthy ranger,
When the moon is decently hiding.   Hark !
What was that ?   Was it just the shiver
Of an eerie wind or a clammy hand ?
The rustle of grass, or the passing quiver
Of one of the ghosts of No Man's Land ?

It's only at night when the ghosts awaken,
And gibber and whisper horrible things ;
For to every foot of this God-forsaken
Zone of jeopard some horror clings.
Ugh !   What was that ?   It felt like a jelly,
That flattish mound in the noisome grass ;
You three big rats running free of its belly,
Out of my way and let me pass !

But if there's horror, there's beauty, wonder ;
The trench lights gleam and the rockets play.
That flood of magnificent orange yonder
Is a battery blazing miles away.
With a rush and a singing a great shell passes ;
The rifles resentfully bicker and brawl,
And here I crouch in the dew-drenched grasses,
And look and listen and love it all.

God ! what a life ! But I must make haste now,
Before the shadow of night be spent.
It's little the time there is to waste now,
If I'd do the job for which I was sent.
My bombs are right and my clippers ready,
And I wriggle out to the chosen place,
When I hear a rustle. . . . Steady ! . . . Steady !
Who am I staring slap in the face ?

There in the dark I can hear him breathing,
A foot away, and as still as death ;
And my heart beats hard, and my brain is seething,
And I know he's a Hun by the smell of his
    breath.
Then : " Will you surrender ? " I whisper hoarsely,
For it's death, swift death to utter a cry.
" English schwein-hund ! " he murmurs coarsely.
" Then we'll fight it out in the dark," say I.

So we grip and we slip and we trip and wrestle
There in the gutter of No Man's Land ;
And I feel my nails in his wind-pipe nestle,
And he tries to gouge, but I bite his hand.
And he tries to squeal, but I squeeze him tighter :
" Now," I say, " I can kill you fine ;
But tell me first, you Teutonic blighter !
Have you any children ? " He answers : " Nein."

Nine ! Well, I cannot kill such a father,
So I tie his hands and I leave him there.
Do I finish my little job ? Well, rather ;
And I get home safe with some light to spare.
Heigh-ho ! by day it's just prosy duty,
Doing the same old song and dance ;
But oh ! with the night—joy, glory, beauty :
Over the parapet—Life, Romance !

THE BALLAD OF SOULFUL SAM

You want me to tell you a story, a yarn of the
    firin' line,
Of our thin red kharki 'eroes, out there where the
    bullets whine ;
Out there where the bombs are bustin', and the
    cannons like 'ell-doors slam—
Just order another drink, boys, and I'll tell you of
    Soulful Sam.

Oh, Sam, he was never 'ilarious, though I've 'ad
    some mates as was wus ;
He 'adn't C.B. on his programme, he never was
    known to cuss.
For a card or a skirt or a beer-mug he 'adn't a
    friendly word ;
But when it came down to Scriptures, say ! wasn't
    he just a bird !

He always 'ad tracts in his pocket, the which he
    would haste to present,
And though the fellers would use them in ways that
    they never was meant,

I used to read 'em religious, and frequent I've been
    impressed
By some of them bundles of 'oly dope he carried
    around in his vest.

For I—and oh, 'ow I shudder at the 'orror the
    word conveys!
'Ave been—let me whisper it 'oarsely—a gambler
    'alf of me days;
A gambler you 'ear—a gambler. It makes me
    wishful to weep,
And yet 'ow it's true, my brethren!—I'd rather
    gamble than sleep.

I've gambled the 'ole world over, from Monte
    Carlo to Maine;
From Dawson City to Dover, from San Francisco
    to Spain.
Cards! They 'ave been me ruin. They've taken
    me pride and me pelf,
And when I'd no one to play with—why, I'd go
    and I'd play by meself.

And Sam 'e would sit and watch me, as I shuffled a
    greasy deck,
And 'e'd say: " You're bound to Perdition." And
    I'd answer: " Git off me neck! "

And that's 'ow we came to get friendly, though
    built on a different plan,
Me wot's a desprite gambler, 'im sich a good young
    man.

But on to me tale.   Just imagine . . . Darkness!
    The battle-front!
The furious 'Uns attackin'!   Us ones a-bearin' the
    brunt!
Me crouchin' be'ind a sandbag, tryin' 'ard to keep
    calm,
When I 'ears someone singin' a 'ymn toon; be'old!
    it is Soulful Sam.

Yes; right in the crash of the combat, in the fury
    of flash and flame,
'E was shootin' and singin' serenely as if 'e enjoyed
    the same.
And there in the 'eat of the battle, as the 'ordes of
    demons attacked,
He dipped down into 'is tunic, and 'e 'anded me
    out a tract.

Then a star-shell flared, and I read it: Oh, Flee
    From the Wrath to Come!
Nice cheerful subject, I tell yer, when you're 'earin'
    the bullets 'um.

And before I 'ad time to thank 'im, just one of
    them bits of lead
Comes slingin' along in a 'urry, and it 'its my
    partner. . . . Dead ?

No, siree ! not by a long sight ! For it plugged
    'im 'ard on the chest,
Just where 'e'd tracts for a army corps stowed
    away in 'is vest.
On its mission of death that bullet 'ustled along,
    and it caved
A 'ole in them tracts to 'is 'ide, boys—but the life o'
    me pal was saved.

And there as 'e showed me in triumph, and 'orror
    was chokin' me breath,
On came another bullet on its 'orrible mission of
    death ;
On through the night it cavorted, seekin' its 'aven
    of rest,
And it zipped through a crack in the sandbags, and
    it wolloped me bang in the breast.

Was I killed, do you ask ?   Oh no, boys.   Why
    am I sittin' 'ere
Gazin' with mournful vision at a mug long empty
    of beer ?

With a throat as dry as a—oh. thanky! I don't
 much mind if I do.
Beer with a dash of 'Ollands, that's my particular
 brew.

Yes, that was a terrible moment.   It 'ammered me
 'ard o'er the 'eart ;
It bowled me down like a ninepin, and I looked for
 the gore to start ;
And I saw in the flash of a moment, in that thunder
 of hate and strife,
Me wretched past like a pitchur—the sins of a
 gambler's life.

For I 'ad no tracts to save me, to thwart that mad
 missile's doom ;
I 'ad no pious pamphlets to 'elp me to cheat the
 tomb ;
I 'ad no 'oly leaflets to baffle a bullet's aim ;
I'd only—a deck of cards, boys, but . . . *it seemed
 to do just the same.*

ONLY A BOCHE

WE brought him in from between the lines : we'd
    better have let him lie :
For what's the use of risking one's skin for a *type*
    that's going to die ?
What's the use of tearing him loose under a gruel-
    ling fire,
When he's shot in the head, and worse than dead,
    and all messed up on the wire ?
However, I say, we brought him in. *Diable !*
    The mud was bad ;
The trench was crooked and greasy and high, and
    oh, what a time we had !
And often we slipped, and often we tripped, but
    never he made a moan ;
And how we were wet with blood and with sweat !
    But we carried him in like our own.

Now there he lies in the dug-out dim, awaiting the
    ambulance,
And the doctor shrugs his shoulders at him, and
    remarks : " He hasn't a chance."

533

And we squat and smoke at our game of bridge on
    the glistening, straw-packed floor,
And above our oaths we can hear his breath deep
    drawn in a kind of snore.

For the dressing station is long and low, and the
    candles gutter dim,
And the mean light falls on the cold clay walls and
    our faces bristly and grim ;
And we flap our cards on the lousy straw, and we
    laugh and jibe as we play,
And you'd never know that the cursed foe was less
    than a mile away.
As we con our cards in the rancid gloom, op
    pressed by that snoring breath,
You'd never dream that our broad roof-beam was
    swept by the broom of death.

Heigh-ho ! My turn for the dummy hand ; I rise
    and I stretch a bit ;
The fetid air is making me yawn, and my cigarette's
    unlit,
So I go to the nearest candle flame, and the man
    we brought is there,
And his face is white in the shabby light, and I
    stand at his feet and stare.

Stand for awhile, and quietly stare : for strange
though it seems to be,
The dying Boche on the stretcher there has a queer
resemblance to me.

It gives one a kind of a turn, you know, to come
on a thing like that.
It's just as if I were lying there, with a turban of
blood for a hat,
Lying there in a coat grey-green instead of a coat
grey-blue,
With one of my eyes all shot away, and my brain
half tumbling through ;
Lying there with a chest that heaves like a bellows
up and down,
And a cheek as white as snow on a grave, and lips
that are coffee brown.

And confound him, too ! He wears, like me, on
his finger a wedding ring,
And around his neck, as around my own, by a
greasy bit of string,
A locket hangs with a woman's face, and I turn it
about to see :
Just as I thought . . . on the other side the faces
of children three ;

Clustered together cherub-like, three little laugh-
      ing girls,
With the usual tiny rosebud mouths and the usual
      silken curls.
" Zut ! " I say, " he has beaten me ; for me, I have
      only two,"
And I push the locket beneath his shirt, feeling a
      little blue.

Oh, it isn't cheerful to see a man, the marvellous
      work of God,
Crushed in the mutilation mill, crushed to a smeary
      clod ;
Oh, it isn't cheerful to hear him moan, but it isn't
      that I mind,
It isn't the anguish that goes with him, it's the
      anguish he leaves behind.
For his going opens a tragic door that gives on a
      world of pain,
And the death he dies, those who live and love will
      die again and again.

So here I am at my cards once more, but it's kind
      of spoiling my play
Thinking of those three brats of his so many a mile
      away.

War is war, and he's only a Boche, and we all of
    us take our chance ;
But all the same I'll be mighty glad when I'm hear-
    ing the ambulance.
One foe the less, but all the same I'm heartily glad
    I'm not
The man who gave him his broken head, the sniper
    who fired the shot. . . .
No trumps you make it, I think you said ?   You'll
    pardon me if I err ;
For a moment I thought of other things. . . . *Mon
    Dieu ! Quelle vache de guerre.*

PILGRIMS

For oh, when the war will be over
We'll go and we'll look for our dead;
We'll go when the bee's on the clover,
And the plume of the poppy is red:
We'll go when the year's at its gayest,
When meadows are laughing with flow'rs;
And there where the crosses are greyest,
We'll seek for the cross that is ours.

For they cry to us: *Friends, we are lonely,*
A-weary the night and the day;
But come in the blossom-time only,
Come when our graves will be gay:
When daffodils all are a-blowing,
And larks are a-thrilling the skies,
Oh, come with the hearts of you glowing,
And the joy of the Spring in your eyes.

But never, oh, never come sighing,
For ours was the Splendid Release;
And oh, but 'twas joy in the dying
To know we were winning you Peace !

So come when the valleys are sheening,
And fledged with the promise of grain ;
And here where our graves will be greening,
Just smile and be happy again.

And so, when the war will be over,
We'll seek for the Wonderful One ;
And maiden will look for her lover,
And mother will look for her son ;
And there will be end to our grieving,
And gladness will gleam over loss,
As—glory beyond all believing !
We point . . . to a name on a cross.

MY PRISONER

WE was in a crump-'ole, 'im and me;
Fightin' wiv our bayonets was we;
Fightin' 'ard as 'ell we was,
Fightin' fierce as fire because
It was 'im or me as must be downed;
'E was twice as big as me;
I was 'arf the weight of 'e;
We was like a terryer and a 'ound.

'Struth! But 'e was sich a 'andsome bloke.
Me—I'm 'andsome as a chunk o' coke.
Did I give it 'im? Not 'arf!
Why, it fairly made me laugh,
'Cos 'is bloomin' bellows wasn't sound.
Couldn't fight for monkey nuts.
Soon I gets 'im in the guts,
There 'e lies a-floppin' in the ground.

In I goes to finish up the job.
Quick 'e throws 'is 'ands above 'is nob;

Speakin' English good as me :
" 'Tain't no use to kill," says 'e ;
" Can't yer tyke me prisoner instead ? "
" Why, I'd like to, sir," says I ;
" But—yer knows the reason why :
If we pokes our noses out we're dead.

" Sorry, sir. Then, on the other 'and
(As a gent like you must understand),
If I 'olds you longer 'ere,
Wiv yer pals so werry near,
It's me 'oo'll 'ave a free trip to Berlin ;
If I lets yer go away,
Why, you'll fight another day :
See the sitooation I am in.

" Anyway I'll tell you wot I'll do,
Bein' kind and seein' as it's you,
Knowin' 'ow it's cold, the feel
Of a 'alf a yard o' steel,
I'll let yer 'ave a rifle ball instead ;
Now, jist think yerself in luck. . . .
'Ere, ol' man ! You keep 'em stuck,
Them saucy dooks o' yours, above yer 'ead."

'Ow 'is mits shot up, it made me smile !
'Ow 'e seemed to ponder for a while !

Then 'e says : " It seems a shyme,
Me, a man wot's known ter Fyme ;
Give me blocks of stone, I'll give yer gods.
Whereas, pardon me, I'm sure
You, my friend, are still obscure. . . ."
" In war," says I, " that makes no blurry odds."

Then says 'e : " I've painted picters too. . , .
Oh, dear God ! the work I planned to do,
And to think this is the end ! "
" 'Ere," says I, " my hartist friend,
Don't you give yeself no friskin' airs,
Picters, statoos, is that why
You should be let off to die ?
That the best ye done ?   Just say yer prayers."

Once again 'e seems ter think awhile.
Then 'e smiles a werry 'aughty smile :
" Why, no, sir, it's not the best ;
There's a locket next me breast,
Picter of a gel 'oo's eyes are blue.
That's the best I've done," says 'e.
" That's me darter, aged three. . . ."
" Blimy ! " says I.   " I've a nipper, too."

Straight I chucks my rifle to one side ;
Shows 'im wiv a lovin' father's pride

Me own little Mary Jane.
Proud 'e shows me 'is Elaine,
And we talks as friendly as can be ;
Then I 'elps 'im on 'is way,
'Opes 'e's sife at 'ome to-day,
Wonders—*'ow would 'e 'ave treated me ?*

TRI-COLOUR

POPPIES, you try to tell me, glowing there in the
   wheat ;
Poppies ! Ah no ! You mock me : it's blood, I tell
   you, it's blood.
It's gleaming wet in the grasses ; it's glist'ning
   warm in the wheat ;
It dabbles the ferns and the clover ; it brims in an
   angry flood ;
It leaps to the startled heavens ; it smothers the
   sun ; it cries
With scarlet voices of triumph from blossom and
   bough and blade.
See the bright horror of it ! It's roaring out of
   the skies,
And the whole red world is a-welter. . . . Oh
   God ! I'm afraid ! I'm afraid !

Cornflowers, you say, just cornflowers, gemming
   the golden grain ;
Ah no ! You can't deceive me. Can't I believe
   my eyes ?

Look! It's the dead, my comrades, stark on the
   dreadful plain,
All in their dark-blue blouses, staring up at the
   skies.
Comrades of canteen laughter, dumb in the yellow
   wheat.
See how they sprawl and huddle! See how their
   brows are white!
Goaded on to the shambles, there in death and
   defeat. . . .
Father of Pity, hide them! Hasten, O God, Thy
   night!

Lilies (the light is waning), only lilies you say,
Nestling and softly shining there where the spear-
   grass waves.
No, my friend, I know better; brighter I see than
   day:
It's the poor little wooden crosses over their quiet
   graves.
Oh, how they're gleaming, gleaming! See! each
   cross has a crown.
Yes, it's true I am dying; little will be the loss. . . .
Darkness . . . but look! In Heaven a light, and
   it's shining down. . . .
God's accolade! Lift me up, friends. I'm going
   to win *my Cross*.

A POT OF TEA

You make it in your mess-tin by the brazier's rosy
    gleam ;
You watch it cloud, then settle amber clear ;
You lift it with your bay'nit and you sniff the fra-
    grant steam ;
The very breath of it is ripe with cheer.
You're awful cold and dirty, and a-cursin' of your
    lot ;
You scoff the blushin' 'alf of it, so rich and rippin'
    'ot ;
It bucks you up like anythink, just seems to touch
    the spot :
      God bless the man that first discovered Tea !

Since I came out to fight in France, which ain't the
    other day,
I think I've drunk enough to float a barge ;
All kinds of fancy foreign dope, from caffy and
    doo lay,
To rum they serves you out before a charge.

In back rooms of estaminays I've gurgled pints of
    cham ;
I've swilled down mugs of cider till I've felt a
    bloomin' dam ;
But 'struth ! they all ain't in it with the vintage of
    Assam :
      God bless the man that first invented Tea !

I think them lazy lumps o' gods wot kips on
    asphodel
Swigs nectar that's a flavour of Oolong ;
I only wish them sons o' guns a-grillin' down in 'ell,
Could 'ave their daily ration of Suchong.
Hurrah ! I'm off to battle, which is 'ell and 'eaven
    too ;
And if I don't give some poor bloke a sexton's
    job to do,
To-night, by Fritz's camp fire, won't I 'ave a
    gorgeous brew
      (For fightin' mustn't interfere with Tea).
To-night we'll all be tellin' of the Boches that we
    slew,
      As we drink the giddy victory in Tea.

THE REVELATION

THE same old sprint in the morning, boys, to the
same old din and smut ;
Chained all day to the same old desk, down in the
same old rut ;
Posting the same old greasy books, catching the
same old train :
Oh, how will I manage to stick it all, if I ever get
back again ?

We've bidden good-bye to life in a cage, we're
finished with pushing a pen ;
They're pumping us full of bellicose rage, they're
showing us how to be men.
We're only beginning to find ourselves ; we're
wonders of brawn and thew ;
But when we go back to our Cissy jobs—oh, what
are we going to do ?

For shoulders curved with the counter stoop will
    be carried erect and square ;
And faces white from the office light will be
    bronzed by the open air ;
And we'll walk with the stride of a new-born pride,
    with a new-found joy in our eyes,
Scornful men who have diced with death under the
    naked skies.

And when we get back to the dreary grind, and
    the bald-headed boss's call,
Don't you think that the dingy window-blind, and
    the dingier office wall,
Will suddenly melt to a vision of space, of violent,
    flame-scarred night ?
Then . . . oh, the joy of the danger-thrill, and oh,
    the roar of the fight !

Don't you think as we peddle a card of pins the
    counter will fade away,
And again we'll be seeing the sand-bag rims, and
    the barb-wire's misty grey ?
As a flat voice asks for a pound of tea, don't you
    fancy we'll hear instead
The night-wind moan and the soothing drone of
    the packet that's overhead ?

Don't you guess that the things we're seeing now
    will haunt us through all the years ;
Heaven and hell rolled into one, glory and blood
    and tears ;
Life's pattern picked with a scarlet thread, where
    once we wove with a grey,
To remind us all how we played our part in the
    shock of an epic day !

Oh, we're booked for the Great Adventure now
    we're pledged to the Real Romance ;
We'll find ourselves or we'll lose ourselves some-
    where in giddy old France ;
We'll know the zest of the fighter's life ; the best
    that we have we'll give ;
We'll hunger and thirst ; we'll die . . . but first—
    we'll live ; by the gods, we'll live !

We'll breathe free air and we'll bivouac under the
    starry sky ;
We'll march with men, and we'll fight with men,
    and we'll see men laugh and die ;
We'll know such joy as we never dreamed ; we'll
    fathom the deeps of pain :
But the hardest bit of it all will be—when we come
    back home again.

*For some of us smirk in a chiffon shop, and some
    of us teach in a school ;*
*Some of us help with the seat of our pants to polish
    an office stool ;*
*The merits of somebody's soap or jam some of us
    seek to explain,*
*But all of us wonder what we'll do when we have
    to go back again.*

GRAND-PERE

And so when he reached my bed
The General made a stand :
" My brave young fellow," he said,
    " I would shake your hand."

So I lifted my arm, the right,
With never a hand at all ;
Only a stump, a sight
    Fit to appal.

" Well, well.   Now that's too bad !
That's sorrowful luck," he said ;
" But there !   You give me, my lad,
    The left instead."

So from under the blanket's rim
I raised and showed him the other,
A snag as ugly and grim
    As its ugly brother.

He looked at each jagged wrist ;
He looked but he did not speak ;
And then he bent down and kissed
    Me on either cheek.

You wonder now I don't mind
I hadn't a hand to offer. . . .
They tell me (you know I'm blind)
    'Twas Grand-père Joffre.

SON

HE hurried away, young heart of joy, under our
  Devon sky !
And I watched him go, my beautiful boy, and a
  weary woman was I.
For my hair is grey, and his was gold ; he'd the best
  of his life to live ;
And I'd loved him so, and I'm old, I'm old ; and
  he's all I had to give.

Ah yes, he was proud and swift and gay, but oh
  how my eyes were dim !
With the sun in his heart he went away, but he took
  the sun with him.
For look ! How the leaves are falling now, and
  the winter won't be long. . . .
Oh boy, my boy with the sunny brow, and the lips
  of love and of song !

How we used to sit at the day's sweet end, we two
    by the firelight's gleam,
And we'd drift to the Valley of Let's Pretend, on
    the beautiful river of Dream.
Oh dear little heart!   All wealth untold would I
    gladly, gladly pay
Could I just for a moment closely hold that golden
    head to my grey.

For I gaze in the fire, and I'm seeing there a child,
    and he waves to me ;
And I run and I hold him up in the air, and he
    laughs and shouts with glee ;
A little bundle of love and mirth, crying : " Come,
    Mumsie dear ! "
Ah me !   If he called from the ends of the earth I
    know that my heart would hear.

    *   *   *   *   *   *

Yet the thought comes thrilling through all my
    pain : how worthier could he die ?
Yea, a loss like that is a glorious gain, and pitiful
    proud am I.
For Peace must be bought with blood and tears,
    and the boys of our hearts must pay ;
And so in our joy of the after-years, let us bless
    them every day.

And though I know there's a hasty grave with a
    poor little cross at its head,
And the gold of his youth he so gladly gave, yet to
    me he'll never be dead.
And the sun in my Devon lane will be gay, and my
    boy will be with me still.
So I'm finding the heart to smile and say : " Oh
    God, if it be Thy Will ! "

THE BLACK DUDEEN

Humping it here in the dug-out,
Sucking me black dudeen,
I'd like to say in a general way
There's nothing like Nickyteen;
There's nothing like Nickyteen, me boys,
Be it pipes or snipes or cigars;
So be sure that a bloke
Has plenty to smoke,
If you wants him to fight your wars.

When I've eat my fill and my belt is snug,
I begin to think of my baccy plug.
I whittle a fill in my horny palm,
And the bowl of me old clay pipe I cram.
I trim the edges, I tamp it down,
I nurse a light with an anxious frown ;
I begin to draw, and my cheeks tuck in.
And all my face is a blissful grin ;
And up in a cloud the good smoke goes,
And the good pipe glimmers and fades and glows ;

In its throat it chuckles a cheery song,
For I likes it hot and I likes it strong.
Oh, it's good is grub when you're feeling hollow,
But the best of a meal's the smoke to follow.

There was Micky and me on a night patrol,
Having to hide in a fizz-bang hole ;
And sure I thought I was worse than dead
Wi' them crump-crumps hustlin' over me head.
Sure I thought 'twas the dirty spot,
Hammer and tongs till the air was hot.
And mind you, water up to your knees.
And cold ! A monkey of brass would freeze.
And if we ventured our noses out
A " typewriter " clattered its pills about.
The field of glory ! Well, I don't think !
I'd sooner be safe and snug in clink.

Then Micky, he goes and he cops one bad,
He always was having ill-luck, poor lad.
Says he : " Old chummy, I'm booked right
    through ;
Death and me 'as a wrongday voo.
But . . . 'aven't you got a pinch of shag ?—
I'd sell me perishin' soul for a fag."
And there he shivered and cussed his luck,
So I gave him me old black pipe to suck.

And he heaves a sigh, and he takes to it
Like a babby takes to his mammy's tit ;
Like an infant takes to his mother's breast,
Poor little Micky ! he " travelled West."
But the dawn was near, though the night was
    black,
So I left him there and I started back.
And I laughed as the silly old bullets came,
For the bullet ain't made wot's got me name.
Yet some of 'em buzzed onhealthily near,
And one little blighter just chipped me ear.
But there ! I got to the trench all right,
When sudden I jumped wi' a start o' fright,
And a word that doesn't look well in type :
I'd clean forgotten me old clay pipe.

So I had to do it all over again,
Crawling out on that filthy plain.
Through shells and bombs and bullets and all—
Only this time—I do not crawl.
I run like a man wot's missing a train,
Or a tom-cat caught in a plump of rain.
I hear the spit of a quick-fire gun
Tickle my heels, but I run, I run.
Through crash and crackle, and flicker and
    flame,
(Oh, the packet ain't issued wot's got me name !)

T

I run like a man that's no ideer
Of hunting around for a sooveneer.
I run bang into a German chap,
And he stares like an owl, so I bash his map.
And just to show him that I'm his boss,
I gives him a kick on the parados.
And I marches him back with me all serene,
With, *tucked in me gub, me old dudeen.*

> *Sitting here in the trenches*
> *Me heart's a-splittin' with spleen,*
> *For a parcel o' lead comes missing me nead,*
> *But it smashes me old dudeen*
> *God blast that red-headed sniper !*
> *I'll give him somethin' to snipe :*
> *Before the war's through*
> *Just see how I do*
> *That blighter that smashed me pipe.*

THE LITTLE PIOU-PIOU

OH, some of us lolled in the château,
And some of us slinked in the slum ;
But now we are here with a song and a cheer
To serve at the sign of the drum.
They put us in trousers of scarlet,
In big sloppy ulsters of blue ;
In boots that are flat, a box of a hat,
And they call us the little piou-piou,
        Piou-piou,
The laughing and quaffing piou-piou ;
The swinging and singing piou-piou ;
And so with a rattle we march to the battle,
The weary but cheery piou-piou.

   Encore un petit verre de vin,
   Pour nous mettre en route ;
   Encore un petit verre de vin
   Pour nous mettre en train.

They drive us head-on for the slaughter ;
We haven't got much of a chance ;
The issue looks bad, but we're awfully glad
To battle and die for La France.
For some must be killed, that is certain :
There's only one's duty to do ;
So we leap to the fray in the glorious way
They expect of the little piou-piou.
> *En avant !*
The way of the gallant piou-piou ;
The dashing and smashing piou-piou ;
The way grim and gory that leads us to glory
Is the way of the little piou-piou.

> *Allons, enfants de la Patrie,*
> *Le jour de gloire est arrivé.*

To-day you would scarce recognize us,
Such veterans warwise are we ;
So grimy and hard, so calloused and scarred,
So " crummy," yet gay as can be.
We've finished with trousers of scarlet,
They're giving us breeches of blue,
With a helmet instead of a cap on our head,
Yet still we're the little piou-piou.
> *Nous les aurons !*

The jesting, unresting piou-piou ;
The cheering, unfearing piou-piou ;
The keep-your-head-level and fight-like-the-devil,
The dying, defying piou-piou.

> *À la bayonette ! Jusqu'a la mort !*
> *Sonnez la charge, clairons !*

BILL THE BOMBER

THE poppies gleamed like bloody pools through
  cotton-woolly mist ;
The Captain kept a-lookin' at the watch upon his
  wrist ;
And there we smoked and squatted, as we watched
  the shrapnel flame ;
'Twas wonnerful, I'm tellin' you, how fast them
  bullets came.
'Twas weary work the waiting, though ; I tried to
  sleep a wink,
For waitin' means a-thinkin', and it doesn't do to
  think.
So I closed my eyes a little, and I had a niceish
  dream
Of a-standin' by a dresser with a dish of Devon
  cream ;
But I hadn't time to sample it, for suddenlike I
  woke :
" Come on, me lads ! " the Captain says, 'n I climbed
  out through the smoke.

We spread out in the open : it was like a bath of
     lead ;
But the boys they cheered and hollered fit to raise
     the bloody dead,
Till a beastly bullet copped 'em, then they lay
     without a sound,
And it's odd—we didn't seem to heed them corpses
     on the ground.
And I kept on thinkin', thinkin' as the bullets faster
     flew,
How they picks the werry best men, and they lets
     the rotters through ;
So indiscriminatin' like, they spares a man
     of sin,
And a rare lad wot's a husband and a father gets
     done in.
And while havin' these reflections and advancin' on
     the run,
A bullet biffs me shoulder, and says I : " That's
     number one."

Well, it downed me for a jiffy, but I didn't lose me
     calm,
For I knew that I was needed : I'm a bomber, so
     I am.
I 'ad lost me cap and rifle, but I " carried on "
     because

I 'ad me bombs and knew that they was needed, so
    they was.
We didn't 'ave no singin' now, nor many men to
    cheer ;
Maybe the shrapnel drowned 'em, crashin' out so
    werry near ;
And the Maxims got us sideways, and the bullets
    faster flew,
And I copped one on me flipper, and says I :
    " That's number two."

I was pleased it was the left one, for I 'ad me bombs,
    ye see,
And 'twas 'ard if they'd be wasted like, and all along
    o' me.
And I'd lost me 'at and rifle—but I told you that
    before,
So I packed me mit inside me coat and " carried
    on " once more.
But the rumpus it was wicked, and the men were
    scarcer yet,
And I felt me ginger goin', but me jaws I kind
    o' set,
And we passed the Boche first trenches, which was
    'eapin' 'igh with dead,
And we started for their second, which was fifty
    feet ahead ;

When something like a 'ammer smashed me savage
    on the knee,
And down I came all muck and blood : Says I :
    " That's number three."

So there I lay all 'elpless like, and bloody sick at
    that,
And worryin' like anythink, because I'd lost me 'at ;
And thinkin' of me missis, and the partin' words
    she said :
" If you gets killed, write quick, ol' man, and tell
    me as you're dead."
And lookin' at me bunch o' bombs—that was the
    'ardest blow,
To think I'd never 'ave the chance to 'url them at
    the foe.
And there was all our boys in front, a-fightin' there
    like mad,
And me as could 'ave 'elped 'em wiv the lovely
    bombs I 'ad.
And so I cussed and cussed, and then I struggled
    back again,
Into that bit of battered trench, packed solid with
    its slain.

Now as I lay a-lyin' there and blastin' of me lot,
And wishin' I could just dispose of all them bombs
    I'd got,

I sees within the doorway of a shy, retirin'
    dug-out
Six Boches all a-grinnin', and their Captain stuck
    'is mug out ;
And they 'ad a nice machine gun, and I twigged
    what they was at ;
And they fixed it on a tripod, and I watched 'em
    like a cat ;
And they got it in position, and they seemed so
    werry glad,
Like they'd got us in a death-trap, which, condemn
    their souls ! they 'ad.
For there our boys was fightin' fifty yards in front,
    and 'ere
This lousy bunch of Boches they 'ad got us in the
    rear.

Oh it set me blood a-boilin', and I quite forgot me
    pain,
So I started crawlin', crawlin' over all them mounds
    of slain ;
And them barstards was so busy-like they 'ad no
    eyes for me,
And me bleedin' leg was draggin', but me right arm
    it was free. . . .
And now they 'ave it all in shape, and swingin'
    sweet and clear ;
And now they're all excited like, but—I am drawin'
    near ;

And now they 'ave it loaded up, and now they're
    takin' aim. . . .
Rat-tat-tat-tat! Oh here, says I, is where I join
    the game.
And my right arm it goes swingin', and a bomb it
    goes a-slingin',
And that " typewriter " goes wingin' in a thunder-
    bolt of flame.

Then these Boches, wot was left of 'em, they
    tumbled down their 'ole,
And up I climbed a mound of dead, and down on
    them I stole.
And oh that blessed moment when I heard their
    frightened yell,
And I laughed down in that dug-out, ere I bombed
    their souls to hell.
And now I'm in the hospital, surprised that I'm
    alive ;
We started out a thousand men, we came back
    thirty-five.
And I'm minus of a trotter, but I'm most amazin'
    gay,
For me bombs they wasn't wasted, though, you
    might say, " thrown away."

THE WHISTLE OF SANDY McGRAW

You may talk o' your lutes and your dulcimers fine,
Your harps and your tabors and cymbals and a',
But here in the trenches jist gie me for mine
The wee penny whistle o' Sandy McGraw.
Oh it's : " Sandy, ma lad, will you lilt us a tune ? "
And Sandy is willin' and trillin' like mad ;
Sae silvery sweet that we a' throng aroun',
And some o' it's gay, but the maist o' it's sad.
Jist the wee simple airs that sink intae your hert,
And grup ye wi' love and wi' longin' for hame ;
And ye glour like an owl till you're feelin' the stert
O' a tear, and you blink wi' a feelin' o' shame.
For his song's o' the heather, and here in the dirt
You listen and dream o' a land that's sae braw,
And he mak's you forget a' the harm and the hurt.
For he pipes like a laverock, does Sandy McGraw.

*   *   *   *   *   *

At Eepers I mind me when rank upon rank
We rose from the trenches and swept like the gale,
Till the rapid-fire guns got us fell on the flank
And the murderin' bullets came swishin' like hail :
Till a' that were left o' us faltered and broke ;
Till it seemed for a moment a panicky rout,
When shrill through the fume and the flash and
    the smoke
The wee valiant voice o' a whistle piped out.
The Campbells are comin' : then into the fray
We bounded wi' bayonets reekin' and raw,
And oh we fair revelled in glory that day,
Jist thanks to the whistle o' Sandy McGraw.

    *   *   *   *   *   *

At Loose, it wis after a sconnersome fecht,
On the field o' the slain I wis crawlin' aboot ;
And the rockets were burnin' red holes in the
    nicht,
And the guns they were veciously thunderin' oot.
When sudden I heard a bit sound like a sigh,
And there in a crump-hole a kiltie I saw :
"Whit ails ye, ma lad ? Are ye woundit ? "
    says I.
"I've lost ma wee whustle," says Sandy McGraw.
" 'Twas oot by yon bing where we pressed the
    attack,

It drapped frae ma pooch, and between noo and
dawn

There isna much time, so I'm jist crawlin'
back. . . ."

" Ye're daft, man ! " I telt him, but Sandy wis
gone.

Weel, I waited a wee, then I crawled oot masel,

And the big stuff wis gorin' and roarin' around,

And I seemed tae be under the oxter o' hell,

And Creation wis crackin' tae bits by the sound.

And I says in ma mind : " Gang ye back, ye auld
fule ! "

When I thrilled tae a note that wis saucy and
sma' ;

And there in a crater, collected and cool,

Wi' his wee penny whistle, wis Sandy McGraw.

Ay, there he wis playin' as gleg as could be,

And listenin' hard wis a spectacled Boche ;

Then Sandy turned roon' and he noddit tae me,

And he says : " Dinna blab on me, Sergeant
McTosh.

The auld chap is deein'.   He likes me tae play.

It's makin' him happy.   Jist see his een shine ! "

And thrillin' and sweet in the hert o' the fray

Wee Sandy wis playin' *The Watch on the Rhine*

*   *   *   *   *   *

The last scene o' a'—'twas the day that we took
That bit o' black ruin they ca' Labbiesell.
It seemed the hale hillside jist shivered and shook,
And the red skies were roarin' and spewin' oot shell.
And the Sergeants were cursin' tae keep us in
    hand,
And hard on the leash we were strainin' likₐ
    dugs,
When upward we shot at the word o' command,
And the bullets were dingin' their songs in oor
    lugs.

And onward we swept wi' a yell and a cheer,
And a' wis destruction, confusion and din,
And we knew that the trench o' the Boches wis
    near,
And it seemed jist the safest bit hole tae be in.
So we a' tumbled doon, and the Boches were there,
And they held up their hands, and they yelled:
    " Kamarad ! "
And I merched aff wi' ten, wi' their palms in
    the air,
And my ! I wis prood-like, and my ! I wis glad.
And I thocht : if ma lassie could see me jist
    then. . . .

When sudden I sobered at somethin' I saw,
And I stopped and I stared, and I halted ma men,
For there on a stretcher wis Sandy McGraw.

Weel, he looks in ma face, jist as game as ye please :
" Ye ken hoo I hate tae be workin'," says he ;
" But noo I can play in the street for bawbees,
Wi' baith o' ma legs taken aff at the knee."
And though I could see he wis rackit wi' pain,
He reached for his whistle and stertit tae play,
And quaverin' sweet wis the pensive refrain :
The flo'oers o' the forest are a' wede away.
Then sudden he stoppit : " Man, wis it no grand
Hoo we took a' them trenches ? " . . . He shakit
    his heid. . . .
" I'll—no—play—nae—mair——" feebly doon frae
    his hand
Slipped the wee penny whistle and . . . *Sandy wis
    deid.*

     *   *   *   *   *   *

And so ye may talk o' your Steinways and Strads,
Yer wunnerfu' organs and brasses sae braw ;
But oot in the trenches jist gie me, ma lads,
Yon wee penny whistle o' Sandy McGraw.

THE STRETCHER-BEARER

My stretcher is one scarlet stain,
And as I tries to scrape it clean,
I tell you wot—I'm sick with pain
For all I've 'eard, for all I've seen;
Around me is the 'ellish night,
And as the war's red rim I trace,
I wonder if in 'Eaven's height
Our God don't turn away 'Is Face.

    I don't care 'ose the Crime may be;
    I 'olds no brief for kin or clan;
    I 'ymns no 'ate: I only see
    As man destroys his brother man;
    I waves no flag: I only know,
    As 'ere beside the dead I wait,
    A million 'earts is weighed with woe,
    A million 'omes is desolate.

In drippin' darkness, far and near,
All night I've sought them woeful ones.
Dawn shudders up and still I 'ear
The crimson chorus of the guns.
Look, like a ball of blood the sun
'Angs o'er the scene of wrath and wrong. . . .
"Quick! Stretcher-bearers on the run!"
O Prince of Peace! 'Ow long, 'ow long!

WOUNDED

Is it not strange ?   A year ago to-day,
With scarce a thought beyond the humdrum round,
I did my decent job and earned my pay ;
Was averagely happy, I'll be bound.
Ay, in my little groove I was content,
Seeing my life run smoothly to the end,
With prosy days in stolid labour spent,
And jolly nights, a pipe, a glass, a friend.
In God's good time a hearth fire's cosy gleam,
A wife and kids, and all a fellow needs ;
When presto ! like a bubble goes my dream :
I leap upon the Stage of Splendid Deeds.
I yell with rage ; I wallow deep in gore :
I, that was clerk in a drysalter's store.

Stranger than any book I've ever read.
Here on the reeking battlefield I lie,
Under the stars, propped up with smeary dead.
Like too, if no one takes me in, to die.

Hit on the arms, legs, liver, lungs and gall ;
Damn glad there's nothing more of me to hit ;
But calm, and feeling never pain at all,
And full of wonder at the turn of it.
For of the dead around me three are mine,
Three foemen vanquished in the whirl of fight ;
So if I die I have no right to whine,
I feel I've done my little bit all right.
I don't know how—but there the beggars are,
As dead as herrings pickled in a jar.

And here am I, worse wounded that I thought ;
For in the fight a bullet bee-like stings ;
You never heed ; the air is metal-hot,
And all alive with little flicking wings.
But on you charge. You see the fellows fall ;
Your pal was by your side, fair fighting-mad ;
You turn to him, and lo ! no pal at all ;
You wonder vaguely if he's copped it bad.
But on you charge. The heavens vomit death ;
And vicious death is besoming the ground.
You're blind with sweat ; you're dazed, and out of
          breath,
And though you yell, you cannot hear a sound.
But on you charge. Oh, War's a rousing game !
Around you smoky clouds like ogres tower ;

The earth is rowelled deep with spurs of flame,
And on your helmet stones and ashes shower.
But on you charge. It's odd ! You have no fear.
Machine-gun bullets whip and lash your path ;
Red, yellow, black the smoky giants rear ;
The shrapnel rips, the heavens roar in wrath.
But on you charge. Barbed wire all trampled
    down ;

The ground all gored and rent as by a blast ;
Grim heaps of grey where once were heaps of
    brown ;
A ragged ditch—the Hun first line at last,
All smashed to hell. Their second right ahead,
So on you charge. There's nothing else to do.
More reeking holes, blood, barbed wire, gruesome
    dead
(Your puttee strap's undone—that worries you).
You glare around. You think you're all alone.
But no ; your chums come surging left and right.
The nearest chap flops down without a groan,
His face still snarling with the rage of fight.
Ha ! here's the second trench—just like the first,
Only a little more so, more " laid out " ;
More pounded, flame-corroded, death-accurst ;
A pretty piece of work, beyond a doubt.

Now for the third, and there your job is done,
So on you charge. You never stop to think.
Your cursed puttee's trailing as you run ;
You feel you'd sell your soul to have a drink.
The acrid air is full of cracking whips.
You wonder how it is you're going still.
You foam with rage. Oh, God ! to be at grips
With someone you can rush and crush and kill.
Your sleeve is dripping blood ; you're seeing red ;
You're battle-mad ; your turn is coming now.
See ! there's the jagged barbed wire straight ahead,
And there's the trench—you'll get there anyhow.
Your puttee catches on a strand of wire,
And down you go ; perhaps it saves your life,
For over sandbag rims you see 'em fire,
Crop-headed chaps, their eyes ablaze with strife.
You crawl, you cower ; then once again you plunge
With all your comrades roaring at your heels.
Have at 'em, lads ! You stab, you jab, you lunge ;
A blaze of glory, then the red world reels.
A crash of triumph, then . . . you're faint a bit . . .
That cursed puttee ! Now to fasten it. . . .

Well, that's the charge. And now I'm here alone.
I've built a little wall of Hun on Hun,
To shield me from the leaden bees that drone
(It saves me worry, and it hurts 'em none).

The only thing I'm wondering is when
Some stretcher-men will stroll along my way ?
It isn't much that's left of me, but then
Where life is, hope is, so at least they say.
Well, if I'm spared I'll be the happy lad.
I tell you I won't envy any king.
I've stood the racket, and I'm proud and glad ;
I've had my crowning hour.   Oh, War's the thing !
It gives us common, working chaps our chance,
A taste of glory, chivalry, romance.

Ay, War, they say, is hell ; it's heaven, too.
It lets a man discover what he's worth.
It takes his measure, shows what he can do,
Gives him a joy like nothing else on earth.
It fans in him a flame that otherwise
Would flicker out, these drab, discordant days ;
It teaches him in pain and sacrifice
Faith, fortitude, grim courage past all praise.
Yes, War is good.   So here beside my slain,
A happy wreck, I wait amid the din ;
For even if I perish mine's the gain. . . .
Hi there, you fellows !   *Won't* you take me in ?
Give me a fag to smoke upon the way. . . .
We've taken La Boiselle !   The hell, you say !
Well, that would make a corpse sit up and grin. . . ,
Lead on !   I'll live to fight another day.

FAITH

Since all that is was ever bound to be ;
Since grim, eternal laws our Being bind ;
And both the riddle and the answer find,
And both the carnage and the calm decree ;
Since plain within the Book of Destiny
Is written all the journey of mankind
Inexorably to the end ; since blind
And mortal puppets playing parts are we :

Then let's have faith ; good cometh out of ill ;
The power that shaped the strife shall end the
    strife ;
Then let's bow down before the Unknown Will ;
Fight on, believing all is well with life ;
Seeing within the worst of War's red rage
The gleam, the glory of the Golden Age.

THE COWARD

'Ave you seen Bill's mug in the Noos to-day ?
'E's gyned the Victoriar Cross, they say ;
Little Bill wot would grizzle and run away,
    If you 'it 'im a swipe on the jawr.
'E's slaughtered the Kaiser's men in tons ;
'E's captured one of their quick-fire guns,
And 'e 'adn't no practice in killin' 'Uns
    Afore 'e went off to the war.

    Little Bill wot I nussed in 'is by-by clothes ;
    Little Bill wot told me 'is childish woes ;
    'Ow often I've tidied 'is pore little nose
        Wiv the 'em of me pinnyfore.
    And now all the papers 'is praises ring,
    And 'e's been and 'e's shaken the 'and of the
        King,
    And I sawr 'im to-day in the ward, pore thing,
        Where they're patching 'im up once more.

And 'e says : " Wot d'ye think of it, Lizer Ann ? "
And I says : " Well, I can't make it out, old man ;
You'd 'ook it as soon as a scrap began,
    When you was a bit of a kid."
And 'e whispers : " 'Ere, on the quiet, Liz,
They're makin' too much of the 'ole damn biz,
And the papers is printin' me ugly phiz,
    But . . . I'm 'anged if I know wot I did.

" Oh, the Captain comes and 'e says : ' Look 'ere !
They're far too quiet out there : it's queer.
They're up to somethin'—'oo'll volunteer
    To crawl in the dark and see ? '
Then I felt me 'eart like a 'ammer go,
And up jumps a chap and 'e says : ' Right O ! '
But I chips in straight, and I says, ' Oh no !
    'E's a missis and kids—take me.'

    " And the next I knew I was sneakin' out,
    And the oozy corpses was all about,
    And I felt so scared I wanted to shout,
        And my skin fair prickled wiv fear ;
    And I sez : ' You coward ! You 'ad no
      right
    To take on the job of a man this night.'
    Yet still I kept creepin' till ('orrid sight !)
        The trench of the 'Uns was near.

" It was all so dark, it was all so still ;
Yet somethin' pushed me against me will ;
'Ow I wanted to turn !   Yet I crawled until
    I was seein' a dim light shine.
Then thinks I : ' I'll just go a little bit,
And see wot the doose I can make of it,'
And it seemed to come from the mouth of a pit :
    ' Christmas ! ' sez I, ' a *mine.*'

" Then 'ere's the part wot I can't explain :
I wanted to make for 'ome again,
But somethin' was blazin' inside me brain,
    So I crawled to the trench instead ;
Then I saw the bullet 'ead of a 'Un,
And 'e stood by a rapid-firer gun,
And I lifted a rock and I 'it 'im one,
    And 'e dropped like a chunk o' lead.

" Then all the 'Uns that was underground
Comes up with a rush and on with a bound,
And I swings that giddy old Maxim round
    And belts 'em solid and square.
You see I was off me chump wiv fear :
' If I'm sellin' me life,' sez I, ' it's dear.'
And the trench was narrow and they was near,
    So I peppered the brutes for fair.

" So I 'eld 'em back and I yelled with fright,
And the boys attacked and we 'ad a fight,
And we ' captured a section o' trench ' that night
    Which we didn't expect to get ;
And they found me there with me Maxim gun,
And I'd laid out a score if I'd laid out one,
And I fainted away when the thing was done,
    And I 'aven't got over it yet."

So that's the 'istory Bill told me.
Of course it's all on the strict Q.T. ;
It wouldn't do to get out, you see,
    As 'e hacted against 'is will.
But 'e's convalescin' wiv all 'is might,
And 'e 'opes to be fit for another fight—
Say !   Ain't 'e a bit of the real all right ?
    Wot's the matter with Bill !

MISSIS MORIARTY'S BOY

MISSIS MORIARTY called last week, and says she to
    me, says she :
" Sure the heart of me's broken entirely now—it's
    the fortunate woman you are ;
You've still got your Dinnis to cheer up your home,
    but me Patsy boy where is he ?
Lyin' alone, cold as a stone, kilt in the weariful
    wahr.
Oh, I'm seein' him now as I looked on him last, wid
    his hair all curly and bright,
And the wonderful, tenderful heart he had, and his
    eyes as he wint away,
Shinin' and lookin' down on me from the pride of
    his proper height :
Sure I'll remember me boy like that if I live to me
    dyin' day."

And just as she spoke them very same words me
    Dinnis came in at the door,
Came in from McGonigle's ould shebeen, came in
    from drinkin' his pay ;
And Missis Moriarty looked at him, and she didn't
    say anny more,
But she wrapped her head in her ould black shawl,
    and she quietly wint away.
And what was I thinkin', I ask ye now, as I put me
    Dinnis to bed,
Wid him ravin' and cursin' one half o' the night, as
    cold by his side I sat ;
Was I thinkin' the poor ould woman she was, wid
    her Patsy slaughtered and dead ?
Was I weepin' for Missis Moriarty ? I'm not so
    sure about that.

Missis Moriarty goes about wid a shinin' look on
    her face ;
Wid her grey hair under her ould black shawl, and
    the eyes of her mother-mild ;
Some say she's a little bit off her head ; but anny-
    way it's the case
Her timper's so swate that you nivver would tell
    she'd be losin' her only child.
And I think, as I wait up ivery night for me Dinnis
    to come home blind,

And I'm hearin' his stumblin' foot on the stair
    along about half-past three :
Sure there's many a way of breakin' a heart, and I
    haven't made up me mind—
Would I be Missis Moriarty, or Missis Moriarty
    me ?

MY FOE

A *Belgian Priest-Soldier speaks :*

GURR ! you *cochon* !   Stand and fight !
Show your mettle !   Snarl and bite !
Spawn of an accursed race,
Turn and meet me face to face !
Here amid the wreck and rout
Let us grip and have it out !
Here where ruins rock and reel
Let us settle, steel to steel !
Look !   Our houses, how they spit
Sparks from brands your friends have lit.
See !   Our gutters running red,
Bright with blood your friends have shed.
Hark !   Amid your drunken brawl
How our maidens shriek and call.
Why have *you* come here alone,
To this hearth's blood-spattered stone ?

Come to ravish, come to loot,
Come to play the ghoulish brute.
Ah, indeed! We well are met,
Bayonet to bayonet.
God! I never killed a man :
Now I'll do the best I can.
Rip you to the evil heart,
Laugh to see the life-blood start.
Bah! you swine! I hate you so.
Show you mercy? No! . . . and no! . . .

There! I've done it. See! he lies
Death a-staring from his eyes ;
Glazing eyeballs, panting breath,
How it's horrible, is Death!
Plucking at his bloody lips
With his trembling finger-tips ;
Choking in a dreadful way
As if he would something say
In that uncouth tongue of his. . . .
Oh, how horrible Death is!

How I wish that he would die!
So unnerved, unmanned am I.
See! His twitching face is white!
See! His bubbling blood is bright.

U

Why do I not shout with glee ?
What strange spell is over me ?
There he lies ; the fight was fair ;
Let me toss my cap in air.
Why am I so silent ?   Why
Do I pray for him to die ?
Where is all my vengeful joy ?
Ugh !   *My foe is but a boy.*

I'd a brother of his age
Perished in the war's red rage :
Perished in the Ypres hell :
Oh, I loved my brother well.
And though I be hard and grim,
How it makes me think of him !
He had just such flaxen hair
As the lad that's lying there.
Just such frank blue eyes were his. . . .
God !   How horrible war is !

I have reason to be gay :
There is one less foe to slay.
I have reason to be glad :
Yet—my foe is such a lad.
So I watch in dull amaze,
See his dying eyes a-glaze,

See his face grow glorified,
See his hands outstretched and wide
To that bit of ruined wall
Where the flames have ceased to crawl,
Where amid the crumbling bricks
Hangs *a blackened crucifix.*

Now, oh now I understand.
Quick I press it in his hand,
Close his feeble finger-tips,
Hold it to his faltering lips.
As I watch his welling blood
I would stem it if I could.
God of Pity, let him live!
God of Love, forgive, forgive.

    *   *   *   *   *   *

His face looked strangely, as he died,
Like that of One they crucified.
And in the pocket of his coat
I found a letter; thus he wrote:
The things I've seen! Oh mother, dear.
I'm wondering can God be here?
To-night amid the drunken brawl
I saw a Cross hung on a wall;
I'll seek it out, and there alone
Perhaps I may atone, atone. . . .

Ah no ! 'tis I who must atone.
No other saw but God alone ;
Yet how can I forget the sight
Of that face so woeful white !
Dead I kissed him as he lay,
Knelt by him and tried to pray ;
Left him lying there at rest,
Crucifix upon his breast.

Not for him the pity be.
Ye who pity, pity me,
Crawling now the ways I trod.
Blood-guilty in the sight of God.

MY JOB

I'VE got a little job on 'and, the time is drawin'
 nigh ;
At seven by the Captain's watch I'm due to go and
 do it ;
I wants to 'ave it nice and neat, and pleasin' to the
 eye,
And I 'opes the God of soldier men will see me
 safely through it.
Because, you see, it's somethin' I 'ave never done
 before ;
And till you 'as experience noo stunts is always
 tryin' ;
The chances is I'll never 'ave to do it any more :
At seven by the Captain's watch my little job is
 . . . *dyin'*.

I've got a little note to write ; I'd best begin it now.
I ain't much good at writin' notes, but here goes :
 " Dearest Mother,
I've been in many 'ot old ' do's ' ; I've scraped
 through safe some'ow,
But now I'm on the very point of tacklin' another.

A little job of hand-grenades; they called for
    volunteers.
They picked me out; I'm proud of it; it seems a
    trifle dicky.
If anythin' should 'appen, well, there ain't no call
    for tears,
And so . . . I 'opes this finds you well.—Your
    werry lovin' Micky."

I've got a little score to settle wiv them swine out
    there.
I've 'ad so many of me pals done in it's quite upset
    me.
I've seen so much of bloody death I don't seem for
    to care,
If I can only even up, how soon the blighters get
    me.
I'm sorry for them perishers that corpses in a bed;
I only 'opes mine's short and sweet, no linger-
    longer-lyin';
I've made a mess of life, but now I'll try to make
    instead . . .
It's seven sharp. Good-bye, old pals! . . . *a*
    decent job in ayin'.

THE SONG OF THE PACIFIST

WHAT do they matter, our headlong hates, when
    we take the toll of our Dead ?
Think ye our glory and gain will pay for the tor-
    rent of blood we have shed ?
By the cheers of our Victory will the heart of the
    mother be comforted ?

If by the Victory all we mean is a broken and
    brooding foe ;
Is the pomp and power of a glitt'ring hour, and
    a truce for an age or so :
By the clay-cold hand on the broken blade we have
    smitten a bootless blow !

If by the Triumph we only prove that the sword
    we sheathe is bright ;
That justice and truth and love endure ; that
    freedom's throned on the height ;
That the feebler folks shall be unafraid ; that Might
    shall never be Right ;

If this be all : by the blood-drenched plains, by the
    havoc of fire and fear,
By the rending roar of the War of Wars, by the
    Dead so doubly dear. . . .
Then our Victory is a vast defeat, and it mocks us
    as we cheer.

Victory ! there can be but one, hallowed in every
    land :
When by the graves of our common dead we who
    were foemen stand ;
And in the hush of our common grief hand is
    tendered to hand.

Triumph ! Yes, when out of the dust in the splen-
    dour of their release
The spirits of those who fell go forth and they
    hallow our hearts to peace,
And, brothers in pain, with world-wide voice, we
    clamour that War shall cease.

Glory ! Ay, when from blackest loss shall be born
    most radiant gain ;
When over the gory fields shall rise a star that
    never shall wane :
Then, and then only, our Dead shall know that
    they have not fall'n in vain.

When our children's children shall talk of War as
    a madness that may not be ;
When we thank our God for our grief to-day, and
    blazon from sea to sea
In the name of the Dead the banner of Peace . . .
    that will be Victory.

THE TWINS

There were two brothers, John and James,
And when the town went up in flames,
To save the house of James dashed John,
Then turned, and lo ! his own was gone.

And when the great World War began,
To volunteer John promptly ran ;
And while he learned live bombs to lob,
James stayed at home and—sneaked his job.

John came home with a missing limb ;
That didn't seem to worry him ;
But oh, it set his brain awhirl
To find that James had—sneaked his girl !

Time passed.   John tried his grief to drown :
To-day James owns one-half the town ;
His army contracts riches yield ;
And John ?   Well, *search the Potter's Field.*

THE SONG OF THE SOLDIER-BORN

Give me the scorn of the stars and a peak defiant ;
Wail of the pines and a wind with the shout of a
*   giant ;*
Night and a trail unknown and a heart reliant.

Give me to live and love in the old, bold fashion ;
A soldier's billet at night and a soldier's ration ;
A heart that leaps to the fight with a soldier's
    passion.

For I hold as a simple faith there's no denying :
The trade of a soldier's the only trade worth
    plying ;
The death of a soldier's the only death worth dying.

So let me go and leave your safety behind me ;
Go to the spaces of hazard where nothing shall bind
    me ;
Go till the word is War—and then you will find me.

Then you will call me and claim me because you
    will need me ;
Cheer me and gird me and into the battle-wrath
    speed me. . . .
And when it's over, spurn me and no longer heed
    me.

For guile and a purse gold-greased are the arms
    you carry ;
With deeds of paper you fight and with pens you
    parry ;
You call on the hounds of the law your foes to
    harry.

You with your " Art for its own sake," posing and
    prinking ;
You with your " Live and be merry," eating and
    drinking ;
You with your " Peace at all hazard," from bright
    blood shrinking.

Fools ! I will tell you now : though the red rain
    patters,
And a million of men go down, it's little it
    matters. . . .
There's the Flag upflung to the stars, though it
    streams in tatters.

There's a glory gold never can buy to yearn and
    to cry for ;
There's a hope that's as old as the sky to suffer and
    sigh for ;
There's a faith that out-dazzles the sun to martyr
    and die for.

Ah no ! it's my dream that War will never be ended ;
That men will perish like men, and valour be
    splendid ;
That the Flag by the sword will be served, and
    honour defended.

That the tale of my fights will never be ancient
    story ;
That though my eye may be dim and my beard be
    hoary,
I'll die as a soldier dies on the Field of Glory.

*So give me a strong right arm for a wrong's swift
    righting ;*
Stave of a song on my lips as my sword is smiting ;
Death in my boots maybe, but fighting, fighting.

AFTERNOON TEA

As I was saying . . . (No, thank you ; I never take
    cream with my tea ;
Cows weren't allowed in the trenches—got out of
    the habit, y'see.)
As I was saying, our Colonel leaped up like a
    youngster of ten :
" Come on, lads ! " he shouts, " and we'll show
    'em." And he sprang to the head of the men.
Then some bally thing seemed to trip him, and he
    fell on his face with a slam. . . .
Oh, he died like a true British soldier, and the last
    word he uttered was " Damn ! "
And hang it ! I loved the old fellow, and some-
    thing just burst in my brain,
And I cared no more for the bullets than I would
    for a shower of rain.
'Twas an awf'ly funny sensation (I say, this is jolly
    nice tea) ;
I felt as if something had broken ; by gad ! I was
    suddenly free.

Free for a glorified moment, beyond regulations
and laws,
Free just to wallow in slaughter, as the chap of the
Stone Age was.
So on I went joyously nursing a Berserker rage of
my own,
And though all my chaps were behind me, feeling
most frightf'ly alone ;
With the bullets and shells ding-donging, and the
" krock " and the swish of the shrap ;
And I found myself humming " Ben Bolt " . . .
(Will you pass me the sugar, old chap ?
Two lumps, please). . . . What was I saying ?
Oh yes, the jolly old dash ;
We simply ripped through the barrage, and on
with a roar and a crash.
My fellows—Old Nick couldn't stop 'em. On, on
they went with a yell,
Till they tripped on the Boches' sand-bags—
nothing much left to tell.
A trench so tattered and battered that even a rat
couldn't live ;
Some corpses tangled and mangled, wire you could
pass through a sieve.
The jolly old guns had bilked us, cheated us out
of our show,

And my fellows were simply yearning for a red
mix-up with the foe.

So I shouted to them to follow, and on we went
roaring again,

Battle-tuned and exultant, on in the leaden
rain.

Then all at once a machine gun barks from a bit
of a bank,

And our Major roars in a fury: "We've got to
take it on flank."

He was running like fire to lead us, when down
like a stone he comes,

As full of "typewriter" bullets as a pudding is full
of plums.

So I took his job and we got 'em. . . . By gad!
we got 'em like rats;

Down in a deep shell crater we fought like Kil-
kenny cats.

'Twas pleasant just for a moment to be sheltered
and out of range,

With some one you *saw* to go for—it made an
agreeable change.

And the Boches that missed my bullets, my chaps
gave the bayonet jolt,

And all the time, I remember, I whistled and
hummed "Ben Bolt."

Well, that little job was over, so hell for leather
    we ran,

On to the second line trenches—that's where the
    fun began.

For though we had strafed 'em like fury, there still
    were some Boches about,

And my fellows, teeth set and eyes glaring, like
    terriers routed 'em out.

Then I stumbled on one of their dug-outs, and I
    shouted : " Is any one there ? "

And a voice, " Yes, one ; but I'm wounded," came
    faint up the narrow stair ;

And my man was descending before me, when
    sudden a cry ! a shot !

(I say, this cake is delicious. You make it your-
    self, do you not ?)

My man ? Oh, they killed the poor devil ; for if
    there was one there was ten ;

So after I'd bombed 'em sufficient I went down at
    the head of my men ;

And four tried to sneak from a bunk-hole, but we
    cornered the rotters all right ;

I'd rather not go into details, 'twas messy, that bit
    of the fight.

But all of it's beastly messy ; let's talk of pleasanter
    things :

The skirts that the girls are wearing, ridiculous
    fluffy things,
So short that they show. . . . Oh, hang it ! Well,
    if I must, I must.
We cleaned out the second trench line, bomb and
    bayonet thrust ;
And on we went to the third one, quite calloused to
    crumping by now ;
And some of our fellows who'd passed us were
    making a deuce of a row ;
And my chaps—well, I just couldn't hold 'em. (It's
    strange how it is with gore ;
In some ways it's just like whisky : if you taste
    it you must have more.)
Their eyes were like beacons of battle ; by gad, sir !
    they *couldn't* be calmed,
So I headed 'em bang for the bomb-belt, racing like
    billy-be-damned.
Oh, it didn't take long to arrive there, those who
    arrived at all ;
The machine guns were certainly chronic, the
    shindy enough to appal.
Oh yes, I omitted to tell you, I'd wounds on the
    chest and the head,
And my shirt was torn to a gun-rag, and my face
    blood-gummy and red.

I'm thinking I looked like a madman ; I fancy I
    felt one too,
Half naked and swinging a rifle. . . . God ! what
    a glorious " do."
As I sit here in old Piccadilly, sipping my afternoon
    tea,
I see a blind, bullet-chipped devil, and it's hard to
    believe that it's me ;
I see a wild, war-damaged demon, smashing out
    left and right,
And humming " Ben Bolt " rather loudly, and
    hugely enjoying the fight.
And as for my men, may God bless 'em ! I've
    loved 'em ever since then :
They fought like the shining angels ; they're the
    pick o' the land, my men.
And the trench was a reeking shambles, not a
    Boche to be seen alive—
So I thought ; but on rounding a traverse I came
    on a covey of five ;
And four of 'em threw up their flippers, but the
    fifth chap, a sergeant, was game,
And though I'd a bomb and revolver he came at
    me just the same.
A sporty thing that, I tell you ; I just couldn't blow
    him to hell,

So I swung to the point of his jaw-bone, and down
like a ninepin he fell.

And then when I'd brought him to reason, he
wasn't half bad, that Hun ;

He bandaged my head and my short-rib as well as
the Doc could have done.

So back I went with my Boches, as gay as a two-
year-old colt,

And it suddenly struck me as rummy, I still was
a-humming " Ben Bolt."

And now, by Jove ! how I've bored you. You've
just let me babble away ;

Let's talk of the things that *matter*—your car or
the newest play. . . .

THE MOURNERS

I LOOK into the aching womb of night ;
I look across the mist that masks the dead ;
The moon is tired and gives but little light,
      The stars have gone to bed.

The earth is sick and seems to breathe with pain ;
A lost wind whimpers in a mangled tree :
I do not see the foul, corpse-cluttered plain,
      The dead I do not see.

The slain I *would* not see . . . and so I lift
My eyes from out the shambles where they lie ;
When lo ! a million woman-faces drift
      Like pale leaves through the sky.

The cheeks of some are channelled deep with tears ;
But some are tearless, with wild eyes that stare
Into the shadow of the coming years
      Of fathomless despair.

611

And some are young, and some are very old ;
And some are rich, some poor beyond belief ;
Yet all are strangely like, set in the mould
      Of everlasting grief.

They fill the vast of Heaven, face on face ;
And then I see one weeping with the rest,
Whose eyes beseech me for a moment's space. . . .
      Oh, eyes I love the best !

Nay, I but dream.   The sky is all forlorn,
And there's the plain of battle writhing red :
God pity them, the womenfolk who mourn !
      How happy are the dead

L'ENVOI

My job is done ; my rhymes are ranked and ready,
My word-battalions marching verse by verse ;
Here stanza-companies are none too steady ;
There print-platoons are weak, but might be worse.
And as in marshalled order I review them,
My type-brigades, unfearful of the fray.
My eyes that seek their faults are seeing through
        them
Immortal visions of an epic day.

It seems I'm in a giant bowling-alley ;
The hidden heavies round me crash and thud ;
A spire snaps like a pipe-stem in the valley ;
The rising sun is like a ball of blood.
Along the road the " fantassins " are pouring,
And some are gay as fire, and some steel-stern. . . .
Then back again I see the red tide pouring,
Along the reeking road from Hebuterne.

And once again I seek Hill Sixty-Seven,
The Hun lines grey and peaceful in my sight ;
When suddenly the rosy air is riven—
A " coal-box " blots the " boyou " on my right.
Or else to evil Carnoy I am stealing,
Past sentinels who hail with bated breath ;
Where not a cigarette spark's dim revealing
May hint our mission in that zone of death.

I see across the shrapnel-seeded meadows
The jagged rubble-heap of La Boiselle ;
Blood-guilty Fricourt brooding in the shadows,
And Thiepval's château empty as a shell.
Down Albert's riven streets the moon is leering :
The Hanging Virgin takes its bitter ray ;
And all the road from Hamel I am hearing
The silver rage of bugles over Bray.

Once more within the sky's deep sapphire hollow
I sight a swimming Taube, a fairy thing ;
I watch the angry shell flame flash and follow
In feather puffs that flick a tilted wing ;
And then it fades, with shrapnel mirror's flashing ;
The flashes bloom to blossoms lily gold ;
The batteries are rancorously crashing,
And life is just as full as it can hold.

Oh spacious days of glory and of grieving !
Oh sounding hours of lustre and of loss !
Let us be glad we lived you, still believing
The God who gave the cannon gave the Cross.
Let us be sure amid the seething passions,
The lusts of blood and hate our souls abhor,
The Power that Order out of Chaos fashions
Smites fiercest in the wrath-red forge of War. . . .
Have faith ! Fight on ! Amid the battle-hell
Love triumphs, Freedom beacons, all is well.

BALLADS OF A BOHEMIAN

PRELUDE

Alas ! upon some starry height,
The Gods of Excellence to please,
This hand of mine will never smite
The Harp of High Serenities.
Mere minstrel of the street am I,
To whom a careless coin you fling :
But who, beneath the bitter sky,
Blue-lipped, yet insolent of eye,
Can shrill a song of Spring ;
A song of merry mansard days,
The cheery chimney-tops among ;
Of rolics and of roundelays
When we were young . . . when we were young ;
A song of love and lilac nights,
Of wit, of wisdom and of wine ;
Of Folly whirling on the Heights,
Of hunger and of hope divine ;
Of Blanche, Suzette and Celestine,
And all that gay and tender band
Who shared with us the fat, the lean,
The hazard of Illusion-land ;
When scores of Philistines we slew
As mightily with brush and pen
We sought to make the world anew,
And scorned the gods of other men :

When we were fools divinely wise,
Who held it rapturous to strive ;
When Art was sacred in our eyes,
And it was Heav'n to be alive. . . .

O days of glamour, glory, truth,
To you to-night I raise my glass ;
O freehold of immortal youth,
Bohemia, the lost, alas !
O laughing lads who led the romp,
Respectable you've grown, I'm told :
Your heads you bow to power and pomp,
You've learned to know the worth of gold.
O merry maids who shared our cheer,
Your eyes are dim, your locks are grey ;
And as you scrub I sadly fear
Your daughters speed the dance to-day.
O windmill land and crescent moon !
O Columbine and Pierrette !
To you my old guitar I tune
Ere I forget, ere I forget. . . .

So come, good men who toil and tire,
Who smoke and sip the kindly cup,
Ring round about the tavern fire
Ere yet you drink your liquor up ;
And hear my simple songs of earth,
Of youth and truth and living things ;
Of poverty and proper mirth,
Of rags and rich imagings ;
Of cock-a-hoop, blue-heavened days,
Of hearts elate and eager breath,
Of wonder, worship, pity, praise,

Of sorrow, sacrifice and death ;
Of lusting, laughter, passion, pain,
Of lights that lure and dreams that thrall . . .
And if a golden word I gain,
Oh, kindly folks, God save you all !
And if you shake your heads in blame . . .
Good friends, God love you all the same.

PART ONE
SPRING

I

MONTPARNASSE,
April 1914.

All day the sun has shone into my little attic, a bitter sunshine that brightened yet did not warm. And so as I toiled and toiled doggedly enough, many were the looks I cast at the three faggots I had saved to cook my evening meal. Now, however, my supper is over, my pipe alight, and as I stretch my legs before the embers I have at last a glow of comfort, a glimpse of peace.

MY GARRET

HERE is my Garret up five flights of stairs;
Here's where I deal in dreams and ply in fancies
Here is the wonder-shop of all my wares,
My sounding sonnets and my red romances.
Here's where I challenge Fate and ring my rhymes,
And grope at glory—aye, and starve at times.

Here is my Stronghold : stout of heart am I,
Greeting each dawn as songful as a linnet;
And when at night on yon poor bed I lie
(Blessing the world and every soul that's in it),
Here's where I thank the Lord no shadow bars
My skylight's vision of the valiant stars.

Here is my Palace tapestried with dreams.
Ah ! though to-night ten *sous* are all my treasure,
While in my gaze immortal beauty gleams,
Am I not dowered with wealth beyond all measure ?
Though in my ragged coat my songs I sing,
King of my soul, I envy not the king.

Here is my Haven : it's so quiet here ;
Only the scratch of pen, the candle's flutter ;
Shabby and bare and small, but O how dear !
Mark you—my table with my work a-clutter,
My shelf of tattered books along the wall,
My bed, my broken chair—that's nearly all.

Only four faded walls, yet mine, all mine.
Oh, you fine folks, a pauper scorns your pity.
Look, where above me stars of rapture shine
See, where below me gleams the siren city . . .
Am I not rich ?—a millionaire no less,
If wealth be told in terms of Happiness.

Ten *sous*. . . . I think one can sing best of poverty when
one is holding it at arm's-length. I'm sure that when I
wrote these lines, fortune had for a moment tweaked me
by the nose. To-night, however, I am truly down to ten
sous. It is for that I have stayed in my room all day,
rolled in my blankets and clutching my pen with clammy
fingers. For I must work, work, work. I must finish my
book before poverty crushes me. I am not only writing for
my living but for my life. Even to-day my Muse was
mutinous. For hours and hours anxiously I stared at a
paper that was blank ; nervously I paced up and down
my garret ; bitterly I flung myself on my bed. Then

suddenly it all came.   Line after line I wrote with hardly a
halt.   So I made another of my Ballads of the Boulevards.
Here it is :

JULOT THE *APACHE*

You'vE heard of Julot the *apache*, and Gigolette, his
 môme. . . .
Montmartre was their hunting-ground, but Belville was
 their home.
A little chap just like a boy, with smudgy black
 moustache,—
Yet there was nothing juvenile in Julot the *apache*.
From head to heel as tough as steel, as nimble as a
 cat,
With every trick of twist and kick, a master of *savate*.
And Gigolette was tall and fair, as stupid as a cow,
With three combs in the greasy hair she banged upon
 her brow.
You'd see her on the Place Pigalle on any afternoon,
A primitive and strapping wench as brazen as the moon.
And yet there is a tale that's told of Clichy after dark,
And two *gendarmes* who swung their arms with Julot
 for a mark.
And oh, but they'd have got him too ; they banged and
 blazed away,
When like a flash a woman leapt between them and
 their prey.
She took the medicine meant for him ; she came down
 with a crash . . .
" Quick now, and make your get-away, O Julot the
 apache / " . .

But no ! He turned, ran swiftly back, his arms around
   her met ;
They nabbed him sobbing like a kid, and kissing
   Gigolette.

Now I'm a reckless painter chap who loves a jamboree,
And one night in Cyrano's bar I got upon a spree ;
And there were trollops all about, and crooks of every
   kind,
But though the place was reeling round I didn't seem
   to mind.
Till down I sank, and all was blank when in the bleary
   dawn
I woke up in my studio to find—my money gone ;
Three hundred francs I'd scraped and squeezed to pay
   my quarter's rent.
" Someone has pinched my wad," I wailed ; " it never
   has been spent."
And as I racked my brains to seek how I could raise
   some more,
Before my cruel landlord kicked me cowering from the
   door :
A knock . . . " Come in," I gruffly groaned ; I did
   not raise my head,
Then lo ! I heard a husky voice, a swift and silky tread :
" You got so blind, last night, *mon vieux*, I collared all
   your cash—
Three hundred francs. . . . There ! *Nom de Dieu !*"
   said Julot the *apache*.

And that was how I came to know Julot and Gigolette,
And we would talk and drink a *bock*, and smoke a
   cigarette.

And I would meditate upon the artistry of crime,
And he would tell of cracking cribs and cops and doing
time ;
Or else when he was flush of funds he'd carelessly
explain
He'd biffed some bloated *bourgeois* on the border of the
Seine.
So gentle and polite he was, just like a man of peace,
And not a desperado and the terror of the police.

Now one day in a *bistro* that's behind the Place Vendôme
I came on Julot the *apache*, and Gigolette his *môme*.
And as they looked so very grave, says I to them, says I,
"Come on and have a little glass, it's good to rinse
the eye.
You both look mighty serious ; you've something on
the heart."
"Ah, yes," said Julot the *apache*, " we've something to
impart.
When such things come to folks like us, it isn't very
gay . . .
It's Gigolette—she tells me that a *gosse* is on the way."
Then Gigolette, she looked at me with eyes like stones
of gall :
" If we were honest folks," said she, " I wouldn't mind
at all.
But then . . . you know the life we lead ; well, any-
way I mean
(That is, providing it's a girl) to call her Angeline."
" Cheer up," said I ; " it's all in life. There's gold
within the dross.
Come on, we'll drink another *verre* to Angeline the
gosse."

And so the weary winter passed, and then one April
  morn
The worthy Julot came at last to say the babe was born.
" I'd like to chuck it in the Seine," he sourly snarled,
  " and yet
I guess I'll have to let it live, because of Gigolette."
I only laughed, for sure I saw his spite was all a bluff,
And he was prouder than a prince behind his manner
  gruff.
Yet every day he'd blast the brat with curses deep and
  grim,
And swear to me that Gigolette no longer thought of
  him.
And then one night he dropped the mask; his eyes were
  sick with dread,
And when I offered him a smoke he groaned and shook
  his head :
" I'm all upset ; it's Angeline . . . she's covered with
  a rash . .
She'll maybe die, my little *gosse,*" cried Julot the
  apache.

But Angeline, I joy to say, came through the test
  all right,
Though Julot, so they tell me, watched beside her
  day and night.
And when I saw him next, says he : " Come up and
  dine with me.
We'll buy a beefsteak on the way, a bottle and some
  brie."
And so I had a merry night within his humble home,
And laughed with Angeline the *gosse* and Gigolette
  the *môme.*

And every time that Julot used a word the least obscene,
How Gigolette would frown at him and point to
    Angeline :
Oh, such a little innocent, with hair of silken floss,
I do not wonder they were proud of Angeline the *gosse*.
And when her arms were round his neck, then Julot
    says to me :
" I must work harder now, *mon vieux*, since I've to
    work for three."
He worked so very hard indeed, the police dropped in
    one day,
And for a year behind the bars they put him safe away.

So dark and silent now, their home ; they'd gone—I
    wondered where,
Till in a laundry near I saw a child with shining hair ;
And o'er the tub a strapping wench, her arms in soapy
    foam ;
Lo ! it was Angeline the *gosse*, and Gigolette the *môme*.
And so I kept an eye on them and saw that all went
    right,
Until at last came Julot home, half crazy with delight.
And when he'd kissed them both, says he : " I've had
    my fill this time.
I'm on the honest now, I am ; I'm all fed up with crime.
You mark my words, the page I turn is going to be clean,
I swear it on the head of her, my little Angeline."

And so, to finish up my tale, this morning as I strolled
Along the boulevard I heard a voice I knew of old.
I saw a rosy little man with walrus-like moustache . . .
I stopped, I stared. . . By all the gods ! 'twas Julot
    the *apache*.

" I'm in the garden way," he said, " and doing mighty
   well ;
I've half an acre under glass, and heaps of truck to sell.
Come out and see. Oh come, my friend, on Sunday,
   wet or shine . . .
Say !—*it's the First Communion of that little girl of mine.*

II

Chez Moi, MONTPARNASSE,
The same evening.

To-day is an anniversary. A year ago to-day I kicked
over an office stool and came to Paris, thinking to make a
living by my pen. I was twenty then, and in my pocket
I had twenty pounds. Of that, my ten *sous* are all that
remain. And so to-night I am going to spend them, not
prudently on bread, but prodigally on beer.

As I stroll down the Boul' Mich' the lingering light has
all the exquisite tenderness of violet ; the trees are in their
first translucent green ; beneath them the lamps are lit
with purest gold, and from the Little Luxembourg comes
a silver jangle of tiny voices. Taking the gay side of the
street, I enter a café. Although it isn't its true name, I
choose to call my café

L'ESCARGOT D'OR

O TAVERN of the Golden Snail !
Ten *sous* have I, so I'll regale ;
Ten *sous* your amber brew to sip
(Eight for the *bock* and two the tip),
And so I'll sit the evening long,
And smoke my pipe and watch the throng.

The giddy crowd that drains and drinks
I'll watch it quiet as a sphinx ;
And who among them all shall buy
For ten poor *sous* such joy as I ?
As I who, snugly tucked away,
Look on it all as on a play,
A frolic scene of love and fun,
To please an audience of One.

O Tavern of the Golden Snail !
You've stuff indeed for many a tale.
All eyes, all ears, I nothing miss :
Two lovers lean to clasp and kiss ;
The merry students sing and shout,
The nimble *garçons* dart about ;
Lo ! here come Mimi and Musette
With : " *S'il vous plait, une cigarette ?* "
Marcel and Rudolf, Schaunard too,
Behold the old rapscallion crew,
With flowing tie and shaggy head . . ·
Who says Bohemia is dead ?
Oh shades of Murger ! prank and clown,
And I will watch and write it down.

O Tavern of the Golden Snail !
What crackling throats have gulped your ale !
What sons of Fame from far and near
Have glowed and mellowed in your cheer !
Within this corner where I sit
Banville and Coppée clashed their wit ;
And hither too, to dream and drain,
And drown despair, came poor Verlaine.

Here Wilde would talk and Synge would muse,
Maybe like me with just ten *sous*.
Ah! one is lucky, is one not?
With ghosts so rare to drain a pot!
So may your custom never fail,
O Tavern of the Golden Snail!

There! my pipe is out. Let me light it again and consider.
I have no illusions about myself. I am not fool enough to
think I am a poet, but I have a knack of rhyme and I love
to make verses. Mine is a tootling, tin-whistle music.
Humbly and afar I follow in the footsteps of Praed and
Lampson, of Field and Riley, hoping that in time my Muse
may bring me bread and butter. So far, however, it has
been all kicks and no coppers. And to-night I am at the
end of my tether. I wish I knew where to-morrow's breakfast
was coming from. Well, since rhyming's been my ruin, let
me rhyme to the bitter end.

IT IS LATER THAN YOU THINK

Lone amid the café's cheer,
Sad of heart am I to-night;
Dolefully I drink my beer,
But no single line I write.
There's the wretched rent to pay,
Yet I glower at pen and ink:
Oh, inspire me, Muse, I pray,
It is later than you think!

Hello! there's a pregnant phrase.
Bravo! let me write it down;
Hold it with a hopeful gaze,
Gauge it with a fretful frown.

Tune it to my lyric lyre . . .
Ah ! upon starvation's brink,
How the words are dark and dire :
It is later than you think.

Weigh them well. . . . Behold yon band,
Students drinking by the door,
Madly merry, *bock* in hand,
Saucers stacked to mark their score.
Get you gone, you jolly scamps ;
Let your parting glasses clink ;
Seek your long neglected lamps :
It is later than you think.

Look again : yon dainty blonde,
All allure and golden grace,
Oh so willing to respond
Should you turn a smiling face.
Play your part, poor pretty doll ;
Feast and frolic, pose and prink ;
There's the Morgue to end it all,
And it's later than you think.

Yon's a playwright—mark his face,
Puffed and purple, tense and tired ;
Pasha-like he holds his place,
Hated, envied and admired.
How you gobble life, my friend ;
Wine, and woman soft and pink !
Well, each tether has its end :
Sir, it's later than you think.

See yon living scarecrow pass
With a wild and wolfish stare
At each empty absinthe glass,
As if he saw Heaven there.
Poor damned wretch, to end your pain
There is still the Greater Drink.
Yonder waits the sanguine Seine . . .
It is later than you think.

Lastly, you who read ; aye, you
Who this very line may scan :
Think of all you planned to do . . .
Have you done the best you can ?
See ! the tavern lights are low ;
Black's the night, and how you shrink
God ! and is it time to go !
Ah ! the clock is always slow ;
It is later than you think ;
Sadly later than you think ;
Far, far later than you think.

Scarcely do I scribble that last line on the back of an old
envelope when a voice hails me. It is a fellow free-lance,
a short-story man called MacBean. He is having a feast
of *Marennes* and he asks me to join him.

MacBean is a Scotsman with the soul of an Irishman.
He has a keen, lean, spectacled face, and if it were not for
his grey hair he might be taken for a student of theology.
However, there is nothing of the Puritan in MacBean. He
loves wine and women, and money melts in his fingers.

He has lived so long in the Quarter he looks at life from
the Parisian angle. His knowledge of literature is such that
he might be a Professor, but he would rather be a vagabond

of letters. We talk shop. We discuss the American short story, but MacBean vows they do these things better in France. He says that some of the *contes* printed every day in the *Journal* are worthy of Maupassant. After that he buys more beer, and we roam airily over the fields of literature, plucking here and there a blossom of quotation. A fine talk, vivid and eager. It puts me into a kind of glow.

MacBean pays the bill from a handful of big notes, and the thought of my own empty pockets for a moment damps me. However, when we rise to go, it is well after midnight, and I am in a pleasant daze. The rest of the evening may be summed up in the following jingle :

NOCTAMBULE

Zut ! it's two o'clock.
See ! the lights are jumping.
Finish up your *bock*,
Time we all were humping.
Waiters stack the chairs,
Pile them on the tables ;
Let us to our lairs
Underneath the gables.

Up the old Boul' Mich'
Climb with steps erratic.
Steady . . . how I wish
I was in my attic !
Full am I with cheer ;
In my heart the joy stirs ;
Couldn't be the beer,
Must have been the oysters.

In obscene array
Garbage cans spill over;
How I wish that they
Smelled as sweet as clover!
Charing women wait;
Cafés drop their shutters;
Rats perambulate
Up and down the gutters!

Down the darkened street
Market carts are creeping;
Horse with wary feet,
Red-faced driver sleeping.
Loads of vivid greens,
Carrots, leeks, potatoes,
Cabbages and beans,
Turnips and tomatoes.

Pair of dapper chaps,
Cigarettes and sashes,
Stare at me, perhaps
Desperate *apaches*.
" Needn't bother me,
Jolly well you know it;
Parceque je suis
Quartier Latin poète.

" Give you villanelles
Madrigals and lyrics
Ballades and rondels,
Odes and panegyrics.

Poet pinched and poor,
Pricked by cold and hunger;
Trouble's troubadour,
Misery's balladmonger."

Think how queer it is!
Every move I'm making,
Cosmic gravity's
Centre I am shaking;
Oh, how droll to feel
(As I now am feeling),
Even as I reel,
All the world is reeling.

Reeling too the stars,
Neptune and Uranus,
Jupiter and Mars,
Mercury and Venus;
Suns and moons with me,
As I'm homeward straying,
All in sympathy
Swaying, swaying, swaying.

Lord! I've got a head.
Well, it's not surprising.
I must gain my bed
Ere the sun be rising;
When the merry lark
In the sky is soaring,
I'll refuse to hark,
I'll be snoring, snoring.

Strike a sulphur match . . .
Ha ! at last my garret.
Fumble at the latch,
Close the door and bar it.
Bed, you graciously
Wait, despite my scorning . . .
So, bibaciously
Mad old world, good morning.

III

MY GARRET, MONTPARNASSE,
April.

INSOMNIA

HEIGH HO ! to sleep I vainly try ;
Since twelve I haven't closed an eye,
And now it's three, and as I lie,
From Notre Dame to St. Denis
The bells of Paris chime to me ;
" You're young," they say, " and strong and free."

I do not turn with sighs and groans
To ease my limbs, to rest my bones,
As if my bed were stuffed with stones.
No peevish murmur tips my tongue—
Ah no ! for every sound upflung
Says : " Lad, you're free and strong and young."

And so beneath the sheet's caress
My body purrs with happiness ;
Joy bubbles in my veins. . . . Ah yes,

My very blood that leaps along
Is chiming in a joyous song,
Because I'm young and free and strong.

Maybe it is the springtide. I am so happy I am afraid.
The sense of living fills me with exultation. I want to sing,
to dance ; I am dithyrambic with delight.

I think the moon must be to blame :
It fills the room with fairy flame ;
It paints the wall, it seems to pour
A dappled flood upon the floor.
I rise and through the window stare . . !
Ye gods ! how marvellously fair !
From Montrouge to the Martyr's Hill,
A silver city rapt and still ;
Dim, drowsy deeps of opal haze,
And spire and dome in diamond blaze ;
The little lisping leaves of spring
Like sequins softly glimmering ;
Each roof a plaque of argent sheen,
A gauzy gulf the space between ;
Each chimney-top a thing of grace,
Where merry moonbeams prank and chase ;
And all that sordid was and mean,
Just Beauty, deathless and serene.

O magic city of a dream !
From glory unto glory gleam ;
And I will gaze and pity those
Who on their pillows drowse and doze

And as I've nothing else to do,
Of tea I'll make a rousing brew,
And coax my pipes until they croon,
And chant a ditty to the moon.

There ! my tea is black and strong. Inspiration comes
with every sip. Now for the moon.

The moon peeped out behind the hill
As yellow as an apricot ;
Then up and up it climbed until
Into the sky it fairly got ;
The sky was vast and violet ;
The poor moon seemed to faint in fright,
And pale it grew and paler yet,
Like fine old silver, rinsed and bright.
And yet it climbed so bravely on
Until it mounted heaven-high ;
Then earthward it serenely shone,
A silver sovereign of the sky,
A bland sultana of the night,
Surveying realms of lily light.

MOON SONG

A CHILD saw in the morning skies
The dissipated-looking moon,
And opened wide her big blue eyes,
And cried : " Look, look, my lost balloon
And clapped her rosy hands with glee :
" Quick, mother ! Bring it back to me."

A poet in a lilied pond
Espied the moon's reflected charms,
And ravished by that beauty blonde,
Leapt out to clasp her in his arms.
And as he'd never learnt to swim,
Poor fool! that was the end of him.

A rustic glimpsed amid the trees
The bluff moon caught as in a snare.
"They say it do be made of cheese,"
Said Giles, "and that a chap bides there. . . .
That Blue Boar ale be strong, I vow—
The lad's a-winkin' at me now."

Two lovers watched the new moon hold
The old moon in her bright embrace.
Said she: "There's mother, pale and old,
And drawing near her resting place."
Said he: "Be mine, and with me wed,"
Moon-high she stared . . . she shook her head.

A soldier saw with dying eyes
The bleared moon like a ball of blood,
And thought of how in other skies,
So pearly bright on leaf and bud
Like peace its soft white beams had lain;
Like Peace! . . . He closed his eyes again.

Child, lover, poet, soldier, clown,
Ah yes, old Moon, what things you've seen!
I marvel now, as you look down,
How can your face be so serene?
And tranquil still you'll make your round,
Old Moon, when we are underground.

" And now, blow out your candle, lad, and get to bed.
See, the dawn is in the sky. Open your window and let
its freshness rouge your cheek. You've earned your rest.
Sleep."

Aye, but before I do so, let me read again the last
of my *Ballads*.

THE SEWING-GIRL

THE humble garret where I dwell
Is in that Quarter called the Latin ;
It isn't spacious—truth to tell,
There's hardly room to swing a cat in.
But what of that ! It's there I fight
For food and fame, my Muse inviting,
And all the day and half the night
You'll find me writing, writing, writing.

Now, it was in the month of May
As, wrestling with a rhyme rheumatic,
I chanced to look across the way,
And lo ! within a neighbour attic,
A hand drew back the window shade,
And there, a picture glad and glowing,
I saw a sweet and slender maid,
And she was sewing, sewing, sewing.

So poor the room, so small, so scant,
Yet somehow oh, so bright and airy
There was a pink geranium plant,
Likewise a very pert canary.
And in the maiden's heart it seemed
Some fount of gladness must be springing,
For as alone I sadly dreamed
I heard her singing, singing, singing.

God love her ! how it cheered me then
To see her there so brave and pretty ;
So she with needle, I with pen,
We slaved and sang above the city.
And as across my streams of ink
I watched her from a poet's distance,
She stitched and sang . . . I scarcely think
She was aware of my existence.

And then one day she sang no more.
That put me out, there's no denying.
I looked—she laboured as before,
But, bless me ! she was crying, crying.
Her poor canary chirped in vain ;
Her pink geranium drooped in sorrow ;
" Of course," said I, " she'll sing again.
Maybe," I sighed, " she will to-morrow."

Poor child ! 'twas finished with her song :
Day after day her tears were flowing ;
And as I wondered what was wrong
She pined and peaked above her sewing.
And then one day the blind she drew,
Ah ! though I sought with vain endeavour
To pierce the darkness, well I know
My sewing-girl had gone for ever.

And as I sit alone to-night
My eyes unto her room are turning . . .
I'd give the sum of all I write
Once more to see her candle burning,

Once more to glimpse her happy face,
And while my rhymes of cheer I'm ringing,
Across the sunny sweep of space
To hear her singing, singing, singing.

Heigh ho! I realize I am very weary. It's nice to be so
tired, and to know one can sleep as long as one wants. The
morning sunlight floods in at my window, so I draw the
blind and throw myself on my bed. . . .

IV

MY GARRET, MONTPARNASSE,
April.

Hurrah! As I opened my eyes this morning to a hard,
unfeeling world, little did I think what a surprise awaited
me. A big blue envelope had been pushed under my door.
Another rejection, I thought, and I took it up distastefully.
The next moment I was staring at my first cheque.

It was an express order for two hundred francs, in payment
of a bit of verse. . . . So to-day I will celebrate. I will
lunch at the D'Harcourt, I will dine on the Grand Boulevard,
I will go to the theatre.

Well, here's the thing that has turned the tide for me.
It is somewhat in the vein of " Sourdough " Service, the
Yukon bard. I don't think much of his stuff, but they
say he makes heaps of money. I can well believe it, for
he drives a Hispano-Suiza in the Bois every afternoon. The
other night he was with a crowd at the Dome Café, a chubby
chap who sits in a corner and seldom speaks. I was dis-
appointed. I thought he was a big, hairy man who swore

like a trooper and mixed brandy with his beer.   He only
drank Vichy, poor fellow !

LUCILLE

OF course you've heard of the *Nancy Lee*, and how she
 sailed away
On her famous quest of the Arctic flea, to the wilds
 of Hudson's Bay ?
For it was a foreign Prince's whim to collect this tiny cuss,
And a golden quid was no more to him than a copper
 to coves like us.
So we sailed away and our hearts were gay as we gazed
 on the gorgeous scene ;
And we laughed with glee as we caught the flea of the
 wolf and the wolverine ;
Yea, our hearts were light as the parasite of the ermine
 rat we slew,
And the great musk ox, and the silver fox, and the
 moose and the cariboo.
And we laughed with zest as the insect pest of the
 marmot crowned our zeal,
And the wary mink and the wily " link," and the walrus
 and the seal.
And with eyes aglow on the scornful snow we danced
 a rigadoon,
Round the lonesome lair of the Arctic hare, by the
 light of the silver moon.
But the time was nigh to homeward hie, when, imagine
 our despair !
For the best of the lot we hadn't got—the flea of the
 polar bear.

Oh, his face was long and his breath was strong, as
the Skipper he says to me:

"I wants you to linger 'ere, my lad, by the shores of
the Hartic Sea;

I wants you to 'unt the polar bear the perishin' winter
through,

And if flea ye find of its breed and kind, there's a
'undred quid for you."

But I shook my head: "No, Cap," I said; "it's
yourself I'd like to please,

But I tells ye flat I wouldn't do that if ye went on yer
bended knees."

Then the Captain spat in the seething brine, and he
says: "Good luck to you,

If it can't be did for a 'undred quid, supposin' we call
it two?"

So that was why they said good-bye, and they sailed
and left me there—

Alone, alone in the Arctic Zone to hunt for the polar
bear.

Oh, the days were slow and packed with woe, till I
thought they would never end;

And I used to sit when the fire was lit, with my pipe
for my only friend.

And I tried to sing some rollicky thing, but my song
broke off in a prayer,

And I'd drowse and dream by the driftwood gleam:
I'd dream of a polar bear;

I'd dream of a cloudlike polar bear that blotted the
stars on high,

With ravenous jaws and fienzing claws, and the flames
of hell in his eye.

And I'd trap around on the frozen ground, as a proper hunter ought,

And beasts I'd find of every kind, but never the one I sought.

Never a track in the white ice-pack that humped and heaved and flawed,

Till I came to think : " Why, strike me pink ! if the creature ain't a fraud."

And then one night in the waning light, as I hurried home to sup,

I hears a roar by the cabin door, and a great white hulk heaves up.

So my rifle flashed, and a bullet crashed ; dead, dead as a stone fell he,

And I gave a cheer, for there in his ear—Gosh ding me !—a tiny flea.

At last, at last ! Oh, I clutched it fast, and I gazed on it with pride ;

And I thrust it in-to a biscuit-tin, and I shut it safe inside ;

With a lid of glass for the light to pass, and space to leap and play ;

Oh, it kept alive ; yea, seemed to thrive, as I watched it night and day.

And I used to sit and sing to it, and I shielded it from harm,

And many a feed it had at need on the heft of my hairy arm.

For you'll never know in that land of snow how lonesome a man can feel ;

So I made a fuss of the little cuss, and I christened it " Lucille."

But the longest winter has its end, and the ice went
    out to sea,

And I saw one day a ship in the bay, and there was the
    Nancy Lee.

So a boat was lowered and I went aboard, and they
    opened wide their eyes—

Yes, they gave a cheer when the truth was clear, and
    they saw my precious prize.

And then it was all like a giddy dream ; but to cut
    my story short,

We sailed away on the fifth of May to the foreign
    Prince's court ;

To a palmy land and a palace grand, and the little
    Prince was there,

And a fat Princess in a satin dress with a crown of
    gold on her hair.

And they showed me into a shiny room, just him and
    her and me,

And the Prince he was pleased and friendly-like, and
    he calls for drinks for three.

And I shows them my battered biscuit-tin, and I
    makes my modest spiel,

And they laughed, they did, when I opened the lid,
    and out there popped Lucille.

Oh, the Prince was glad, I could soon see that, and the
    Princess she was too ;

And Lucille waltzed round on the tablecloth as she
    often used to do.

And the Prince pulled out a purse of gold, and he put
    it in my hand ;

And he says : " It was worth all that, I'm told, to stay
    in that nasty land."

And then he turned with a sudden cry, and he clutched
　　at his royal beard ;
And the Princess screamed, and well she might—for
　　Lucille had disappeared.

" She must be here," said his Noble Nibbs, so we hunted
　　all around ;
Oh, we searched that place, but never a trace of the
　　little beast we found.
So I shook my head, and I glumly said : " Gol darn the
　　saucy cuss !
It's mighty queer, but she isn't here ; so . . . she
　　must be on one of us.
You'll pardon me if I make so free, but—there's just
　　one thing to do :
If you'll kindly go for a half a mo' I'll search me
　　garments through."
Then all alone on the shiny throne I stripped from head
　　to heel ;
In vain, in vain ; it was very plain that I hadn't got
　　Lucille.
So I garbed again, and I told the Prince, and he scratched
　　his august head ;
"I suppose if she hasn't selected you, it must be me,"
　　he said.
So *he* retired ; but he soon came back, and his features
　　showed distress :
" Oh, it isn't you and it isn't me." . . . Then we looked
　　at the Princess.
So *she* retired ; and we heard a scream, and she opened
　　wide the door ;
And her fingers twain were pinched to pain, but a
　　radiant smile she wore :

" It's here," she cries, " our precious prize. Oh, I
    found it right away. . . . "
Then I ran to her with a shout of joy, but I choked
    with a wild dismay.
I clutched the back of the golden throne, and the room
    began to reel . . .
What she held to me was, ah yes! a flea, but . . .
    it wasn't my Lucille.

After all, I did not celebrate. I sat on the terrace of the
Café Napolitain on the Grand Boulevard, half hypnotized
by the passing crowd. And as I sat I fell into conversation
with a god-like stranger who sipped some golden ambrosia.
He told me he was an actor and introduced me to his
beverage, which he called a " Suze-Anni." He soon left me,
but the effect of the golden liquid remained, and there
came over me a desire to write. *C'était plus fort que moi.*
So instead of going to the Folies Bergère I spent all evening in the Omnium Bar near the Bourse, and wrote the
following:

ON THE BOULEVARD

Oh, it's pleasant sitting here,
  Seeing all the people pass ;
You beside your *bock* of beer,
  I behind my *demi-tasse.*
Chatting of no matter what.
You the Mummer, I the Bard ;
Ah, it's jolly, is it not ?—
Sitting on the Boulevard.

More amusing than a book,
If a chap has eyes to see;
For, no matter where I look,
Stories, stories jump at me.
Moving tales my pen might write;
Poems plain on every face;
Monologues you could recite
With inimitable grace.

(Ah! Imagination's power)
See yon *demi-mondaine* there,
Idly toying with a flower,
Smiling with a pensive air . . .
Well, her smile is but a mask,
For I saw within her muff
Such a wicked little flask:
Vitriol—ugh! the beastly stuff.

Now look back beside the bar.
See yon curled and scented *beau*,
Puffing at a fine cigar—
Sale espèce de maquereau.
Well (of course, it's all surmise),
It's for him she holds her place;
When he passes she will rise,
Dash the vitriol in his face.

Quick they'll carry him away,
Pack him in a Red Cross car;
Her they'll hurry, so they say,
To the cells of St. Lazare.

What will happen then, you ask ?
What will all the sequel be ?
Ah ! Imagination's task
Isn't easy . . . let me see . . .

She will go to gaol, no doubt,
For a year, or maybe two ;
But as soon as she gets out
Start her bawdy life anew.
He will lie within a ward,
Harmless as a man can be,
With his face grotesquely scarred,
And his eyes that cannot see.

Then amid the city's din
He will stand against a wall,
With around his neck a tin
Into which the pennies fall.
She will pass (I see it plain,
Like a cinematograph),
She will halt and turn again,
Look and look, and maybe laugh.

Well, I'm not so sure of that—
Whether she will laugh or cry.
He will hold a battered hat
To the lady passing by.
He will smile a cringing smile,
And into his grimy hold,
With a laugh (or sob) the while,
She will drop a piece of gold.

" Bless you, lady," he will say,
And get grandly drunk that night.
She will come and come each day,
Fascinated by the sight.
Then somehow he'll get to know
(Maybe by a kindly friend)
Who she is, and so . . . and so
Bring my story to an end.

How his heart will burst with hate !
He will curse and he will cry.
He will wait and wait and wait,
Till again she passes by.
Then like tiger from its lair
He will leap from out his place,
Down her, clutch her by the hair,
Smear the vitriol on her face.

(Ah ! Imagination rare)
See . . . he takes his hat to go ;
Now he's level with her chair ;
Now she rises up to throw. . . .
God ! and she has done it too . . .
Oh, those screams ! those hideous screams !
I imagined and . . . it's true :
How his face will haunt my dreams !

What a sight ! It makes me sick
Seems I am to blame somehow.
Garçon, fetch a brandy quick . . '
There ! I'm feeling better now.

Let's collaborate, we two,
You the Mummer, I the Bard;
Oh, what stunning stuff we'll do,
Sitting on the Boulevard!

It is strange how one works easily at times. I wrote
this so quickly that I might almost say I had reached the
end before I had come to the beginning. In such a mood
I wonder why everybody does not write poetry. Get a
Roget's *Thesaurus*, a rhyming dictionary; sit before your
typewriter with a strong glass of coffee at your elbow,
and just click the stuff off.

FACILITY

So easy 'tis to make a rhyme,
That did the world but know it,
Your coachman might Parnassus climb,
Your butler be a poet.

Then, 'oh, how charming it would be
If, when in haste hysteric
You called the page, you learned that he
Was grappling with a lyric.

Or else what rapture it would yield,
When cook sent up the salad,
To find within its depths concealed
A touching little ballad.

Or if for tea and toast you yearned,
What joy to find upon it
The chambermaid had coyly laid
A palpitating sonnet.

z

Your baker could the fashion set;
Your butcher might respond well;
With every tart a triolet,
With every chop a rondel.

Your tailor's bill . . . well, I'll be blowed!
Dear chap! I never knowed him . . .
He's gone and written me an ode,
Instead of what I *owed* him.

So easy 'tis to rhyme . . . yet stay!
Oh, terrible misgiving!
Please do not give the game away . . .
I've got to make my living.

V

MY GARRET,
May 1914

GOLDEN DAYS

ANOTHER day of toil and strife,
Another page so white,
Within that fateful Log of Life
That I and all must write;
Another page without a stain
To make of as I may,
That done, I shall not see again
Until the Judgment Day.

Ah, could I, could I backward turn
The pages of that Book,
How often would I blench and burn!
How often loathe to look!

What pages would be meanly scrolled ;
What smeared as if with mud ;
A few, maybe, might gleam like gold,
Some scarlet seem as blood.

O Record grave, God guide my hand
And make me worthy be,
Since what I write to-day shall stand
To all eternity ;
Aye, teach me, Lord of Life, I pray,
As I salute the sun,
To bear myself that every day
May be a Golden One.

I awoke this morning to see the bright sunshine flooding
into my garret. No chamber in the palace of a king could
have been more fair. How I sang as I dressed ! How I
lingered over my coffee, savouring every drop ! How
carefully I packed my pipe, gazing serenely over the roofs
of Paris.

Never is the city so lovely as in this month of May, when
all the trees are in the fulness of their foliage. As I look, I
feel a freshness of vision in my eyes. Wonder wakes in
me. The simplest things move me to delight.

THE JOY OF LITTLE THINGS

It's good the great green earth to roam,
Where sights of awe the soul inspire ;
But oh, it's best, the coming home,
The crackle of one's own hearth-fire !

You've hob-nobbed with the solemn Past ;
You've seen the pageantry of kings ;
Yet oh, how sweet to gain at last
The peace and rest of Little Things !

Perhaps you're counted with the Great ;
You strain and strive with mighty men ;
Your hand is on the helm of State ;
Colossus-like you stride . . . and then
There comes a pause, a shining hour,
A dog that leaps, a hand that clings :
O Titan, turn from pomp and power ;
Give all your heart to Little Things.

Go couch you childwise in the grass,
Believing it's some jungle strange,
Where mighty monsters peer and pass,
Where beetles roam and spiders range.
Mid gloom and gleam of leaf and blade,
What dragons rasp their painted wings !
O magic world of shine and shade !
O beauty land of Little Things !

I sometimes wonder, after all,
Amid this tangled web of fate,
If what is great may not be small,
And what is small may not be great.
So wondering I go my way,
Yet in my heart contentment sings . . .
O may I ever see, I pray,
God's grace and love in Little Things.

So give to me, I only beg,
A little roof to call my own,
A little cider in the keg,
A little meat upon the bone ;
A little garden by the sea,
A little boat that dips and swings . . .
Take wealth, take fame, but leave to me,
O Lord of Life, just Little Things.

Yesterday I finished my tenth ballad. When I have
done about a score I will seek a publisher. If I cannot find
one, I will earn, beg or steal the money to get them printed.
Then if they do not sell I will hawk them from door to door.
Oh, I'll succeed, I know I'll succeed. And yet I don't want
an easy success ; give me the joy of the fight, the thrill
of the adventure. Here's my last ballad :

THE ABSINTHE DRINKERS

HE's yonder, on the terrace of the Café de la Paix,
The little wizened Spanish man, I see him every day.
He's sitting with his Pernod on his customary chair ;
He's staring at the passers with his customary stare.
He never takes his piercing eyes from off that moving
    throng,
That current cosmopolitan meandering along :
Dark diplomats from Martinique, pale Rastas from
    Peru,
An Englishman from Bloomsbury, a Yank from
    Kalmazoo ;
A poet from Montmartre's heights, a dapper little Jap.
Exotic citizens of all the countries on the map ;

A tourist horde from every land that's underneath the
    sun—
That little wizened Spanish man, he misses never one.
Oh, foul or fair he's always there, and many a drink he
    buys,
And there's a fire of red desire within his hollow eyes.
And sipping of my Pernod, and a-knowing what I know,
Sometimes I want to shriek aloud and give away the
    show.
I've lost my nerve; he's haunting me; he's like a
    beast of prey,
That Spanish man that's watching at the Café de la Paix.

Say ! Listen and I'll tell you all . . . the day was
    growing dim,
And I was with my Pernod at the table next to him;
And he was sitting soberly as if he were asleep,
When suddenly he seemed to tense, like tiger for a leap.
And then he swung around to me, his hand went to
    his hip,
My heart was beating like a gong—my arm was in
    his grip;
His eyes were glaring into mine; aye, though I shrank
    with fear,
His fetid breath was on my face, his voice was in my ear:
" Excuse my *brusquerie*," he hissed; " but, sir, do
    you suppose—
That portly man who passed us had a *wen upon his
    nose ?* "

And then at last it dawned on me, the fellow must be
    mad ;
And when I soothingly replied: "I do not think he had,"

The little wizened Spanish man subsided in his chair,
And shrouded in his raven cloak resumed his owlish
    stare.
But when I tried to slip away he turned and glared
    at me,
And oh, that fishlike face of his was sinister to see:
"Forgive me if I startled you; of course you think
    I'm queer;
No doubt you wonder who I am, so solitary here;
You question why the passers-by I piercingly review . . .
Well, listen, my bibacious friend, I'll tell my tale to you.

"It happened twenty years ago, and in another land:
A maiden young and beautiful, two suitors for her
    hand.
My rival was the lucky one; I vowed I would repay;
Revenge has mellowed in my heart, it's rotten ripe
    to-day.
My happy rival skipped away, vamoosed, he left no
    trace;
And so I'm waiting, waiting here to meet him face to
    face;
For has it not been ever said that all the world one
    day
Will pass in pilgrimage before the Café de la Paix?"

"But, sir," I made remonstrance, "if it's twenty
    years ago,
You'd scarcely recognize him now, he must have altered
    so."
The little wizened Spanish man he laughed a hideous
    laugh,
And from his cloak he quickly drew a faded photograph.

"You're right," said he ; "but there are traits (oh, this you must allow)
That never change; Lopez was fat, he must be fatter now.
His paunch is senatorial, he cannot see his toes,
I'm sure of it ; and then, behold ! that wen upon his nose.
I'm looking for a man like that. I'll wait and wait until . . . "
"What will you do ? " I sharply cried ; he answered me : "Why, kill !
He robbed me of my happiness—nay, stranger, do not start ;
I'll firmly and politely put—a bullet in his heart."

And then that little Spanish man, with big cigar alight,
Uprose and shook my trembling hand and vanished in the night.
And I went home and thought of him and had a dreadful dream
Of portly men with each a wen, and woke up with a scream.
And sure enough, next morning, as I prowled the Boulevard,
A portly man with wenny nose roamed into my regard ;
Then like a flash I ran to him and clutched him by the arm :
"Oh, sir," said I, "I do not wish to see you come to harm ;
But if your life you value aught, I beg, entreat and pray—
Don't pass before the terrace of the Café de la Paix."

That portly man he looked at me with such a startled
    air,
Then bolted like a rabbit down the rue Michaudière.
" Ha ! ha ! I've saved a life," I thought ; and laughed
    in my relief,
And straightway joined the Spanish man o'er his
    apéritif.
And thus each day I dodged about and kept the strictest
    guard
For portly men with each a wen upon the Boulevard.
And then I hailed my Spanish pal, and sitting in the sun,
We ordered many Pernods and we drank them every one.
And sternly he would stare and stare until my hand
    would shake,
And grimly he would glare and glare until my heart
    would quake.
And I would say : " Alphonso, lad, I must expostulate ;
Why keep alive for twenty years the furnace of your
    hate ?
Perhaps his wedded life was hell ; and you, at least,
    are free . . . "
" That's where you've got it wrong," he snarled ;
    " the fool she took was *me.*
My rival sneaked, threw up the sponge, betrayed himself
    a churl :
'Twas he who got the happiness, I only got—the girl."
With that he looked so devil-like he made me creep
    and shrink,
And there was nothing else to do but buy another
    drink.

Now yonder like a blot of ink he sits across the way,
Upon the smiling terrace of the Café de la Paix ;

That little wizened Spanish man, his face is ghastly
white,
His eyes are staring, staring like a tiger's in the night.
I know within his evil heart the fires of hate are fanned.
I know his automatic's ready waiting to his hand.
I know a tragedy is near, I dread, I have no peace . . .
Oh, don't you think I ought to go and call upon the
police ?
Look there . . . he's rising up . . . my God ! He leaps
from out his place . . .
Yon millionaire from Argentine . . . the two are face
to face . . .
A shot ! A shriek ! A heavy fall ! A huddled heap !
Oh, see
The little wizened Spanish man is dancing in his glee. . . .
I'm sick . . . I'm faint . . . I'm going mad. . . . Oh,
please take me away . . .
There's BLOOD upon the terrace of the Café de la
Paix. . . .

And now I'll leave my work and sally forth. The
city is *en fête*. I'll join the crowd and laugh and sing with
the best.

> The sunshine seeks my little room
> To tell me Paris streets are gay ;
> That children cry the lily bloom
> All up and down the leafy way ;
> That half the town is mad with May,
> With flame of flag and boom of bell :
> For Carnival is King to-day ;
> So pen and page, awhile farewell.

PART TWO

EARLY SUMMER

I

THE RELEASE

To-day within a grog-shop near
I saw a newly captured linnet,
Who beat against his cage in fear,
And fell exhausted every minute;
And when I asked the fellow there
If he to sell the bird were willing,
He told me with a careless air
That I could have it for a shilling.

And so I bought it, cage and all
(Although I went without my dinner),
And where some trees were fairly tall
And houses shrank and smoke was thinner,
The tiny door I open threw,
As down upon the grass I sank me:
Poor little chap! How quick he flew . . .
He didn't even wait to thank me.

Life's like a cage; we beat the bars,
We bruise our breasts, we struggle vainly;
Up to the glory of the stars
We strain with flutterings ungainly.

666

And then—God opens wide the door;
Our wondrous wings are arched for flying;
We poise, we part, we sing, we soar . . .
Light, freedom, love. . . . Fools call it—Dying.

Yes, that wretched little bird haunted me. I had to let it go. Since I have seized my own liberty I am a fanatic for freedom. It is now a year ago I launched on my great adventure. I have had hard times, been hungry, cold, weary. I have worked harder than ever I did and discouragement has slapped me on the face. Yet the year has been the happiest of my life.

And all because I am free. By reason of filthy money no one can say to me: Do this, or do that. "Master" doesn't exist in my vocabulary. I can look any man in the face and tell him to go to the devil. I belong to myself. I am not for sale. It's glorious to feel like that. It sweetens the dry crust and warms the heart in the icy wind. For that I will hunger and go threadbare; for that I will live austerely and deny myself all pleasure. After health, the best thing in life is freedom.

Here is the last of my ballads. It is by way of being an experiment. Its theme is commonplace, its language that of every day. It is a bit of realism in rhyme.

THE WEE SHOP

She risked her all, they told me, bravely sinking
The pinched economies of thirty years;
And there the little shop was, meek and shrinking,
The sum of all her dreams and hopes and fears.
Ere it was opened I would see them in it,
The grey-haired dame, the daughter with her crutch;
So fond, so happy, hoarding every minute,
Like artists, for the final tender touch.

The opening day ! I'm sure that to their seeming
Was never shop so wonderful as theirs ;
With pyramids of jam-jars rubbed to gleaming ;
Such vivid cans of peaches, prunes and pears ;
And chocolate, and biscuits in glass cases,
And bon-bon bottles, many-hued and bright ;
Yet nothing half so radiant as their faces,
Their eyes of hope, excitement and delight.

I entered : how they waited all a-flutter !
How awkwardly they weighed my acid-drops !
And then with all the thanks a tongue could utter
They bowed me from the kindliest of shops.
I'm sure that night their customers they numbered ;
Discussed them all in happy, breathless speech ;
And though quite worn and weary, ere they slumbered,
Sent heavenward a little prayer for each.

And so I watched with interest redoubled
That little shop, spent in it all I had ;
And when I saw it empty I was troubled,
And when I saw them busy I was glad.
And when I dared to ask how things were going,
They told me, with a fine and gallant smile :
" Not badly . . . slow at first . . . There's never
    knowing . . .
'Twill surely pick up in a little while."

I'd often see them through the winter weather.
Behind the shutters by a light's faint speck,
Poring o'er books, their faces close together,
The lame girl's arm around her mother's neck,

They dressed their window not one time but twenty,
Each change more pinched, more desperately neat;
Alas! I wondered if behind that plenty
The two who owned it had enough to eat.

Ah, who would dare to sing of tea and coffee?
The sadness of a stock unsold and dead;
The petty tragedy of melting toffee,
The sordid pathos of stale gingerbread.
Ignoble themes! And yet—those haggard faces!
Within that little shop. . . . Oh, here I say
One does not need to look in lofty places
For tragic themes, they're round us every day.

And so I saw their agony, their fighting,
Their eyes of fear, their heartbreak, their despair;
And there the little shop is, black and blighting,
And all the world goes by and does not care.
They say she sought her old employer's pity,
Content to take the pittance he would give.
The lame girl? yes, she's working in the city;
She coughs a lot—she hasn't long to live.

Last night MacBean introduced me to Saxon Dane the
Poet. Truly, he is more like a blacksmith than a Bard—
a big, bearded man whose black eyes brood sombrely or
flash with sudden fire. We talked of Walt Whitman, and
then of others.

"The trouble with poetry," he said, "is that it is too
exalted. It has a phraseology of its own; it selects themes
that are quite outside of ordinary experience. As a medium
of expression it fails to reach the great mass of the people."

Then he added: "To hell with the great mass of the
people! What have they got to do with it? Write to

please yourself, as if not a single reader existed. The moment a man begins to be conscious of an audience he is artistically damned. You're not a Poet, I hope ? "

I meekly assured him I was a mere maker of verse.

" Well," said he, " better good verse than middling poetry. And maybe even the humblest of rhymes has its uses. Happiness is happiness, whether it be inspired by a Rossetti sonnet or a ballad by G. R. Sims. Let each one who has something to say, say it in the best way he can, and abide the result. . . . After all," he went on, " what does it matter ? We are living in a pigmy day. With Tennyson and Browning the line of great poets passed away, perhaps for ever. The world to-day is full of little minstrels, who echo one another and who pipe away tunefully enough. But with one exception they do not matter."

I dared to ask who was his one exception. He answered, " Myself, of course."

Here's a bit of light verse which it amused me to write to-day, as I sat in the sun on the terrace of the Closerie de Lilas :

THE PHILISTINE AND THE BOHEMIAN

SHE was a Philistine spick and span,
He was a bold Bohemian.
She had the *mode*, and the last at that ;
He had a cape and a brigand hat.
She was so *riante* and *chic* and trim ;
He was so shaggy, unkempt and grim.
On the rue de la Paix she was wont to shine ;
The rue de la Gaîté was more his line.
She doted on Barclay and Dell and Caine ;
He quoted Malarmé and Paul Verlaine.
She was a triumph at Tango teas ;
At Vorticist's suppers he sought to please.

She thought that Franz Lehar was utterly great;
Of Strauss and Stravinski he'd piously prate.
She loved elegance, he loved art;
They were as wide as the poles apart:
Yet—Cupid and Caprice are hand and glove—
They met at a dinner, they fell in love.

Home he went to his garret bare,
Thrilling with rapture, hope, despair.
Swift he gazed in his looking-glass,
Made a grimace and murmured: " Ass ! "
Seized his scissors and fiercely sheared,
Severed his buccaneering beard;
Grabbed his hair, and clip ! clip ! clip !
Off came a bunch with every snip.
Ran to a tailor's in startled state,
Suits a dozen commanded straight;
Coats and overcoats, pants in pairs,
Everything that a dandy wears;
Socks and collars, and shoes and ties,
Everything that a dandy buys.
Chums looked at him with wondering stare,
Fancied they'd seen him before somewhere;
A Brummell, a D'Orsay, a *beau* so fine,
A shining, immaculate Philistine.

Home she went in a raptured daze,
Looked in a mirror with startled gaze,
Didn't seem to be pleased at all;
Savagely muttered: " Insipid Doll ! "
Clutched her hair and a pair of shears,
Cropped and bobbed it behind the ears;

Aimed at a wan and willowy-necked
Sort of a Holman Hunt effect ;
Robed in subtile and sage-green tones,
Like the dames of Rossetti and F. B. Jones ;
Girdled her garments billowing wide,
Moved with an undulating glide ;
All her frivolous friends forsook,
Cultivated a soulful look ;
Gushed in a voice with a creamy throb
Over some weirdly Futurist daub—
Did all, in short, that a woman can
To be a consummate Bohemian.

A year went past with its hopes and fears,
A year that seemed like a dozen years.
They met once more. . . . Oh, at last ! At last !
They rushed together, they stopped aghast.
They looked at each other with blank dismay,
They simply hadn't a word to say.
He thought with a shiver : " Can this be she ? "
She thought with a shudder : " This can't be he ? "
This simpering dandy, so sleek and spruce ;
This languorous lily in garments loose ;
They sought to brace from the awful shock :
Taking a seat, they tried to talk.
She spoke of Bergson and Pater's prose,
He prattled of dances and ragtime shows ;
She purred of pictures, Matisse, Cezanne,
His tastes to the girls of Kirchner ran ;
She raved of Tschaikowsky and Cæsar Franck,
He owned that he was a jazz-band crank !
They made no headway.   Alas ! alas !
He thought her a bore, she thought him an ass.

And so they arose and hurriedly fled ;
Perish Illusion, Romance, you're dead.
He loved elegance, she loved art,
Better at once to part, to part.

And what is the moral of all this rot ?
Don't try to be what you know you're not.
And if you're made on a muttonish plan,
Don't seek to seem a Bohemian ;
And if to the goats your feet incline,
Don't try to pass for a Philistine.

II

A Small Café in a Side Street,
June 1914.

THE BOHEMIAN DREAMS

Because my overcoat's in pawn,
I choose to take my glass
Within a little *bistro* on
The rue du Montparnasse ;
The dusty bins with bottles shine,
The counter's lined with zinc,
And there I sit and drink my wine,
And think and think and think.

I think of hoary old Stamboul,
Of Moslem and of Greek,
Of Persian in coat of wool,
Of Kurd and Arab sheikh ;

Of all the types of weal and woe,
And as I raise my glass,
Across Galata bridge I know
They pass and pass and pass.

I think of citron-trees aglow,
Of fan-palms shading down,
Of sailors dancing heel and toe
With wenches black and brown;
And though it's all an ocean far
From Yucatan to France,
I'll bet beside the old bazaar
They dance and dance and dance.

I think of Monte Carlo, where
The pallid croupiers call,
And in the gorgeous, guilty air
The gamblers watch the ball;
And as I flick away the foam
With which my beer is crowned,
The wheels beneath the gilded dome
Go round and round and round.

I think of vast Niagara,
Those gulfs of foam a-shine,
Whose mighty roar would stagger a
More prosy bean than mine;
And as the hours I idly spend
Against a greasy wall,
I know that green the waters bend
And fall and fall and fall.

I think of Nijni Novgorod
And Jews who never rest;
And womenfolk with spade and hod
Who slave in Buda Pest;
Of squat and sturdy Japanese
Who pound the paddy soil,
And as I loaf and smoke at ease
They toil and toil and toil.

I think of shrines in Hindustan.
Of cloistral glooms in Spain,
Of minarets in Ispahan,
Of St. Sophia's fane,
Of convent towers in Palestine,
Of temples in Cathay,
And as I stretch and sip my wine
They pray and pray and pray.

And so my dreams I dwell within,
And visions come and go,
And life is passing like a Cin-
Ematographic Show;
Till just as surely as my pipe
Is underneath my nose,
Amid my visions rich and ripe
I doze and doze and doze.

Alas! it is too true. Once more I am counting the coppers,
living on the ragged edge. My manuscripts come back to
me like boomerangs, and I have not the postage, far less
the heart, to send them out again.

MacBean seems to take an interest in my struggles. I
often sit in his room in the rue Saint-Julien-le-Pauvre.

smoking and sipping whisky into the small hours. He is an old hand, who knows the market and frankly manufactures for it.

"Give me short pieces," he says; "things of three verses that will fill a blank half-page of a magazine. Let them be sprightly, and, if possible, have a snapper at the end. Give me that sort of article. I think I can place it for you."

Then he looked through a lot of my verse: "This is the kind of stuff I might be able to sell," he said:

A DOMESTIC TRAGEDY

CLORINDA met me on the way
As I came from the train;
Her face was anything but gay,
In fact, suggested pain.
"Oh hubby, hubby dear!" she cried,
"I've awful news to tell. . . ."
"What is it, darling?" I replied;
"Your mother—is she well?"

"Oh no! oh no! it is not that,
It's something else," she wailed,
My heart was beating pit-a-pat,
My ruddy visage paled.
Like lightning flash in heaven's dome
The fear within me woke:
"Don't say," I cried, "our little home
Has all gone up in smoke!"

She shook her head. Oh, swift I clasped
And held her to my breast;
"The children! Tell me quick," I gasped,
"Believe me, it is best."

Then, then she spoke ; mid sobs I caught
These words of woe divine :
" It's coo-coo-cook has gone and bought
A new hat just like mine."

At present I am living on bread and milk. By doing this I can rub along for another ten days. The thought pleases me. As long as I have a crust I am master of my destiny. Some day, when I am rich and famous, I shall look back on all this with regret. Yet I think I shall always remain a Bohemian. I hate regularity. The clock was never made for me. I want to eat when I am hungry, sleep when I am weary, drink—well, any old time.

I prefer to be alone. Company is a constraint on my spirit. I never make an engagement if I can avoid it. To do so is to put a mortgage on my future. I like to be able to rise in the morning with the thought that the hours before me are all mine, to spend in my own way—to work, to dream, to watch the unfolding drama of life.

Here is another of my ballads. It is longer than most, and gave me more trouble, though none the better for that.

THE PENCIL SELLER

A PENCIL, sir ; a penny—won't you buy ?
I'm cold and wet and tired, a sorry plight ;
Don't turn your back, sir ; take one just to try ;
I haven't made a single sale to-night.
Oh, thank you, sir ; but take the pencil too ;
I'm not a beggar, I'm a business man.
Pencils I deal in, red and black and blue ;
It's hard, but still I do the best I can.
Most days I make enough to pay for bread,
A cup o' coffee, stretching room at night.
One needs so little—to be warm and fed,
A hole to kennel in—oh, one's all right . . .

Excuse me, you're a painter, are you not ?
I saw you looking at that dealer's show,
The *croûtes* he has for sale, a shabby lot—
What do I know of Art ? What do I know . . .
Well, look ! That David Strong so well displayed,
" White Sorcery " it's called, all gossamer,
And pale moon-magic and a dancing maid
(You like the little elfin face of her ?)—
That's good ; but still, the picture as a whole,
The values.—Pah ! He never painted worse ;
Perhaps because his fire was lacking coal,
His cupboard bare, no money in his purse.
Perhaps . . . they say he laboured hard and long,
And see now, in the harvest of his fame,
When round his pictures people gape and throng,
A scurvy dealer sells this on his name.
A wretched rag, wrung out of want and woe ;
A soulless daub, not David Strong a bit,
Unworthy of his art. . . . How should I know ?
How should I know ? I'm *Strong*—I painted it.

There now, I didn't mean to let that out.
It came in spite of me—aye, stare and stare.
You think I'm lying, crazy, drunk, no doubt—
Think what you like, it's neither here nor there.
It's hard to tell so terrible a truth,
To gain to glory, yet be such as I.
It's true ; that picture's mine, done in my youth,
Up in a garret near the Paris sky.
The child's my daughter ; aye, she posed for me.
That's why I come and sit here every night.
The painting's bad, but still—oh, still I see
Her little face all laughing in the light.

So now you understand.—I live in fear
Lest one like you should carry it away ;
A poor, pot-boiling thing, but oh, how dear !
" Don't let them buy it, pitying God ! " I pray !
And hark ye, sir—sometimes my brain's awhirl.
Some night I'll crash into that window pane
And snatch my picture back, my little girl,
And run and run. . . .

                   I'm talking wild again ;
A crab can't run. I'm crippled, withered, lame,
Palsied, as good as dead all down one side.
No warning had I when the evil came :
It struck me down in all my strength and pride.
Triumph was mine, I thrilled with perfect power ;
Honour was mine, Fame's laurel touched my
    brow ;
Glory was mine—within a little hour
I was a god and . . . what you find me now.

My child, that little, laughing girl you see,
She was my nurse for all ten weary years ;
Her joy, her hope, her youth she gave for me ;
Her very smiles were masks to hide her tears.
And I, my precious art, so rich, so rare,
Lost, lost to me — what could my heart but
    break !
Oh, as I lay and wrestled with despair,
I would have killed myself but for her sake. . . .

By luck I had some pictures I could sell,
And so we fought the wolf back from the door ;
She painted too, aye, wonderfully well.
We often dreamed of brighter days in store.

And then quite suddenly she seemed to fail
I saw the shadows darken round her eyes.
So tired she was, so sorrowful, so pale,
And oh, there came a day she could not rise.
The doctor looked at her ; he shook his head,
And spoke of wine and grapes and Southern air :
" If you can get her out of this," he said,
" She'll have a fighting chance with proper care."

" With proper care ! " When he had gone away,
I sat there, trembling, twitching, dazed with grief.
Under my old and ragged coat she lay,
Our room was bare and cold beyond belief.
" Maybe," I thought, " I still can paint a bit,
Some lilies, landscape, anything at all."
Alas ! My brush, I could not steady it.
Down from my fumbling hand I let it fall.
" With proper care "—how could I give her that,
Half of me dead ? . . . I crawled down to the street.
Cowering beside the wall, I held my hat
And begged of everyone I chanced to meet.
I got some pennies, bought her milk and bread,
And so I fought to keep the Doom away ;
And yet I saw with agony of dread
My dear one sinking, sinking day by day.
And then I was awakened in the night :
" Please take my hands, I'm cold," I heard her sigh ;
And soft she whispered, as she held me tight :
" Oh, daddy, we've been happy, you and I ! "
I do not think she suffered any pain,
She breathed so quietly . . . but though I tried,
I could not warm her little hands again :
And so there in the icy dark she died. . . .

The dawn came groping in with fingers grey
And touched me, sitting silent as a stone ;
I kissed those piteous lips, as cold as clay—
I did not cry, I did not even moan.
At last I rose, groped down the narrow stair ;
An evil fog was oozing from the sky ;
Half-crazed I stumbled on, I knew not where,
Like phantoms were the folks that passed me by.
How long I wandered thus I do not know,
But suddenly I halted, stood stock-still—
Beside a door that spilled a golden glow
I saw a name, *my name*, upon a bill.
" A Sale of Famous Pictures," so it read,
" A Notable Collection, each a gem,
Distinguished Works of Art by painters dead."
The folks were going in, I followed them.
I stood upon the outskirts of the crowd,
I only hoped that none might notice me.
Soon, soon I heard them call my name aloud :
" A ' David Strong,' his *Fête in Brittany*."
(A brave big picture that, the best I've done,
It glowed and kindled half the hall away,
With all its memories of sea and sun,
Of pipe and bowl, of joyous work and play.
I saw the sardine nets blue as the sky,
I saw the nut-brown fisher-boats put out.)
" Five hundred pounds !" rapped out a voice near by ;
" Six hundred ! "   " Seven !"   " Eight ! "   And then a
     shout :
" A thousand pounds !"   Oh, how I thrilled to hear !
Oh, how the bids went up by leaps, by bounds !
And then a silence ; then the auctioneer :
" It's going ! Going ! Gone ! *Three thousand pounds !* "

Three thousand pounds ! A frenzy leapt in me.
" That picture's mine," I cried; "I'm David Strong.
I painted it, this famished wretch you see ;
I did it, I, and sold it for a song.
And in a garret three small hours ago
My daughter died for want of Christian care.
Look, look at me ! . . . Is it to mock my woe
You pay three thousand for my picture there ?" . . .

O God ! I stumbled blindly from the hall ;
The city crashed on me, the fiendish sounds
Of cruelty and strife, but over all
" Three thousand pounds ! " I heard ; " Three thousand
    pounds ! "

There, that's my story, sir ; it isn't gay.
Tales of the Poor are never very bright . . .
You'll look for me next time you pass this way . . .
I hope you'll find me, sir ; good-night, good-night.

III

THE LUXEMBOURG,
June 1914.

On a late afternoon, where the sunlight is mellow on the
leaves, I often sit near the Fontaine de Medicis, and watch
the children at their play. Sometimes I make bits of verse
about them, such as :

FI-FI IN BED

Up into the sky I stare ;
All the little stars I see ;
And I know that God is there
O, how lonely He must be !

Me, I laugh and leap all day,
Till my head begins to nod ;
He's so great, He cannot play :
I am glad I am not God.

Poor kind God upon His throne,
Up there in the sky so blue,
Always, always all alone . . .
" *Please, dear God, I pity You.*"

Or else, sitting on the terrace of a café on the Boul' Mich',
I sip slowly a Dubonnet or a Byrrh, and the charm of the
Quarter possesses me. I think of men who have lived and
loved there, who have grovelled and gloried, who have drunk
deep and died. And then I scribble things like this :

GODS IN THE GUTTER

I DREAMED I saw three demi-gods who in a café sat ;
And one was lean and satyr-like, and one was large
      and fat ;
And one was eaten up with vice and verminous at
      that.

The first he spoke of secret sins, and gems and perfumes
    rare ;
And velvet cats and courtesans voluptuously fair :
" Who is the Sybarite ? " I asked. They answered :
    " Baudelaire."

The second talked in tapestries, by fantasy beguiled ;
As frail as bubbles, hard as gems, his pageantries he
    piled ;
" This Lord of Language, who is he ? " They whis-
    pered " Oscar Wilde."

The third was staring at his glass from out abysmal
    pain ;
With tears his eyes were bitten in beneath his bulbous
    brain.
" Who is the derelict ? " said I. They told me : " Paul
    Verlaine."

Oh Wilde, Verlaine and Baudelaire, their lips were wet
    with wine ;
Oh poseur, pimp and libertine ! Oh cynic, sot and
    swine !
Oh votaries of velvet vice ! . . . Oh gods of light
    divine !

Oh Baudelaire, Verlaine and Wilde, they knew the
    sinks of shame ;
Their sun-aspiring wings they scorched at passion's
    altar flame ;
Yet lo ! enthroned, enskied they stand, Immortal
    Sons of Fame.

I dreamed I saw three demi-gods who walked with
    feet of clay,
With cruel crosses on their backs, along a miry way ;
Who climbed and climbed the bitter steep . . . to
    which men turn and pray.

   And while I am on the subject of the Quarter, let me
repeat this, which is included in my Ballads of the
Boulevards :

THE DEATH OF MARIE TORO

WE'RE taking Marie Toro to her home in Père-La-
    Chaise ;
We're taking Marie Toro to her last resting-place.
Behold ! her hearse is hung with wreaths till everything
    is hid
Except the blossoms heaping high upon her coffin lid.
A week ago she roamed the street, a draggle and a slut,
A by-word of the Boulevard and everybody's butt ;
A week ago she haunted us, we heard her whining cry,
We brushed aside the broken blooms she pestered us
    to buy ;
A week ago she had not where to rest her weary
    head . . .
But now, oh, follow, follow on, for Marie Toro's dead.

Oh Marie, she was once a queen—ah yes, a queen of
    queens.
High-throned above the Carnival she held her splendid
    sway.
For four-and-twenty crashing hours she knew what
    glory means,

The cheers of half a million throats, the *délire* of a day.
Yet she was only one of us, a little sewing-girl,
Though far the loveliest and best of all our laughing
band ;
Then Fortune beckoned ; off she danced, amid the
dizzy whirl,
And we who once might kiss her cheek were proud to
kiss her hand.
For swiftly as a star she soared ; she had her every
wish ;
We saw her roped with pearls of price, with princes
at her call ;
And yet, and yet I think her dreams were of the old
Boul' Mich',
And yet I'm sure within her heart she loved us best of
all.
For one night in the Purple Pig, upon the rue Saint-
Jacques,
We laughed and quaffed . . . a limousine came swishing
to the door ;
Then Raymond Jolicœur cried out : " It's Queen Marie
come back,
In satin clad to make us glad, and witch our hearts
once more."
But no, her face was strangely sad, and at the evening's
end :
" Dear lads," she said ; " I love you all, and when
I'm far away,
Remember, oh, remember, little Marie is your friend,
And though the world may lie between, I'm coming
back some day."
And so she went, and many a boy who's fought his
way to Fame,

Can look back on the struggle of his garret days and
    bless
The loyal heart, the tender hand, the Providence that
    came
To him and all in hour of need, in sickness and distress.
Time passed away. She won their hearts in London,
    Moscow, Rome ;
They worshipped her in Argentine, adored her in Brazil ;
We smoked our pipes and wondered when she might be
    coming home,
And then we learned the luck had turned, the things
    were going ill.
Her health had failed, her beauty paled, her lovers
    fled away ;
And someone saw her in Peru, a common drab at last.
So years went by, and faces changed ; our beards were
    sadly grey,
And Marie Toro's name became an echo of the past.

You know that old and withered man, that derelict
    of art,
Who for a paltry franc will make a crayon sketch of
    you ?
In slouching hat and shabby cloak he looks and is the
    part,
A sodden old Bohemian, without a single *sou*.
A boon companion of the days of Rimbaud and Verlaine,
He broods and broods, and chews the cud of bitter
    souvenirs ;
Beneath his mop of grizzled hair his cheeks are gouged
    with pain,
The saffron sockets of his eyes are hollowed out with
    tears.

Well, one night in the D'Harcourt's din I saw him in
    his place,
When suddenly the door was swung, a woman halted
    there ;
A woman cowering like a dog, with white and haggard
    face,
A broken creature, bent of spine, a daughter of
    Despair.
She looked and looked, as to her breast she held some
    withered bloom ;
" Too late ! Too late ! . . . they all are dead and gone,"
    I heard her say.
And once again her weary eyes went round and round
    the room ;
" Not one of all I used to know . . . " she turned to
    go away . . .
But quick I saw the old man start : " Ah no ! " he cried,
    " Not all.
Oh Marie Toro, queen of queens, don't you remember
    Paul ? "

" Oh Marie, Marie Toro, in my garret next the sky,
Where many a day and night I've crouched with not
    a crust to eat,
A picture hangs upon the wall a fortune couldn't
    buy,
A portrait of a girl whose face is pure and angel-
    sweet."
Sadly the woman looked at him : " Alas ! it's true,"
    she said ;
" That little maid, I knew her once. It's long ago—
    she's dead."

He went to her ; he laid his hand upon her wasted arm :
" Oh, Marie Toro, come with me, though poor and sick
am I.
For old times' sake I cannot bear to see you come to
harm ;
Ah ! there are memories, God knows, that never,
never die. . . . "
" Too late ! " she sighed ; " I've lived my life of splendour
and of shame ;
I've been adored by men of power, I've touched the
highest height ;
I've squandered gold like heaps of dirt—oh, I have
played the game ;
I've had my place within the sun . . . and now I
face the night."
Look ! look ! you see I'm lost to hope ; I live no
matter how . . .
To drink and drink and so forget . . . that's all I
care for now."

And so she went her heedless way, and all our help
was vain.
She trailed along with tattered shawl and mud-corroded
skirt ;
She gnawed a crust and slept beneath the bridges of
the Seine,
A garbage thing, a composite of alcohol and dirt.
The students learned her story and the cafés knew her
well,
The Pascal and the Panthéon, the Sufflot and Vachette
She shuffled round the tables with the flowers she tried
to sell,
A living mask of misery that no one will forget.

And then last week I missed her, and they found her
 in the street
One morning early, huddled down, for it was freezing
 cold ;
But when they raised her ragged shawl her face was
 still and sweet ;
Some bits of broken bloom were clutched within her
 icy hold.
That's all. . . . Ah yes, they say that saw : her blue,
 wide-open eyes
Were beautiful with joy again, with radiant surprise. . . .

A week ago she begged for bread : we've bought for
 her a stone,
And a peaceful place in Père-La-Chaise where she'll be
 well alone.
She cost a king his crown, they say ; oh, wouldn't
 she be proud
If she could see the wreaths to-day, the coaches and the
 crowd !
So follow, follow, follow on with slow and sober tread,
For Marie Toro, gutter waif and queen of queens, is
 dead.

IV

THE CAFÉ DE DEUX MAGOTS,
June 1914.

THE BOHEMIAN

Up in my garret bleak and bare
I tilted back on my broken chair,
And my three old pals were with me there,
 Hunger and Thirst and Cold ;

Hunger scowled at his scurvy mate:
Cold cowered down by the hollow grate,
And I hated them with a deadly hate
    As old as life is old.

So up in my garret that's near the sky
I smiled a smile that was thin and dry:
" You've roomed with me twenty year," said I,
    " Hunger and Thirst and Cold;
But now, begone down the broken stair!
I've suffered enough of your spite . . . so
    there ! "
Bang! Bang! I slapped on the table bare
    A glittering heap of gold.

" Red flames will jewel my wine to-night;
I'll loose my belt that you've lugged so tight;
Ha! Ha! Dame Fortune is smiling bright;
    The stuff of my brain I've sold;
Canaille of the gutter, up! Away!
You've battened on me for a bitter-long day;
But I'm driving you forth, and forever and aye,
    Hunger and Thirst and Cold."

So I kicked them out with a scornful roar;
Yet, oh, they turned at the garret door;
Quietly there they spoke once more:
    " The tale is not all told.
It's *au revoir*, but it's not good-bye;
We're yours, old chap, till the day you die;
Laugh on, you fool! Oh, you'll never defy
    Hunger and Thirst and Cold."

Hurrah! The crisis in my financial career is over. Once more I have weathered the storm, and never did money jingle so sweetly in my pocket. It was MacBean who delivered me. He arrived at the door of my garret this morning, with a broad grin of pleasure on his face.

"Here," said he; "I've sold some of your rubbish. They'll take more too, of the same sort."

With that he handed me three crisp notes. For a moment I thought that he was paying the money out of his own pocket, as he knew I was desperately hard up; but he showed me the letter enclosing the cheque he had cashed for me.

So we sought the Grand Boulevard, and I had a Pernod, which rose to my head in delicious waves of joy. I talked ecstatic nonsense, and seemed to walk like a god on clouds of gold. We dined on frogs' legs and Vouvray, and then went to see the Revue at the Marigny. A very merry evening.

Such is the life of Bohemia, up and down, fast and feast; its very uncertainty its charm.

Here is my latest ballad, another attempt to express the sentiment of actuality:

THE AUCTION SALE

HER little head just topped the window-sill;
She even mounted on a stool, maybe;
She pressed against the pane, as children will,
And watched us playing, oh so wistfully!
And then I missed her for a month or more,
And idly thought: "She's gone away, no doubt,"
Until a hearse drew up beside the door . . .
I saw a tiny coffin carried out.

And after that, towards dusk I'd often see
Behind the blind another face that looked:
Eyes of a young wife watching anxiously,
Then rushing back to where her dinner cooked.

She often gulped it down alone, I fear,
Within her heart the sadness of despair,
For near to midnight I would vaguely hear
A lurching step, a stumbling on the stair.

These little dramas of the common day!
A man weak-willed and fore-ordained to fail . . .
The window's empty now, they've gone away,
And yonder, see, their furniture's for sale.
To all the world their door is open wide,
And round and round the bargain-hunters roam,
And peer and gloat, like vultures avid-eyed,
Above the corpse of what was once a home.

So reverent I go from room to room,
And see the patient care, the tender touch,
The love that sought to brighten up the gloom,
The woman-courage tested overmuch.
Amid those things so intimate and dear,
Where now the mob invades with brutal tread,
I think : " What happiness is buried here,
What dreams are withered and what hopes are dead ! "

Oh, woman dear, and were you sweet and glad
Over the lining of your little nest !
What ponderings and proud ideas you had !
What visions of a shrine of peace and rest !
For there's his easy-chair upon the rug,
His reading-lamp, his pipe-rack on the wall,
All that you could devise to make him snug—
And yet you could not hold him with it all.

Ah, patient heart, what homelike joys you planned
To stay him by the dull domestic flame !
Those silken cushions that you worked by hand
When you had time, before the baby came.
Oh, how you wove around him cosy spells,
And schemed so hard to keep him home of nights !
Aye, every touch and turn some story tells
Of sweet conspiracies and dead delights.

And here upon the scratched piano stool,
Tied in a bundle, are the songs you sung ;
That cosy that you worked in coloured wool,
The Spanish lace you made when you were young,
And lots of modern novels, cheap reprints,
And little dainty knick-knacks everywhere ;
And silken bows and curtains of gay chintz . . .
And oh, her tiny crib, her folding chair !

Sweet woman dear, and did your heart not break,
To leave this precious home you made in vain ?
Poor shabby things ! so prized for old times' sake,
With all their memories of love and pain.
Alas ! while shouts the raucous auctioneer,
And rat-faced dames are prying everywhere,
The echo of old joy is all I hear,
All, all I see just heartbreak and despair.

Imagination is the great gift of the gods. Given it, one
does not need to look afar for subjects. There is a romance
in every face.

Those who have Imagination live in a land of enchant-
ment which the eyes of others cannot see. Yet if it brings

marvellous joy it also brings exquisite pain. Who lives a hundred lives must die a hundred deaths.

I do not know any of the people who live around me. Sometimes I pass them on the stairs. However, I am going to give my imagination rein, and string some rhymes about them.

Before doing so, having money in my pocket and seeing the prospect of making more, let me blithely chant about.

THE JOY OF BEING POOR

I

LET others sing of gold and gear, the joy of being rich ;
But oh, the days when I was poor, a vagrant in a ditch !
When every dawn was like a gem, so radiant and rare,
And I had but a single coat, and not a single care ;
When I would feast right royally on bacon, bread and
        beer,
And dig into a stack of hay and doze like any peer ;
When I would wash beside a brook my solitary shirt,
And though it dried upon my back I never took a hurt;
When I went romping down the road contemptuous of
        care,
And slapped Adventure on the back—by Gad ! we
        were a pair ;
When, though my pockets lacked a coin, and though
        my coat was old,
The largess of the stars was mine, and all the sunset
        gold ;
When time was only made for fools, and free as air
        was I,
And hard I hit and hard I lived beneath the open sky;

When all the roads were one to me, and each had its
    allure . . .
Ye Gods ! these were the happy days, the days when
    I was poor.

II

Or else, again, old pal of mine, do you recall the
    times
You struggled with your storyettes, I wrestled with my
    rhymes ;
Oh, we were happy, were we not ?—we used to live so
    " high "
(A little bit of broken roof between us and the sky);
Upon the forge of art we toiled with hammer and with
    tongs ;
You told me all your ripping yarns, I sang to you my
    songs.
Our hats were frayed, our jackets patched, our boots
    were down at heel,
But oh, the happy men were we, although we lacked
    a meal.
And if I sold a bit of rhyme, or if you placed a tale,
What feasts we had of tenderloins and apple-tarts
    and ale !
And yet how often we would dine as cheerful as you
    please,
Beside our little friendly fire on coffee, bread and
    cheese.
We lived upon the ragged edge, and grub was never
    sure,
But oh, these were the happy days, the days when
    we were poor.

III

Alas ! old man, we're wealthy now, it's sad beyond a
   doubt ;
We cannot dodge prosperity, success has found us out.
Your eye is very dull and drear, my brow is creased
   with care,
We realize how hard it is to be a millionaire.
The burden's heavy on our backs—you're thinking of
   your rents,
I'm worrying if I'll invest in five or six per cents.
We've limousines, and marble halls, and flunkeys by
   the score,
We play the part . . . but say, old chap, oh, isn't it
   a bore ?
We work like slaves, we eat too much, we put on
   evening dress ;
We've everything a man can want, I think . . . but
   happiness.

Come, let us sneak away, old chum ; forget that we
   are rich,
And earn an honest appetite, and scratch an honest itch.
Let's be two jolly garreteers, up seven flights of stairs,
And wear old clothes and just pretend we aren't
   millionaires ;
And wonder how we'll pay the rent, and scribble ream
   on ream,
And sup on sausages and tea, and laugh and loaf and
   dream.

And when we're tired of that, my friend, oh, you will
   come with me ;
And we will seek the sunlit roads that lie beside the sea.

We'll know the joy the gipsy knows, the freedom
    nothing mars,
The golden treasure-gates of dawn, the mintage of the
    stars.
We'll smoke our pipes and watch the pot, and feed the
    crackling fire,
And sing like two old jolly boys, and dance to heart's
    desire ;
We'll climb the hill and ford the brook and camp upon
    the moor . . .
Old chap, let's haste, I'm mad to taste the Joy of Being
    Poor.

V

My Garret, Montparnasse,
        June 1914.

MY NEIGHBOURS

To rest my fagged brain now and then,
When wearied of my proper labours,
I lay aside my lagging pen
And get to thinking on my neighbours ;
For, oh, around my garret den
There's woe and poverty a-plenty,
And life's so interesting when
A lad is only two-and-twenty.

Now, there's that artist gaunt and wan,
A little card his door adorning ;
It reads : " Je ne suis pour personne,"
A very frank and fitting warning.

I fear he's in a sorry plight ;
He starves, I think, too proud to borrow
I hear him moaning every night :
Maybe they'll find him dead to-morrow.

ROOM 4

THE PAINTER CHAP

HE gives me such a bold and curious look,
That young American across the way,
As if he'd like to put me in a book
(Fancies himself a poet, so they say).
Ah well ! He'll make no " document " of me.
I lock my door. Ha ! ha ! Now none shall see. . . .

Pictures, just pictures piled from roof to floor,
Each one a bit of me, a dream fulfilled,
A vision of the beauty I adore,
My own poor glimpse of glory, passion-thrilled . . .
But now my money's gone, I paint no more.

For three days past I have not tasted food ;
The jewelled colours run . . . I reel, I faint ;
They tell me that my pictures are no good,
Just crude and childish daubs, a waste of paint.
I burned to throw on canvas all I saw—
Twilight on water, tenderness of trees,
Wet sands at sunset and the smoking seas,
The peace of valleys and the mountain's awe :
Emotion swayed me at the thought of these.
I sought to paint ere I had learned to draw,

And that's the trouble. . . .

                    Ah well ! here am I,
Facing my failure after struggle long ;
And there they are, my *croûtes* that none will buy
(And doubtless they are right and I am wrong);
Well, when one's lost one's faith it's time to die. . . .

This knife will do . . . and now to slash and slash ;
Rip them to ribands, rend them every one,
My dreams and visions—tear and stab and gash,
So that their crudeness may be known to none ;
Poor, miserable daubs ! Ah ! there, it's done. . . .

And now to close my little window tight.
Lo ! in the dusking sky, serenely set,
The evening star is like a beacon bright.
And see ! to keep her tender tryst with night
How Paris veils herself in violet. . . .

Oh, why does God create such men as I ?—
All pride and passion and divine desire,
Raw, quivering nerve-stuff and devouring fire,
Foredoomed to failure though they try and try ;
Abortive, blindly to destruction hurled ;
Unfound, unfit to grapple with the world. . . .

And now to light my wheezy jet of gas ;
Chink up the window-crannies and the door,
So that no single breath of air may pass ;
So that I'm sealed air-tight from roof to floor.
There, there, that's done ; and now there's nothing
      more. . . .

Look at the city's myriad lamps a-shine ;
See, the calm moon is launching into space . . .
There will be darkness in these eyes of mine
Ere it can climb to shine upon my face.
Oh, it will find such peace upon my face ! . . .

City of Beauty, I have loved you well,
A laugh or two I've had, but many a sigh ;
I've run with you the scale from Heav'n to Hell.
Paris, I love you still . . . good-bye, good-bye.
Thus it all ends—unhappily, alas !
It's time to sleep, and now . . . *blow out the gas.* . .

* * * * *

Now there's that little midinette
Who goes to work each morning daily ;
I choose to call her Blithe Babette,
Because she's always humming gaily ;
And though the Goddess " Comme-il-faut '
May look on her with prim expression,
It's Pagan Paris where, you know,
The queen of virtues is Discretion

Room 6

THE LITTLE WORKGIRL

THREE gentlemen live close beside me—
A painter of pictures bizarre,
A poet whose virtues might guide me
A singer who plays the guitar ;
And there on my lintel is Cupid ;
I leave my door open, and yet
These gentlemen, aren't they stupid
They never make love to Babette.

I go to the shop every morning ;
I work with my needle and thread
Silk, satin and velvet adorning,
Then luncheon on coffee and bread.
Then sewing and sewing till seven ;
Or else, if the order I get,
I toil and I toil till eleven—
And such is the day of Babette.

It doesn't seem cheerful, I fancy ;
The wage is unthinkably small ;
And yet there is one thing I can say :
I keep a bright face through it all.
I chaff though my head may be aching;
I sing a gay song to forget ;
I laugh though my heart may be breaking—
It's all in the life of Babette.

That gown, O my lady of leisure,
You begged to be " finished in haste."
It gives you an exquisite pleasure,
Your lovers remark on its taste.
Yet . . . oh, the poor little white faces,
The tense midnight toil and the fret . . .
I fear that the foam of its laces
Is salt with the tears of Babette.

It takes a brave heart to be cheery
With no gleam of hope in the sky ;
The future's so utterly dreary,
I'm laughing—in case I should cry.

And if, where the gay lights are glowing,
I dine with a man I have met,
And snatch a bright moment—who's going
To blame a poor little Babette?

And you, Friend beyond all the telling,
Although you're an ocean away,
Your pictures, they tell me, are selling
You're married and settled, they say.
Such happiness one wouldn't barter;
Yet, oh, do you never regret
The Springtide, the roses, Montmartre
Youth, poverty, love and—Babette?

* * * * *

That blond-haired chap across the way
With sunny smile and voice so mellow
He sings in some cheap cabaret,
Yet what a gay and charming fellow!
His breath with garlic may be strong,
What matters it? his laugh is jolly;
His day he gives to sleep and song:
His night's made up of song and folly.

ROOM 5

THE CONCERT-SINGER

I'M one of these haphazard chaps
Who sit in cafés drinking;
A most improper taste, perhaps.
Yet pleasant, to my thinking.
For, oh, I hate discord and strife;
I'm sadly, weakly human;
And I do think the best of life
Is wine and song and woman.

Now, there's that youngster on my right
Who thinks himself a poet,
And so he toils from morn to night
And vainly hopes to show it ;
And there's that dauber on my left,
Within his chamber shrinking—
He looks like one of hope bereft ;
He lives on air, I'm thinking.

But me, I love the things that are,
My heart is always merry ;
I laugh and tune my old guitar :
Sing ho ! and hey-down-derry.
Oh, let them toil their lives away
To gild a tawdry era,
But I'll be gay while yet I may :
Sing tira-lira-lira.

I'm sure you know that picture well,
A monk, all else unheeding,
Within a bare and gloomy cell
A musty volume reading ;
While through the window you can see
In sunny glade entrancing,
With cap and bells beneath a tree
A jester dancing, dancing.

Which is the fool and which the sage
I cannot quite discover ;
But you may look in learning's page
And I'll be laughter's lover.

For this our life is none too long,
And hearts were made for gladness;
Let virtue lie in joy and song,
The only sin be sadness.

So let me troll a jolly air,
Come what come will to-morrow;
I'll be no *cabotin* of care,
No *souteneur* of sorrow.
Let those who will indulge in strife,
To my most merry thinking,
The true philosophy of life
Is laughing, loving, drinking.

*   *   *   *   *

And there's that weird and ghastly hag
Who walks head bent, with lips a-mutter ;
With twitching hands and feet that drag,
And tattered skirts that sweep the gutter.
An outworn harlot, lost to hope,
With staring eyes and hair that's hoary
I hear her gibber, dazed with dope :
I often wonder what's her story.

Room 7

THE COCO-FIEND

I LOOK at no one, me ;
I pass them on the stair ;
Shadows ! I don't see ;
Shadows ! everywhere.
Haunting, taunting, staring, glaring,
Shadows ! I don't care.

Once my room I gain
Then my life begins
Shut the door on pain ;
How the Devil grins !
Grin with might and main ;
Grin and grin in vain ;
Here's where Heav'n begins :
Cocaine ! Cocaine !

A whiff ! Ah, that's the thing.
How it makes me gay !
Now I want to sing,
Leap, laugh, play.
Ha ! I've had my fling !
Mistress of a king
In my day.
Just another snuff . . .
Oh, the blessed stuff !
How the wretched room
Rushes from my sight ;
Misery and gloom
Melt into delight ;
Fear and death and doom
Vanish in the night.
No more cold and pain,
I am young again,
Beautiful again,
Cocaine ! Cocaine !

Oh, I was made to be good, to be good,
For a true man's love and a life that's sweet ;
Fireside blessings and motherhood,
Little ones playing around my feet.

How it all unfolds like a magic screen,
Tender and glowing and clear and glad,
The wonderful mother I might have been,
The beautiful children I might have had ;
Romping and laughing and shrill with glee,
Oh, I see them now and I see them plain.
Darlings ! Come nestle up close to me,
You comfort me so, and you're just . . . Cocaine.

It's Life that's all to blame :
We can't do what we will :
She robes us with her shame,
She crowns us with her ill.
I do not care, because
I see with bitter calm,
Life made me what I was,
Life makes me what I am.
Could I throw back the years,
It all would be the same :
Hunger and cold and tears
Misery, fear and shame,
And then the old refrain,
Cocaine ! Cocaine !

A love-child I, so here my mother came,
Where she might live in peace with none to blame.
And how she toiled ! Harder than any slave,
What courage ! patient, hopeful, tender, brave.
We had a little room at Lavilette,
So small, so neat, so clean, I see it yet.
Poor mother ! sewing, sewing late at night,
Her wasted face beside the candlelight,

This Paris crushed her. How she used to sigh!
And as I watched her from my bed I knew
She saw red roofs against a primrose sky
And glistening fields and apples dimmed with dew.
Hard times we had. We counted every *sou*,
We sewed sacks for a living. I was quick . . .
Four busy hands to work instead of two.
Oh, we were happy there, till she fell sick. . . .

My mother lay, her face turned to the wall,
And I, a girl of sixteen, fair and tall,
Sat by her side, all stricken with despair,
Knelt by her bed and faltered out a prayer.
A doctor's order on the table lay,
Medicine for which, alas! I could not pay;
Medicine to save her life, to soothe her pain.
I sought for something I could sell, in vain . . .
All, all was gone! The room was cold and bare;
Gone blankets and the cloak I used to wear;
Bare floor and wall and cupboard, every shelf—
Nothing that I could sell . . . except myself.

I sought the street, I could not bear
To hear my mother moaning there.
I clutched the paper in my hand.
'Twas hard. You cannot understand . . .
I walked as martyr to the flame,
Almost exalted in my shame.
They turned, who heard my voiceless cry,
" For Sale, a virgin, who will buy ? "
And so myself I fiercely sold,
And clutched the price, a piece of gold.

Into a pharmacy I pressed ;
I took the paper from my breast.
I gave my money . . . how it gleamed !
How precious to my eyes it seemed !
And then I saw the chemist frown,
Quick on the counter throw it down,
Shake with an angry look his head :
" Your *louis d'or* is bad," he said.

Dazed, crushed, I went into the night,
I clutched my gleaming coin so tight.
No, no, I could not well believe
That anyone could so deceive.
I tried again and yet again—
Contempt, suspicion and disdain ;
Always the same reply I had :
" Get out of this. Your money's bad."

Heart-broken to the room I crept,
To mother's side. All still . . . she slept . . .
I bent, I sought to raise her head . . .
" Oh, God have pity ! " she was dead.

That's how it all began.
Said I : Revenge is sweet.
So in my guilty span
I've ruined many a man.
They've grovelled at my feet,
I've pity had for none ;
I've bled them every one.
Oh, I've had interest for
That worthless *louis d'or*.

But now it's over ; see,
I care for no one, me ;
Only at night sometimes
In dreams I hear the chimes
Of wedding-bells and see
A woman without stain,
With children at her knee.
Ah, how you comfort me.
Cocaine ! . . .

PART THREE

LATE SUMMER

The Omnium Bar, near the Bourse,
Late July 1914.

MacBean, before he settled down to the manufacture of mercantile fiction, had ideas of a nobler sort, which bore their fruit in a slender book of poems. In subject they are either erotic, mythologic, or descriptive of nature. So polished are they that the mind seems to slide over them; so faultless in form that the critics hailed them with highest praise, and as many as a hundred copies were sold.

Saxon Dane, too, has published a book of poems, but he, on the other hand, defies tradition to an eccentric degree. Originality is his sin. He strains after it in every line. I must confess I think much of the free verse he writes is really prose, and a good deal of it blank verse chopped up into odd lengths. He talks of assonance and colour, of stress and pause and accent, and bewilders me with his theories.

He and MacBean represent two extremes, and at night, as we sit in the Café du Dôme, they have the hottest of arguments. As for me, I listen with awe, content that my medium is verse, and that the fashions of Hood, Thackeray and Bret Harte are the fashions of to-day.

Of late I have been doing light stuff, " fillers " for Mac-Bean. Here are three of my specimens:

THE PHILANDERER

Oh, have you forgotten those afternoons
With riot of roses and amber skies,
When we thrilled to the joy of a million Junes,
And I sought for your soul in the deeps of your eyes?

I would love you, I promised, for ever and aye,
And I meant it too ; yet, oh, isn't it odd ?
When we met in the Underground to-day
I addressed you as Mary instead of as Maude.

Oh, don't you remember that moonlit sea,
With us on a silver trail afloat,
When I gracefully sank on my bended knee
At the risk of upsetting our little boat ?
Oh, I vowed that my life was blighted then,
As friendship you proffered with mournful mien ;
But now as I think of your children ten,
I'm glad you refused me, Evangeline.

Oh, is that moment eternal still
When I breathed my love in your shell-like ear,
And you plucked at your fan as a maiden will,
And you blushed so charmingly, Guinevere ?
Like a worshipper at your feet I sat ;
For a year and a day you made me mad ;
But now, alas ! you are forty, fat,
And I think : What a lucky escape I had !

Oh, maidens I've set in a sacred shrine,
Oh, Rosamond, Molly and Mignonette,
I've deemed you in turn the most divine,
In turn you've broken my heart . . . and yet
It's easily mended. What's past is past.
To-day on Lucy I'm going to call ;
For I'm sure that I know true love at last,
And *She* is the fairest girl of all.

THE *PETIT VIEUX*

"Sow your wild oats in your youth," so we're always
    told ;
But I say with deeper sooth : "Sow them when you're
    old."
I'll be wise till I'm about seventy or so :
Then, by Gad ! I'll blossom out as an ancient *beau*.

I'll assume a dashing air, laugh with loud Ha ! ha ! . . .
How my grandchildren will stare at their grandpapa !
Their perfection aurioled I will scandalize :
Won't I be a hoary old sinner in their eyes !

Watch me, how I'll learn to chaff barmaids in a bar
Scotches daily, gaily quaff, puff a fierce cigar.
I will haunt the Tango teas, at the stage-door stand ;
Wait for Dolly Dimpleknees, bouquet in my hand.

Then at seventy I'll take flutters at roulette ;
While at eighty hope I'll make good at poker yet ;
And in fashionable togs to the races go,
Gayest of the gay old dogs, ninety years or so.

"Sow your wild oats while you're young," that's what
    you are told ;
Don't believe the foolish tongue—sow 'em when you're
    old.
Till you've threescore years and ten, take my humble
    tip,
Sow your nice tame oats and then . . . Hi, boys !
    Let 'er rip.

MY MASTERPIECE

IT's slim and trim and bound in blue;
Its leaves are crisp and edged with gold;
Its words are simple, stalwart too;
Its thoughts are tender, wise and bold.
Its pages scintillate with wit;
Its pathos clutches at my throat:
Oh, how I love each line of it!
That Little Book I Never Wrote.

In dreams I see it praised and prized
By all, from ploughman unto peer;
It's pencil-marked and memorized,
It's loaned (and not returned, I fear);
It's worn and torn and travel-tossed,
And even dusky natives quote
That classic that the world has lost,
The Little Book I Never Wrote.

Poor ghost! For homes you've failed to cheer,
For grieving hearts uncomforted,
Don't haunt me now. . . . Alas! I fear
The fire of Inspiration's dead.
A humdrum way I go to-night,
From all I hoped and dreamed remote:
Too late . . . a better man must write
That Little Book I Never Wrote.

Talking about writing books, there is a queer character
who shuffles up and down the little streets that neighbour
the Place Maubert, and who they say has been engaged

on one for years. Sometimes I see him cowering in some
cheap *bouge*, and his wild eyes gleam at me through the
tangle of his hair. But I do not think he ever sees me.
He mumbles to himself, and moves like a man in a dream.
His pockets are full of filthy paper on which he writes from
time to time. The students laugh at him and make him
tipsy; the street-boys pelt him with ordure; the better
cafés turn him from their doors. But who knows? At
least, this is how I see him:

MY BOOK

BEFORE I drink myself to death,
God, let me finish up my Book!
At night I fear, I fight for breath,
And wake up whiter than a spook;
And crawl off to a *bistro* near,
And drink until my brain is clear.

Rare Absinthe! Oh, it gives me strength
To write and write; and so I spend
Day after day, until at length
With joy and pain I'll write The End:
Then let this carcase rot; I give
The world my Book—my Book will live.

For every line is tense with truth,
There's hope and joy on every page;
A cheer, a clarion call to Youth,
A hymn, a comforter to Age:
All's there that I was meant to be,
My part divine, the God in me.

It's of my life the golden sum ;
Ah ! who that reads this Work of mine,
In stormy centuries to come,
Will dream I rooted with the swine ?
Behold ! I give mankind my best :
What does it matter, all the rest ?

It's this that makes sublime my day ;
It's this that makes me struggle on.
Oh, let them mock my mortal clay,
My spirit's deathless as the dawn ;
Oh, let them shudder as they look . . .
I'll be immortal in my Book.

And so beside the sullen Seine
I fight with dogs for filthy food,
Yet know that from my sin and pain
Will soar serene a Something Good ;
Exultantly from shame and wrong
A Right, a Glory and a Song.

How charming it is, this Paris of the summer skies. Each
morning I leap up with joy in my heart, all eager to begin
the day of work. As I eat my breakfast and smoke my
pipe, I ponder over my task. Then in the golden sunshine
that floods my little attic I pace up and down, absorbed
and forgetful of the world. As I compose I speak the words
aloud. There are difficulties to overcome ; thoughts that
will not fit their mould ; rebellious rhymes. Ah ! those
moments of despair and defeat.

Then suddenly the mind grows lucid, imagination glows,
the snarl unravels. In the end is always triumph and
success. O delectable *métier !* Who would not be a rhyme-
smith in Paris, in Bohemia, in the heart of youth !

I have now finished my twentieth ballad. Five more
and they will be done. In quiet corners of cafés, on benches
of the Luxembourg, on the sunny Quays I read them over
one by one. Here is my latest:

MY HOUR

DAY after day behold me plying
My pen within an office drear;
The dullest dog, till homeward hying,
Then lo! I reign a king of cheer.
A throne have I of padded leather,
A little court of kiddies three,
A wife who smiles whate'er the weather,
A feast of muffins, jam and tea.

The table cleared, a romping battle,
A fairy tale, a " Children, bed,"
A kiss, a hug, a hush of prattle
(God save each little drowsy head!),
A cosy chat with wife a-sewing,
A silver lining clouds that lour,
Then she too goes, and with her going,
I come again into my Hour.

I poke the fire, I snugly settle,
My pipe I prime with proper care;
The water's purring in the kettle,
Rum, lemon, sugar, all are there.
And now the honest grog is steaming,
And now the trusty briar's aglow:
Alas! in smoking, drinking, dreaming,
How sadly swift the moments go!

Oh, golden hour! 'twixt love and duty,
All others I to others give;
But you are mine to yield to Beauty,
To glean Romance, to greatly live.
For in my easy-chair reclining . . .
I feel the sting of ocean spray ;
And yonder wondrously are shining
The Magic Isles of Far Away.

Beyond the comber's crashing thunder
Strange beaches flash into my ken ;
On jetties heaped head-high with plunder
I dance and dice with sailor-men.
Strange stars swarm down to burn above me
Strange shadows haunt, strange voices greet ;
Strange women lure and laugh and love me,
And fling their bastards at my feet.

Oh, I would wish the wide world over,
In ports of passion and unrest,
To drink and drain, a tarry rover
With dragons tattooed on my chest,
With haunted eyes that hold red glories
Of foaming seas and crashing shores,
With lips that tell the strangest stories
Of sunken ships and gold moidores ;

Till sick of storm and strife and slaughter,
Some ghostly night when hides the moon,
I slip into the milk-warm water,
And softly swim the stale lagoon.

Then through some jungle python-haunted,
Or plumed morass, or woodland wild,
I win my way with heart undaunted,
And all the wonder of a child.

The pathless plains shall swoon around me,
The forests frown, the floods appal ;
The mountains tiptoe to confound me,
The rivers roar to speed my fall.
Wild dooms shall daunt, and dawns be gory,
And Death shall sit beside my knee ;
Till after terror, torment, glory,
I win again the sea, the sea. . . .

Oh, anguish sweet ! Oh, triumph splendid !
Oh, dreams adieu ! my pipe is dead.
My glass is dry, my Hour is ended,
It's time indeed I stole to bed.
How peacefully the house is sleeping !
Ah ! why should I strange fortunes plan ?
To guard the dear ones in my keeping—
That's task enough for any man.

So though dim seas I'll ne'er go spoiling ;
The red Tortugas never roam ;
Please God ! I'll keep the pot a-boiling,
And make at least a happy home.
My children's path shall gleam with roses,
Their grace abound, their joy increase.
And so my Hour divinely closes
With tender thoughts of praise and peace.

II

THE GARDEN OF THE LUXEMBOURG,
Late July 1914.

When on some scintillating summer morning I leap lightly up to the seclusion of my garret, I often think of those lines : " In the brave days when I was twenty-one."

True, I have no loving, kind Lisette to pin her petticoat across the pane, yet do I live in hope. Am I not in Bohemia the Magical, Bohemia of Murger, of de Musset, of Verlaine ? Shades of Mimi Pinson, of Trilby, of all that immortal line of laughterful grisettes, do not tell me that the days of love and fun are for ever at an end !

Yes, youth is golden, but what of age ? Shall it too not testify to the rhapsody of existence ? Let the years between be those of struggle, of sufferance—of disillusion if you will ; but let youth and age affirm the ecstasy of being. Let us look forward all to a serene sunset, and in the still skies " a late lark singing."

This thought comes to me as, sitting on a bench near the band-stand, I see an old savant who talks to all the children. His clean-shaven face is alive with kindliness ; under his tall silk hat his white hair falls to his shoulders. He wears a long black cape over a black frock-coat, very neat linen, and a flowing tie of black silk. I call him " Silvester Bonnard." As I look at him I truly think the best of life are the years between sixty and seventy.

A SONG OF SIXTY-FIVE

BRAVE Thackeray has trolled of days when he was twenty-one,

And bounded up five flights of stairs, a gallant garreteer ;

And yet again in mellow vein when youth was gaily run,

Has dipped his nose in Gascon wine, and told of Forty Year.

But if I worthy were to sing a richer, rarer time,
I'd tune my pipes before the fire and merrily I'd
  strive
To praise that age when prose again has given way to
  rhyme,
The Indian Summer days of life when I'll be Sixty-five.

For then my work will all be done, my voyaging be
  past,
And I'll have earned the right to rest where folding
  hills are green ;
So in some glassy anchorage I'll make my cable
  fast,—
Oh, let the seas show all their teeth, I'll sit and smile
  serene.
The storm may bellow round the roof, I'll bide beside
  the fire,
And many a scene of sail and trail within the flame
  I'll see ;
For I'll have worn away the spur of passion and
  desire. . .
Oh yes, when I am Sixty-five, what peace will come to
  me.

I'll take my breakfast in my bed, I'll rise at half-past
  ten,
When all the world is nicely groomed and full of golden
  song ;
I'll smoke a bit and joke a bit, and read the news, and
  then
I'll potter round my peach-trees till I hear the luncheon
  gong.

And after that I think I'll doze an hour, well, maybe
    two,
And then I'll show some kindred soul how well my
    roses thrive ;
I'll do the things I never yet have found the time to
    do. . . .
Oh, won't I be the busy man when I am Sixty-five.

I'll revel in my library ; I'll read De Morgan's books ;
I'll grow so garrulous I fear you'll write me down a
    bore ;
I'll watch the ways of ants and bees in quiet sunny
    nooks,
I'll understand Creation as I never did before.
When gossips round the tea-cups talk I'll listen to it all ;
On smiling days some kindly friend will take me for
    a drive :
I'll own a shaggy collie dog that dashes to my call :
I'll celebrate my second youth when I am Sixty-Five.

Ah, though I've twenty years to go, I see myself quite
    plain,
A wrinkling, twinkling, rosy-cheeked, benevolent old
    chap ;
I think I'll wear a tartan shawl and lean upon a cane ;
I hope that I'll have silver hair beneath a velvet cap.
I see my little grandchildren a-romping round my
    knee ;
So gay the scene, I almost wish 'twould hasten to arrive.
Let others sing of Youth and Spring, still will it seem
    to me
The golden time's the olden time, some time round
    Sixty-five.

From old men to children is but a step, and there too, in the shadow of the Fontaine de Medicis, I spend much of my time watching the little ones. Childhood, so innocent, so helpless, so trusting, is somehow pathetic to me.

There was one jolly little chap who used to play with a large white Teddy Bear. He was always with his mother, a sweet-faced woman, who followed his every movement with delight. I used to watch them both, and often spoke a few words.

Then one day I missed them, and it struck me I had not seen them for a week, even a month, maybe. After that I looked for them a time or two and soon forgot.

Then this morning I saw the mother in the rue D'Assas. She was alone and in deep black. I wanted to ask after the boy, but there was a look in her face that stopped me.

I do not think she will ever enter the garden of the Luxembourg again.

TEDDY BEAR

O TEDDY BEAR ! with your head awry
And your comical twisted smile,
You rub your eyes—do you wonder why
You've slept such a long, long while ?
As you lay so still in the cupboard dim,
And you heard on the roof the rain,
Were you thinking . . . what has become of *him* ?
And when will he play again ?

Did you sometimes long for a chubby hand,
And a voice so sweetly shrill ?
O Teddy Bear ! don't you understand
Why the house is awf'ly still ?

You sit with your muzzle propped on your paws,
And your whimsical face askew.
Don't wait, don't wait for your friend . . . because
He's sleeping and sleeping too.

Aye, sleeping long. . . . You remember how
He stabbed our hearts with his cries ?
And oh, the dew of pain on his brow,
And the deeps of pain in his eyes !
And, Teddy Bear ! you remember, too,
As he sighed and sank to his rest,
How all of a sudden he smiled to you,
And he clutched you close to his breast.

I'll put you away, little Teddy Bear,
In the cupboard far from my sight ;
Maybe he'll come and he'll kiss you there,
A wee white ghost in the night.
But me, I'll live with my love and pain
A weariful lifetime through ;
And my Hope : will I see him again, again ?
Ah, God ! If I only knew !

After old men and children I am greatly interested in
dogs. I will go out of my way to caress one who shows
any desire to be friendly. There is a very filthy fellow who
collects cigarette stubs on the Boul' Mich', and who is
always followed by a starved yellow cur. The other day
I came across them in a little side street. The man was
stretched on the pavement brutishly drunk and dead to
the world. The dog, lying by his side, seemed to look at
me with sad, imploring eyes. Though all the world despise
that man, I thought, this poor brute loves him and will be
faithful unto death.

From this incident I wrote the verses that follow :

THE OUTLAW

A WILD and woeful race he ran
Of lust and sin by land and sea ;
Until, abhorred of God and man,
They swung him from the gallows-tree.
And then he climbed the Starry Stair,
And dumb and naked and alone,
With head unbowed and brazen glare,
He stood before the Judgment Throne.

The Keeper of the Records spoke :
" This man, O Lord, has mocked Thy Name
The weak have wept beneath his yoke,
The strong have fled before his flame.
The blood of babes is on his sword ;
His life is evil to the brim :
Look down, decree his doom, O Lord !
Lo ! there is none will speak for him."

The golden trumpets blew a blast
That echoed in the crypts of Hell,
For there was Judgment to be passed,
And lips were hushed and silence fell.
The man was mute ; he made no stir,
Erect before the Judgment Seat . . .
When all at once a mongrel cur
Crept out and cowered and licked his feet.

It licked his feet with whining cry.
Come Heav'n, come Hell, what did it care ?
It leapt, it tried to catch his eye ;
Its master, yea, its God was there.

Then, as a thrill of wonder sped
Through throngs of shining seraphim,
The Judge of All looked down and said :
" Lo ! here is ONE who pleads for him.

" And who shall love of these the least,
And who by word or look or deed
Shall pity show to bird or beast,
By Me shall have a friend in need.
Aye, though his sin be black as night,
And though he stand mid men alone,
He shall be softened in My sight,
And find a pleader by My Throne.

" So let this man to glory win ;
From life to life salvation glean ;
By pain and sacrifice and sin,
Until he stand before Me—*clean.*
For he who loves the least of these
(And here I say and here repeat)
Shall win himself an angel's pleas
For Mercy at My Judgment Seat."

I take my exercise in the form of walking. It keeps
me fit and leaves me free to think. In this way I have come
to know Paris like my pocket. I have explored its large
and little streets, its stateliness and its slums.

But most of all I love the Quays, between the leafage
and the sunlit Seine. Like shuttles the little steamers dart
up and down, weaving the water into patterns of foam.
Cigar-shaped barges stream under the lacework of the
many bridges and make me think of tranquil days and
willow-fringed horizons.

But what I love most is the stealing in of night, when

the sky takes on that strange, elusive purple; when eyes
turn to the evening star and marvel at its brightness ; when
the Eiffel Tower becomes a strange, shadowy stairway
yearning in impotent effort to the careless moon.

Here is my latest ballad, short if not very sweet :

THE WALKERS

(*He speaks.*)

WALKING, walking, oh, the joy of walking !
Swinging down the tawny lanes with head held high ;
Striding up the green hills, through the heather stalking,
Swishing through the woodlands where the brown
    leaves lie ;
Marvelling at all things—windmills gaily turning,
Apples for the cider-press, ruby-hued and gold ;
Tails of rabbits twinkling, scarlet berries burning,
Wedge of geese high-flying in the sky's clear cold,
Lights in little windows, field and furrow darkling ;
Home again returning, hungry as a hawk ;
Whistling up the garden, ruddy-cheeked and sparkling,
Oh, but I am happy as I walk, walk, walk !

(*She speaks.*)

Walking, walking, oh, the curse of walking !
Slouching round the grim square, shuffling up the street,
Slinking down the by-way, all my graces hawking,
Offering my body to each man I meet.
Peering in the gin-shop where the lads are drinking,
Trying to look gay-like, crazy with the blues ;
Halting in a doorway, shuddering and shrinking
(Oh, my draggled feather and my thin, wet shoes).

Here's a drunken drover : " Hullo, there, old dearie ! "
No, he only curses, can't be got to talk. . . .
On and on till daylight, famished, wet and weary,
God in Heaven help me as I walk, walk, walk !

III

THE CAFÉ DE LA SOURCE,
Late in July, 1914.

The other evening MacBean was in a pessimistic mood.
" Why do you write ? " he asked me gloomily.

" Obviously," I said, " to avoid starving. To produce
something that will buy me food, shelter, raiment."

" If you were a millionaire, would you still write ? "

" Yes," I said, after a moment's thought. " You get
an idea. It haunts you. It seems to clamour for expression. It begins to obsess you. At last in desperation
you embody it in a poem, an essay, a story. There ! it is
disposed of. You are at rest. It troubles you no more.
Yes ; if I were a millionaire I should write, if it were only to
escape from my ideas."

" You have given two reasons why men write," said Mac-
Bean : " for gain, for self-expression. Then, again, some
men write to amuse themselves, some because they conceive
they have a mission in the world, some because they have
real genius, and are conscious they can enrich the literature
of all time. I must say I don't know of any belonging to
the latter class. We are living in an age of mediocrity.
There is no writer of to-day who will be read twenty years
after he is dead. That's a truth that must come home
to the best of them."

" I guess they're not losing much sleep over it," I
said.

" Take novelists," continued MacBean. " The line of
first-class novelists ended with Dickens and Thackeray.
Then followed some of the second class, Stevenson, Meredith,
Hardy. And to-day we have three novelists of the third

class, good, capable craftsmen. We can trust ourselves comfortably in their hands. We read and enjoy them, but do you think our children will ? "

" Yours won't, anyway," I said.

" Don't be so sure. I may surprise you yet. I may get married and turn *bourgeois*."

The best thing that could happen to MacBean would be that. It might change his point of view. He is so painfully discouraging. I have never mentioned my ballads to him. He would be sure to throw cold water on them. And as it draws near to its end the thought of my book grows more and more dear to me. How I will get it published I know not ; but I will. Then even if it doesn't sell, even if nobody reads it, I will be content. Out of this brief, perishable Me I will have made something concrete, something that will preserve my thought within its dusty covers long after I am dead and dust.

Here is one of my latest :

POOR PETER

BLIND Peter Piper used to play
All up and down the city ;
I'd often meet him on my way,
And throw a coin for pity.
But all amid his sparkling tones
His ear was quick as any
To catch upon the cobble-stones
The jingle of my penny.

And as upon a day that shone
He piped a merry measure :
" How well you play ! " I chanced to say ;
Poor Peter glowed with pleasure.

You'd think the words of praise I spoke
Were all the pay he needed ;
The artist in the player woke,
The penny lay unheeded.

Now Winter's here ; the wind is shrill,
His coat is thin and tattered ;
Yet hark ! he's playing trill on trill
As if his music mattered.
And somehow though the city looks
Soaked through and through with shadows,
He makes you think of singing brooks
And larks and sunny meadows.

Poor chap ! he often starves, they say
Well, well, I can believe it ;
For when you chuck a coin his way
He'll let some street-boy thieve it.
I fear he freezes in the night ;
My praise I've long repented,
Yet look ! his face is all alight. . . .
Blind Peter seems contented.

A day later.

On the terrace of the Closerie de Lilas I came on Saxon
Dane. He was smoking his big briar and drinking a huge
glass of brown beer. The trees gave a pleasant shade,
and he had thrown his sombrero on a chair. I noted how
his high brow was bronzed by the sun and there were golden
lights in his broad beard. There was something massive
and imposing in the man as he sat there in brooding
thought.

MacBean, he told me, was sick and unable to leave his
room. Rheumatism. So I bought a cooked chicken and

a bottle of Barsac, and mounting to the apartment of
the invalid, I made him eat and drink. MacBean was very
despondent, but cheered up greatly.

I think he rather dreads the future. He cannot save
money, and all he makes he spends. He has always
been a rover, often tried to settle down but could not.
Now I think he wishes for security. I fear, however, it
is too late.

THE WISTFUL ONE

I SOUGHT the trails of South and North,
I wandered East and West;
But pride and passion drove me forth
And would not let me rest.

And still I seek, as still I roam,
A snug roof overhead;
Four walls, my own; a quiet home. . . '
" You'll have it—*when you're dead.*"

MacBean is one of Bohemia's victims. It is a country
of the young. The old have no place in it. He will gradually
lose his grip, go down and down. I am sorry. He is my
nearest approach to a friend. I do not make them easily.
I have deep reserves. I like solitude. I am never so
surrounded by boon companions as when I am all alone.

But though I am a solitary, I realize the beauty of friendship, and on looking through my note-book I find the
following :

IF YOU HAD A FRIEND

IF you had a friend strong, simple, true,
Who knew your faults and who understood;
Who believed in the very best of you,
And who cared for you as a father would;

Who would stick by you to the very end,
Who would smile however the world might frown :
I'm sure you would try to please your friend,
You never would think to throw him down.

And supposing your friend was high and great,
And he lived in a palace rich and tall,
And sat like a King in shining state,
And his praise was loud on the lips of all ;
Well then, when he turned to you alone,
And he singled you out from all the crowd,
And he called you up to his golden throne,
Oh, wouldn't you just be jolly proud ?

If you had a friend like this, I say,
So sweet and tender, so strong and true,
You'd try to please him in every way,
You'd live at your bravest—now, wouldn't you ?
His worth would shine in the words you penned ;
You'd shout his praises . . . yet now it's odd !
You tell me you haven't got such a friend ;
You haven't ? I wonder . . . *What of God ?*

To how few is granted the privilege of doing the work
which lies closest to the heart, the work for which one is
best fitted.

The happy man is he who knows his limitations, yet
bows to no false gods.

MacBean is not happy. He is overridden by his
appetites, and to satisfy them he writes stuff that in his
heart he despises.

Saxon Dane is not happy. His dream exceeds his grasp.
His twisted, tortured phrases mock the vague grandiosity
of his visions.

I am happy. My talent is proportioned to my ambition. The things I like to write are the things I like to read. I prefer the lesser poets to the greater, the cackle of the barn-yard fowl to the scream of the eagle. I lack the divinity of discontent.

True Contentment comes from within. It dominates circumstance. It is resignation wedded to philosophy, a Christian quality seldom attained except by the old. There is such a one I sometimes see being wheeled about in the Luxembourg. His face is beautiful in its thankfulness.

THE CONTENTED MAN

" How good God is to me," he said;
" For have I not a mansion tall,
With trees and lawns of velvet tread,
And happy helpers at my call ?
With beauty is my life abrim,
With tranquil hours and dreams apart ;
You wonder that I yield to Him
That best of prayers, a grateful heart ? "

" How good God is to me," he said ;
" For look ! though gone is all my wealth,
How sweet it is to earn one's bread
With brawny arms and brimming health.
Oh, now I know the joy of strife !
To sleep so sound, to wake so fit.
Ah yes, how glorious is life !
I thank Him for each day of it."

" How good God is to me," he said ;
" Though health and wealth are gone, it's true ;
Things might be worse, I might be dead,
And here I'm living, laughing too

> Serene beneath the evening sky
> I wait, and every man's my friend ;
> God's most contented man am I . . .
> He keeps me smiling to the End."

To-day the basin of the Luxembourg is bright with little boats. Hundreds of happy children romp around it. Little ones everywhere ; yet there is no other city with so many childless homes.

THE SPIRIT OF THE UNBORN BABE

THE Spirit of the Unborn Babe peered through the
window-pane,
Peered through the window-pane that glowed like
beacon in the night ;
For, oh, the sky was desolate and wild with wind and
rain ;
And how the little room was crammed with cosiness
and light !
Except the flirting of the fire there was no sound at all ;
The Woman sat beside the hearth, her knitting on her
knee ;
The shadow of her husband's head was dancing on the
wall ;
She looked with staring eyes at it, she looked yet did
not see.
She only saw a childish face that topped the table rim,
A little wistful ghost that smiled and vanished quick
away ;
And then because her tender eyes were flooding to the brim,
She lowered her head. . . "Don't sorrow, dear," she
heard him softly say ;

" It's over now.   We'll try to be as happy as before
(Ah ! they who little children have, grant hostages
    to pain).
We gave Life chance to wound us once, but never, never
    more. . ."
The Spirit of the Unborn Babe fled through the night
    again.

The Spirit of the Unborn Babe went wildered in the
    dark ;
Like termagants the winds tore down and whirled it
    with the snow.
And then amid the writhing storm it saw a tiny
    spark,
A window broad, a spacious room all goldenly
    aglow,
A woman slim and Paris-gowned and exquisitely
    fair,
Who smiled with rapture as she watched her jewels
    catch the blaze ;
A man in faultless evening dress, young, handsome,
    debonnaire,
Who smoked his cigarette and looked with frank
    admiring gaze.
" Oh, we are happy, sweet," said he ; " youth, health,
    and wealth are ours.
What if a thousand toil and sweat that we may live
    at ease !
What if the hands are worn and torn that strew our
    path with flowers !
Ah, well ! we did not make the world : let us not think
    of these.

Let's seek the beauty-spots of earth, Dear Heart,
   just you and I ;
Let other women bring forth life with sorrow and with
   pain,
Above our door we'll hang the sign : " *No children
   need apply.* . . ."
The Spirit of the Unborn Babe sped through the night
   again.

The Spirit of the Unborn Babe went whirling on
   and on ;
It soared above a city vast, it swept down to a slum ;
It saw within a grimy house a light that dimly shone ;
It peered in through a window-pane and lo ! a voice
   said : " Come ! "
And so a little girl was born amid the dirt and din,
And lived in spite of everything, for life is ordered so ;
A child whose eyes first opened wide to swinishness and
   sin,
A child whose love and innocence met only curse and
   blow.
And so in due and proper course she took the path of
   shame,
And gladly died in hospital, quite old at twenty years ;
And when God comes to weigh it all, ah ! whose shall
   be the blame
For all her maimed and poisoned life, her torture and
   her tears ?
For oh, it is not what we do, but what we have not done !
And on that day of reckoning, when all is plain and clear,
What if we stand before the Throne, blood-guilty
   every one ? . . .
Maybe the blackest sins of all are Selfishness and Fear.

IV

THE CAFÉ DE LA PAIX,
August 1, 1914.

Paris and I are out of tune. As I sit at this famous corner the faint breeze is stale and weary; stale and weary too the faces that swirl around me; while overhead the electric sign of Somebody's Chocolate appears and vanishes with irritating insistency. The very trees seem artificial, gleaming under the arc-lights with a raw viridity that rasps my nerves.

" Poor little trees," I mutter, " growing in all this grime and glare, your only dryads the loitering ladies with the complexions of such brilliant certainty, your only Pipes of Pan orchestral echoes from the clamorous cafés. Exiles of the forest! what know you of full-bosomed winds, of red-embered sunsets, of the gentle admonition of spring rain! Life, that would fain be a melody, seems here almost a malady. I crave for the balm of Nature, the anodyne of solitude, the breath of Mother Earth. Tell me, O wistful trees, what shall I do ? "

Then that stale and weary wind rustles the leaves of the nearest sycamore, and I am sure it whispers : " Brittany."

So to-morrow I am off, off to the Land of Little Fields.

FINISTÈRE

HURRAH! I'm off to Finistère, to Finistère, to Finistère;

My satchel's swinging on my back, my staff is in my hand;

I've twenty *louis* in my purse, I know the sun and sea are there,

And so I'm starting out to-day to tramp the golden land.

I'll go alone and glorying, with on my lips a song of
    joy ;
I'll leave behind the city with its canker and its care ;
I'll swing along so sturdily—oh, won't I be the happy
    boy !
A-singing on the rocky roads, the roads of Finistère.

Oh, have you been to Finistère, and do you know a
    whin-grey town
That echoes to the clatter of a thousand wooden
    shoes ?
And have you seen the fisher-girls go galivantin' up
    and down,
And watched the tawny boats go out, and heard the
    roaring crews ?
Oh, would you sit with pipe and bowl, and dream upon
    some sunny quay,
Or would you walk the windy heath and drink the
    caller air ;
Oh, would you seek a cradled cove and tussle with the
    topaz sea !—
Pack up your kit to-morrow, lad, and haste to Finistère.

Oh, I will go to Finistère, there's nothing that can hold
    me back.
I'll laugh with Yves and Léon, and I'll chaff with Rose
    and Jeanne ;
I'll seek the little, quaint *buvette* that's kept by Mother
    Merdrinac,
Who wears a cap of many frills, and swears just like
    a man.

I'll yarn with hearty, hairy chaps who dance and leap
  and crack their heels ;
Who swallow cupfuls of cognac and never turn a
  hair ;
I'll watch the nut-brown boats come in with mullet,
  plaice and conger eels,
The jewelled harvest of the sea they reap in Finistère.

Yes, I'll come back from Finistère with memories of
  shining days,
Of scaly nets and salty men in overalls of brown ;
Of ancient women knitting as they watch the tethered
  cattle graze
By little nestling beaches where the gorse goes blazing
  down ;
Of headlands silvering the sea, of Calvarys against the
  sky,
Of scorn of angry sunsets, and of Carnac grim and
  bare ;
Oh, won't I have the leaping veins, and tawny cheek
  and sparkling eye,
When I come back to Montparnasse and dream of
  Finistère.

Two days later.
  Behold me with staff and scrip, footing it merrily in the
Land of Pardons. I have no goal. When I am weary
I stop at some *auberge ;* when I am rested I go on again.
Neither do I put any constraint on my spirit. No subduing
of the mind to the task of the moment. I dream to heart's
content.
  My dreams stretch into the future. I see myself a
singer of simple songs, a laureate of the under-dog. I

will write books, a score of them. I will voyage far and
wide. I will . . .

But there! Dreams are dangerous. They waste the
time one should spend on making them come true. Yet
when we do make them come true, we find the vision sweeter
than the reality. How much of our happiness do we owe
to dreams? I have in mind one old chap who used to herd
the sheep on my uncle's farm.

OLD DAVID SMAIL

HE dreamed away his hours in school;
He sat with such an absent air,
The master reckoned him a fool,
And gave him up in dull despair.

When other lads were making hay
You'd find him loafing by the stream
He'd take a book and slip away,
And just pretend to fish . . . and dream.

His brothers passed him in the race;
They climbed the hill and clutched the prize.
He did not seem to heed, his face
Was tranquil as the evening skies.

He lived apart, he spoke with few;
Abstractedly through life he went;
Oh, what he dreamed of no one knew,
And yet he seemed to be content.

I see him now, so old and grey,
His eyes with inward vision dim ;
And though he faltered on the way,
Somehow I almost envied him.

At last beside his bed I stood :
" And is Life done so soon ? " he sighed ;
" It's been so rich, so full, so good,
I've loved it all . . ."—and so he died.

Another day.

Framed in hedgerows of emerald, the wheat glows with
a caloric fervour, as if gorged with summer heat. In the
vivid green of pastures old women are herding cows. Calm
and patient are their faces as with gentle industry they
bend over their knitting. One feels that they are necessary
to the landscape.

To gaze at me the field-workers suspend the magnificent
lethargy of their labours. The men with the reaping-hooks
improve the occasion by another pull at the cider bottle
under the stook ; the women raise apathetic brown faces
from the sheaf they are tying ; everyone is a study in
deliberation, though the crop is russet ripe and crying to
be cut.

Then on I go again amid high banks overgrown with fern
and honeysuckle. Sometimes I come on an old mill that
seems to have been constructed by Constable, so charmingly
does Nature imitate Art. By the deserted house, half
drowned in greenery, the velvety wheel, dipping in the
crystal water, seems to protest against this prolongation
of its toil.

Then again I come on its brother, the Mill of the Wind,
whirling its arms so cheerily, as it turns its great white stones
for its master, the floury miller by the door.

These things delight me. I am in a land where Time has
lagged, where simple people timorously hug the Past. How
far away now seems the welter and swelter of the city, the

hectic sophistication of the streets. The sense of wonder is strong in me again, the joy of looking at familiar things as if one were seeing them for the first time.

THE WONDERER

I wish that I could understand
The moving marvel of my Hand;
I watch my fingers turn and twist,
The supple bending of my wrist,
The dainty touch of finger-tip,
The steel intensity of grip;
A tool of exquisite design,
With pride I think: " It's mine ! It's mine ! "

Then there's the wonder of my Eyes,
Where hills and houses, seas and skies,
In waves of light converge and pass,
And print themselves as on a glass.
Line, form and colour live in me;
I am the Beauty that I see;
Ah ! I could write a book of size
About the wonder of my Eyes.

What of the wonder of my Heart,
That plays so faithfully its part ?
I hear it running sound and sweet;
It does not seem to miss a beat;
Between the cradle and the grave
It never falters, stanch and brave.
Alas ! I wish I had the art
To tell the wonder of my Heart.

Then oh ! but how can I explain
The wondrous wonder of my Brain ?
That marvellous machine that brings
All consciousness of wonderings ;
That lets me from myself leap out
And watch my body walk about ;
It's hopeless—all my words are vain
To tell the wonder of my Brain.

But do not think, O patient friend,
Who read these stanzas to the end,
That I myself would glorify. . . .
You're just as wonderful as I,
And all Creation in our view
Is quite as marvellous as you.
Come, let us on the sea-shore stand
And wonder at a grain of sand ;
And then into the meadow pass
And marvel at a blade of grass ;
Or cast our vision high and far
And thrill with wonder at a star ;
A host of stars—night's holy tent
Huge-glittering with wonderment.

If wonder is in great and small,
Then what of Him who made it all ?
In eyes and brain and heart and limb
Let's see the wondrous work of Him.
In house and hill and sward and sea,
In bird and beast and flower and tree,
In everything from sun to sod,
The wonder and the awe of God.

August 9, 1914.

For some time the way has been growing wilder. Thick-set hedges have yielded to dykes of stone, and there is every sign that I am approaching the rugged region of the coast. At each point of vantage I can see a Cross, often a relic of the early Christians, stumpy and corroded. Then I come on a slab of grey stone upstanding about fifteen feet. Like a sentinel on that solitary plain it overwhelms me with a sense of mystery.

But as I go on through this desolate land these stones become more and more familiar. Like soldiers they stand in rank, extending over the moor. The sky is cowled with cloud, save where a sullen sunset shoots blood-red rays across the plain. Bathed in that sinister light stands my army of stone, and a wind swooping down seems to wail amid its ranks. As in a glass darkly I can see the skin-clad men, the women with the tangled hair, the beast-like feast, the cowering terror of the night. Then the sunset is cut off suddenly, and a clammy mist shrouds that silent army. So it is almost with a shudder I take my last look at the Stones of Carnac.

But now my pilgrimage is drawing to an end. A painter friend who lives by the sea has asked me to stay with him awhile. Well, I have walked a hundred miles, singing on the way. I have dreamed and dawdled, planned, exulted. I have drunk buckets of cider, and eaten many an omelette that seemed like a golden glorification of its egg. It has all been very sweet, but it will also be sweet to loaf awhile.

OH, IT IS GOOD

Oh, it is good to drink and sup,
And then beside the kindly fire
To smoke and heap the faggots up,
And rest and dream to heart's desire.

Oh, it is good to ride and run,
To roam the greenwood wild and free;
To hunt, to idle in the sun,
To leap into the laughing sea.

Oh, it is good with hand and brain
To gladly till the chosen soil,
And after honest sweat and strain
To see the harvest of one's toil.

Oh, it is good afar to roam,
And seek adventure in strange lands;
Yet oh, so good the coming home,
The velvet love of little hands.

So much is good. . . . We thank Thee, God,
For all the tokens Thou hast given,
That here on earth our feet have trod
Thy little shining trails of Heaven.

V

August 10, 1914.

I am living in a little house so near the sea that at high tide I can see on my bedroom wall the reflected ripple of the water. At night I waken to the melodious welter of waves; or maybe there is a great stillness, and then I know that the sand and sea-grass are lying naked to the moon. But soon the tide returns, and once more I hear the roistering of the waves.

Calvert, my friend, is a lover as well as a painter of nature. He rises with the dawn to see the morning mist kindle to coral and the sun's edge clear the hill-crest. As he munches his coarse bread and sips his white wine, what dreams are his beneath the magic changes of the sky! He will paint the same scene under a dozen conditions of light. He has looked so long for Beauty that he has come to see it everywhere.

I love this friendly home of his. A peace steals over my spirit, and I feel as if I could stay here always. Some day I hope that I too may have such a one, and that I may write like this:

I HAVE SOME FRIENDS

I HAVE some friends, some worthy friends,
And worthy friends are rare:
These carpet slippers on my feet,
That padded leather chair;
This old and shabby dressing-gown,
So well the worse of wear.

I have some friends, some honest friends,
And honest friends are few;
My pipe of briar, my open fire,
A book that's not too new;
My bed so warm that nights of storm
I love to listen to.

I have some friends, some good, good friends
Who faithful are to me:
My wrestling partner when I rise,
The big and burly sea;
My little boat that's riding there
So saucy and so free.

I have some friends, some golden friends,
Whose worth will not decline :
A tawny Irish terrier, a purple shading pine,
A little red-roofed cottage that
So proudly I call mine.

All other friends may come and go,
All other friendships fail ;
But these, the friends I've worked to win,
Oh, they will never stale ;
And comfort me till Time shall write
The finish to my tale.

Calvert tries to paint more than the thing he sees ; he
tries to paint behind it, to express its spirit. He believes
that Beauty is God made manifest, and that when we discover Him in Nature we discover Him in ourselves.

But Calvert did not always see thus. At one time he
was a Pagan, content to paint the outward aspect of things.
It was after his little child died he gained in vision. Maybe
the thought that the dead are lost to us was too unbearable.
He had to believe in a coming together again.

THE QUEST

I SOUGHT Him on the purple seas,
I sought Him on the peaks aflame ;
Amid the gloom of giant trees
And canyons lone I called His name ;
The wasted ways of earth I trod :
In vain ! In vain ! I found not God.

I sought Him in the hives of men,
The cities grand, the hamlets grey,
The temples old beyond my ken,
The tabernacles of to-day ;
All life that is, from cloud to clod
I sought. . . . Alas ! I found not God.

Then after roamings far and wide,
In streets and seas and deserts wild,
I came to stand at last beside
The death-bed of my little child.
Lo ! as I bent beneath the rod
I raised my eyes . . . and there was God.

A golden mile of sand swings hammock-like between two
tusks of rock. The sea is sleeping sapphire that wakes to
cream and crash upon the beach. There is a majesty in
the detachment of its lazy waves, and it is good in the night
to hear its friendly roar. Good, too, to leap forth with the
first sunshine and fall into its arms, to let it pummel the
body to living ecstasy and send one to breakfast glad-eyed
and glowing.

Behind the house the greensward slopes to a wheat-field
that is like a wall of gold. Here I lie and laze away the time,
or dip into a favourite book, Stevenson's *Letters* or Belloc's
Path to Rome. Bees drone in the wild thyme ; a cuckoo
keeps calling, a lark spills jewelled melody. Then there
is a seeming silence, but it is the silence of a deeper sound.

After all, Silence is only man's confession of his deafness.
Like Death, like Eternity, it is a word that means nothing.
So lying there I hear the breathing of the trees, the
crepitation of the growing grass, the seething of the sap
and the movements of innumerable insects. Strange how
I think with distaste of the spurious glitter of Paris, of
my garret, even of my poor little book.

I watch the wife of my friend gathering poppies in the

wheat. There is a sadness in her face, for it is only a year ago they lost their little one. Often I see her steal away to the village graveyard, sitting silent for long and long.

THE COMFORTER

As I sat by my baby's bed
That's open to the sky,
There fluttered round and round my head
A radiant butterfly.

And as I wept—of hearts that ache
The saddest in the land—
It left a lily for my sake,
And lighted on my hand.

I watched it, oh, so quietly,
And though it rose and flew,
As if it fain would comfort me
It came and came anew.

Now, where my darling lies at rest,
I do not dare to sigh,
For look! there gleams upon my breast
A snow-white butterfly.

My friends will have other children, and if some day they should read this piece of verse, perhaps they will think of the city lad who used to sit under the old fig-tree in the garden and watch the lizards sun themselves on the time-worn wall.

THE OTHER ONE

"GATHER around me, children dear;
The wind is high and the night is cold;
Closer, little ones, snuggle near:
Let's seek a story of ages old;
A magic tale of a bygone day,
Of lovely ladies and dragons dread;
Come, for you're all so tired of play,
We'll read till it's time to go to bed."

So they all are glad, and they nestle in,
And squat on the rough old nursery rug,
And they nudge and hush as I begin,
And the fire leaps up and all's so snug;
And there I sit in the big arm-chair,
And how they are eager and sweet and wise,
And they cup their chins in their hands and stare
At the heart of the flame with thoughtful eyes.

And then, as I read by the ruddy glow
And the little ones sit entranced and still .
He's drawing near, ah! I know, I know
He's listening too, as he always will.
He's there—he's standing beside my knee;
I see him so well, my wee, wee son. . . .
Oh, children dear, don't look at me—
I'm reading now for—the Other One.

For the firelight glints in his golden hair,
And his wondering eyes are fixed on my face,
And he rests on the arm of my easy-chair,
And the book's a blur and I lose my place:

And I touch my lips to his shining head,
And my voice breaks down and—the story's done. . .
Oh, children, kiss me and go to bed:
Leave me to think of the Other One.

Of the One who will never grow up at all,
Who will always be just a child at play,
Tender and trusting and sweet and small,
Who will never leave me and go away;
Who will never hurt me and give me pain;
Who will comfort me when I'm all alone;
A heart of love that's without a stain,
Always and always my own, my own.

Yet a thought shines out from the dark of pain,
And it gives me hope to be reconciled:
That each of us must be born again,
And live and die as a little child;
So that with souls all shining white,
White as snow and without one sin,
We may come to the Gates of Eternal Light,
Where only children may enter in.

So, gentle mothers, don't ever grieve
Because you have lost, but kiss the rod;
From the depths of your woe be glad, believe
You've given an angel unto God.
Rejoice! You've a child whose youth endures,
Who comes to you when the day is done,
Wistful for love, oh, yours, just yours,
Dearest of all, the Other One.

CATASTROPHE

BRITTANY,
August First, 1914.

And now I fear I must write in another strain. Up to this time I have been too happy. I have existed in a magic Bohemia, largely of my own making. Hope, faith, enthusiasm have been mine. Each day has had its struggle, its failure, its triumph. However, that is all ended. During the past week we have lived breathlessly. For in spite of the exultant sunshine our spirits have been under a cloud, a deepening shadow of horror and calamity. . . . WAR.

Even as I write, in our little village steeple the bells are ringing madly, and in every little village steeple all over the land. As he listens, the harvester checks his scythe on the swing; the clerk throws down his pen; the shopkeeper puts up his shutters. Only in the cafés there is a clamour of voices and a drowning of care.

For here every man must fight, every home give tribute. There is no question, no appeal. By heredity and discipline all minds are shaped to this great hour. So to-morrow each man will seek his barracks and become a soldier as completely as if he had never been anything else. With the same docility as he dons his baggy red trousers will he let some muddle-headed General hurl him to destruction for some dubious gain. To-day a father, a home-maker; to-morrow fodder for cannon. So they all go without hesitation, without bitterness; and the great military machine that knows not humanity swings them to their fate. I marvel at the sense of duty, the resignation, the sacrifice. It is magnificent, it is FRANCE.

And the Women. Those who wait and weep. Ah! to-day I have not seen one who did not weep. Yes, one. She was very old, and she stood by her garden gate with her hand on the uplifted latch. As I passed she looked at me with eyes that did not see. She had no doubt sons and grandsons who must fight, and she had good reason, perhaps, to remember the war of *soixante-dix*. When I passed an hour later she was still there, her hand on the uplifted latch.

August 30th.

The men have gone. Only remain greybeards, women and children. Calvert and I have been helping our neighbours to get in the harvest. No doubt we aid; but there with the old men and children a sense of uneasiness and even shame comes over me. I would like to return to Paris, but the railway is mobilized. Each day I grow more discontented. Up there in the red North great things are doing and I am out of it. I am thoroughly unhappy.

Then Calvert comes to me with a plan. He has a Ford car. We will all three go to Paris. He intends to offer himself and his car to the Red Cross. His wife will nurse. So we are very happy at the solution, and to-morrow we are off.

PARIS.

Back again. Closed shutters, deserted streets. How glum everything is! Those who are not mobilized seem uncertain how to turn. Everyone buys the papers and reads grimly of disaster. No news is bad news.

I go to my garret as to a beloved friend. Everything is just as I left it, so that it seems I have never been away. I sigh with relief and joy. I will take up my work again. Serene above the storm I will watch and wait. Although I have been brought up in England I am American born. My country is not concerned.

So, going to the Dôme Café, I seek some of my comrades. Strange! They have gone. MacBean, I am told, is in Scotland. By dyeing his hair and lying about his age he has managed to enlist in the Seaforth Highlanders. Saxon Dane too. He has joined the Foreign Legion, and even now may be fighting.

Well, let them go. I will keep out of the mess. But why did they go? I wish I knew. War is murder. Criminal folly. Against Humanity. Imperialism is at the root of it. We are fools and dupes. Yes, I will think and write of other things. . . .

MacBean has enlisted.

I hate violence. I would not willingly cause pain to

anything breathing. I would rather be killed than kill. I will stand above the Battle and watch it from afar.

Dane is in the Foreign Legion.

How disturbing it all is! One cannot settle down to anything. Every day I meet men who tell the most wonderful stories in the most casual way. I envy them. I too want to have experiences, to live where life's beat is most intense. But that's a poor reason for going to war.

And yet, though I shrink from the idea of fighting, I might in some way help those who are. MacBean and Dane, for example. Sitting lonely in the Dôme, I seem to see their ghosts in the corner. MacBean listening with his keen, sarcastic smile, Saxon Dane banging his great hairy fist on the table till the glasses jump. Where are they now? Living a life that I will never know. When they come back, if they ever do, shall I not feel shamed in their presence? Oh, this filthy war! Things were going on so beautifully. We were all so happy, so full of ambition, of hope; laughing and talking over pipe and bowl, and in our garrets seeking to realize our dreams. Ah, these days will never come again!

Then, as I sit there, Calvert seeks me out. He has joined an ambulance corps that is going to the Front. Will I come in?

"Yes," I say; "I'll do anything."

So it is all settled. To-morrow I give up my freedom.

PART FOUR

WINTER

✗

THE SOMME FRONT,
January 1915.

THERE is an avenue of noble beeches leading to the Château,
and in the shadow of each glimmers the pale oblong of an
ambulance. We have to keep them thus concealed, for
only yesterday morning a Taube flew over. The beggars
are rather partial to Red Cross cars. One of our chaps,
taking in a load of wounded, was chased and pelted the
other day.

The Château seems all spires and towers, the glorified
dream of a Parisian pastrycook. On its terrace figures in
khaki are lounging. They are the volunteers, the owner-
drivers of the Corps, many of them men of wealth and title.
Curious to see one who owns all the coal in two counties
proudly signing for his *sou* a day; or another, who lives in
a Fifth Avenue palace, contentedly sleeping on the straw-
strewn floor of a hovel.

Here is a rhyme I have made of such a one:

PRISCILLA

JERRY MACMULLEN, the millionaire,
Driving a red-meat bus out there—
How did he win his *Croix de Guerre*?
Bless you, that's all old stuff:
Beast of a night on the Verdun road,
Jerry stuck with a woful load,
Stalled in the mud where the red lights glowed,
Prospect devilish tough.

758

"Little Priscilla" he called his car,
Best of our battered bunch by far,
Branded with many a bullet scar,
Yet running so sweet and true.
Jerry he loved her, knew her tricks ;
Swore : "She's the beat of the best big six,
And if ever I get in a deuce of a fix
Priscilla will pull me through."

"Looks pretty rotten right now," says he :
"Hanged if the devil himself could see.
Priscilla, it's up to you and me
To show 'em what we can do."
Seemed that Priscilla just took the word ;
Up with a leap like a horse that's spurred,
On with the joy of a homing bird,
Swift as the wind she flew.

Shell-holes shoot at them out of the night ;
A lurch to the left, a wrench to the right,
Hands grim-gripping and teeth clenched tight,
Eyes that glare through the dark.
"Priscilla, you're doing me proud this day ;
Hospital's only a league away,
And, honey, I'm longing to hit the hay,
So hurry, old girl. . . . But hark ! "

Howl of a shell, harsh, sudden, dread ;
Another . . . another. . . . "Strike me dead
If the Huns ain't strafing the road ahead
So the convoy can't get through !

A barrage of shrap, and us alone :
Four rush-cases—you hear 'em moan ?
Fierce old messes of blood and bone.　.
Priscilla, what shall we do ? "

Again it seems that Priscilla hears.
With a rush and a roar her way she clears,
Straight at the hell of flame she steers,
Full at its heart of wrath.
Fury of death and dust and din !
Havoc and horror ! She's in, she's in ;
She's almost over, she'll win, she'll win !
Woof ! Crump ! right in the path.

Little Priscilla skids and stops,
Jerry MacMullen sways and flops ;
Bang in his map the crash he cops ;
Shriek from the car : " Mon Dieu ! "
One of the *blessés* hears him say,
Just at the moment he faints away :
" Reckon this isn't my lucky day,
Priscilla, it's up to you."

Sergeant raps on the doctor's door ;
" Car in the court with *couchés* four ;
Driver dead on the dashboard floor ;
Strange how the bunch got here."
" No," says the Doc, " this chap's alive ;
But tell me, how could a man contrive
With both arms broken, a car to drive ?
Thunder of God ! it's queer."

Same little *blessé* makes a spell;
Says he: " When I saw our driver reel,
A Strange Shape leapt to the driving wheel
And sped us safe through the night."
But Jerry, he says in his drawling tone:
" Rats ! Why, Priscilla came in on her own.
Bless her, she did it alone, alone. . . ."
Hanged if I know who's right.

As I am sitting down to my midday meal an orderly
gives me a telegram:

Hill 71. *Two couchés. Send car at once.*

The uptilted country-side is a checker-board of green
and grey, and, except where groves of trees rise like
islands, cultivated to the last acre. But as we near the
firing-line all efforts to till the land cease, and the ungathered
beets of last year have grown to seed. Amid rank unkempt
fields I run over a road that is pitted with obus-holes; I
pass a line of guns painted like snakes, and drawn by horses
dyed khaki-colour; then soldiers coming from the trenches,
mud-caked and ineffably weary; then a race over a bit of
road that is exposed; then, buried in the hill-side, the dressing
station.

The two wounded are put into my car. From hip to heel
one is swathed in bandages; the other has a great white
turban on his head, with a red patch on it that spreads and
spreads. They stare dully, but make no sound. As I
crank the car there is a shrill screaming noise. . . . About
thirty yards away I hear an explosion like a mine-blast,
followed by a sudden belch of coal-black smoke. I stare
at it in a dazed way. Then the doctor says: " Don't
trouble to analyse your sensations. Better get off.
You're only drawing their fire."

Here is one of my experiences:

A CASUALTY

THAT boy I took in the car last night,
With the body that awfully sagged away,
And the lips blood-crisped, and the eyes flame-
    bright,
And the poor hands folded and cold as clay—
Oh, I've thought and I've thought of him all the
    day.

For the weary old doctor says to me:
" He'll only last for an hour or so.
Both of his legs below the knee
Blown off by a bomb. . . . So, lad, go slow,
And please remember, he doesn't know."

So I tried to drive with never a jar ;
And there was I cursing the road like mad,
When I hears a ghost of a voice from the car :
" Tell me, old chap, have I ' copped it ' bad ? "
So I answers " No," and he says, " I'm glad."

" Glad," says he, " for at twenty-two
Life's so splendid, I hate to go.
There's so much good that a chap might do,
And I've fought from the start and I've suffered
    so.
Twould be hard to get knocked out now, you
    know."

" Forget it," says I ; then I drove awhile,
And I passed him a cheery word or two ;
But he didn't answer for many a mile,
So just as the hospital hove in view,
Says I : " Is there nothing that I can do ? "

Then he opens his eyes and he smiles at me ;
And he takes my hand in his trembling hold :
" Thank you— you're far too kind," says he :
" I'm awfully comfy—stay . . . let's see :
I fancy my blanket's come unrolled—
My *feet*, please wrap 'em—they're cold . . . they're
    cold."

There is a city that glitters on the plain. Afar off we
can see its tall cathedral spire, and there we often take our
wounded from the little village hospitals to the rail-head.
Tragic little buildings, these emergency hospitals—town-
halls, churches, schools ; their cots are never empty, their
surgeons never still.

So every day we get our list of cases and off we go, a long
line of cars swishing through the mud. Then one by one
we branch off to our village hospital, puzzling out the road
on our maps. Arrived there, we load up quickly.

The wounded make no moan. They lie, limp, heavily
bandaged, with bare legs and arms protruding from their
blankets. They do not know where they are going ; they
do not care. Like live stock, they are labelled and numbered. An orderly brings along their battle-scarred equipment, throwing open their rifles to see that no charge
remains. Sometimes they shake our hands and thank us
for the drive.

In the streets of the city I see French soldiers wearing
the *fourragère*. It is a cord of green, yellow or red, and
corresponds to the *Croix de Guerre*, the *Médaille militaire*

and the Legion of Honour. The red is the highest of all, and has been granted only to one or two regiments. This incident was told to me by a man who saw it:

THE BLOOD-RED *FOURRAGÈRE*

WHAT was the blackest sight to me
Of all that campaign ?
A naked woman tied to a tree
With jagged holes where her breasts should be,
Rotting there in the rain.

On we pressed to the battle fray,
Dogged and dour and spent.
Sudden I heard my Captain say :
" *Voilà !* Kultur has passed this way,
And left us a monument."

So I looked and I saw our Colonel there,
And his grand head, snowed with the years,
Unto the beat of the rain was bare ;
And, oh, there was grief in his frozen stare,
And his cheeks were stung with tears !

Then at last he turned from the woful tree
And his face like stone was set ;
"Go, march the Regiment past," said he,
"That every father and son may see,
And none may ever forget."

Oh, the crimson strands of her hair downpoured
Over her breasts of woe ;
And our grim old Colonel leaned on his sword,
And the men filed past with their rifles lowered,
Solemn and sad and slow.

But I'll never forget till the day I die,
As I stood in the driving rain,
And the jaded columns of men slouched by,
How amazement leapt into every eye,
Then fury and grief and pain.

And some would like madmen stand aghast,
With their hands upclenched to the sky ;
And some would cross themselves as they passed,
And some would curse in a scalding blast,
And some like children cry.

Yea, some would be sobbing, and some would pray,
And some hurl hateful names ;
But the best had never a word to say ;
They turned their twitching faces away,
And their eyes were like hot flames.

They passed ; then down on his bended knee
The Colonel dropped to the Dead :
" Poor martyred daughter of France ! " said he,
" O dearly, dearly avenged you'll be
Or ever a day be sped ! "

Now they hold that we are the best of the best,
And each of our men may wear,
Like a gash of crimson across his chest,
As one fierce-proved in the battle-test,
The blood-red *Fourragère*.

For each as he leaps to the top can see,
Like an etching of blood on his brain,
A wife or a mother lashed to a tree,
With two black holes where her breasts should be,
Left to rot in the rain.

So we fight like fiends, and of us they say
That we neither yield nor spare.
Oh, we have the bitterest debt to pay. . . .
Have we paid it ?—Look—how we wear to-day
Like a trophy, gallant and proud and gay,
Our blood-red *Fourragère*.

It is often weary waiting at the little *poste de secours*. Some of us play solitaire, some read a " sixpenny," some doze or try to talk in bad French to the *poilus*. Around us is discomfort, dirt and drama.

For my part, I pass the time only too quickly, trying to put into verse the incidents and ideas that come my way. In this way I hope to collect quite a lot of stuff which may some day see itself in print.

Here is one of my efforts :

JIM

NEVER knew Jim, did you ? Our boy Jim ?
Bless you, there was the likely lad ;
Supple and straight and long of limb,
Clean as a whistle, and just as glad.

Always laughing, wasn't he, dad ?
Joy, pure joy to the heart of him,
And, oh, but the soothering ways he had,
                                    Jim, our Jim!

But I see him best as a tiny tot,
A bonny babe, though it's me that speaks ;
Laughing there in his little cot,
With his sunny hair and his apple cheeks.
And my ! but the blue, blue eyes he'd got,
And just where his wee mouth dimpled dim
Such a fairy mark like a beauty spot—
                                    That was Jim.

Oh, the war, the war ! How my eyes were wet !
But he says : " Don't be sorrowing, mother dear ;
You never knew me to fail you yet,
And I'll be back in a year, a year."
'Twas at Mons he fell, in the first attack ;
For so they said, and their eyes were dim ;
But I laughed in their faces : " He'll come back,
                                    Will my Jim."

Now, we'd been wedded for twenty year,
And Jim was the only one we'd had ;
So when I whispered in father's ear,
He wouldn't believe me—would you, dad ?
There ! I must hurry . . . . hear him cry !
My new little baby. . . . See ! that's him.
What are we going to call him ? Why,
                                    Jim, just Jim.

Jim ! For look at him laughing there
In the same old way in his tiny cot,
With his rosy cheeks and his sunny hair,
And look, just look . . . his beauty spot
In the selfsame place. . . . Oh, I can't explain,
And of course you think it's a mother's whim,
But I know, I know it's my boy again,

>> Same wee Jim.

Just come back as he said he would ;
Come with his love and his heart of glee.
Oh, I cried and I cried, but the Lord was good ;
From the shadow of Death he set Jim free.
So I'll have him all over again, you see.
Can you wonder my mother-heart's a-brim ?
Oh, how happy we're going to be !

>> Aren't we, Jim ?

II

IN PICARDY,
January 1915.

The road lies amid a malevolent heath. It seems to lead
us right into the clutch of the enemy ; for the star-shells,
that at first were bursting overhead, gradually encircle us.
The fields are strangely sinister ; the splintered trees are
like giant toothpicks. There is a lisping and a twanging
overhead.

As we wait at the door of the dugout that serves as a
first-aid dressing station, I gaze up into that mysterious
dark, so alive with musical vibrations. Then a small shadow
detaches itself from the greater shadow, and a grey-bearded
sentry says to me : " You'd better come in out of the bullets."

So I keep under cover, and presently they bring my
load. Two men drip with sweat as they carry their comrade.

I can see that they all three belong to the Foreign Legion. I think for a moment of Saxon Dane. How strange if some day I should carry him! Half fearfully I look at my passenger, but he is a black man. Such things only happen in fiction.

This is what I have written of the finest troops in the Army of France :

KELLY OF THE LEGION

Now Kelly was no fighter;
He loved his pipe and glass;
An easygoing blighter,
Who lived in Montparnasse.
But 'mid the tavern tattle
He heard some guinney say :
" When France goes forth to battle,
The Legion leads the way.

> *" The scourings of creation,*
> *Of every sin and station,*
> *The men who've known damnation,*
> *Are picked to lead the way."*

Well, Kelly joined the Legion;
They marched him day and night;
They rushed him to the region
Where largest loomed the fight.
" Behold your mighty mission,
Your destiny," said they;
" By glorious tradition
The Legion leads the way.

" With tattered banners flying
With trail of dead and dying,
On ! On ! All hell defying,
The Legion sweeps the way."

With grim, hard-bitten faces,
With jests of savage mirth,
They swept into their places,
The men of iron worth ;
Their blooded steel was flashing ;
They swung to face the fray ;
Then rushing, roaring, crashing,
The Legion cleared the way.

The trail they blazed was gory ;
Few lived to tell the story ;
Through death they plunged to glory :
But, oh, they cleared the way !

Now Kelly lay a-dying,
And dimly saw advance,
With split new banners flying,
The *fantassins* of France.
Then up amid the *mêlée*
He rose from where he lay ;
" Come on, me boys," says Kelly,
" The Layjun lades the way ! "

Aye, while they faltered, doubting
(Such flames of doom were spouting),
He caught them, thrilled them, shouting :
" The Layjun lades the way !"

They saw him slip and stumble,
Then stagger on once more;
They marked him trip and tumble,
A mass of grime and gore;
They watched him blindly crawling
Amid hell's own affray,
And calling, calling, calling:
"The Layjun lades the way!"

    And even while they wondered,
    The battle-wrack was sundered:
    To Victory they thundered,
    But . . . Kelly led the way.

Still Kelly kept agoing;
Berserker-like he ran;
His eyes with fury glowing,
A lion of a man;
His rifle madly swinging,
His soul athirst to slay,
His slogan ringing, ringing,
"The Layjun lades the way!"

    Till in a pit death-baited,
    Where Huns with Maxims waited,
    He plunged . . . and there, blood-sated
    To death he stabbed his way.

Now Kelly was a fellow
Who simply loathed a fight:
He loved a tavern mellow,
Grog hot and pipe alight;

I'm sure the Show appalled him,
And yet without dismay,
When Death and Duty called him,
He up and led the way.

> *So in Valhalla drinking*
> *(If heroes meek and shrinking*
> *Are suffered there), I'm thinking*
> *'Tis Kelly leads the way.*

We have just had one of our men killed, a young sculptor
of immense promise.

When one thinks of all the fine work he might have
accomplished, it seems a shame. But, after all, to-morrow
it may be the turn of any of us. If it should be mine, my
chief regret will be for work undone.

Ah! I often dream of how I will go back to the Quarter
and take up the old life again. How sweet it will all seem.
But first I must earn the right. And if ever I do go back,
how I will find Bohemia changed! Missing how many a
face!

It was in thinking of our lost comrade I wrote the
following:

THE THREE TOMMIES

THAT Barret, the painter of pictures, what feeling for
    colour he had!
And Fanning, the maker of music, such melodies mirth-
    ful and mad!
And Harley, the writer of stories, so whimsical,
    tender and glad!

To hark to their talk in the trenches, high heart
    unfolding to heart,
Of the day when the war would be over, and each
    would be true to his part,
Upbuilding a Palace of Beauty to the wonder and
    glory of Art . . .

Yon's Barret, the painter of pictures, yon carcass that
    rots on the wire ;
His hand with its sensitive cunning is crisped to a
    cinder with fire ;
His eyes with their magical vision are bubbles of
    glutinous mire.

Poor Fanning ! He sought to discover the symphonic
    note of a shell ;
There are bits of him broken and bloody, to show you
    the place where it fell ;
I've reason to fear on his exquisite ear the rats have
    been banqueting well.

And speaking of Harley, the writer, I fancy I looked
    on him last,
Sprawling and staring and writhing in the roar of the
    battle blast ;
Then a mad gun-team crashed over, and scattered his
    brains as it passed.

Oh, Harley and Fanning and Barret, they were bloody
    good mates o' mine ;
Their bodies are empty bottles ; Death has guzzled
    the wine ;
What's left of them's filth and corruption. . . . Where
    is the Fire Divine ?

I'll tell you. . . . At night in the trenches, as I watch
    and I do my part,
Three radiant spirits I'm seeing, high heart revealing
    to heart,
And they're building a peerless palace to the splendour
    and triumph of Art.

Yet, alas! for the fame of Barret, the glory he might
    have trailed!
And alas! for the name of Fanning, a star that beaconed
    and paled,
Poor Harley, obscure and forgotten. . . . Well, who
    shall say that they failed!

No, each did a Something Grander than ever he dreamed
    to do;
And as for the work unfinished, all will be paid their
    due;
The broken ends will be fitted, the balance struck will
    be true.

So painters, and players, and penmen, I tell you: Do
    as you please;
Let your fame outleap on the trumpets, you'll never
    rise up to these—
To three grim and gory Tommies, down, down on your
    bended knees.

    Daventry, the sculptor, is buried in a little graveyard
near one of our posts. Just now our section of the line
is quiet, so I often go and sit there. Stretching myself on
a flat stone, I dream for hours.

Silence and solitude ! How good the peace of it all seems ! Around me the grasses weave a pattern, and half hide the hundreds of little wooden crosses. Here is one with a single name :

AUBREY.

Who was Aubrey I wonder ? Then another :

To Our Beloved Comrade.

Then one which has attached to it, in the cheapest of little frames, the crude water-colour daub of a child, three purple flowers standing in a yellow vase. Below it, painfully printed, I read :

To My Darling Papa—Thy Little Odette.

And beyond the crosses many fresh graves have been dug. With hungry open mouths they wait. Even now I can hear the guns that are going to feed them. Soon there will be more crosses, and more and more. Then they will cease, and wives and mothers will come here to weep.

Ah ! Peace so precious must be bought with blood and tears. Let us honour and bless the men who pay, and envy them the manner of their dying ; for not all the jewelled orders on the breasts of the living can vie in glory with the little wooden cross the humblest of these has won. . . .

THE TWA JOCKS

SAYS Bauldy MacGreegor frae Gleska tae Hecky
    MacCrimmon frae Skye :
"That's whit I hate maist aboot fechtin'—it maks ye
    sae deevilish dry ;
Noo jist hae a keek at yon ferm-hoose them Gairmans
    are poundin' sae fine,
Weel, think o' it, doon in the dunnie there's bottles
    and bottles o' wine.

A' hell's fairly belchin' oot yonner, but oh, lad, I'm
    ettlin' tae try. . . ."
" *If it's poose she'll be with ye whateffer,*" *says Hecky*
    MacCrimmon frae Skye.

Says Bauldy MacGreegor frae Gleska : " Whit price
    fur a funeral wreath ?
We're dodgin' a' kinds o' destruction, an' jist by the
    skin o' oor teeth.
Here, spread yersel oot on yer belly, and slither along
    in the glaur ;
Confoond ye, ye big Hielan' deevil ! Ye don't realize
    there's a war.
Ye think that ye're back in Dunvegan, and herdin,
    the wee bits o' kye."
" *She'll neffer trink wine in Dunfegan,*" *says Hecky*
    MacCrimmon frae Skye.

Says Bauldy MacGreegor frae Gleska : " Thank good-
    ness ! the ferm-hoose at last ;
There's no muckle left but the celler, an' even that's
    vanishin' fast.
Look oot, there's the corpse o' a wumman, sair mangelt
    and deid by her lane.
Quick ! Strike a match. . . . Whit did I tell ye ! A
    hale bonny box o' shampane ;
Jist knock the heid aff o' a bottle. . . . Haud on,
    mon, I'm hearing a cry. . . ."
" *She'll think it's a wean that wass greetin',*" *says Hecky*
    MacCrimmon frae Skye.

Says Bauldy MacGreegor frae Gleska: "Ma con-
science! I'm hanged but yer richt.

It's yin o' thae waifs of the war-field, a' sobbin' and
shakin' wi' fricht.

Wheesht noo, dear, we're no gaun tae hurt ye. We're
takin' ye hame, my wee doo!

We've got tae get back wi' her, Hecky. Whit mercy
we didna get fou!

We'll no touch a drap o' that likker—that's hard, man,
ye canna deny. . . ."

*"It's the last thing she'll think o' denyin'," says Hecky
MacCrimmon frae Skye.*

Says Bauldy MacGreegor frae Gleska: "If I should
get struck frae the rear,

Ye'll tak' and ye'll shield the wee lassie, and rin for the
lines like a deer.

God! Wis that the breenge o' a bullet? I'm thinkin'
it's cracket ma spine.

I'm doon on ma knees in the glabber; I'm fearin', auld
man, I've got mine.

Here, quick! Pit yer erms roon the lassie. Noo, rin,
lad! good luck and good-bye. . . .

*" Hoots, mon! it's ye baith she'll be takin'," says Hecky
MacCrimmon frae Skye.*

Says Corporal Muckle frae Rannoch: "Is that no' a
picture tae frame?

Twa sair woundit Jocks wi' a lassie jist like ma wee
Jeannie at hame.

We're prood o' ye baith, ma brave heroes.   We'll gie
    ye a medal, I think "
Says Bauldy MacGreegor frae Gleska : " I'd raither
    ye gied me a drink.
I'll no speak for Private MacCrimmon, but oh, mon,
    I'm perishin' dry. . . ."
" *She'll wush that Loch Lefen wass whuskey,*" *says Hecky*
    MacCrimmon frae Skye.

III

NEAR ALBERT,
February 1915.

Over the spine of the ridge a horned moon of reddish
hue peers through the splintered, hag-like trees.   Where
the trenches are, rockets are rising, green and red.   I hear
the coughing of the maxims, the peevish nagging of the
rifles, the boom of a " heavy " and the hollow sound of its
exploding shell.

Running the car into the shadow of a ruined house, I
try to sleep.   But a battery starts to blaze away close by,
and the flame lights up my shelter.   Near me some soldiers
are in deep slumber ; one stirs in his sleep as a big rat runs
over him, and I know by experience that when one is
sleeping a rat feels as heavy as a sheep.

But how *can* one possibly sleep ?   Out there in the dark
there is the wild tattoo of a thousand rifles; and hark !
that dull roar is the explosion of a mine.   There ! the purring
of the rapid firers.   Desperate things are doing.   There
will be lots of work for me before this night is over.   What
a cursed place !

As I cannot sleep, I think of a story I heard to-day.   It
is of a Canadian Colonel, and in my mind I shape it like
this :

HIS BOYS

"I'M going, Billy, old fellow. Hist, lad! Don't make
any noise.
There's Boches to beat all creation, the pitch of a
bomb away.
I've fixed the note to your collar, you've got to get
back to my Boys,
You've got to get back to warn 'em before it's the
break of day."

The order came to go forward to a trench-line traced
on the map;
I knew the brass-hats had blundered, I knew and I
told 'em so;
I knew if I did as they ordered I would tumble into a trap,
And I tried to explain, but the answer came like a
pistol: "Go."

Then I thought of the Boys I commanded—I always
called them "my Boys"—
The men of my own recruiting, the lads of my countryside;
Tested in many a battle, I knew their sorrows and joys,
And I loved them all like a father, with more than a
father's pride.

To march my Boys to a shambles as soon as the dawn
of day;
To see them helplessly slaughtered, if all that I guessed
was true;
My Boys that trusted me blindly, I thought and I tried
to pray,
And then I arose and I muttered: "It's either them
or it's you."

I rose and I donned my rain-coat ; I buckled my helmet
   tight.
I remember you watched me, Billy, as I took my cane
   in my hand ;
1 vaulted over the sandbags into the pitchy night,
Into the pitted valley that served us as No Man's Land.

I strode out over the hollow of hate and havoc and
   death,
From the heights the guns were angry, with a vengeful
   snarling of steel ;
And once in a moment of stillness I heard hard panting
   breath,
And I turned . . . it was you, old rascal, following
   hard on my heel.

I fancy I cursed you, Billy ; but not so much as I
   ought !
And so we went forward together, till we came to the
   valley rim,
And then a star-shell sputtered . . . it was even worse
   than I thought,
For the trench they told me to move in was packed
   with Boche to the brim.

They saw me too, and they got me ; they peppered me
   till I fell ;
And there I scribbled my message with my life-blood
   ebbing away ;
"Now, Billy, you fat old duffer, you've got to get back
   like hell ;
And get them to cancel that order before it's the dawn
   of day.

"Billy, old boy, I love you, I kiss your shiny black nose ;
Now, home there. . . . Hurry, you devil, or I'll cut
  you to ribands. . . . See . . ."
Poor brute ! he's off ! and I'm dying. . . . I go as a
  soldier goes.
I'm happy. My Boys, God bless 'em ! . . . It had to
  be them or me.

Ah ! I never was intended for a job like this. I realize
it more and more every day, but I will stick it out till I
break down. To be nervous, over-imaginative, terribly
sensitive to suffering, is a poor equipment for the man who
starts out to drive wounded on the battlefield. I am
haunted by the thought that my car may break down
when I have a load of wounded. Once indeed it did, and a
man died while I waited for help. Now I never look at
what is given me. It might unnerve me.

I have been at it for over six months without a rest.
When an attack has been going on I have worked day and
night, until as I drove I wanted to fall asleep at the wheel.

The winter has been trying ; there is rain one day, frost
the next. Mud up to the axles. One sleeps in lousy barns
or dripping dugouts. Cold, hunger, dirt, I know them all
singly and together. My only consolation is that the war
must soon be over, and that I will have helped. When
I have time and am not too tired, I comfort myself with
scribbling.

THE BOOBY-TRAP

I'M crawlin' out in the mangolds to bury wot's left
  o' Joe—
Joe, my pal, and a good un (God ! 'ow it rains and rains).
I'm sick o' seein' him lyin' like a 'eap o' offal, and so
I'm crawlin' out in the beet-field to bury 'is last
  remains.

'E might 'a bin makin' munitions—'e 'adn't no need
    to go ;
An' I tells 'im strite, but 'e arnsers, " 'Tain't no use
    chewin' the fat ;
I've got to be doin' me dooty wiv the rest o' the
    boys " . . . an' so
Yon's 'im, yon blob on the beet-field wot I'm tryin'
    so 'ard to git at.

There was five of us lads from the brickyard ; 'Enry
    was gassed at Bapome,
Sydney was drowned in a crater, 'Erbert was 'alved
    by a shell ;
Joe was the pick o' the posy, might 'a bin sifely at
    'ome,
Only son of 'is mother, 'er a widder as well.

She used to sell bobbins and buttons—'ad a plice near
    the Waterloo Road ;
A little, old, bent-over lydy, wiv glasses an' silvery
    'air ;
Must tell 'er I planted 'im nicely, cheer 'er up like. . .
    (Well, I'm blowed,
That bullet near catched me a biffer)—I'll see the old
    gel if I'm spared.

She'll tike it to 'eart, pore ol' lydy, fer 'e was 'er 'ope
    and 'er joy ;
'Is dad used to drink like a knot-'ole, she kept the 'ome
    goin', she did :
She pinched and she scriped fer 'is scoolin', 'e was sich
    a fine 'andsome boy
('Alf Flanders seems packed on me panties)—'e's 'and-
    some no longer, pore kid !

This bit o' a board that I'm packin' and draggin' around
in the mire,
I was tickled to death when I found it. Says I, " 'Ere's
a nice little glow."
I was chilled and wet through to the marrer, so I started
to make me a fire ;
And then I says : " No; 'ere, Goblimy, it'll do for a
cross for Joe."

Well, 'ere 'e is. Gawd ! 'Ow one chinges a-lyin' six
weeks in the rain.
Joe, me old pal, 'ow I'm sorry; so 'elp me, I wish I
could pray.
An' now I 'ad best get a-diggin' 'is grave (it seems
more like a drain)—
And I 'opes that the Boches won't git me till I gits
'im safe planted away.

*(As he touches the body there is a tremendous
explosion. He falls back shattered.)*

A booby-trap ! Ought to 'a known it ! If that's not a
bastardly trick !
Well, one thing, I won't be long goin'. Gawd ! I'm
a 'ell of a sight.
Wish I'd died fightin' and killin' ; that's wot it is makes
me sick. . . .
Ah, Joe ! we'll be pushin' up dysies . . . together,
old Chummie . . . good-night !

To-day I heard that MacBean had been killed in Belgium.
I believe he turned out a wonderful soldier. Saxon Dane,
too, has been missing for two months. We know what
that means.

It is odd how one gets callous to death, a mediæval callousness. When we hear that the best of our friends have gone West, we have a moment of the keenest regret; but how soon again we find the heart to laugh! The saddest part of loss, I think, is that one so soon gets over it.

Is it that we fail to realize it all? Is it that it seems a strange and hideous dream, from which we will awake and rub our eyes?

Oh, how I feel bitter as the days go by! It is creeping more and more into my verse. Read this:

BONEHEAD BILL

I WONDER 'oo and wot 'e was,
That 'Un I got so slick.
I couldn't see 'is face because
The night was 'ideous thick.
I just made out among the black
A blinkin' wedge o' white;
Then *biff!* I guess I got 'im *crack*—
The man I killed last night.

I wonder if account o' me
Some wench will go unwed,
And 'eaps o' lives will never be
Because 'e's stark and dead?
Or if 'is missis damns the war,
And by some candle light,
'Tow-headed kids are prayin' for
The Fritz I copped last night.

I wonder, 'struth, I wonder why
I 'ad that 'orful dream ?
I saw up in the giddy sky
The gates o' God agleam ;
I saw the gates o' 'eaven shine
Wiv everlastin' light :
And then . . . I knew that I'd got mine,
As 'e got 'is last night.

Aye, bang beyond the broodin' mists
Where spawn the mother stars,
I 'ammered wiv me bloody fists
Upon them golden bars ;
I 'ammered till a devil's doubt
Fair froze me wiv affright :
To fink wot God would say about
The bloke I corpsed last night.

I 'ushed ; I wilted wiv despair,
When, like a rosy flame,
I sees a angel standin' there
'Oo calls me by me name.
'E 'ad such soft, such shiny eyes ;
'E 'eld 'is 'and and smiled ;
And through the gates o' Paradise
'E led me like a child.

'E led me by them golden palms
Wot 'ems that jewelled street ;
And seraphs was a-singin' psalms,
You've no ideer 'ow sweet ;

Wiv cheroobs crowdin' closer round
Than peas is in a pod,
'E led me to a shiny mound
Where beams the throne o' God.

And then I 'ears God's werry voice:
" Bill Fagan, 'ave no fear.
Stand up and glory and rejoice
For 'im 'oo led you 'ere."
And in a nip I seemed to see:
Aye, like a flash o' light,
My angel pal I knew to be
The chap I plugged last night.

Now, I don't claim to understand—
They calls me Bonehead Bill ;
They shoves a rifle in me 'and,
And shows me 'ow to kill.
Me job's to risk me life and limb,
But . . . be it wrong or right,
This cross I'm makin', it's for 'im,
The cove I croaked last night.

IV

A LAPSE OF TIME AND A WORD OF EXPLANATION

THE AMERICAN HOSPITAL, NEUILLY.
                    January 1919.
Four years have passed and it is winter again.   Much
has happened.   When I last wrote, on the Somme in 1915,

I was sickening with typhoid fever. All that spring I was in hospital.

Nevertheless, I was sufficiently recovered to take part in the Champagne battle in the Fall of that year, and to "carry on" during the following winter. It was at Verdun I got my first wound.

In the spring of 1917 I again served with my Corps; but on the entry of the United States into the War I joined the army of my country. In the Argonne I had my left arm shot away.

As far as time and health permitted, I kept a record of these years, and also wrote much verse. All this, however, has disappeared under circumstances into which there is no need to enter here. The loss was a cruel one, almost more so than that of my arm; for I have neither the heart nor the power to rewrite this material.

And now, in default of something better, I have bundled together this manuscript, and have added to it a few more verses, written in hospitals. Let it represent me. If I can find a publisher for it, *tant mieux*. If not, I will print it at my own cost, and anyone who cares for a copy can write to me—

STEPHEN POORE,
12 *bis*, RUE DES PETITS MOINEAUX,
PARIS.

MICHAEL

" THERE'S something in your face, Michael, I've seen
   it all the day;
There's something quare that wasn't there when first
   ye wint away. . . ."

"It's just the Army life, mother, the drill, the left
and right,
That puts the stiffinin' in yer spine and locks yer jaw
up tight. . . ."

"There's something in your eyes, Michael, an' how
they stare and stare—
You're lookin' at me now, me boy, as if I wasn't
there. . . ."

"It's just the things I've seen, mother, the sights
that come and come,
A bit o' broken, bloody pulp that used to be a
chum. . . ."

"There's something on your heart, Michael, that makes
ye wake at night,
And often when I hear ye moan, I trimble in me
fright. . . ."

"It's just a man I killed, mother, a mother's son like
me ;
It seems he's always hauntin' me, he'll never let me
be. . . ."

"But maybe he was bad, Michael, maybe it was
right
To kill the inimy you hate in fair and honest
fight. . . ."

" I did not hate at all, mother ; he never did me
 harm ;
I think he was a lad like me, who worked upon a
 farm. . . ."

" And what's it all about, Michael ; why did you have
 to go,
A quiet, peaceful lad like you, and we were happy
 so ? . . ."

" It's thim that's up above, mother, it's thim that sits
 an' rules ;
We've got to fight the wars they make, it's us as are
 the fools. . . ."

" And what will be the end, Michael, and what's the
 use, I say,
Of fightin' if whoever wins it's us that's got to pay ? . . ."

" Oh, it will be the end, mother, when lads like him
 and me,
That sweat to feed the ones above, decide that we'll
 be free. . . ."

" And when will that day come, Michael, and when will
 fightin' cease,
And simple folks may till their soil and live and love
 in peace ? . . ."

" It's coming soon and soon, mother, it's nearer every day,
When only men who earn their wage will have a word
 to say ;

When all who gain their honest bread in every land
    and soil
Will claim the Brotherhood of Man, the Comradeship
    of Toil ;
When we, the Workers, all demand : ' What are we
    fighting for ? ' . . .
Then, then we'll end that stupid crime, that devil's
    madness—War."

THE WIFE

" TELL Annie I'll be home in time
To help her with her Christmas-tree."
That's what he wrote, and hark ! the chime
Of Christmas bells, and where is he ?
And how the house is dark and sad,
And Annie's sobbing on my knee !

The page beside the candle-flame
With cruel type was overfilled ;
I read and read until a name
Leapt at me and my heart was stilled :
My eye crept up the column—up
Unto its hateful heading : *Killed.*

And there was Annie on the stair :
" And will he not be long ? " she said.
Her eyes were bright and in her hair
She'd twined a bit of riband red ;
And every step was daddy's sure,
Till tired out she went to bed.

And there alone I sat so still,
With staring eyes that did not see;
The room was desolate and chill,
And desolate the heart of me;
Outside I heard the news-boys shrill:
"Another Glorious Victory!"

A victory. . . . Ah! what care I?
A thousand victories are vain.
Here in my ruined home I cry
From out my black despair and pain,
I'd rather, rather damned defeat,
And have my man with me again.

They talk to us of pride and power,
Of Empire vast beyond the sea;
As here beside my hearth I cower,
What mean such words as these to me?
Oh, will they lift the clouds that lour,
Or light my load in years to be?

What matters it to us poor folk?
Who win or lose, it's we who pay.
Oh, I would laugh beneath the yoke
If I had *him* at home to-day;
One's home before one's country comes:
Aye, so a million women say.

"Hush, Annie dear, don't sorrow so."
(How can I tell her?) "See, we'll light
With tiny star of purest glow
Each little candle pink and white."
(They make mistakes. I'll try to think
I did not read that name aright.)

Come, dearest one; come, let us pray
Beside our gleaming Christmas-tree;
Just fold your little hands and say
These words so softly after me:
" God pity mothers in distress,
And little children fatherless."

" *God pity mothers in distress,*
And little children fatherless."

*   *   *   *   *

What's that ?—a step upon the stair;
A shout !—the door thrown open wide !
My hero and my man is there,
And Annie's leaping by his side. . . .
The room reels round, I faint, I fall. . . ·
" O God ! Thy world is glorified."

VICTORY STUFF

WHAT d'ye think, lad; what d'ye think,
As the roaring crowds go by ?
As the banners flare and the brasses blare
And the great guns rend the sky ?
As the women laugh like they'd all gone mad,
And the champagne glasses clink:
Oh, you're grippin' me hand so tightly, lad,
I'm a-wonderin' : what d'ye think ?

D'ye think o' the boys we used to know,
And how they'd have topped the fun ?
Tom and Charlie, and Jack and Joe—
Gone now, every one.

How they'd have cheered as the joy-bells chime,
And they grabbed each girl for a kiss !
And now—they're rottin' in Flanders slime,
And they gave their lives—for *this*.

Or else d'ye think of the many a time
We wished we too was dead,
Up to our knees in the freezin' grime,
With the fires of hell overhead.
When the youth and the strength of us sapped away,
And we cursed in our rage and pain—
And yet—we haven't a word to say. . .
We're glad. We'd do it again.

I'm scared that they pity us. Come, old boy,
Let's leave them their flags and their fuss.
We'd surely be hatin' to spoil their joy
With the sight of such wrecks as us.
Let's slip away quietly, you and me,
And we'll talk of our chums out there :
You with your eyes that'll never see,
Me that's wheeled in a chair.

WAS IT YOU ?

" HULLO, young Jones ! with your tie so gay
And your pen behind your ear ;
Will you mark my cheque in the usual way ?
For I'm overdrawn, I fear."
Then you look at me in a manner bland,
As you turn your ledger's leaves,
And you hand it back with a soft white hand,
And the air of a man who grieves. . . .

" Was it you, young Jones, was it you I saw
(And I think I see you yet)
With a live bomb gripped in your grimy paw
And your face to the parapet ?
With your lips asnarl and your eyes gone mad
With a fury that thrilled you through. . . .
Oh, I look at you now and I think, my lad,
Was it you, young Jones, was it you ?

"Hullo, young Smith, with your well-fed look
And your coat of dapper fit,
Will you recommend me a decent book
With nothing of War in it ? "
Then you smile as you polish a finger-nail,
And your eyes serenely roam,
And you suavely hand me a thrilling tale
By a man who stayed at home.

" Was it you, young Smith, was it you I saw
In the battle's storm and stench,
With a roar of rage and a wound red-raw
Leap into the reeking trench ?
As you stood like a fiend on the firing-shelf
And you stabbed and hacked and slew. . . .
Oh, I look at you and I ask myself,
Was it you, young Smith, was it you ?

"Hullo, old Brown, with your ruddy cheek
And your tummy's rounded swell,
Your garden's looking jolly *chic*
And your kiddies awf'ly well.

Then you beam at me in your cheery way
As you swing your water-can ;
And you mop your brow and you blithely say :
' What about golf, old man ? '

" *Was it you, old Brown, was it you I saw*
Like a bull-dog stick to your gun,
A cursing devil of fang and claw
When the rest were on the run ?
Your eyes aflame with the battle-hate. . . .
As you sit in the family pew,
And I see you rising to pass the plate,
I ask : Old Brown, was it you ?

" Was it me and you ? Was it you and me ?
(Is that grammar, or is it not ?)
Who grovelled in filth and misery,
Who gloried and groused and fought ?
Which is the wrong and which is the right ?
Which is the false and the true ?
The man of peace or the man of fight ?
Which is the ME and the YOU ? "

V

LES GRANDS MUTILES

I saw three wounded of the war :
And the first had lost his eyes ;
And the second went on wheels and had
No legs below the thighs ;

And the face of the third was featureless,
And his mouth ran cornerwise.

So I made a rhyme about each one,
And this is how my fancies run.

THE SIGHTLESS MAN

Out of the night a crash,
A roar, a rampart of light;
A flame that leaped like a lash,
Searing for ever my sight;
Out of the night a flash,
Then, oh, for ever the Night!

Here in the dark I sit,
I who so loved the sun;
Supple and strong and fit,
In the dark till my days be done;
Aye, that's the hell of it,
Stalwart and twenty-one.

Marie is stanch and true,
Willing to be my wife;
Swears she has eyes for two . . :
Aye, but it's long, is Life.
What is a lad to do
With his heart and his brain at strife?

There now, my pipe is out;
No one to give me a light;
I grope and I grope about. . . .
Well, it is nearly night;
Sleep may resolve my doubt,
Help me to reason right. . . .

(He sleeps and dreams.)

I heard them whispering there by the bed . . .
Oh, but the ears of the blind are quick !
Every treacherous word they said
Was a stab of pain and my heart turned sick.
Then lip met lip and they looked at me,
Sitting bent by the fallen fire,
And they laughed to think that I couldn't see;
But I felt the flame of their hot desire.
He's helping Marie to work the farm,
A dashing, upstanding chap, they say ;
And look at me with my flabby arm,
And the fat of sloth, and my face of clay—
Look at me as I sit and sit,
By the side of a fire that's seldom lit,
Sagging and weary the livelong day,
When everyone else is out on the field,
Sowing the seed for a golden yield,
Or tossing around the new-mown hay. . . .

Oh, the shimmering wheat that frets the sky,
Gold of plenty and blue of hope,
I'm seeing it all with an inner eye
As out of the door I grope and grope.
And I hear my wife and her lover there,
Whispering, whispering, round the rick,
Mocking me and my sightless stare,
As I fumble and stumble everywhere,
Slapping and tapping with my stick ;
Old and weary at thirty-one,
Heartsick, wishing it all was done.

Oh, I'll tap my way around to the byre,
And I'll hear the cows as they chew their hay;
There at least there is none to tire,
There at least I am not in the way.
And they'll look at me with their velvet eyes
And I'll stroke their flanks with my woman's hand,
And they'll answer to me with soft replies,
And somehow I fancy they'll understand.
And the horses too, they know me well;
I'm sure that they pity my wretched lot,
And the big fat ram with the jingling bell . . .
Oh, the beasts are the only friends I've got.
And my old dog, too, he loves me more,
I think, than ever he did before.
Thank God for the beasts that are all so kind,
That know and pity the helpless blind!

Ha! they're coming, the loving pair.
My hand's a-shake as my pipe I fill.
What if I steal on them unaware
With a reaping-hook, to kill, to kill? . . .
I'll do it . . . they're there in the mow of hay,
I hear them saying: "He's out of the way!"
Hark! how they're kissing and whispering. . . .
Closer I creep . . . I crouch . . . I spring. . . .

(He wakes.)

Ugh! What a horrible dream I've had!
And it isn't real . . . I'm glad, I'm glad!
Marie is good and Marie is true . . .
But now I know what it's best to do.

I'll sell the farm and I'll seek my kind,
I'll live apart with my fellow-blind,
And we'll eat and drink, and we'll laugh and
    joke,
And we'll talk of our battles, and smoke and
    smoke ;
And brushes of bristle we'll make for sale,
While one of us reads a book of Braille.
And there will be music and dancing too,
And we'll seek to fashion our life anew ;
And we'll walk the highways hand in hand,
The Brotherhood of the Sightless Band ;
Till the years at last shall bring respite
And our night is lost in the Greater Night.

THE LEGLESS MAN

(*The Dark Side.*)

*My mind goes back to Fumin Wood, and how we stuck
    it out,*
*Eight days of hunger, thirst and cold, mowed down by
    steel and flame ;*
*Waist-deep in mud and mad with woe, with dead men
    all about,*
*We fought like fiends and waited for relief that never
    came.*
*Eight days and nights they rolled on us in battle-frenzied
    mass !*
*" Debout les morts ! " We hurled them back. By God !
    they did not pass.*

They pinned two medals on my chest, a yellow and a
  brown,
And lovely ladies made me blush, such pretty words
  they said.
I felt a cheerful man, almost, until my eyes went down,
And there I saw the blankets—how they sagged upon
  my bed.
And then again I drank the cup of sorrow to the dregs :
Oh, they can keep their medals if they give me back
  my legs.

I think of how I used to run and leap and kick the
  ball
And ride and dance and climb the hills and frolic in
  the sea ;
And all the thousand things that now I'll never do at
  all. . . .
Alas ! there's nothing left in life, it often seems to me.
And as the nurses lift me up and strap me in my
  chair,
If they would chloroform me off, by God I wouldn't care.

Ah yes ! we're " heroes all " to-day—they point to us
  with pride ;
To-day their hearts go out to us, the tears are in their
  eyes !
But wait a bit ; to-morrow they will blindly look aside ;
They'll cease to talk of what they owe, the dues of
  sacrifice
(One hates to be reminded of an everlasting debt).
It's all in human nature. Ah ! the world will soon
  forget.

*My mind goes back to where I lay wound-rotted on the
    plain,*
*And ate the muddy mangold roots, and drank the drops
    of dew,*
*And dragged myself for miles and miles when every move
    was pain,*
And over me the carrion-crows were retching as they flew.
Oh, ere I closed my eyes and stuck my rifle in the air
*I wish that those who picked me up had passed and left
    me there.*

(*The Bright Side.*)

Oh, one gets used to everything !
I hum a merry song,
And up the street and round the square
I wheel my chair along ;
For look you, how my chest is sound
And how my arms are strong !

Oh, one gets used to anything !
It's awkward at the first,
And jolting o'er the cobbles gives
A man a grievous thirst ;
But of all ills that one must bear
That's surely not the worst.

For there's the café open wide,
And there they set me up ;
And there I smoke my *caporal*
Above my cider cup ;
And play *manille* a while before
I hurry home to sup.

At home the wife is waiting me
With smiles and pigeon-pie ;
And little Zi-Zi claps her hands
With laughter loud and high ;
And if there's cause to growl, I fail
To see the reason why.

And all the evening by the lamp
I read some tale of crime,
Or play my old accordion
With Marie keeping time,
Until we hear the hour of ten
From out the steeple chime.

Then in the morning bright and soon,
No moment do I lose ;
Within my little cobbler's shop
To gain the silver *sous*
(Good luck one has no need of legs
To make a pair of shoes).

And every Sunday—oh, it's then
I am the happy man ;
They wheel me to the river-side,
And there with rod and can
I sit and fish and catch a dish
Of *goujons* for the pan.

Aye, one gets used to everything,
And doesn't seem to mind ;
Maybe I'm happier than most
Of my two-legged kind ;
For look you at the darkest cloud,
Lo ! how it's silver-lined.

THE FACELESS MAN

I'm dead.
Officially I'm dead. Their hope is past.
How long I stood as missing ! Now, at last
                                    I'm dead.
Look in my face—no likeness can you see,
No tiny trace of him they knew as "me."
How terrible the change !
Even my eyes are strange.
So keyed are they to pain,
That if I chanced to meet
My mother in the street
She'd look at me in vain.   . .

When she got home I think she'd say :
"I saw the saddest sight to-day—
A *poilu* with no face at all.
Far better in the fight to fall
Than go through life like that, I think.
Poor fellow ! how he made me shrink.
No face. Just eyes that seemed to stare
At me with anguish and despair.
This ghastly war ! I'm almost cheered
To think my son who disappeared,
My boy so handsome and so gay,
Might have come home like him to-day."

I'm dead. I think it's better to be dead
When little children look at you with dread ;
And when you know your coming home again
Will only give the ones who love you pain.

Ah ! who can help but shrink ? One cannot
    blame.
They see the hideous husk, not, not the flame
Of sacrifice and love that burns within ;
While souls of satyrs, raddled through with sin,
Have bodies fair and excellent to see.
Mon Dieu ! how different we all would be
If this our flesh was ordained to express
Our spirit's beauty or its ugliness.

(Oh, you who look at me with fear to-day,
And shrink despite yourselves, and turn away—
It was for you I suffered woe accurst ;
For you I braved red battle at its worst ;
For you I fought and bled and maimed and slew ;
                       For you, for you
For you I faced hell-fury and despair ;
The reeking horror of it all I knew :
I flung myself into the furnace there ;
I faced the flame that scorched me with its glare ;
I drank unto the dregs the devil's brew—
Look at me now—for *you* and *you* and *you*. . . .)

       *   *   *   *   *

I'm thinking of the time we said good-bye :
We took our dinner in Duval's that night,
Just little Jacqueline, Lucette and I ;
We tried our very utmost to be bright.
We laughed. And yet our eyes, they weren't gay
I sought all kinds of cheering things to say.

"Don't grieve," I told them. "Soon the time will
    pass ;
My next permission will come quickly round ;
We'll all meet at the Gare du Montparnasse ;
Three times I've come already, safe and sound."
(But oh, I thought, it's harder every time,
After a home that seems like Paradise,
To go back to the vermin and the slime,
The weariness, the want, the sacrifice.
"Pray God," I said, "the war may soon be done,
But no, oh never, never till we've won!")

Then to the station quietly we walked ;
I had my rifle and my haversack,
My heavy boots, my blankets on my back ;
And though it hurt us, cheerfully we talked.
We chatted bravely at the platform gate.
I watched the clock. My train must go at eight.
One minute to the hour . . . we kissed good-bye,
Then, oh, they both broke down, with piteous cry
I went. . . . Their way was barred; they could not
    pass.
I looked back as the train began to start ;
Once more I ran with anguish at my heart
And through the bars I kissed my little lass. . . ·

Three years have gone; they've waited day by day
I never came. I did not even write.
For when I saw my face was such a sight
I thought that I had better . . . stay away.
And so I took the name of one who died,
A friendless friend who perished by my side.

In Prussian prison camps three years of hell
I hugged my secret; oh, I kept it well!
And now I'm free, but none shall ever know;
They think I died out there . . . it's better so.

To-day I met my wife in widow's weeds.
I brushed her arm. She did not even look.
So white, so pinched her face, my heart still bleeds,
And at the touch of her, oh, how I shook!
And then last night I passed the window where
They sat together; I could see them clear,
The lamplight softly gleaming on their hair,
And all the room so full of cosy cheer.
My wife was sewing, while my daughter read;
I even saw my portrait on the wall.
I wanted to rush in, to tell them all;
And then I cursed myself: "You're dead, you're
    dead!"
God! how I watched them from the darkness
    there,
Clutching the dripping branches of a tree,
Peering as close as ever I might dare,
And sobbing, sobbing, oh, so bitterly!

But no, it's folly; and I mustn't stay
To-morrow I am going far away.
I'll find a ship and sail before the mast;
In some wild land I'll bury all the past.
I'll live on lonely shores and there forget,
Or tell myself that there has never been
The gay and tender courage of Lucette,
The little loving arms of Jacqueline.

A lonely man upon a lonely isle,
Sometimes I'll look towards the North and smile
To think they're happy, and they both believe
I died for France, and that I lie at rest ;
And for my glory's sake they've ceased to grieve,
And hold my memory sacred. Ah ! that's best.
And in that thought I'll find my joy and peace
As there alone I wait the Last Release.

L'ENVOI

We've finished up the filthy war;
We've won what we were fighting for . . .
(Or have we? I don't know).
But anyway I have my wish:
I'm back upon the old Boul' Mich',
And how my heart's aglow!
Though in my coat's an empty sleeve,
Ah! do not think I ever grieve
(The pension for it, I believe,
Will keep me on the go).

So I'll be free to write and write,
And give my soul to sheer delight,
Till joy is almost pain;
To stand aloof and watch the throng,
And worship youth and sing my song
Of faith and hope again;
To seek for beauty everywhere,
To make each day a living prayer
That life may not be vain.

To sing of things that comfort me,
The joy in mother-eyes, the glee
Of little ones at play;

The blessed gentleness of trees,
Of old men dreaming at their ease
Soft afternoons away;
Of violets and swallows' wings,
Of wondrous, ordinary things
In words of every day.

To rhyme of rich and rainy nights,
When like a legion leap the lights
And take the town with gold;
Of taverns quaint where poets dream,
Of cafés gaudily agleam,
And vice that's overbold;
Of crystal shimmer, silver sheen,
Of soft and soothing nicotine,
Of wine that's rich and old.

Of gutters, chimney-tops and stars,
Of apple-carts and motor-cars,
The sordid and sublime;
Of wealth and misery that meet
In every great and little street,
Of glory and of grime;
Of all the living tide that flows—
From princes down to puppet shows—
I'll make my humble rhyme.

So if you like the sort of thing
Of which I also like to sing,
Just give my stuff a look;

And if you don't, no harm is done—
In writing it I've had my fun;
Good luck to you and everyone—
And so . . .

HERE ENDS MY BOOK.

PRINTED IN GREAT BRITAIN BY PURNELL AND SONS, LTD.
PAULTON (SOMERSET) AND LONDON